Writer's Guide to Magazine Editors and Publishers, 1997–1998

Judy Mandell

PRIMA PUBLISHING

PRIMA PUBLISHING and colophon are registered trademarks of Prima Communications, Inc. Information contained in this book has been obtained by Author from sources believed to be reliable. However, because of the possibility of human or mechanical error, or because such information may change after the publication of this book, the Author and Publisher do not guarantee the accuracy, adequacy, or completeness of such information and are not responsible for any errors or omission caused by the use of such information.

ISBN: 0-7615-0409-5
ISSN: 1089-2494

96 97 98 99 00 01 AA 10 9 8 7 6 5 4 3 2 1
Printed in the United States of America

How to Order

Single copies may be ordered from Prima Publishing, P.O. Box 1260BK, Rocklin, CA 95677; telephone (916) 632-4400. Quantity discounts are also available. On your letterhead, include information concerning the intended use of the books and the number of books you wish to purchase.

Visit us online at http://www.primapublishing.com

Contents

Acknowledgments

I wish to thank the magazine editors who responded to my questionnaire. I'm especially grateful to those editors who took precious time to write extensive essays and offer tips to writers. Their remarks give writers a clear look at what it's like to be on the receiving end of query letters and manuscripts, and their "from-the-horse's-mouth" advice is invaluable. Freelancers who can empathize with editors and know what they are looking for will have a better shot at getting published.

Introduction

More than 10,000 magazines are published in North America each year. Magazines abound for every imaginable interest, hobby, and profession. There are city, state, and regional publications, there are magazines for and about airlines and cruise lines, vacations and vocations, mystery and humor, and there are those with an emphasis on health, science, computers, arts, literature, leisure, women's interests, men's interests, and prurient interests. Magazines are produced to entertain, to teach, and to titillate. If an idea exists, a magazine can be found to cover it.

Writer's Guide to Magazine Editors and Publishers provides information about 327 nationally recognized publications and represents most magazine categories. All magazines listed accept freelance submissions and are excellent markets for freelance writers.

Each magazine entry covers essential information that writers need—name, address, phone, fax, e-mail address, circulation, availability, history, and mission, as well as material that will help writers angle their stories—the target audience, article interests and needs, and sections of the magazine open to freelancers. Other pertinent data includes the portion of the magazine that is nonfiction and/or fiction, the percentage that is freelance-written, the number of articles bought annually, average article length, pay scale, and time of payment (on acceptance or publication), expenses covered (if any), photographs, response time to queries, rights bought, kill fees, and availability of writer's guidelines and sample issues.

I also asked editors to write short essays answering what I thought were freelance writers' most-asked questions:

What sparks your interest in a query and/or a freelance writer?

What are the key elements of a good, professional query?

Do you always want clips from new writers? How many do you want?

What do you look for in the writer's clips?

Will you look at completed manuscripts?

Is a SASE always necessary?

Are phone calls from writers OK? If yes, under what circumstances?

Is it OK if writers fax or e-mail queries to you?

What is the best way to break into your magazine?

What are the keys to breaking in to magazines in general?

What are the best things writers do?

What are the worst things writers do (pet peeves)?

How can writers angle their stories for your magazine?

What overall advice would you give writers who want to get published?

In addition, I encouraged editors to discuss other topics that they thought were important.

Editors who complied gave readers the inside scoop—the secrets to breaking into the business. They expressed what they love about writers and what they hate, what sparks their interest in a query and what they find abominable, what they look for in a writer's clips, and what's unimpressive. They gave their honest impressions and advice. I edited these essays lightly—mainly for spelling or grammatical errors—so that the editors' personas might be revealed. Many editors are talented writers and were once successful freelancers. It shows. For those who didn't write essays but jotted short answers to my guiding questions, I created a Q & A section following their entry.

I encourage readers to thoroughly read *all* of the essays in this book. Even if a magazine is geared to a specialty that is not yours, you will find hints in its profile that are applicable to other publications.

Writer's Guide to Magazine Editors and Publishers should serve as a priceless tool for novice and professional writers, students, scholars, and teachers of writing. It provides everything any writer would ever need to get published—the facts about the magazines and constructive advice from the editors.

PART ONE

Writing for Publication

So You Want to Be
a Freelance Writer

JAMIE MILLER

Before becoming the editor of Albemarle *magazine in Charlottesville, Virginia, Jamie Miller was a freelance writer publishing with* The Washington Post *and National Public Radio's* All Things Considered, *where he wrote and produced commentary. Additionally, he has published with* The Daily Progress, Blue Ridge Country, Virginia, Acoustic Performer, The Virginia Journal of Education, The C-Ville Review, GameDay, The Real Estate Weekly, Acoustic Guitar, HealthSense, *and* The Observer.

You have learned your postman's patterns. The side yard cut-throughs, the aspects of his summer dress—indeed, all habits postal have come under your scrutiny, especially that most important of habits: the time of delivery. Yes, in the time you've spent on front-porch stakeout waiting for the mail, you could well qualify for an FBI surveillance team. But your heart lies elsewhere. Your study is nothing personal; it's purely business because you know the letter carrier carries more than the mail, he carries hopes and dreams in the shape of crisp white envelopes: he carries acceptance, he carries that check, he carries the sweetest three words a writer can imagine: notice of publication.

He also carries rejection.

But for the freelance writer, the one posting the queries and penning the texts, rejection is as unlikely a vision as a missed slam dunk by Michael Jordan—and therein lies perhaps the most important skill a freelance writer can possess: eternal optimism. And you'll need it.

When I began my freelance career, the only thing I knew for sure was that I'd need to get accustomed to rejections. Old girlfriends aside, I had not dealt with a great deal of rejection, so I decided to initiate myself into the brother and sisterhood of writer-dom. I crafted a short story and sent it to the top, to the best, to the Big Apple: I sent it to *The New Yorker*. (An aside: my choice was fiction, but it could have been any form of writing, the point being that the good freelancer must attain competency in all forms of rejection.) I sent my work to *The New Yorker* because I figured that if I were to be rejected, I may as well be rejected by the best and then work my way down.

In short order, the good people at *The New Yorker* agreed and, within only a few weeks, I received a lovely rejection slip along with my unread manuscript. "We are sorry to say," it began "that this submission isn't quite right for us, in spite of it's obvious merit. Unfortunately, we are receiving so many manuscripts that it has become impossible for us to make specific comments about as many of them as we would like to. We do thank you for the chance to consider the work." Signed, "The Editors."

I was on my way.

And what a way to go, because there was a lovely irony in that rejection. While I may have considered the vaunted *New Yorker* to be the publishing pinnacle, it wasn't until several years later, when I was teaching a writing class, that a student saw that rejection note and pointed out an editing impossibility. Yes, Michael Jordan had indeed flubbed his slam dunk, because right there in the first sentence, The Editors missed a major mistake: they spelled "its" as "it's."

The error highlights an important point—that behind the guise of power and perfection lurks the undeniable, immeasurable fallibility—even to the point of humanity—of all editors. If the *New Yorkers* let that one slip by, you can bet that their country cousins have done the same, and to the tenth. We editors make mistakes. We only admit it under oath, but we do err.

THAT FIRST STEP

With all the obstacles in the way, with all the frowning editors and frightening odds, how does one begin a freelance career? Well, think of it this way: consider your career to be a staircase. You're certainly not going to get to the top by leaping fifteen feet in the air, so take it one step at a time. Start at the bottom and be patient.

By the way, if you don't have patience, you don't have a prayer. It can be argued that for the freelance writer, patience and persistence are more valuable than talent. Sounds cold, but it's true . . . the tortoise didn't beat the rabbit because he was fast.

Of course, breaking into print by starting at the bottom is a feat subject to the laws of that age-old chicken-and-egg conundrum. For in order to receive an assignment from an editor, one must show that editor published materials. To get published, you must already be published. Or just be lucky.

Therefore, taking the first step into the publishing realm probably means seeking out the most elementary of venues and working for, at best, peanuts.

First, look into the newsletter market. Contact your church and see if they need any help with the newsletter. Do the same with real estate companies, private schools, and auto dealerships, even the senior center—any organization putting the public foot forward. And be creative; look for any company that might produce a newsletter and offer them your services. Volunteer to write about anything, about everything. Offer your time to the chamber of commerce to write press releases, to the fire department to write the safety manual. Anything.

At the same time, write letters to the editor. Read your local papers and think of brief letters you could send that would display your incredible wisdom and brilliant writing style. Work on Op Ed pieces as well, political or social or satirical comment on events of our time. If you can get a 600-word essay accepted, great. It's print, it's ink, it's a byline. It's a clip.

A *clip* is, in case you've not heard, publishing jargon for *clipping*, which is your article once it's published. All occupations use annoying buzzword jargon, and this is one of many in the freelance game.

The next step is the local weekly newspaper. Take your press release and your newsletter profile and your letter to the editor, and send a query to the editor of the weekly. I say weekly newspaper because that publication is typically a bare-bones operation using a great deal of freelancers and paying them, typically, not a great deal. Perfect for you.

Petition the editor for anything. Suggest a story or two, a profile on a local clock repairman or a war hero, whatever, but tell the editor that you will be happy to take an assignment on any topic. Your area may have one or two weeklies, and they are your target publications, but keep in mind the surrounding area. Many counties have weekly newspapers and they can sometimes be even barer at the bones than the city papers. That's good. Offer to cover the high school sports beat, or write book or movie reviews, or a food-and-wine column. Don't know much about food and wine? You're the only one who knows that. Through interviews and research, the true freelance writer can become an expert on any subject—at least for a thousand words—so study up on the baseball stats and the vintage news and dive in. When you're further along in your career you can be a little more picky, but for now take anything an editor offers.

When you start getting published clips and sending them to editors, send photocopies. No editor expects the original, and actually, the original can be a glaring flag that says, "Hey, I'm a serious rookie!" The experienced writers send photocopies. This is a significantly minute point, but as we'll discuss later, when your query letter is one of a dozen the editor may review that day, image is very important. In other words, if you have the opportunity NOT to shoot yourself in the foot, take it.

Once your persistence yields a couple of clips, you can begin targeting larger publications. See if the local daily papers accept freelancers, and if so, query them. At this point, you are also ready to contact local magazines.

Go to the library and browse the possibilities. Again, the smaller the magazine the better—that means that it has fewer people on staff and fewer dollars, and thus, fewer chances of drawing in the more experienced writers who could edge you out. Am I being too negative with all this talk of magazine and newspaper slumming? Nope. I'm saying the little guy gets picked last, and if last isn't good enough, then "not at all" is always waiting. The truth is, freelance writing is so competitive that you've got to get your foot in the door by any means possible.

I have walked every step I am detailing here. I want to be as encouraging as possible—and yes, the good news is you can do it, you can succeed!—but in guiding your path, I also want to steer you clear of the gopher holes and cow pies. Again, why cross the field with the CAUTION: BULL sign on the fence? Find the path of least resistance and keep moving.

Therefore, look for the city magazine, the regional magazine, the state magazine. Check out the genre publications: is there a statewide business magazine, a tristate farming publication, nature mag, a sports mag, an auto mag? These are the publications that need freelancers. Write down addresses and send off for copies.

Think of all the possibilities in these magazines. Why, they've got a department on running, and you run! They have a back-page essay section, and you write essays! They cover hog births in Minnesota—hey, you're rich! Send off the queries.

Needless to say, at this point, you have begun climbing the stairs. You have built up your clips and are using one publication to climb to the next. This stage will lead you as high as you can climb. It will lead you into a steady freelance writing career.

WHAT'S A QUERY LETTER?

There are two ways to contact an editor in solicitation of work: the query and the wrong way. Editors are very busy people (and they love to say that), so they can't be dealing with constant phone distractions. Picture this. The editor of your dreams, the person who is going to say "yes!" to your 20,000-word story on the history of air, this person is sitting at a computer editing one of a dozen stories due tomorrow. In addition, he or she is taking emergency calls from the printer, the ad agency, and the cleaner. This is the ninth in a row of fourteen-hour days and the Chinese takeout is stacked waist high. This dream editor, mid-word, gets a call from you.

Are you very pleasant with phone solicitors who interrupt your dinner—are you as excited about their pitch as they are? I'm an experienced writer with some national credits, I'm a *magazine* editor, and I wouldn't take those chances. Sure I may think I'm a hot ticket, but unless I'm John Updike, I'm small potatoes to just about any editor I could imagine—at least over the phone.

But the mail is the great equalizer. On the page, you and I can be kings. Each page starts out blank and a great many editors are going to consider queries on a case-by-case basis.

While we're on the subject of approaching an editor through the mail, let me recommend a letterhead and business cards. In the same way that you don't want to diminish your chances, you also don't want to miss the opportunity to enhance them. One very simple and easy method of doing that is to invest a little money in some professional-looking stationery. Keep it simple, nothing scented and embossed, just your name and address in letterhead font at the top of the page showing that this is what you do. Black ink on white paper says you did it yesterday, you'll do it tomorrow. Under your name on the business card, it says writer.

You would be surprised at the lack of professionalism we editors see in the mail and on the phone every day. Writers misspell our magazines, misspell our names, and confuse our genders.

Yes, our genders. My first name is Jamie—is that male or female? If you're sending me a letter that says "Dear Ms. Miller," you'd better be right, so call the office and find out. It's an understandable mistake, and I've accepted stories sent to my alternate gender, but some editors will turn you down for it.

Along these same lines, if a writer dates a letter by stating the year as 1896, the editor may think twice about trusting that same person with fact gathering in a feature story. So always do your homework and proof your correspondence—and think about getting that letterhead, it could be just the edge to make you stand out in a positive, professional manner.

As you begin to write your query letter, make sure you keep it brief. Tell the editor who you are, what you want, and what you can do. First, take one or two paragraphs to detail your story idea. Next, who are you and what have you done? Well, you're a freelance writer living over in Anytown who has published with this, that, and the other. And by the way, if this story doesn't suit, you'll be happy to cover any topic the editor has a need for, because you've written about everything from this to that.

With your query, enclose a few of your best clips, a resume if you like, and an SASE. The latter stands for self-addressed, stamped envelope. In other words, the editor doesn't want to take the time to address and pay postage for dozens and dozens of requests each week. It sounds petty, but many publications will tell you they don't even respond to queries without an SASE. Again, following this procedure will streamline your chances at publication acceptance, and bucking the system only increases the risk of failure. Looking back to the opening passage of this chapter, remember: you don't want to wait one more day than absolutely necessary to get a response, and you certainly don't want to wait for something that's in the trash can instead of the U.S. mail.

Once the query is in the mail, how long do you wait? Unfortunately, one to three months. That seems like a long time, but it's standard in the publishing business. Deadlines dictate much of the editorial calendar, so editors have very little free time to consider new material. They review manuscripts and query letters when they can, every few weeks or months. If you haven't heard anything after about two months, you can post a reminder letter—a very nice reminder letter—telling the editor that you sent your proposal back when and that you hope to receive consideration soon.

If you send an angry note, though, you'll ensure rejection. I know: as a freelancer, I have sailed rude and impatient into these waters and been suitably drenched.

Now it's time to review the content of the query. Some writers try to write in the tone of the story they're proposing. They will actually write a lead to the article and try to draw the editor into the idea the same way they would try to draw the reader into the article. Not a bad idea. If you can interest an editor in the story this way, chances are good you'll get the assignment.

So what does that mean—to write it in the tone of the story? Well, consider this scenario. Say you are proposing a piece on some old barns in one part of the county, and the fact that they were all built by the same family over a period of 150 years; legend has it that this same family follows the tradition of using the barns for, among other things, family weddings—just like the great, great grandparents did. Given that information, try something like this:

> John Hampton said "I do" just as his father had, and just as his father before him, and his before that. While most of us follow in traditional footsteps when it comes

to the wedding day, few can claim the same doorstep, and fewer still have been married where the Hampton clan has—in a barn. Especially in a barn built by grandpa's grandpa.

I propose an article. . . .

Something along those lines. The same query could also be written a million ways:

1. All across the nation, barns are being torn down as progress passes through, but right here in southern Anywhere, history itself is being threatened.
2. Married at the courthouse? Yes. Married at the church? Yes. Married at the barn—well, Yes!
3. The Hamptons have been building barns *their* way for 150 years, and time tells us their way works. Perhaps just as interesting, though, is what happens in the barn after it's raised.

You get the idea. Sell the tone, the writing style along with the story idea.

Now, you may choose to inform the editor in a different way, by simply describing the story and what you propose to highlight. That method is fine, too. The key is to send out the best letter you can, the best letter for you. If you feel you're forcing it to create a lead and a tone in the query, stay with the basic information statement and let your clips speak for themselves.

Do that and you'll never be rejected.

Sorry, I couldn't resist. Fact is, you could send the finest query ever written, a query constructed by God's own angels, or better, by Hemingway himself, and some bonehead editor like me will find a way to reject it. That's life; that's playing the writing odds. I have no doubt that as an editor I've rejected good ideas—maybe too many cups of coffee, maybe too few—I'm human. The point is you will see neon NO's. What you must do is learn how to handle them.

The secret is in the numbers.

Years ago, I found myself selling radio advertising. I hated it and it hated me; we were short-lived. But there were moments. One of them came in the numbers. An older, wiser salesman told me that so much of success in sales came in the volume of the attempt, that is, if you walk into ten establishments touting your product's value, nine will throw you out and the tenth will buy. The secret is in the sets of ten—or whatever the percentage—in making sure you contact patrons and get rid of the rejections. He said he'd say thank you to the folks who said no, because that just meant he was one call closer to a yes.

Translating that into the freelance business, that means rejection is a given and you've got to be able to move on. Yes, each of those rejected ideas will sting, but take the advice of my old friend and say thank you so you can bring your talents to another source. A lot of freelancers suggest having a game plan mapped out to the point of a waiting response letter and addressed envelope. When the rejection slip arrives, date the letter and send it out.

The importance of hope has lived at cliché levels for years, but it's true, hope does spring eternal. If you get the whopping big rejection one day, the hope of the whopping big acceptance leaves in the mail the next. Hope soothes, keep hope in the mail.

What happens, though, if you only have two good query ideas? Fiction happens, essays happen. As a freelance writer, you need to develop your craft, so write, write, write. One kind of writing serves another. Your goal may be the publishing of feature stories, but that doesn't mean you can't use your creativity to write and publish short stories, to write essays—which every editor respects—and to look for numerous publishing opportunities. The great thing about fiction and essays is that you can write them as you choose and keep the manuscripts constantly revolving in the mail. Try the same thing with poetry. (And by the way, if you want to be a better writer, study some of the top poetry around today—look at the language, the subtlety, the sparseness, the speed. It will only benefit your prose.)

So, if you have a number of things in the mail, some to literary journals, some to genre magazines, you can keep the hopeful flames burning, and burning brighter than if you've just got a few article queries in circulation. Again, there's safety in numbers.

BUSINESS, YES, BUT WHAT ABOUT WRITING?

We have looked at the business of freelancing—the query, the editor, the postman, the numbers. But just as important as all of that is the art, the actual writing.

I say *just as important* instead of *more* important because I want to make a sad point. You can be a John Casey or a Gregg Orr or an Annie Dillard—three of the most wonderful and unappreciated writers alive today—but unless you're a John Grisham, you will need to live and die by the marketable idea: with few exceptions, people buy books and magazines for their topics, not their prose.

In other words, and this is no slam on Grisham—he's a much better writer than many of his best-seller peers—you get your foot in the door with ideas, not with writing technique. The editor generally looks for the story and assumes the writer can handle the topic. When I think back about the best articles I've accepted as an editor, my initial vision is always of the story topic and how it meshed with our marketing plan to sell magazines. Only after that does my memory move to the tone of the piece and the craft of the writing. That's because I have to be a businessman. I can love the art of writing all I like, but if I don't sell magazines on the newsstand, I won't have a job on Monday morning.

So is it better to be lucky than good? Or translated into publishing terms, *persistent* than good? Again sadly, yes.

That's not to say that craft is of no consequence. Writers for *The New Yorker* and *Atlantic* and *Sports Illustrated* are not there because they're lucky, but because they're good. Well, they're lucky first, to get the opportunity, then they're good enough to deliver great writing—this balance will always apply.

Oftentimes, editors live on the good-enough edge. No matter what level of editorial sophistication, each magazine works with the good-enough writers, those who fit into an ability range that's appropriate in dollars and cents and marketing for that magazine. And that is where you come in. You want to make it to the good-enough pile—the writers regularly assigned by the editor. It's great to get a story idea and sell it to an editor, but it's better to be in a more consistent rotation where the editor comes to you, not the other way around. Your ticket to those good graces will be your query letter and clips. Even if the editor doesn't want the query, if it's presented well and backed up by good clips, he or she will know that you are a capable writer. Then, with pleasant persistence, with other queries and occasional check-ins through the mail, the phone may ring one day with an offer to write something from the editor's assignment list.

But how do you develop that good-enough ability? And how do you pass good-enough and move to great? Every industry has trade manuals, and writing's no different. Because it is *writers* who stock the writing business, though, the how-to material is particularly good and plentiful. Most libraries and bookstores will have dozens of books on writing—the one you're reading, *Writer's Guide to Magazine Editors and Publishers,* by Judy Mandell, is case in point. These books provide a tremendous amount of information on all facets of the writer's life. You can focus on the ones that deal with prose: how to write a lead, how to tell a story, how to create effective images and metaphors and scenes.

As well as books, you can also find trade magazines. It's safe to say that for the beginning freelance writer, one magazine, *Writers Digest*, truly stands out. You'll do well to read this publication cover to cover, including the classifieds, and then look for the next issue. It contains all the above-mentioned topics and more, and it's written with a freelance writer's concerns in mind.

Other books are published each year which detail the publishing policies of just about every magazine in the country. You'll get the names of editors, the types of articles they publish, the rates they pay, the turnaround time, and a great deal more. This sounds like a commercial, but I've got to say, these publications can be invaluable to the freelancer.

You will grow as a writer when you read about how to write, but don't forget to read the good writing itself. Read everything, from classics to sci-fi, from poetry to plays. Especially read the contemporary authors, those mentioned in this chapter and many more. Read Dillard for language, read Grisham for story, read Casey for everything. And read the national magazines and newspapers. See what you like, which leads work for you, which blocks of quotations seem to drag, which endings sing.

Then sit down and write. Try to write every day, even if it's just for five minutes. I once read a book on writing that claimed to have a surefire test for determining whether you have the stuff to be a writer. It said that you should write every day, and if you didn't, if you didn't have the discipline to be consistent, then you were NOT a writer. Wrong. Sure, it's important to develop discipline, but not all of us have the time and energy to hit the keyboard daily. Just do what you can, knowing that the greater the frequency, the greater the growing.

Try writing a journal. Many people keep daily journals of their insights and reflections. If that's not for you, work on essays—your trip to the vet, your cousin's bad breath, your bout with the flu. Carve your experience into essays that show your take on life. And write fiction. Two out of every three people in the checkout line at Kroger have a novel in the works—join them. Maybe you'll never publish, but it's a good exercise for your prose. If the novel is too long, write the story. There are hundreds of literary journals spread out across America today, and they all accept short stories based on merit, not name, so the playing field is quite level.

As you pursue your career, look also for classes. Many community colleges offer writing workshops, try them out. Universities often have continuing education curricula offering night classes once a week. You can study and get feedback on feature writing, creative writing, play writing, and even business or technical writing. All of these will help you develop your craft. Keep at it, stoke the hope by playing the numbers, and someday soon, perhaps when you least expect it, the postman may bring you cause for celebration.

The Answers to Freelance Writers' Most-Asked Questions

An Interview with Mary Ann Cavlin, Executive Editor, of *Modern Bride*

JUDY MANDELL

Mary Ann Cavlin was a history major in college. After graduation, she joined Parade *magazine as an assistant in reader mail and worked her way up to Associate Editor. After five years, she went to* Harper's Bazaar *and two years later moved to* Mademoiselle. *In 1982 Cavlin joined* Modern Bride *as Managing Editor. She was promoted to Executive Editor in 1995.*

Q: What is the best way for unestablished writers to pitch articles to editors at top magazines?

A: It's difficult because the top magazines usually have a stable of established writers. New writers have to work harder to gain recognition. First, study several issues of the magazine. Then, develop a few article ideas, as concisely as possible. It's vital that you know the magazine's audience.

Recently I received a query from a writer who offered to write an article titled "How to Grow Your Own Bridal Bouquet." If she had read enough bridal magazines, she'd know that the last thing most brides want to worry about is whether the flowers she wants for her wedding will be in bloom the day she's getting married.

Q: What do inexperienced writers do that hinder them from getting published?

A: Inexperienced writers will send in a completed manuscript, bypassing the query letter. The query letter is paramount to breaking in. Less experienced writers will take longer to present their ideas and often do not remain as focused on the topic.

Also they usually will not send clips. Professional writers usually include a variety of recent clips. The more variety, the more interested I will be.

Q: *If the query letter is paramount to a writer's breaking in, what's the secret of a good query letter?*
A: It's the first paragraph. If you lose the editor after the first paragraph, that's it. If the first paragraph is good, it whets the editor's appetite to read more.

The first paragraph should be about the topic, not about the writer. Professionals usually conclude their letter with a brief summary of their credentials and writings.

Q: *Do you think that in some cases queries are not read?*
A: No, that has not been my experience.

Q: *When should writers inquire about their query?*
A: It depends on the magazine. We try to respond in 4 to 6 weeks.

Q: *Is it OK for new writers to ask for more money than an editor offers them when negotiating a contract?*
A: They can try. Most editors are quite reasonable.

Q: *When is it appropriate for a writer to ask for expense money?*
A: During the initial conversation, when the writer is discussing the details of the assignment.

Q: *How important are deadlines to magazine editors?*
A: That depends on the magazine. I have an inventory of articles, so I can be flexible. But if I've given a writer an assignment for a certain issue, I expect the writer to meet my deadline.

Q: *If a writer can't make a deadline, what do you advise?*
A: Contact the editor immediately and explain the reason for the delay. This industry is small, and the last thing a freelance writer wants is to be considered unreliable.

Q: *How close to the assigned length must the writer come?*
A: Within a hundred words or so. For me, 10% over the assigned length is fine.

Q: *What about kill fees?*
A: We give writers a 25% kill fee for assigned articles that do not meet our editorial requirements. I always give a writer an opportunity to rewrite or accept the kill fee.

Q: *Do you have any advice for freelance writers?*
A: Know the market you're interested in writing for and present your ideas in a concise, one-page query letter.

Navigating the Slush Pile

AMY WEAVER

Assistant Editor, *Travel & Leisure*

As long as there have been people who have wanted to write, and magazines and publishing houses to publish them, there have been readers of "slush," usually students or publishing upstarts who are paid meagerly to sift through the piles of stories, articles, book manuscripts, and letters to find the rare hidden gem. Often it is one of the main duties of the editorial assistant, and some editors, when hiring, will even dangle that job as a carrot of creativity to lighten the drudgery of filing, expense reports, and answering phones.

Publishing is a notoriously difficult business to break into, from both sides. New York is full of recent graduates and more seasoned editors scrambling for jobs in magazines and books, and the hopeful payoff in that for the freelance or would-be freelance writer is that those who get in will have a nugget of sympathy for others on the outside. But probably not. All the sympathy in the world doesn't change the fact that the majority of writing sent in to magazines is just not that great. But this is not meant to be defeating—it's meant to inspire. Even well-known writers are often asked to revise their work, and more often than not, editors must do quite a lot of tinkering themselves to get the revision into working order. Without naming names, I must say I've heard many an editor complain about the uninspired copy a famous writer sent in. This is simply reassurance to the amateur that it takes awhile to get it right and to understand what the editors want. Magazine writing especially must adhere to the particular tone or voice of the given publication (more on that later). No one understands this better than the dues-paying assistants, junior staffers, and fledgling editors who have to work hard to get something published in the magazine they work for.

By now you might have figured out that I've done my time in the slush piles. I've worked with them in many capacities—as a freelance fiction reader for *Redbook*, as an intern at *New Woman,* as an assistant at a highly selective literary quarterly, and finally, as an editorial assistant at my present employer, *Travel & Leisure.* Plus all those years of creative writing classes (reading and critiquing the work of fellow students). All this experience makes me grateful for one thing. I am quite happy to be on this side of the pile, rather than a freelance writer trying to break into the business. I won't lie and say that many or even 5% of published stories and articles are discovered through unsolicited mailings. Most writers are discovered through other publications, word of mouth, or familiarity—they just always seem to have been around. Nonetheless, every place has its ubiquitous slush pile, and each one is different in its regard of that ever-present, always growing mound.

In fact, one of my first jobs in New York was reading for *Redbook,* which meant going into the offices once a month with a big shopping bag, cramming it full of unsolicited fiction manuscripts, carting them home, reading them as quickly as possible, sealing the rejection slips into the self-addressed stamped envelopes, and then dumping them all into a mailbox. All of this for $.50 a manuscript. Out of each bagful, maybe eight were turned back in to the editor, with a little summary from me. Hence, I spent many a long evening buried in short stories by amateur fiction writers from all over the country. Some of them were good; most of them were well-intentioned, but poorly structured or disciplined. Though I (like most slush readers) am usually able to tell after one or two paragraphs if a story is even a "maybe," I often found myself reading the whole thing, because, even though most of the writing was not of a professional enough caliber for publication in a national magazine, a lot of it was very compelling. But for $.50, I tried to keep the pace ruthlessly brisk. In Mary McCarthy's novel of New York in the thirties, "*The Group,*" book publisher Gus LeRoy tells Libby, one of his readers, that "the function of the first reader is to save the second reader's time. And his own." He fired her because she spent too much time on novels she ultimately rejected, for being "uneconomic." That is one reality that works against the unsolicited writer—especially when it comes to fiction or longer stories. Sadly, of all the manuscripts I plowed through in that year, only one even almost made it into the magazine. Apparently, the editor told me later, the story fell apart in the revision.

Later, while still a graduate student, I had the good fortune to work with Gordon Lish, then an editor at Alfred A. Knopf, and more pertinent to me, the editor and creator of a very risky literary magazine called *The Quarterly.* Two days a week for about a year, I sat on the floor of his very small office on East 50th Street, tearing through hundreds of fiction and poetry submissions while he talked on the phone to his writers, questioned me about my goals in life or my own writing, or quite often, read right alongside me. As a man passionately involved in language (he himself has written several novels and teaches a workshop for writers of fiction and poetry), he gave every submission consideration. He never glanced at a query letter, didn't care who the person was, or who they'd written for, as long as they did something real with the language. While working for him, I too, learned to throw letters of introduction into the trash. Often he scribbled a personal note on the rejection slip—"Send us more," or something to that effect, with a few return stamps out of courtesy. On the rejection slips for the *Redbook* submissions I also often wrote a little note when a story moved me, or the writer was someone I felt a straight, formal rejection might deflate. Of course, those little slips from publishers are famous for the devastating effect they can have even on established writers. In *A Moveable Feast,* Hemingway writes autobiographically about meeting with other struggling writers in Cafe de Flore to nurse their wounds over the rejections. I've gotten a few myself, but we won't talk about that. If your rejection is personalized, take it as a good sign, and perhaps send some more ideas.

There are ways, however, to lessen the threat of immediate rejection. Basically, before you approach a national magazine, have a portfolio, or at least a couple of clips from a smaller publication (newspaper, trade magazine) to back you up. Unpublished writers are never given assignments "on spec" (that is, before the article is written), and on the flip side, completed, unsolicited manuscripts are almost never published as is. Call the magazine and ask who would be the best person to send a proposal on whatever your topic is. Be specific, but don't attempt to pitch the idea over the phone. It won't get you anywhere. Then type a friendly, concise letter giving a rundown of your credentials and short, punchy paragraphs describing your idea. Don't include a resume or life history—your clips and the freshness of your ideas tell the editor everything he or she needs to know. Assume that as a novice, you have a small chance of breaking into a national magazine, and armed with that modesty, approach with a light touch. Despite old adages and clichés about the Darwinian struggle in the publishing business, aggressive behavior on the part of the writer is rarely endearing. Remember— getting a writing assignment is almost like getting a job. The editor has to like you. If they're interested, they'll probably call and ask you to send the completed article for consideration, no guarantees. Big rule: *don't* call them.

As for how your manuscript should look—well, preparing a good magazine submission is a lot like what my mother always said about housework—no one notices your efforts until you stop. A beautifully typed letter with the properly spelled name of the current editor (we still get queries addressed to an editor who left seven years ago) won't get you published, or necessarily get you noticed, but the sloppily handled version will irritate the receiver and can be taken as a bad omen. After all, if a writer isn't savvy enough to pick up the most current issue on the newsstand to see who works here now, how savvy will they be when it comes to ideas, style, and factual detail? It is also not flattering to see another publication's name typed on the cover letter. If you are doing a mass mailing, at least be careful enough not to mix up the letters.

More importantly, know inside and out the publication you are pitching. If you read a magazine every month, you will start to recognize the underlying voice that ties the entire magazine together; in fact, in most articles, the writer's voice is secondary to the subject matter. Once you have decided which magazine to pursue, pitch first to the "departments" or shorter, front-of-the-book or back-of-the-book sections. These are usually a combination of staff and freelance written material, and a novice has a much better chance of breaking in with a 200-word piece than a full-length feature. It's best if you stick with an area you have some interest in, like health, or sports, or computer technology. Most magazines have a "news" or "in brief" column and if you start thinking along those lines, you can constantly be looking for ideas. You might not even get a byline, but once you've published one of these short briefs, you may very well be called to write another. Editors need writers they can count on to do the work quickly, thoroughly, and according to instructions.

Follow this advice, and you are at least guaranteed the editor's consideration, if momentary, and if your story is rejected, remember how many stories and proposals those editors see each day, and keep trying. Make it better, and more polished each time, and if you never get a response from a certain magazine, move on to another one. There are lots of us out there.

Deciphering the Masthead

C. MICHAEL CURTIS
Senior Editor, *The Atlantic Monthly*

When I joined *The Atlantic* in 1963, it had no masthead. The question of who was who, I discovered, was sorted out more or less informally. We had an editor-in-chief, who was very much in charge. Under him were a managing editor, responsible for all production matters, and an associate editor, who worked directly with authors, read a great many manuscripts, and dealt with both literary agents and publishers soliciting our interest in excerpting from forthcoming books. The rest of us were "assistants to the editor," and that was that. Very soon after my arrival, the editor-in-chief retired and was replaced by a longtime *Time* magazine editor and bureau chief; *The Atlantic* soon had a masthead, a listing of all editors and, approximately, their areas of special responsibility. The new *Atlantic* followed the pattern established in most other magazines, assigning "associate" status to editors working closely with acquisition. The managing editor was the person looking after production (chiefly though not exclusively), and assistant editors were relatively new or junior hires, whatever their job assignments.

With a masthead and staff enlargement, however, come sensitivities and new distinctions. Thus was born the "executive editor," someone who often has a major voice in hiring and firing, and in the formation of editorial policy—or simply wants a little daylight between him(her)self and other editors near the top of the editorial pyramid. Similarly, "senior" editors are often editors at a plateau significantly higher than associates, usually because of seniority or particular skills. "Contributing editors" are normally not on the premises, but write frequently for the magazine, and maintain a friendly relationship with its editors. An "articles editor" is likely to be someone who sees to the details of assignments (fees, guarantees, expenses, deadlines, and so on), and a "fiction editor" is most likely someone whose chief responsibility is weeding through an overwhelming number of fiction manuscripts, in search of the handful that can be published. "Editorial assistants" are likely to be new hires, assisting someone or even a department. Their duties may be clerical. Someone has to type letters, answer the phone, see to the filing system, or perform other duties. On the other hand, today's editorial assistant may be tomorrow's associate editor. At *The Atlantic*, as at many other periodicals, even the newest and most poorly paid editorial personnel may well be evaluating manuscripts, editing specialized sections of the magazine, even writing for their own or other magazines.

My guess is that magazines will be more alike than not, with respect to the relationship between job title and actual work responsibility. Some are more explicit in their labeling of copy editors, proof readers, fact-checkers, and office managers. Others lump those job categories under the more general titles, "associate" or "assistant" or "staff" editors, depending on time served and salary level. In general, however, senior and associate editors concern themselves with acquiring and editing pieces for the magazine. Once the acquiring editors have done their job, the managing editor and the technicians who work with him/her take over. In virtually all cases that I know of, the editor-in-chief has the last word on what gets accepted; other senior editors have a *de facto* veto in that their job is, in part, to reduce the number of decisions that must be made by the editor-in-chief.

Some magazines have a precise and easily articulated editorial purpose or formula, based on a targeted set of readers with predictable tastes and interests. In such cases, the editor-in-chief is less valued for inspired taste and judgment than for managerial efficiency and a comfort level with the magazine's stated editorial ambitions. In the case of a general magazine like *The Atlantic*, the taste and judgment of the editor-in-chief are the defining characteristics of the magazine. What appears in each issue is a reflection of what the editor-in-chief and his or her senior editors find interesting and editorially palatable.

How are editors trained? Virtually all of the skilled editors I've worked with or know anything about have wide-ranging interests, a keen curiosity, and what is probably an instinctive sense of how the language works. They may or may not know what grammar is in the technical sense, but show them a bad sentence and they'll show you how to fix it. Many of them worked for newspapers early in their print careers, and, while newspapering, encountered deadlines, tight writing, broad choices of subject matter, editorial ethics, and the need to compose swiftly and regularly. Some editors spent time in graduate school, whether or not they earned an advanced degree. As graduate students they became specialists, and they learned something about both intellectual rigor and interdisciplinary thinking. If lucky, they also developed a visceral dislike for academic evasions and an appreciation for prose that makes its point clearly and directly. At least a few editors were simply very bright people, whether university-educated or not, who began their careers in entry-level jobs and demonstrated, repeatedly and convincingly, that they had the lively minds and editorial instincts that are the currency of the profession.

Editors don't earn the right to do what they do by passing a certification exam, like so many other professionals. Their eligibility for doing the job they do is tested daily and they are either helpful to those they work for or they look for employment elsewhere. Judgment is all, and dissonance—at least in the chronic sense—is fatal.

Freelance writers who don't know the magazine they're approaching are usually safe sending proposals to any senior editor (including associate, managing, articles, department, senior, or editor-in-chief). Proposals that reach the wrong desk will quickly reach the right one. Generally speaking, however, the higher the editor is on the masthead the more likely that he or she is actively involved in reading, assigning, and editing material for the magazine.

A writer will likely work closely with at least one line editor (someone who edits the piece line by line) and perhaps a fact-checker. In most cases, that will be the writer's only direct contact with the magazine, for other than administrative issues (such as payment schedules, arrangements for complimentary copies, author bios, and the like). The line editor will normally explain what major editing issues need to be addressed and will negotiate specific changes with the author. Eventually, the line editor will send galleys, explain and defend cuts and other word changes, and respond to expressions of authorial dismay. The fact-checker, normally someone other than the line editor, will want documentation of virtually every assertion of fact in the manuscript, a process that can be daunting, but will spare the author (and the magazine) a great many problems down the line. In most rigorously edited magazines, the line editor (often supported by a number of other unseen but grammatically fastidious hands) works to make sure the final product is concise, coherently organized, defensible at the factual level, and accessible to general readers. Those efforts are often subtle, sometimes bruising, but in most cases they are supportive and transforming, and help present the work of the writer in the best possible light.

I think writers should trust that editors have their best interests in mind, but should not abdicate responsibility for the final product. Once the process is understood, editor and writer ought to be able to work together amicably; the editor should expect to be required to explain and defend any changes; the writer should expect to be heard if he or she feels that the intent of the manuscript has been changed in substantive ways or that what was artful has now become laborious, even if technically correct. In general, I think writers ought to have the final say—even if that means the manuscript has to be withdrawn. A writer should not be compelled to accept editorial changes that seem unjustified and not obviously helpful. And an editor should feel obliged to explain, persuasively, any changes proposed.

Beyond Good Writing Style

An Editor's Top 10 Lists

CINDY T. MCDANIEL
AND SARA HORTON

Cindy McDaniel is editor of Arthritis Today, *the Arthritis Foundation's national consumer magazine. She directed the feasibility study that led to the magazine's establishment in 1987, and has served as its editor since. During that time, the magazine's circulation has grown to almost 600,000. In the past three years,* Arthritis Today *has won more than 65 awards of editorial and design excellence.*

McDaniel's previous experience was in public relations and marketing for the Arthritis Foundation and for Baptist Medical Center-Montclair in Birmingham, Alabama. She holds an undergraduate degree in public relations/journalism from Auburn University and an MBA in marketing from the University of Alabama in Birmingham.

Sara Horton is coordinating editor for Arthritis Today. *She started working with the Arthritis Foundation in 1994 as editorial assistant for the Publications Department. She has an undergraduate degree in liberal studies from Emory University and is completing her master's degree in English from Georgia State University.*

You've sent out a dozen query letters for the idea of the decade, proofed and spell checked to make sure there are no errors, and attached your five fave clips—yet you've received a dozen equally grammatically correct rejections. Or you have finally landed that big assignment and written a personal masterpiece, but after you received your comp copies in the mail, you have never heard from that editor again. Worse yet, you have ended up with a kill fee when your sterling manuscript was rejected because it's not what the editor expected.

What's going on here? You did your homework, wrote a convincing query letter, researched and wrote a literary triumph, and submitted it with all the requested documentation, disks, and data. In essence, you dotted all the i's, crossed all the t's, and basically did everything asked of you. So what went wrong? Chances are, you hit upon one of the intangibles that can send a writer into never-never land with a particular editor.

Although the specifics vary from editor to editor, most of us have a personal list of "do's" and "don'ts" that can either endear a writer to us for the long haul—or alienate us from the get-go. In the following sections, we have outlined our own "Top 10s." Another editor might add or delete items, or place the priorities differently, but this general road map should help you not only sell your great ideas, but engender long-lasting and mutually beneficial relationships with editors for whom you really want to write.

10 THINGS EDITORS LOVE MOST ABOUT FREELANCE WRITERS

1. **Knowledge of the target audience.** Before you approach a magazine with a query, take the time to find out about the publication. Request a copy of their writer's guidelines and a sample issue of the publication and familiarize yourself with it. Know who their audience is and what the message or mission of the publication is before you even approach them. When you do approach the publication with an idea, you can then better tailor that idea to its readers' needs. A writer who shows respect for the publication sets up a friendly, professional relationship with the staff of that publication.

2. **Clear and thorough queries.** A query letter is the editor's first impression of your writing ability. Remember, editors receive hundreds of queries from freelance writers—perhaps some with the same ideas as you. The one who presents the idea in the most concise and accurate way will get the assignment. A detailed query should be no longer than one page and should include a clear explanation of the story, demonstrate your knowledge about the subject, and list sources of information you plan to use in the article. It should show that you have given the idea enough thought to know there is a story and that you know how to get the information needed for that story. You should also include clips of your previous work if you are a first-time writer for the magazine. The easier you make it for the editor to see that you are qualified, the sooner the assignment will be made.

3. **Listening to and understanding the assignment.** A writer's best asset is often the ability to listen. Don't rush the editor when she is making the assignment. Preconceived ideas of how the publication plans to use your idea or what its needs are can backfire when the assignment is made. The editor might change your query a little or angle your idea differently to better fit the needs of the publication at that time. You need to make sure you understand what the editor expects from the story. If the editor has not made that clear to you, take the time to ask questions until you feel you understand the focus of the assignment. Don't try to figure it out on your own.

4. **Asking for background information.** Before a story is assigned, editors usually spend a lot of time researching and planning the article. Chances are the publication you're writing for has information about the subject on which you are writing. The topic may have even been covered in an earlier issue of the publication. Editors often have information and sources that you might not have access to—

especially if you are writing for a publication with a specialized topic. A writer who asks for background information indicates that he or she wants to know as much as possible about the subject and the publication's history with that subject, and to do a thorough job covering it.

5. **Staying in touch.** Editors get nervous if they don't hear from a writer after the assignment is made. An editor has as much at stake with an article as the writer does. A story that doesn't deliver what is expected can leave the publication with a hole in the lineup. Editors often must give updates on a story's progress at weekly staff meetings. It is essential that a writer stay in close contact with the editor when working on a story. Call the editor when you are doing research to let her know what information you're finding and how it will effect the direction of the story. Check in periodically while writing to make sure the article is on target with the assignment. This lets the editors know that the assignment is as important to you as it is to them.

6. **Enthusiasm for the project.** Not every assignment is exciting, but it is important that the editor knows you will give 100% to each story you write. Any editor wants to feel that the assignment he gives you will be important enough for you to do a complete and thorough job. Passion and excitement about your work indicate to the editor that you will put that energy into the article.

7. **Double-checking facts and information.** With most publications becoming financially driven, staff sizes are being cut. Because staffs often aren't large, it is more important than ever to an editor to know that you are delivering a story that is as accurate as possible. Always include a source list with full contact information so the staff can check quotes and facts. Also, be willing to double-check any information that the editor might question. The editor will probably be knowledgeable about the subject matter, and nothing impresses him less than an article that is filled with errors and inaccuracies.

8. **Professionalism.** It is important to remember that this is a business relationship, and you are delivering a product—not a work of art. While the old saying, "The customer is always right" may be a little harsh, it is important to keep in mind that the editor is your customer who is paying you for a service. The editor is more familiar with the agenda of the publication than you are. He will cut, question, criticize, and change your original manuscript to fit the tone and style of the magazine; that is what an editor does. Expect it and be willing to work in the changes required to make your product fit the needs of your customer.

9. **Flexibility.** A writer who shows the willingness to go the extra mile to make the story the best it can be is one that an editor will employ again and again. An editor might want to get to know your ability by assigning you smaller pieces at first. The writer who eagerly accepts smaller assignments and does a good job with them generally will be given larger, more involved assignments later. If a writer is "too busy" to spend the time needed on a smaller piece, the editor might wonder how time will be made to do a larger piece and thus give the assignment to someone with more time. If you don't want the job, you are guaranteed that someone else will. It is important to build a relationship of respect and trust between the writer and the editor—and that can take time.

10. **Prompt delivery of the product.** Putting together a publication is a business based on deadlines. Everyone involved has to meet specific deadlines in order for the publication to go to the consumer on time. This starts with the writer. Editors and writers need to work out deadlines that they both can live with and need to understand that the deadline will be met. Just as a writer would have a problem if the editor suddenly decided she wanted an article earlier than agreed upon, receiving a late article throws off the schedule for the rest of the production of the publication. Extensions of a deadline can be made in special circumstances, but the later that article is, the worse it reflects on you. The best writer in the world won't find work if she can't produce the product on time.

10 THINGS EDITORS HATE ABOUT FREELANCERS

1. **Sloppy, unfocused query letters.** Query letters are not insignificant. Editors look to these as an introduction to the writer and pay careful attention to what the query letter says about the writer who sent it. A sloppy query, full of misspelled words and grammatical errors, is almost insulting to the editor and often will not even get read. Any query with inadequate or incomplete information shows the writer has not given much thought to the article. If you have a story idea, use the query to tell the editor what that story is. It is not enough to say you want to write an article about the healthcare system. You have tell the editor what your angle is. What do you want to say about it? What is the story? And, please, a query should fit the publication to which you are sending it. Blanket queries often are rejected simply because there is nothing that would lend itself to the uniqueness of the publication.

2. **Exaggeration of abilities and experience.** A writer can't get away with lying about their ability. Sooner or later, the editor will see the lack of knowledge in the final product and reject the story. It is better to become an expert in an area and only take assignments that you know you can handle. If the assignment is something you are not interested in or have no knowledge of, the editor will appreciate your honesty. Saying you are not the right person for this job opens the way for you to pitch the story that you are right for.

3. **Disappearing.** Don't do it. There is not a faster way to lose an assignment. If the editor calls you, return the call promptly. Perception is important in business, and everyone needs to know that work is being done. As a freelance writer, part of your job is customer service—letting the editor know everything is on target. Even if you are not proceeding as quickly as you should, a good editor can help you get back on track. If the editor doesn't hear from you, he may think it is because you can't do the story. He might then reassign to another writer to cover his deadline, and you could be out of a job.

4. **Changing direction of the story without consultation.** If your research starts pointing you away from the original focus of the assignment, you need to consult with the editor before you change the direction of the story. Many publications have very detailed ideas about where the story is going. Artwork and companion articles might be assigned based on the original premise of your article. If the

story leads in a different direction, it may no longer be useful to the publication. Writers often stumble upon another exciting topic while research a story. Don't change the current assignment without checking it with the editor. Your editor may say go with it or save it for another issue. You have then created another assignment. Or you can keep that angle for another publication and go ahead an finish the original story for the current editor.

5. **Defensiveness about rewrites.** Any professional writer should expect and plan on revisions to a story. It is common for an editor to ask for more information or different sources. It is part of a freelancer's job to be available to make the story fit the needs of the publication. Usually rewrites don't involve an extensive amount of work—especially if you are careful to let the editor know what is going on with the story while you are researching and writing it. And, remember that it is a business decision—not a personal problem with you or your writing. If an editor doesn't think you have the talent and ability to get the story where he needs it, he might just kill the story without giving you a chance to do a rewrite. A writer that creates a fuss about revisions will leave a bad taste in the editor's mouth.

6. **Misunderstanding the assignment.** The time to let the editor know that you didn't understand the assignment is not after you turn in the story. Spending the time up front to make sure everything is clear will save you time and effort later. If a writer decides late in the game that she didn't understand the assignment, it sounds like an excuse for not doing the story right the first time. At worst, the editor will feel you can't follow through on an assignment. At best, he will think that the communication problem is with you since you didn't ask questions in the beginning.

7. **Insensitivity to the subject.** This is especially frustrating for editors working with special topics. It is extremely important that the writer be aware of whom he is writing for and about. You need to know your audience and keep the reader in mind when you are writing a story. An insensitivity to the subject, such as the use of nonpolitically correct language and slurs, can almost guarantee the article will be killed.

8. **Phone queries.** Because editors have busy schedules and many deadlines to meet, it is best not to query them over the phone. If you telephone an editor to talk about a query, more than likely you will be told to write a query letter and send it in. Decisions about assigning articles are rarely made by one person and probably not by the person you get on the phone. Several editors will read your query and clips and decide as a group if the idea is usable in the publication and if you are the right person for the assignment. It is easier to do this if your qualifications and clips are in writing. That way, the editors can decide for themselves about your ability. It is generally thought that writers who query by phone do not have enough experience to put their ideas down on paper or have not thought through their ideas and want help from an editor to flesh it out. Editors do not have time for this.

9. **Presentation of clips that misrepresent abilities.** Writers know if a story has been heavily edited. Do not give editors clips that do not represent your writing

style. If your clip was heavily edited by another publication's editors, it is probably not a good indication of what you can do. Clips should be of pieces that you truly feel ownership of and know are your best work. Don't leave an editor with expectations you can't live up to. You won't get more than one assignment; and, if you don't pull that off, the story might not be bought.

10. **Missing deadlines.** This is the industry taboo. Deadlines should be set in stone. If an editor gives you a deadline you can't meet, be honest about it in the beginning. Try to negotiate a deadline that better fits your schedule; if that can't be found, don't accept the assignment. The editor will appreciate and remember your honesty when it comes to future assignments. If you take the assignment and miss the deadline, rest assured the editor will remember that as well.

Magazine Contracts, Rights, and Electronic Publishing

An Interview with Lawyer Jonathan Kirsch

JUDY MANDELL

Jonathan Kirsch's college major was history, but his undergraduate education centered around writing for his local newspaper and for the Time-Life *News Bureau. After graduation, he wrote and published two novels while working at the* Los Angeles Times. *Kirsch followed the advice of his editor to acquire a topical specialty and attended law school at night. He passed the California bar in 1976, but remained in journalism until 1983, when he decided to practice law. Kirsch worked for two law firms before going out on his own in 1988. As a partner in the firm of Kirsch and Mitchell, Kirsch's present focus is intellectual property—copyrights and trademarks with a specialty in publishing law. He continues to actively freelance for magazines and newspapers. His book,* Kirsch's Handbook of Publishing Law for Authors, Editors, Publisher, and Agents, *was published in February 1995.*

Q: Let's talk about specific contractual terms. What are "first rights"?
A: The phrase first rights is an extremely shorthand phrase. It doesn't give you enough information and it would be dangerous to make an arrangement based on the phrase "first rights." All that says is that [the publisher] is going to have the first opportunity to use the author's work but it doesn't say anything about what format or what medium. "First rights" is not an adequate phrase.

Q: What are "first serial rights"?
A: First serial rights are the exclusive right to publish the author's work in a serial publication, such as a magazine or newspaper, for the first time.

Q: Under what circumstances are "first serial rights" bought?
A: First serial rights come up in two different ways. One is if you're doing a free-lance article, photograph, or piece of artwork for a magazine or newspaper. It [also] comes up in a separate context if you're writing a book. First serial rights in a book setting means the right to prepublication—the right to publish material in the magazine before it's published in the book. The definition is internally consistent. One suggests the other, but there are slightly different nuances.

Q: What are "second serial rights"?
A: "Second serial rights" means literally the second time.

Q: How does the meaning change when the words "North American" are prefaced?
A: North American added means that those rights are confined to North America.

Q: What other rights could a publisher buy?
A: You could have first serial rights worldwide, first European serial rights, first Asian serial rights, first English language serial rights. You could subdivide serial rights into a whole bunch of different markets. That just describes where you could exercise the rights.

Q: Tell me about onetime publishing rights?
A: Onetime is another way of saying "you have the right to publish it once only," but that doesn't tell you in what format or in what market. A more complete [phrase] would be "first North American serial rights one time only" or "first onetime only North American serial rights." If you put that phrase together it would mean you, the author or freelancer, are giving the publisher the right to be the very first one to print the work, but . . . only print it in North America and . . . only print it once. [The publisher] can't anthologize it, . . . can't reprint it, . . . can't sell to an online database.

Q: If a writer gives first North American serial rights to a publisher, at what point can that writer sell the piece somewhere else?
A: If the publisher is getting first North American serial rights only, once the magazine or newspaper has published it, the best argument is that they may not publish that piece any more. The author controls the rest of the rights.

Q: Can the writer in that case sell that piece to a syndicate or a book publisher the day after it's published?
A: Yes.

Q: Can writers rely on what you've just said?
A: It's a little simplistic to rely on what I've just said because you also have to look to the Custom and Practice of the publishing industry and the changing definitions.

Q: What is the meaning of "Custom and Practice"?
A: The terms under which magazine publishers acquire rights were defined for many years by what many lawyers call Custom and Practice. Custom and Practice means the general rules that apply and are understood in a particular industry.

Q: How have rights that publishers buy from freelancers changed in the last 50 years?

A: There was a time when most freelance work was done without any contract at all. It was very rare that a publisher would go to the trouble of asking a freelancer to sign a contract, especially newspapers, which deal with huge volumes of material. Nowadays, because of lawyers like me, publishers are more careful and offer freelancers contracts or assignment letters that are to be countersigned.

Fifty years ago the primary rights that a magazine or newspaper publisher needed and acquired in a freelancer's work was the right to set it into type and print it on paper. Today that definition is changing because it's becoming increasingly common that publishers not only print an article on paper and sell it as part of [a] magazine by subscription or on newsstands, they also may make back issues available online as well as facts on demand or specific articles from back issues. The standard meanings of the terms like "first North American serial rights" or "first world rights" now are in the process of being redefined. Publishers are beginning to change their standard freelance contracts so that they have those rights. The Custom and Practice is changing because of electronic media.

It's naive of the writer to assume that because the phrase first North American serial rights has been used, the day after it's published the newspaper or magazine publisher can do nothing more with the article. It's more realistic for the writer to know that the publisher is assuming it can do lots of things with it. It's the responsibility of the freelancer to define what limitations he or she is placing on that work and that everybody understands what those limitations are.

Q: Are magazines buying more rights today than they used to?

A: Yes. The rule of thumb is that publishers and freelancers are waking up to the complexities of freelance writing contracts and they are paying more attention to defining what's being bought and sold in contract documents.

Q: How are publishers changing standard freelance contracts?

A: Publishers are changing standard freelance contracts to make it clear that not only can they print the freelancer's article or photograph or artwork in the pages of the magazine, they can also use it in electronic media, they can anthologize it, they can use it for facts on demand—things like that.

Q: Are publishers essentially buying all rights from freelance writers?

A: They're buying more and more rights up to all rights. There's a very hot controversy as of this moment in which *The New York Times* is trying to characterize all freelance submissions as work for hire. Work for hire is the most comprehensive acquisition of rights. It takes every single right there is and ever will be. That's one solution that one publisher has come up with. Other publishers are a little more reasonable and saying "we won't take all rights but we need to take a bunch of rights—more rights than we used to."

Q: Let's explore the contractual words "work for hire."

A: There are two ways to convey rights in a copyrighted work from one person to another. One approach is that the author sells or licenses some or all of the rights to another person or a publisher. The other way is work for hire.

In a sale or license, the author can impose a limitation on what rights are given and when they come back and to whom they revert. There are a lot of limitations and restrictions that can be written into an agreement for the sale or license of copyrights. Work for hire, by contrast, takes 100% of all rights forever and gives them to the publisher. There's no limitation, there's no reservation of right, there's no reversion of rights. It all goes to the publisher. Under the law of copyright in the United States, the author of a work for hire is considered to be the commissioning party, not the actual living person who authored the work. So if I'm XYZ Publishing Company, and I go to Judy Mandell and get an article on a work for hire basis, when I fill out the copyright registration form, in the blank that says "author," I write XYZ Publishing Company, not Judy Mandell.

Q: How can freelancers protect themselves and their work in this day of electronic publishing and electronic rights?
A: Electronic rights are not as exotic as you may think. They're just the rights to use a work of authorship in a new medium. There was a time when the only medium was scribes copying manuscripts. Then came the printing press. Then came audio, audio visual, and all kinds of technology. This is just the latest technological wrinkle. Unless he has sold the work as work for hire, the author starts out with all rights and can restrict how the work is used in any particular medium, including electronic media.

Q: What if somebody takes a writer's work and uses it improperly? Either they post it to a bulletin board or they find it on an Internet site and download and copy it?
A: That's garden variety copyright infringement—it's nothing new, it's nothing fancy, it's very simple. The courts have made it very clear that the laws of copyright, trademark, libel, and invasion of privacy all apply in cyberspace.

Q: What can authors do to protect their rights in cyberspace?
A: Not a lot. It's very hard to trace where information has come from, where it's going, and it's hard to track down who is actually infringing. My only practical advice is anything made available in cyberspace should bear proper copyright notices and warnings against reproduction. This has been done for a hundred years in books and sometimes in newspapers and magazines. The copyright notice should say [something like] "All rights reserved. Any copying, downloading, and disseminating is prohibited without the consent of the author." But that doesn't take you very far because of the speed and anonymity of Internet communications. If somebody wants to blast your work all over the Internet, it's going to be very hard to track them down. If you do track them down, you can sue them for copyright infringement. You have all of the remedies you would have if they were doing it on a photocopy machine or on a printer. This has been done. *Playboy* magazine has done it, as has Tsuga, the game manufacturer. Many people with copyrighted words have filed and won lawsuits in electronic infringement cases. But it's a very difficult and expensive process.

Q: Are writers protected by copyright laws if they don't put a copyright notice with their work?
A: Yes. Copyright law does not require registration and does not require notice as a condition for ownership. But there are good reasons to register your work and use

copyright notices. If you register your work and someone infringes it, you have some very impressive legal remedies that you can bring to bear. If you don't register it, you have many fewer remedies. You have some, but it's a harder case to prosecute.

Q: Can writers register their work after the fact? That is, after someone has infringed on it?

A: Registration benefits apply to infringements which take place before the date of registration. If somebody infringes and you run to the copyright office and register your work, that registration will only apply to infringements which take place after the date of registration. However, there is a special rule which says, "if you file your registration within 90 days after publication, the benefits will apply to both infringement before and after registration." It is very much in the interest of an author to make sure that his or her work is registered within 90 days after publication.

Q: Should writers formally register every magazine article?

A: Your publisher is probably registering the entire work. That is effective in protecting everything in it. You're protected. You don't have to do it. But you can. It's very simple. You call the copyright office. You get the copyright form and you register.

Q: Are copyright laws changing because of the Internet and cyberspace?

A: They're changing in small and subtle ways. There's a little fine tuning and fix-up going on in technical areas that don't affect most writers, artists, or photographers.

Q: What should freelance writers watch out for when signing a contract?

A: First and foremost, understand which rights you are selling and those you are keeping. You (the author) must study the contract or assignment letter that the publisher sends. You need to negotiate if the publisher is getting rights that you don't want them to have.

If a writer receives no assignment letter or an informal one that is silent on the question of rights acquired by the publisher, he or she should write to the editor saying "Dear Editor, Let me confirm that you are acquiring the following rights in my freelance work" and list those rights. It would be best if that editor would sign the writer's letter and send a copy back. Most editors won't sign—they don't want to sign legal contracts without their boss's permission. They'll probably ignore it. But sending that letter is better than nothing.

Q: What if the publisher puts material online without the author's consent?

A: Start by looking at rights the publisher says it's acquiring in the assignment letter or contract. Unless you've done something about it, those are probably the rights they've got.

When the freelancer [assumes that the publisher's only right] is to print it on paper, the publisher's argument will be, "when you sent your article in, you knew or should have known that we're not just a print publisher. We also make our magazine available online. We also sell reprints of articles from back issues. We publish an anthology every five years. We have a news service that distributes our articles. You should have known that we were going to make those uses of your article because that's the business we're in."

That's where the definition of serial rights is changing. Five years ago the freelancer had the better argument. I think that's changing now.

Q: Give me give me an example of the ways rights are changing.

A: Let's say you were freelancing for a newspaper in the days before home delivery, when newspapers were bought at newsstands or from newsboys on street corners. Then a new mode of distribution began—delivery boys threw papers on the reader's front porch. Is that a new use? Can the freelancer step up and say "No you can't do that. That's a new form of distribution and I didn't authorize you to do that"? We're in that kind of situation right now. Publishers are beginning to realize that there are other ways to see the magazine or newspaper. [This time] it's a different technological format. We're presently in the middle of a process of change.

Q: Are some publishers paying writers more when they require more rights?

A: Some publishers throw something more in the pot. But here's another wrinkle. I don't think publishers are making more money on the Internet. They assume, in some vague way, that there is a promotional benefit to having the magazine or newspaper online. If the publisher is making money by licensing the publication, that should be shared with the author.

Q: What are important principles to keep in mind with regard to electronic publishing?

A: First and foremost—the law of publishing applies in cyberspace. Any legal right or remedy that potentially arises in a published work, arises in a work that appears in electronic form. That includes copyright, trademark, defamation, invasion of privacy, and the right of publicity.

Second principle—the freelancer starts out with all rights, including electronic rights. It's the responsibility of the freelancer to understand what rights he or she is giving up to the publisher. That can be done in a formal contract, in an assignment letter, in a letter that the freelancer writes back to the publisher. But there should be some effort made to define and agree upon what rights the publisher is getting and how the publisher is going to pay for those rights.

Third principle—the words electronic media or electronic rights cover a huge, growing, and changing body of technology. It's important to go beyond the phrase "electronic rights" and define exactly what uses of the freelancer's work are going to be permitted. For instance, the magazine or newspaper publisher may offer articles from back issues, which they print and fax or e-mail to their readers. That right can be separately defined. Or the publisher may want the right to put the entire issue online, on a subscription data base like Prodigy, America Online, or CompuServe. That's another and different right. The publisher wants to sell the magazine on CD-ROM—another electronic right. Or the publisher may want to license someone to create a multimedia or interactive product with sound and images from bits and pieces of back issues. That's yet another right. Each of those rights should be separately negotiated.

Q: What about the writer who won't give the publisher any electronic rights?

A: That freelancer will be told by the publisher "in that case, we don't want your work." The publisher can't have one version of the magazine available on the newsstand and another version online. "There's Jonathan Kirsch's article—it has to come off. We have to somehow figure out how to delete it before we put the magazine on-line." That's not going to happen.

Q: How would you advise writers in this new era of cyberspace publishing?

A: It is reasonable for a writer to say "you have the right to post my article if you put your magazine online as long as you pay me some agreed-upon percentage or some additional fee, but you don't have the right to create a multimedia product or interactive product based on my article." Not only do you have to define who gets electronic rights, you have to define what electronic rights you're talking about.

It is harder to protect the integrity of work that gets onto the electronic media. But the methods of protecting it are the same as by the print media—use copyright notices, . . . warnings, and text blocks that announce what the user can and cannot do with the material. That's one way of slowing down or discouraging the misuse of material.

Q: How would you advise writers in general when it comes to contracts?

A: The most important and fundamental thing a writer can do is to know in advance what rights the publisher is intending to acquire. If the writer wants to put limits on it, he or she must negotiate up front what those limits will be. With the caveat, most publishers will probably say "we're not going to accept your limits."

PART TWO

The Magazines

Consumer Magazines

Alternative/Astrology/Metaphysical/New Age

GNOSIS: A JOURNAL OF THE WESTERN INNER TRADITIONS

P.O. Box 14217
San Francisco, CA 94114

Phone number   415-974-0600
Fax number   415-974-0366
E-mail address   Editorial inquiries to smoley@well.com
Parent company   Lumen Foundation
Circulation   16,000
Magazine availability   Newsstands and subscription
Target audience   Anyone interested in mysticism, occultism, and esotericism
Magazine's history and mission   Founded in 1985 by Jay Kinney (now publisher) Mission: to provide reliable, intelligent, impartial information on the mystical and esoteric traditions of the world
Nonfiction   100%
Percent of articles freelance-written   75%
Number of articles bought annually   80 (including short items and book reviews)
Sections of the magazine open to freelance writers   All
Article interests and needs   According to their Writer's Guidelines, *Gnosis* is interested in articles on esoteric traditions and practices, current events in spirituality, and book reviews of new spiritual and occult books.
Queries should be directed to   Richard Smoley, Editor
Length of articles   750 to 5,000 words, depending on section of magazine
Payment $75 to $250 per article; $40 per book reviewed
Time of payment   On publication
Expenses   No
Photographs   Yes; payment $50 to $125 per photo
Response time to queries   1 to 2 months

Rights bought   First-time
Kill fees   None
Writer's guidelines   Yes, with SASE
Sample issues $8 per issue (includes shipping). California residents should add $.48 per issue sales tax.

TIPS FOR WRITERS
Richard Smoley, Editor

I can only say that the best advice for breaking into *Gnosis* is to become familiar with it. Though we are found on an increasing number of newsstands, we remain an alternative publication, with the quirkiness that that generally implies. As a result, even more than mainstream publications, the decisions have largely to do with personal tastes and what we happen to be interested in at present.

Hence I'd strongly encourage people to send for a sample issue ($8, including shipping; we do not give out free sample issues to potential writers). Our contributors are by and large people who already know and love the magazine. In addition, we do issues on specific themes and strongly favor articles that fit into these themes (themes are listed both in the issue and in the writer's guidelines).

Written queries, accompanied by clips, are the best way for new writers to introduce themselves; we will, however, read unsolicited submissions and attempt to reply promptly (if an SASE is included). We have run stories of first-person experiences, though this is the exception rather than the rule.

We are a nonsectarian publication and try to provide a forum for intelligent, objective discussions of spirituality from a wide number of viewpoints. Our subhead is "a journal of the Western inner traditions." Our goal has been to cover the mystical, esoteric, and occult traditions of the West, including Christianity, Judaism, Islam, Paganism, as well as more marginal faiths. At present, however, we are shifting our editorial focus slightly to include more on Eastern (i.e. Asian) traditions (this will begin in earnest with our spring 1996 issue, entitled "East Meets West").

HOROSCOPE
1540 Broadway
New York, NY 10036

Phone number   212-782-8532
Fax number   212-782-8309
Parent company   Dell Magazines (Bantam Doubleday Dell)
Circulation   273,600
Magazine availability   Newsstands and subscription
Target audience   Astrologers/students
Nonfiction   100%

Percent of articles freelance-written   100%
Number of articles bought annually   Approximately 40
Sections of the magazine open to freelance writers   Articles
Article interests and needs   Current events
Queries should be directed to   (Ms.) Ronnie Grishman, Editor-in-Chief
Length of articles   2,000 to 3,000 words, generally
Payment $.10 per word
Time of payment   On acceptance
Writer's guidelines   Available

IMPORTANT QUESTIONS ANSWERED

Q: Is an SASE always necessary?
A: Yes
Q: Are phone calls from writers OK?
A: Yes
Q: Is it OK if writers fax or e-mail queries to you?
A: Yes

PARABOLA: THE MAGAZINE OF MYTH AND TRADITION

656 Broadway
New York, NY 10012

Phone number   212-505-9037
Fax number   212-979-7325
E-mail address   parabola@panix.com
Parent company   The Society for the Study of Myth and Tradition
Circulation   40,000
Online status   Web site at http://members.aol.com/parabmag/ParabolaWWW/
Magazine availability   Newsstands and subscription
Target audience   Educated general reader
Magazine's history and mission   Founded in 1976 by D. M. Dooling to explore the myths, symbols, rituals, and art of the world's religious and cultural traditions.
Nonfiction   90%+
Fiction   10% (if that—usually less)
Percent of articles freelance-written   80%+
Number of articles bought annually   Approximately 50
Sections of the magazine open to freelance writers   Articles, retellings of traditional stories, reviews, and comments
Article interests and needs   See essay; must address upcoming theme (list available; send SASE).

Queries should be directed to   The Editors
Length of articles   1,000 to 3,000 words (shorter preferred); 500 to 1,500, reviews and stories
Payment   Usually ranges from $75 to $300 depending on the length of the article and the number of articles in the issue.
Time of payment   On publication
Expenses   Only if previously agreed upon with editor
Photographs   Submit copies with article.
Response time to queries   Variable—depends on how near deadline is
Rights bought   According to its writer's guidelines, "*Parabola* purchases the right to use an article in all substantially complete versions (including non-print versions) of a single issue of our journal. We also request the right to use the piece in the promotion of *Parabola,* and to authorize single-copy reproductions for academic purposes. All other rights are retained by the author."
Kill fees   *Only* for articles solicited by the editors
Writer's guidelines   Yes—send SASE.
Sample issues $6 current issue; $8 back issue

TIPS FOR WRITERS
Natalie Baan, Managing Editor

Your query letter should be brief and to the point. Since we are a theme-driven magazine, it should state which theme you would like to address and how your article explores that theme. A couple of lines of biographical information are always helpful.

Clips are not a major factor in our consideration of a query. If you would like to send one along, fine; but we will be just as likely to request an article if you don't. Usually the query letter itself tells us all we need to know about an author's writing.

A chatty or "clever" query letter, or a letter that tells us how great you or your article are, generally doesn't impress us at all. Don't try to "sell" yourself or "market" your article. Don't send us your glowing rejection letters from other publishers, or letters from people who admire your work. *Parabola* is not about personalities; we pay no more attention to a heavily self-promoted writer than to someone who sends us a brief and to-the-point query. It is acceptable to send a manuscript with no query letter, although we do prefer to receive queries. Please be sure to state in your cover letter which theme you are addressing. If the article is *not* directed to one of our upcoming themes, it will be put in a folder and read when time permits. Our turnaround time for not-for-theme manuscripts is officially three months, but can be much longer.

Articles submitted for a theme usually will be read when we begin work on that issue, although occasionally they do get looked at earlier. The main period of reading for each theme is the month surrounding the deadline: for example, the month of April for our April 15 deadline issue. If you send your manuscript three months early, you may have to wait three months for us to look at it.

Since we have a small staff, we may not be able to return manuscripts immediately after making final decisions, but you can reasonably expect to hear from us by the end of the month following the deadline (May in the example above). Sometimes acceptances take as long to go out as rejections, so don't panic.

Whether you are mailing a query or an article, please include an SASE for response. It is also acceptable to fax or e-mail your query; however, do *not* fax or e-mail your article unless we have already indicated that we would like to see it.

If you have just discovered that a deadline is tomorrow, call us. Otherwise, please do not phone in your query as we will not be able to give it proper consideration. While we are always happy to talk to authors, we are usually on deadline and very busy, so please don't call repeatedly to see if we've read your manuscript or to find out what we think of it. At best, we will be able to tell you if we have received it, and when you should be hearing from us.

Unfortunately, we are not often able to offer feedback or constructive criticism on submissions. Please do not call asking for an explanation of our rejection—usually we do not recall offhand. If you would urgently like to know, send us a brief note. Be sure to remind us of the title of your article, and which theme it addressed.

The best way to be published in *Parabola* is to be intimately familiar with our style and content. Read more than one of our issues, paying attention to the kinds of material that we publish. Send an SASE for our writer's guidelines and list of themes. Be sure to follow our guidelines for presentation and length.

Parabola's specific needs vary depending on the editor; however, we usually look for articles which illuminate some aspect of the spiritual search in a fresh and insightful way. We prefer material which grows from a specific religious or cultural tradition, instead of from generic "spirituality." The article can focus on more than one tradition, but it must do more than skim the surface of each. Articles on other subjects, such as science, the arts, or personal experiences, are also acceptable, providing they touch on some element of the universal search for meaning.

We also publish retellings of myths, fairy tales, and traditional stories. Please be sure to mention the culture from which the story originated.

Parabola does not publish made-up mythology, "fakelore," fantasy fiction, or recountings of vision experiences. We do not publish self-help, "pop" psychology, or Ten Ways to Make Your Life Better. Though we often include esoteric material, we generally do not publish "occult" or magical studies.

Parabola is aimed at the general reader, and therefore prefers material which is not too academic. Avoid scholarly jargon on the one hand, and careless or "flip" writing on the other.

We receive more unsolicited fiction and poetry than anything else. *Parabola* rarely publishes either (perhaps one or two per year out of a selection of over two hundred submissions), and we are very conservative in what we do accept. Please do not send "experimental" works.

Things to avoid:

"I know you only publish articles that fit your theme, but maybe you can use this piece anyway" or "Can you read my work and tell me if it might fit one of your upcoming themes?" (Shows laziness on the part of the author.)

"This article could work for your issue on 'X theme' or your issue on 'Y theme.'" (If it's vague enough to fit multiple themes, we probably can't use it.)

If you plan to send us material for one theme and *different* material for another theme, please make each submission separately with an appropriate cover letter and SASE.

Do not send very long pieces or books, saying "Perhaps you can find something in this which will suit your theme." (We don't have the time or staff to read them.)

Don't send us simultaneous submissions. We prefer articles to be written specifically with *Parabola* in mind.

SHEPHERD EXPRESS

1123 North Water Street
Milwaukee, WI 53202

Phone number   414-276-2222
Fax number   414-276-3312
E-mail address   scott@shepherd.express.com
Parent company   API—Alternative Publications, Inc.
Circulation   55,000
Online status   Web site at http://www.shepherd-express.com
Magazine availability   Newsstands and subscription
Target audience   Movers and shakers of the galaxy
Magazine's history and mission   Started in May 1982. In September 1994, the employees, through Alternative Publications Employees Cooperative, bought controlling interest in API, thus making it the only employee-owned alternative newspaper.
Nonfiction   100%
Percent of articles freelance-written   40%
Number of articles bought annually   200
Sections of the magazine open to freelance writers   Music (rock 'n' roll, alternative national acts), film, book reviews
Article interests and needs   Current issues and culture
Queries should be directed to   Scott Kerr, Editor
Length of articles   800 to 2,400 words
Payment $50 to $200
Time of payment   2 weeks after publication
Expenses   Sometimes—negotiated
Photographs   Query by mail or e-mail
Response time to queries   2 weeks
Rights bought   First-time
Kill fees   50%

Writer's guidelines   No
Sample issues $2.00

IMPORTANT QUESTIONS ANSWERED

Q: Are phone calls from writers OK?
A: No
Q: Is it OK if writers fax or e-mail queries to you?
A: Yes
Q: What is your overall advice to writers who want to get published?
A: Rigorous thinking, vigorous prose

Animal/Pet

ANIMALS
350 South Huntington Avenue
Boston, MA 92130

Phone number   617-541-5065
Fax number   617-522-4885
Parent company   MSPCA/AHES
Circulation   95,000
Online status   Available online from Elosco On-line, American Cybercasting, the Electronic Newsstand, and University Microfilms, Inc.
Magazine availability   Newsstands and subscription
Target audience   Average age 41, 86% female, average income $38,000, 92% pet owners, 44% city, 29% rural, 27% suburb
Magazine's history and mission   Founded in 1868 by the Massachusetts Society for the Prevention of Cruelty to Animals. Mission: ". . . to deliver timely, reliable, and provocative coverage of pet-care topics, animal-protection concerns, and wildlife issues . . . Our goal is to develop a well-informed readership that can help create positive change for animals."
Nonfiction   100%
Percent of articles freelance-written   95%
Number of articles bought annually   40 to 60
Article interests and needs   Profiles, books/reviews, features
Queries should be directed to   Wildlife and/or animal protection to Joni Praded, Director and Editor. Pets or issues that affect companion animals to Paula Abend, Managing Editor.

Length of articles   300 to 2,000 words
Payment $75 to $125 depending on length of article and amount of research needed.
Expenses   Reasonable agreed-upon expenses, such as phone and fax fees
Photographs $125 to $300
Writer's guidelines   Yes
Sample issues   Send $3.95 payable to *Animals* magazine.

CATS MAGAZINE

P.O. Box 290037
Port Orange, FL 32129-0037

Phone number   904-788-2770
Fax number   904-788-2710
E-mail address   cats@pwr.com
Parent company   Cats Magazine, Inc.
Circulation   130,000
Online status   Web site at http://www.catsmag.com
Magazine availability   Newsstands and subscription
Target audience   We have readers in virtually every age group, but statistically the majority is made up of educated women, ages 35 to 54. Most have owned cats for over 10 years.
Magazine's history and mission   Founded in 1945 by Charles Kenny. In April 1951, it was purchased by the Smith/Copeland family, who still publish the magazine today. *CATS Magazine* provides our cat-loving audience with timely, practical, and well-researched information, delivered in an understandable, enjoyable style. We confront controversial issues and encourage responsible pet ownership through ongoing education. We pay tribute to individuals and organizations that improve the lives of cats and owners, and we incorporate reader contributions that extol the virtues and pleasures of being friends with our favorite subject—cats.
Nonfiction   95%
Fiction   5%
Percent of articles freelance-written   80%
Number of articles bought annually   47 feature articles, 36 short stories, 12 Remarkable Cat stories
Sections of the magazine open to freelance writers   Features, Tails & Tales (short stories), Few Lines 'Bout Felines (poems), Remarkable Cats
Article interests and needs   Feature topics must be cat-related, well-written, and well-researched. Include: behavior, health, nutrition, profiles of people and organizations, how-to/instructional, cat-oriented events and places.
Queries should be directed to   Tracey Copeland, Editor
Length of articles   Remarkable Cats: 1,000 to 1,200 words; Short Stories: 1,000 words max; Features: Query first (if assigned, 1,500 to 2,000 words)

Payment   Remarkable Cats: $100 (including photos); Short Stories: $25 to $50; Features: $250 to $500
Time of payment   On publication
Expenses   Must be minimal *and* preapproved
Photographs   Send for guidelines
Response time to queries   Approximately 3 months (sometimes less, sometimes more)
Rights bought   First-time
Kill fees   30% for *assigned* articles not used for publication
Writer's guidelines   Send SASE with request.
Sample issues   Send self-addressed, 9 × 12 envelope with $3 check or money order for shipping and handling.

TIPS FOR WRITERS
Becky Bridges, Assistant Editor

We *prefer* to receive queries for feature articles—if we're interested in the idea, we'll ask to see more. Do not query for short stories, just send the actual manuscript on speculation. If we have not worked with you before, we want to see published clips and a resume in addition to your query/cover letter. The queries that catch our attention are neat, typically one-page (single-spaced) in length (concise, yet long enough to impart a good sense of what the proposed article would really be like), well-written, clear, and include something that tells us just who this writer is and why we should hire him or her to write this particular article. It is also good to give us some idea of the types of sources you have access to and plan to utilize for the proposed article.

Freelancers who hope to have features published in our magazine should present queries that are well thought-out and that prove they have better-than-average writing and research abilities. *Creative*, cat-related feature ideas are a plus, since we often see the same ideas over and over, sometimes on topics that we have recently published articles about (and usually we won't cover the same topic again for the next year or two). It is strongly recommended that writers request our writer's guidelines and thoroughly familiarize themselves with our publication (by reading several issues) *before* submitting materials to our publication.

It is always necessary to send an SASE with any submission, whether it's a manuscript or a query. It is best if writers wait for a positive response to a manuscript or query before they contact us by telephone or fax. For a writer to take our editorial staff's time just to see if we received a submission or to question our response time *does not help* their chances for having their materials selected for publication; patience is a virtue, especially in the field of publishing. To receive confirmation that materials have been received at our office, writers should enclose a self-addressed, stamped postcard (in addition to the SASE, not instead of one) for this purpose. Writers who give us a deadline by which we must respond to their submission usually receive a negative response, and freelancers who ignore our word count and format specifications find their materials receive immediate rejection. Be creative and organized while following our guidelines and your chances for publication will be increased.

THE CHRONICLE OF THE HORSE

P.O. Box 46
301 West Washington Street
Middleburg, VA 22117

Phone number   540-687-6341
Fax number   540-687-3937
E-mail address   staff@chronofhorse.com
Circulation   22,000
Magazine availability   Newsstands and subscription
Target audience   National and international, competitors in English-riding horse sports
Magazine's history and mission   Founded in 1937 by Stacy B. Lloyd Jr. and Gerry Webb. Mission: to cover horse showing dressage, eventing, endurance riding, driving, vaulting, pony club, steeple chasing, and fox hunting in North America and abroad through news reports, features, and informed commentary.
Nonfiction   99%
Fiction   1%
Percent of articles freelance-written   75%
Number of articles bought annually   Over 500
Sections of the magazine open to freelance writers   All but editors' commentary
Article interests and needs   Anything relating to sports we cover.
Queries should be directed to   John Strassburger, Editor; Tricia Booker, Assistant Editor
Length of articles   100 to 3,000 words
Payment $25 to $200
Time of payment   On acceptance and on publication
Expenses   None available to freelancers
Photographs   Required for news and most features
Response time to queries   4 to 6 weeks
Rights bought   We buy first North American rights
Kill fees   None
Writer's guidelines   Yes
Sample issues   Yes

TIPS FOR WRITERS
John Strassburger, Editor

We accept queries and completed manuscripts, although we prefer queries. A good query comes from a writer who's truly familiar with the magazine's content and is not suggesting an article on a subject that's been covered in detail. A good query will also give us time to respond. All news reports on competitions are assigned prior to the event by a member of our staff.

We prefer to receive a resume and one or two recent clips from new writers. We look for equestrian knowledge and background in our writers. Knowledge of the subject is even more important than writing ability—our writers need to be nearly experts.

An SASE isn't always necessary. We do accept phone calls from writers if a time factor is involved with their query, although we're not likely to grant an assignment to an unknown writer over the phone. Writers may fax their queries, but we do not yet have an e-mail address.

The key to breaking into *Chronicle* is to know the magazine and the subject. We receive many submissions from writers who don't have a clue. Our readers are experts themselves, and a very large percentage have a college or advanced degree. So our articles are technical and in-depth—they are not puff pieces about how beautiful horses are. Our news, features, and commentary contain information equestrian competitors can use. To be published, writers need to demonstrate their knowledge and reliability.

HOOF PRINT

P.O. Box 2157
Glens Falls, NY 12801-2157

Phone number   518-792-3131
Fax number   518-792-0407
E-mail address   jobryant@global1.net
Parent company   Glens Falls Newspapers, Inc.
Circulation   15,000
Magazine availability   Newsstands, subscription, tack shops/feed stores
Target audience   Horse people in the Northeast
Magazine's history and mission   Founded in 1992 as a resource for Northeastern horse people.
Nonfiction   100%
Percent of articles freelance-written   90%
Number of articles bought annually   120
Sections of the magazine open to freelance writers   Almost all
Article interests and needs   Equine-related articles and info relevant to the Northeast
Queries should be directed to   Jennifer Bryant, Editor
Length of articles   500 to 2,500 words
Payment $15 to $100
Time of payment   On publication
Expenses   No
Photographs   Yes—$15
Response time to queries   6 to 8 weeks
Rights bought   First North American English-language serial rights and electronic rights
Kill fees   Negotiable

Writer's guidelines   Available for SASE
Sample issues $2.00

IMPORTANT QUESTIONS ANSWERED

Q: What sparks your interest in a query?
A: A well-written letter about an interesting topic.
Q: Do you always want clips from new writers?
A: Not necessary
Q: Will you look at completed manuscripts?
A: Yes
Q: Is an SASE always necessary?
A: Yes
Q: Are phone calls from writers OK?
A: Yes
Q: Is it OK if writers fax or e-mail queries to you?
A: Yes
Q: What is the best way to break into your magazine?
A: Think of a topic that hasn't been done before.
Q: What is the worst thing writers do?
A: Fail to understand our geographic market.
Q: What is your overall advice to writers who want to get published in your magazine?
A: Read *Hoof Print!*

HORSE ILLUSTRATED

P.O. Box 6050
Mission Viejo, CA 92690

Phone number   714-855-8822
Fax number   714-855-0654
Parent company   Fancy Publications
Circulation   186,000
Magazine availability   Newsstands and subscription
Target audience   Women, 20 to 45, who are horse owners (in North America); riders of both English and Western disciplines
Magazine's history and mission   First began publishing in 1976. Magazine's mission is to promote responsible horse ownership.
Nonfiction   100%
Percent of articles freelance-written   20%
Number of articles bought annually   5 to 10 regular features, 10 to 15 news items (800 words)
Sections of the magazine open to freelance writers   Regular features, news column

Article interests and needs   We require articles (max. 2,000 words) regarding horse care and management. This includes medical, training, and riding features. All must be written by an authority or backed up by an authority in the equine industry.
Queries should be directed to   Audrey Pavia, Editor
Length of articles   Articles: 2,000 words max.; News items: 800 words max
Payment $300 to $350 (more with excellent quality photos); $50 to $75 for news item
Time of payment   On publication
Expenses   No
Photographs   Negotiable, depending upon quality of photos and number provided
Response time to queries   4 to 6 weeks
Rights bought   We buy First North American serial rights
Kill fees   30%
Writer's guidelines   Free, provided with an SASE only
Sample issues $4.00 or cover price ($2.95) sent with large envelope and sufficient postage

TIPS FOR WRITERS

Query: One that is well-written without a lot of "formula" hooks. We want writers to show us that they are authorities on the subject they wish to write about. We would like to see at least one clip, but we don't base our entire decision on any clip, since it has gone through an editor. We will look at completed manuscripts, provided that they are accompanied by an SASE.

  Professional etiquette: SASE is always necessary, due to the high volume of unsolicited work we receive. Even Canadian authors, please send at least an IRC and an envelope. No phone calls please. Once a relationship with an author has been established, then we can be contacted by phone. No faxed or e-mail queries.

  Best ways to break into magazine: Send in smaller items for our news column so that we can get a feel for your style.

  Keys: Following our style (generally AP), writing professionally, sending clean copy. If you are a reporter in the industry, just make sure that you back up your information with a real authority (not just someone that you think is a good source because he or she lives close by).

  Pet peeves: Interviews or profiles on a friend that you think has a really super story; "dead horse" stories; poetry; articles that have nothing to do with our focus, such as "horses on stamps" or "carousels"; quizzes on horses through history. Writers should not explain their whole article on the phone. They should not send us back the same article we rejected a year later, hoping we changed our minds. Writers who ignore our guidelines.

  Etc.: Our magazine has moved away slightly from accepting large amounts of freelance work. However, we are always looking for new, fresh voices for our features. If you would like a more open critique of your manuscript, you may contact us for that information (in writing, please). Our field is highly competitive, so we look for people who have done their homework and have tailored their articles to meet our needs.

REPTILE & AMPHIBIAN MAGAZINE

RD #3 Box 3709-A
Pottsville, PA 17901

Phone number   717-622-6050
Fax number   717-622-5858
E-mail address   eramus@postoffice.ptd.net
Parent company   Ramus Publishing, Inc.
Circulation   15,000
Online status   Web site at http://petstation.com/repamp.html
Magazine availability   Newsstands and subscription
Target audience   Advanced amateur hobbyists; college level
Magazine's history   Founded in 1989 by Norman Frank, DVM.
Nonfiction   100%
Percent of articles freelance-written   90%
Number of articles bought annually   60
Sections of the magazine open to freelance writers   All
Article interests and needs   Captive care, breeding, natural history
Queries should be directed to   Erica Ramus, Editor
Length of articles   1,500 to 2,500 words
Payment $100
Time of payment   On acceptance
Expenses   No
Photographs $25 each upon publication
Response time to queries   2 weeks
Kill fees   No
Writer's guidelines   Free
Sample issues $5

IMPORTANT QUESTIONS ANSWERED

Q: What sparks your interest in a query?
A: Familiarity with my topic.
Q: Do you always want clips from new writers?
A: No
Q: Is an SASE always necessary?
A: Yes
Q: Is it OK if writers fax or e-mail queries to you?
A: Yes
Q: Are phone calls from writers OK?
A: Only if [I] already work with you.
Q: What is the worst thing writers do?
A: Ignore guidelines

Q: How should writers angle their stories for your magazine?
A: *Advanced* amateur level

Art and Music

AMERICAN INDIAN ART MAGAZINE

7314 East Osborn Drive
Scottsdale, AZ 85251

Phone number   602-946-9691
Circulation   30,000
Magazine availability   Newsstands and subscription
Target audience   Collectors, dealers, scholars, and students of American Indian art north of the U.S.-Mexico border
Nonfiction   100%
Percent of articles freelance-written   100% (columns written in-house)
Number of articles bought annually   16 to 20
Sections of the magazine open to freelance writers   All editorial
Queries should be directed to   Roanne P. Goldfein
Length of articles   12 to 18 pages, double-spaced
Payment $300 for original research; $150 for museum features
Time of payment   On publication
Photographs   Writer to get permissions, magazine will pay.
Response time to queries   3 months
Rights bought   AIA retains rights to all articles
Kill fees   No
Writer's guidelines   Available with SASE
Sample issues   Available for $6

AN IMPORTANT QUESTION ANSWERED

Q: Is it OK if writers fax or e-mail queries to you?
A: No

JUXTAPOZ

1303 Underwood Avenue
San Francisco, CA 94124

Phone number   415-822-3083
Fax number   415-822-8359
E-mail address   juxtamag@aol.com
Parent company   High Speed Productions
Circulation   50,000
Magazine availability   Newsstands and subscription
Magazine's history and mission   Founded by artist Robert Williams in 1994, *Juxtapoz* is dedicated to presenting the best in underground and alternative art.
Nonfiction   100%
Percent of articles freelance-written   75%
Number of articles bought annually   40
Sections of the magazine open to freelance writers   Features, Beat Down (an art news department)
Article interests and needs   Artist profiles, art movement histories, unusual art events
Queries should be directed to   Shay Nowick, Managing Editor
Length of articles   Usually 1,000 to 2,000 words
Payment   Negotiable, ranges from $100 to $300
Time of payment   On publication
Expenses   Considered part of project
Photographs   Usually not required. Payment for photos is extra.
Response time to queries   4 to 6 weeks
Rights bought   No
Kill fees   No
Writer's guidelines   Send SASE with clips, info.
Sample issues   Send SASE.

TIPS FOR WRITERS

Juxtapoz is interested in writers who can bring new and unusual art and artists to our attention. Writers should be able to provide snapshots of the artist's (or artists') work along with their ideas. Clips and previously published works are important but we do read unpublished manuscripts providing they are relevant. Clips demonstrate writing style, skill, and ability, but since we are primarily interested in the art itself, enthusiasm for the subject is probably most important.

SASEs are required if manuscripts are to be returned. Follow-up phone calls and e-mail are OK, but faxes are much preferred. The best way to break into *Juxtapoz* is to present original article ideas that are fresh, timely, and interesting; the accompanying art must be visually appealing and stimulating.

STRINGS

P.O. Box 767
San Anselmo, CA 94979

Phone number   415-485-6946
Fax number   415-485-0831
E-mail address   strings1@aol.com
Parent company   String Letter Publishing
Circulation   Approximately 13,000
Magazine availability   Newsstands and subscription
Target audience   Players, makers, teachers of the bowed stringed instruments (violin, viola, cello, bass). Professionals and amateurs.
Magazine's history and mission   Founded in 1986 by David A. Lusterman, current publisher. To provide enjoyment and useful information about all aspects of the string-playing world.
Nonfiction   100%
Percent of articles freelance-written   Close to 100%
Number of articles bought annually   60+
Queries should be directed to   Mary Van Clay, Editor
Length of articles   1,000 to 3,000 words
Payment $.10 per word
Time of payment   On publication
Expenses   Sometimes
Photographs   We track, research, find those; the writers need not.
Response time to queries   3 months
Rights bought   We retain copyright unless special arrangements are made.
Kill Fees   50% based on assigned length, and no more than $100
Writer's guidelines   Provided with contract upon assignment

TIPS FOR WRITERS

Interest in freelance writers for *Strings* is usually sparked by three things: 1) Are they string players, or at least true fans of the music? 2) Do they have more than passing knowledge of the subject matter (particularly in the realm of classical music)? 3) Can they write?

The most interesting queries consist of fresh ideas concerning subjects that are lively and new, pitched with an eye toward helping and informing our readership. We get more than enough people who want to write about the same old famous (often deceased) stars (Heifetz, etc.), or about their personal experiences practicing the instrument. We're looking for people who closely follow the "scene" and know what is interesting and different, and who understand what types of services our readership needs (i.e., information about new technologies, new products on the market, new groups/performers who have more than mere youthful sex appeal).

Obviously a clear, concise, well-written cover letter is also vital. We always want at least two or three sample clips that show off the journalist's writing ability, organizational skills, fact-checking prowess, etc. Good leads and well-organized storylines are important.

The SASE is not always necessary, though it's helpful. Queries via mail, fax, or e-mail are fine [and] are all preferable to phone calls.

The best thing writers can do to break into writing for us is to demonstrate true interest and knowledge in the subject matter, instead of just hitting us up, along with dozens of other magazines, for writing "gigs." Of course, they should also meet deadlines, understand that their pieces will in fact be edited, and be willing to work with the editors to meet our specific needs with their stories.

The worst thing they can do is pitch ideas that make it obvious they have never bothered to examine our magazine to get some idea of the kinds of pieces we run, the types of departments we have, the length of stories we prefer, etc. (For example, never call and say, "I'm working on quite a long story about XX, a little-known but really interesting harpist from, of all places, Fresno. She's turning 50 this year. Would you like it?" The answer is no on several counts: we don't run "really long" pieces; we don't cover the harp; someone is not interesting merely because he or she is having any kind of anniversary or comes from a specific place, be it rural or urban.)

In general the best approach for pitching stories to any magazine, in my opinion, is to start with a firm understanding of the magazine itself. Research it—go to the library or bookstore and look for copies, or call the subscription department and see if you can order a few back issues if necessary. Editors who already have even a few good writers aren't interested in trying to "help out" someone who obviously hasn't taken the time to carefully consider and get to know their publication.

Bridal

BRIDE'S

140 East 45 Street, 39th Floor
New York, NY 10017

Phone number   212-880-8800
Fax number   212-880-6689
E-mail address   None (mailbox for reader questions only)
Parent company   The Conde Nast Publications, Inc.
Circulation   350,000
Magazine availability   Newsstands and subscription
Target audience   Our average reader is a 25-year-old engaged woman, but older brides (30s) and remarrying couples also read us.
Magazine's history and mission   *Bride's* was founded in 1934 as a magazine for East-coast wedding announcements, more or less. It was bought by Conde Nast in

1959. *Bride's* mission is to help brides, grooms, and their wedding families plan their wedding, as well as their honeymoon and home.

Nonfiction   100%

Fiction   0% (no poetry, either!)

Percent of articles freelance-written   Features: 40 to 50%; Travel: 60 to 75%

Number of articles bought annually   Approximately 30 features. Approximately 60 travel (but more new writers do features).

Sections of the magazine open to freelance writers   Wedding planning, relationship articles

Article interests and needs   Same as above

Queries should be directed to   Nancy Mattia, Features Editor; Tracy Guth Jr., Associate Features Editor; Laura Begley, Associate Travel Editor

Length of articles   Features: 500 to 800 words; Travel: 200 to 800 words

Payment   Starts at $.50 per word

Time of payment   On acceptance

Expenses   Phone expenses up to $50 reimbursed for features

Photographs   Contact art department. We may sometimes request photos.

Response time to queries   8 weeks tops

Rights bought   We generally buy all rights.

Kill fees   25%

Writer's guidelines   Send an SASE to features department. No travel (honeymoon) guidelines.

Sample issues   No

TIPS FOR WRITERS

Tracy L. Guth, Junior Associate Features Editor

A good query letter shows us the writer has actually looked at the magazine and is aware of what topics we cover and how. For example, we would not do a 1,000-word article on creative ways to depart from the wedding reception; we'd probably do a quick idea list of 350 words or so, set up with bullets and bold lead-ins. We appreciate writers who spell out in their letters how they would tackle the article: who they would interview, studies they would cite, how they would organize the piece. Also, if a writer has looked at the past year of issues, they will know what we have covered recently and will avoid pitching those topics. (Because we're telling our readers how to plan their weddings, we tend to revisit the same subject, but not one issue after another.)

We do appreciate humor and wit, and creative takes on the various wedding-planning and first-year-of-marriage stories that we do again and again. We like to see three or four clips of previously published work, but we are most interested in the quality of the query letter. A brief sentence or two on the writer's background is nice. Bottom line, we're looking for good ideas and the sense that the writer has actually studied the magazine. We will read finished manuscripts—especially first-person essay submissions.

An SASE is always necessary, and we prefer that writers contact us by mail, as opposed to fax or email. Please do not call us—we read queries on a regular basis and get back to the writer within eight weeks tops, but usually within two or three. If we like your idea, we will contact you relatively quickly, usually by phone.

The best things writers do: understand the magazine well enough to come up with relevant ideas and to write stories consistent with our style; make their deadlines.

The worst things writers do: telephone us.

Overall advice to writers who want to get published: know the magazine, and don't assume that because you are married you are qualified to write about weddings and marriage. Although our subject matter is personal, and readers often think of us almost as their friends who are helping them plan their wedding, we work with professional freelance writers.

MODERN BRIDE

249 West 17th Street
New York, NY 10011

Fax number   212-337-7089
Parent company   K-III
Circulation   364,321
Magazine availability   Newsstands and subscription
Target audience   Engaged couples, primarily in their twenties
Magazine's history   Started in 1949
Nonfiction   100%
Percent of articles freelance-written   50%
Number of articles bought annually   15
Sections of the magazine open to freelance writers   Wedding planning and relationship oriented articles
Article interests and needs   Wedding planning, quizzes (dealing with relationships and lifestyle issues).
Queries should be directed to   Mary Ann Cavlin, Executive Editor
Length of articles   1,200 to 2,500 words
Payment $650 to $1,500
Time of payment   On acceptance
Expenses   Reasonable phone expenses only
Photographs   No
Response time to queries   4 to 6 weeks
Rights bought   First periodical publishing
Kill fees   25%
Writer's guidelines   Available
Sample issues   No

Business/Personal Finance

AMERICAN DEMOGRAPHICS

P.O. Box 68
Ithaca, NY 14851

Phone number   607-273-6343
Fax number   607-273-3196
Email address   editors@demographics.com
Parent company   Dow Jones & Co., Inc.
Circulation   35,000
Online status   Full text available on Dow Jones News Retrieval, Lexis: Nexis, and on World Wide Web home page
Magazine availability   Newsstands and subscriptions, but over 90% are sold through subscriptions.
Target audience   Business leaders in all industries who are interested in consumer trends. A large percentage of subscribers are CEOs, presidents, vice presidents, and executives. All ages and nationalities.
Magazine's history and mission   Magazine founded in 1979 by Peter Francese, the current president. The magazine's mission is to create a substantial competitive advantage for readers by providing them with the consumer trend information and analysis they need to make better business decisions.
Nonfiction   99% (occasional humor pieces)
Percent of articles freelance-written   50 to 60%
Number of articles bought annually   Articles are assigned to freelancers. We rarely use unsolicited manuscripts.
Sections of the magazine open to freelance writers   All but a few regular departments
Queries should be directed to   Brad Edmondson, Editor-in-Chief; Diane Crispell, Executive Editor
Length of articles   250 to 750 words for departments and sidebars; 2,500 to 4,500 words for feature articles
Payment $.40 per word for short items; $600-plus for features
Time of payment   On acceptance
Expenses   Yes
Photographs   Depends
Response time to queries   Varies
Rights bought   *American Demographics* retains copyright
Kill fees   Yes, if assigned
Writer's guidelines   Available
Sample issues   Available; send $6.

BUSINESS97

125 Auburn Court, Suite 100
Thousand Oaks, CA 91362

Phone number   805-496-6156
Fax number   805-496-5469
Email address   GoSmallBiz@aol.com
Parent company   Group IV Communications
Circulation   500,000
Online status   Just email.
Magazine availability   *Business97* is distributed to the best small business customers of a network of major banks, coast to coast, including Chemical Bank, NationsBank, and Wells Fargo Bank.
Target audience   The target audience is small business owners who are also members of one of the above three banks. There is no preference to age or sex. Geographical area is based on the regions included in the network of banks.
Magazine's history and mission   The magazine was founded in 1994, with Chemical Bank and Wells Fargo bank versions. NationsBank was added in February of 1995. All three are under the parent company Group IV Communications. The magazine's mission is to provide practical "how-to" information [that readers] can use in operating a small business and to do it better than any other publication in the country.
Nonfiction   100%
Percent of articles freelance-written   80%
Number of articles bought annually   50
Sections of the magazine open to freelance writers   All. Sections include regular departments and topics like marketing, advertising, computing, taxation, banking, and finance, among others.
Article interests and needs   Our editorial emphasis is on providing practical, "how-to" information that readers can use in operating a small business. The articles must be written in the voice of the small business owner. Avoid first-person, introductions, and conclusions. Avoid the passive.
Queries should be directed to   Maryann Hammers, Senior Editor
Length of articles   1,800 to 2,000 words
Payment $500 to $1,000
Time of payment   Writers are paid after review and approval by our editorial staff.
Expenses   We pay reasonable, documented expenses
Photographs   We arrange our own photos.
Response time to queries   Up to 6 months
Rights bought   First North American serial rights and nonexclusive reprint rights
Kill fees   25%
Writer's guidelines   Available upon request with an SASE.
Sample issues   Sample issues are available for $4 per issue. Send checks to the above address, payable to IB L.P. with the desired issues described in an attached letter.

TIPS FOR WRITERS

The query: At *Business97* magazine, a query sparks our interest if it is first and foremost a practical, "how-to" technique, idea, or solution to a small business problem. The query should demonstrate that the writer has read several issues of the magazine and understands our writing style. The query should also indicate that the writer understands our audience and is familiar with the magazine. Finally, the query should demonstrate competent writing ability. All of these elements are part of a good, professional query at *Business97*.

Clips: Yes, we always want 2 to 3 clips from new writers. Clips should demonstrate, above all, solid writing skills. If the writer has experience writing, specifically for business publications, he/she should include those clips; however, ability to write well has greater value than simply having written for a similar publication.

We do not look at completed manuscripts, and never consider them for publication in the magazine.

Professional etiquette: Yes, an SASE is always necessary when a writer expects a response. Phone calls from writers are strongly discouraged. Fax and e-mail queries are also discouraged. All queries should be mailed to Group IV Communications, attention Maryann Hammers.

The best way to break in: The best way to break into our magazine is to demonstrate familiarity with the magazine. Request back issues and understand the style.

The best things writers do: Writers should understand and follow the terms of the assignment and do what is required of them. They should follow through on the terms of their contracts. They should meet agreed upon deadlines and refrain from whining and complaining. They should be available for continued research if the editor in charge of the piece requires more information. Above all, a writer should read past issues of the magazine, be familiar with the magazine, and never take an assignment when he/she does not feel all of the terms can be met.

The worst writers: The worst writers are those who do not follow the style of the magazine, complain about every aspect of the assignment, do not meet deadlines, and demonstrate an obvious lack of knowledge about the style of the magazine.

Ways writers can angle their stories for the magazine: Writers should learn to write from a small business person's perspective.

Overall advice to all writers: Always know the market, the style, and the readership for each publication you wish to write for.

BUSINESS ETHICS

52 South 10th Street, Suite 110
Minneapolis, MN 55403-2001

Phone number   612-962-4701
Fax number   612-962-4810
Email address   Bizethics@aol.com
Circulation   22,000
Online status   Yes
Magazine availability   Through subscription and at bookstores and some newsstands
Target audience   Men and women interested in socially responsible business and investing
Percent of articles freelance-written   60%
Number of articles bought annually   60
Sections of the magazine open to freelance writers   All
Queries should be directed to   Dale Kurschner, Editor; Mary Scott, Senior Editor
Writer's Guidelines   Send SASE.
Sample issues   Send 8 × 10 envelope with six first-class stamps for sample issue.

TIPS FOR WRITERS

We get a lot of prewritten articles submitted. Freelancers should remember that editors like to have a say in how stories are written and molded. We prefer a one-page letter with the idea. If we're interested, we will work with the writer to develop the story so that it fits into our format. Also, we get a lot of phone calls and faxes . . . it's best to start off writing, and then following up with a phone call. The best way to break into our magazine is by writing a smaller piece, such as a trend watch or a short book review.

BUSINESS MARKETING

740 Rush Street
Chicago, IL 60611

Phone number   312-649-5260
Fax number   312-649-5462
Parent company   Crain Communications, Inc.
Circulation   30,000
Online status   With *Advertising Age*
Magazine availability   Newsstands and subscription
Target audience   Top management high-tech, business-to-business operations
Magazine's history and mission   Founded in 1916 by G. P. Crain. Mission: covering how businesses sell products, services to other businesses
Nonfiction   100%
Percent of articles freelance-written   90%
Sections of the magazine open to freelance writers   All

Queries should be directed to   Char Koser, Managing Editor
Time of payment   On publication
Expenses   Yes

CRAIN'S CHICAGO BUSINESS

740 North Rush Street
Chicago, IL 60610

Phone number   312-649-5411
E-mail address   ccbmail@aol.com
Parent company   Crain Communications, Inc.
Circulation   50,000
Online status   Online version with America Online/Chicago Online
Magazine availability   Newsstands and subscription
Target audience   Top executives at Chicago-area companies
Nonfiction   100%
Percent of articles freelance-written   30%
Number of articles bought annually   About 500
Sections of the magazine open to freelance writers   All
Article interests and needs   Must be newsy, well written, thoroughly reported, and geared to Chicago biz audience
Queries should be directed to   Glenn Coleman, Managing Editor
Length of articles   Varies
Payment $13.50 per column inch
Time of payment   On acceptance
Expenses   Cleared in advance
Photographs   Assigned to professional photographers
Response time to queries   2 weeks, on average
Rights bought   Crain's purchases all print and electronic rights.
Kill fees   Sometimes

IMPORTANT QUESTIONS ANSWERED

Q: What are the key elements of a good, professional query?
A: A one-page query that clearly describes the story is always welcome.
Q: Do you want clips from new writers?
A: Include clips and rez, if you think it helps your cause.
Q: Are phone calls from writers OK?
A: Phone *after* sending query.
Q: What is the best way to break into your magazine?

A: Read it. Know it. Think like it. Anything less is a waste of our time and yours.

Q: What other advice would you give writers who want to get published in Crain's Chicago Business?

A: We want full-time professional journalists only who live and work in the Chicago area.

ENTREPRENEUR

2392 Morse Avenue
Irvine, CA 92714

Phone number   714-261-2325
Fax number   714-755-4211
Parent company   Entrepreneur Media Group
Circulation   410,000
Online status   CompuServe
Magazine availability   Newsstands and subscription
Target audience   Owners of small businesses nationwide
Magazine's history and mission   Founded in 1977. Mission: to help small business owners run their businesses.
Nonfiction   100%
Percent of articles freelance-written   50%
Number of articles bought annually   50 features
Sections of the magazine open to freelance writers   Features only. We do accept suggestions for new columns, but it is very rare [that] we start a new column.
Article interests and needs   How-to information on small business, profiles of successful business owners with national recognition (see Birth to Billions monthly feature)
Queries should be directed to   Rieva Lesonsky, Editor-in-Chief
Length of articles   2,000 words
Payment $500
Time of payment   On acceptance
Expenses   Phone only
Photographs   We handle photos
Response time to queries   2 to 3 months
Rights bought   First worldwide
Kill fees   20%
Writer's guidelines   Available with SASE
Sample issues   Send check for $6 to "Attn: Customer Svc." at the above address. However, *Entrepreneur* is available at most bookstores/newsstands.

TIPS FOR WRITERS

The query: A query that grabs my interest indicates the finished story will probably do the same. The query should be professionally written (no typos, etc.), should be very specific about the intended article (naming experts with whom they will speak, etc.), and, most of all, should show that they have read our magazine and understand the audience.

Clips: We do not necessarily need clips from new writers, but they are nice to have. However, as editors we realize that finished clips often reflect an editor's, not a writer's, ability. As a result, I always take them with a large grain of salt. I look at them more for evidence that the writer has experience writing on relevant/similar topics than for evidence of good writing.

I'm happy to look at completed manuscripts.

Professional etiquette: We answer everyone in some way, whether or not they send an SASE. However, failing to send an SASE shows me that they are not professional and makes me reluctant to work with them.

Queries: Phone calls are never OK. Faxing is OK. Letters are best.

Best ways to break into magazine: Features are the only area open to freelancers. We are looking for profiles (see the Birth to Billions column; these need to be big names) as well as articles dealing with current issues business owners face (i.e., sexual harassment, smoking in the workplace) or how-to articles on some aspect of operations.

It's essential to be specific ("I propose an article showing readers how to cut costs by leasing office equipment") rather than general ("I propose an article on how to cut costs").

The best way to break in is to send a good query that shows you have read and understood our audience. You also need to read our columns and be familiar with topics we cover there.

Pet peeves:

1. People who call and leave messages even though our voice mail says "Please send queries in writing." Sorry, but the message applies to everyone, even you!
2. Not providing enough information in queries. If you're proposing a profile, don't make us guess who the business owner is. Include sales figures.

Ways to angle stories: Our readers are small-business owners, both men and women, average age in 30s and 40s, primarily owners of service businesses but also retail (less manufacturing), with about 10 to 20 employees. They are looking for hands-on information they can use to run a better business.

FINANCIAL WORLD

1328 Broadway
New York, NY 10001

Phone number   212-594-5030
Fax number   212-629-0021
E-mail address   LettersFW@aol.com
Circulation   500,000
Online status   America Online
Magazine availability   Newsstands and subscription
Target audience   Men and women, 50+ years, national, high income

Magazine's history and mission   Founded in 1902. Mission: to serve individual and professional investors.
Nonfiction   100%
Percent of articles freelance-written   20%
Number of articles bought annually   20
Sections of the magazine open to freelance writers   All
Article interests and needs   Business and finance
Queries should be directed to   Geof Smith, Editor
Length of articles   700 to 3,500 words
Payment $500 per page in the magazine. No negotiations.
Time of payment   On publication
Expenses   Yes
Photographs   Yes
Response time to queries   Varies
Rights bought   Negotiated
Kill fees   Negotiated

HOME OFFICE COMPUTING/SMALL BUSINESS COMPUTING

411 Lafayette Street, 4th Floor
New York, NY 10003

Phone number   212-505-4220 (Do not call in queries)
Fax number   212-505-4260
E-mail address   hoc@aol.com
Parent company   Scholastic, Inc.
Circulation   560,000
Online status   AOL site, CompuServe, Prodigy
Magazine availability   Newsstands and subscription
Target audience   35- to 45-year-old entrepreneurs of any sex, race, color, etc., who live anywhere in North America
Magazine's history and mission   Founded in 1983, this magazine was launched as *Family Computing* by Scholastic, Inc. It has since transformed into a hybrid business/technology publication.
Nonfiction   100%
Percent of articles freelance-written   85%
Number of articles bought annually   Roughly 20—from short news items to 2,500 word features
Sections of the magazine open to freelance writers   All
Article interests and needs   We're looking for anything that helps the small-business owner (below 15 employees) solve their problems and streamline operations.
Queries should be directed to   Cathy Brower, Executive Editor; Gail Gabriel, Managing Editor

Length of articles   Ranging anywhere from 150 to 3,000 words
Payment   Varies according to article
Time of payment   On acceptance
Expenses   Yes
Photographs   Color transparencies
Response time to queries   When an SASE is provided, 3 weeks
Kill fees   25%
Writer's guidelines   Yes

IMPORTANT QUESTIONS ANSWERED

Q: Will you look at completed manuscripts?
A: Don't send completed manuscripts.
Q: Is it OK if writers fax queries to you?
A: Faxed queries are OK.
Q: What is the worst thing writers do?
A: Fail to read the book.
Q: What about writer's clips?
A: Send clips, roughly 3, related to business.
Q: How should writers angle stories for your magazine?
A: *Solutions* for entrepreneurs
Q: What overall advice can you give writers who want to get published in your magazine?
A: In general, read the magazine—at least 6 issues prior to querying. If you're not familiar with the publication, an editor can tell in two minutes. Get to the point quickly.

INDEPENDENT BUSINESS

125 Auburn Court, Suite 100
Thousand Oaks, CA 91362

Phone number   805-496-6156
Fax number   805-496-5469
E-mail address   GoSmallBiz@aol.com
Parent company   Group IV Communications
Circulation   Approximately 600,000
Online status   Just e-mail.
Magazine availability   *Independent Business* magazine is a controlled circulation publication created for the members of the National Federation of Independent Business, the oldest and largest small business organization.
Target audience   The target audience is small business owners throughout the U.S., regardless of age, sex, or geographic area—but note that it is distributed only to members of the National Federation of Independent Business (NFIB).

Magazine's history and mission   The magazine was founded in 1990 as a bimonthly publication by four individuals who make up the parent company, Group IV Communications. The magazine's mission is to provide practical, "how-to" information that small business owners can use in operating a small business—and to do it better than any other publication in the country.

Nonfiction   100%

Percent of articles freelance-written   80%

Number of articles bought annually   50

Sections of the magazine open to freelance writers   All. Sections include regular departments and topics like marketing, advertising, computing, taxation, banking, and finance, among others.

Article interests and needs   Our editorial emphasis is providing practical, "how-to" information [that readers] can use in operating a small business. The articles must be written in the voice of the small business owner. Avoid first-person, introductions, and conclusions. Avoid the passive.

Queries should be directed to   Maryann Hammers, Senior Editor

Length of articles   1,800 to 2,000 words

Payment $500 to $1,000

Time of payment   After review and approval by our editorial staff

Expenses   We pay reasonable, documented expenses.

Photographs   We arrange our own photographs.

Rights bought   Writers are paid for first North American serial rights and non-exclusive reprint rights.

Kill fees   25%

Writer's guidelines   Available on request with an SASE

Sample issues   Sample issues are available for $4.00 per issue. Send checks to the above address, made payable to IB L.P. with the desired issues described in an attached letter.

TIPS FOR WRITERS

The query: At *Independent Business* magazine, a query sparks our interest if it is first and foremost a practical, "how-to" technique, idea, or solution to a small business problem. The query should demonstrate that the writer has read several issues of the magazine, and understands our writing style. The query should also indicate that the writer understands our audience and is familiar with the magazine. Finally, the query should demonstrate competent writing ability. All of these elements are part of a good, professional query at *Independent Business*.

   Clips: Yes, we always want 2 to 3 clips from new writers. Clips should demonstrate, above all, solid writing skills. If the writer has experience writing, specifically for business publications, he/she should include those clips; however, ability to write well has greater value than simply having written for a similar publication.

   We do not look at completed manuscripts, and never consider them for publication in the magazine.

   Professional etiquette: Yes, an SASE is always necessary when a writer expects a response. Phone calls from writers are strongly discouraged. Fax and e-mail queries are also discouraged. All queries should be mailed to Group IV Communications, attention Maryann Hammers.

The best way to break in: The best way to break into our magazine is to demonstrate familiarity with the magazine. Request back issues and understand the style.

The best things writers do: Writers should understand and follow the terms of the assignment and do what is required of them. They should follow through on the terms of their contracts. They should meet agreed upon deadlines and refrain from whining and complaining. They should be available for continued research if the editor in charge of the piece requires more information. Above all, a writer should read past issues of the magazine, be familiar with the magazine, and never take an assignment when he/she does not feel all of the terms can be met.

The worst writers: The worst writers are those who do not follow the style of the magazine, complain about every aspect of the assignment, do not meet deadlines, and demonstrate an obvious lack of knowledge about the style of the magazine.

Ways writers can angle their stories for the magazine: Writers should learn to write from a small business person's perspective.

Overall advice to all writers: Always know the market, the style, and the readership for each publication you wish to write for.

INFORMATION WEEK

CMP Publications
600 Community Drive
Manhasset, NY 11030

Phone number   516-562-5000
Fax number   516-562-5036
E-mail address   Each editor has his/her own.
Parent company   CMP Publications
Circulation   325,000 controlled circulation
Online status   Web site at http://techweb.cmp.com/iwk
Magazine availability   Subscription only
Target audience   Technology managers
Magazine's history and mission   Founded in 1985 by CMP, "For business and technology managers."
Nonfiction   100%
Articles freelance-written   About 33%
Number of articles bought annually   Varies with needs
Sections of the magazine open to freelance writers   Features sections
Article interests and needs   Must relate to technology management
Queries should be directed to   Peter Krass, Assistant Managing Editor, Features (pkrass@cmp.com)
Length of articles   1,500 words and up
Payment $1.00 per word

Time of payment   On acceptance
Expenses   Yes
Photographs   We have our own photo eds.
Response time to queries   A couple of weeks at most
Rights bought   We buy first print rights and Web reprint rights.
Kill fees   One-third
Writer's guidelines   Yes
Sample issues   Yes

IMPORTANT QUESTIONS ANSWERED

Q: Do you always want clips from new writers?
A: Yes. At least three.
Q: Will you look at completed manuscripts?
A: Not usually
Q: Is an SASE always necessary?
A: No
Q: Is it OK if writers fax or e-mail queries to you?
A: E-mail, yes. Fax, no.
Q: When are phone calls from writers OK?
A: After a mail or an e-mail query.
Q: How should writers angle their stories for your magazine?
A: The story must be written for tech managers.

MAY TRENDS

303 South Northwest Highway
Park Ridge, IL 60068-4255

Phone number   847-825-8806, Ext. 239
Fax number   847-825-7937 (Mark for the Attention of Rosaline J. Angell)
E-mail address   Not yet available
Parent company   George S. May International Company
Circulation   20,000 to 30,000 per issue
Online status   Not active
Magazine availability   Free subscription; requests should be submitted on business letterhead.
Target audience   Owners/operators of medium- and small-sized businesses
Magazine's history and mission   Approximately 30 years ago, the magazine was founded by the George S. May International Company as a public service to assist executives in understanding trends and viewpoints through leading authorities.
Nonfiction   100%
Percent of articles freelance-written   Varies

Sections of the magazine open to freelance writers   Open to business and technical writers who submit on speculation. Material must be germane to the interests of owners and managers of medium- and small-sized businesses.

Article interests and needs   Identify economic, marketing, and technological trends that have an impact on small companies and present ideas and viewpoints of individuals familiar with small business challenges.

Queries should be directed to   Rosalind J. Angell, Editor *MAY TRENDS,* Director—Corporate Communications

Length of articles   2,000 to 3,000 words

Payment $150 to $250

Time of payment   On publication or as otherwise negotiated

Expenses   As negotiated

Photographs   Seldom used

Response time to queries   30 to 60 days

Rights bought   With purchase we buy publishing rights and release for use in the management consulting field.

Writer's guidelines   Available with sample issues on receipt of written or telephone request

---

MONEY

Time & Life Building
Rockefeller Center
New York, NY 10020

Phone number   212-522-3292

Fax number   212-522-0189

E-mail address   moneymag.com

Parent company   Time, Inc.

Circulation   1.95 million

Online status   CompuServe, Pathfinder site on World Wide Web of Internet

Magazine availability   Newsstands and subscription

Target audience   Age 30 to 70, male and female, U.S.A., middle income and higher

Magazine's history and mission   Founded in 1972 by Time, Inc. Mission: help Americans invest, save, borrow, spend wisely, and lower their taxes.

Nonfiction   100%

Percent of articles freelance-written   10%

Number of articles bought annually   About 3 features and 8 department items

Sections of the magazine open to freelance writers   Newsline, Smart Spending, Money Monitor, and features

Queries should be directed to   Frank Lalli, Managing Editor

Length of articles   Varies

Payment   Varies, but department items typically get $250 to $1,000 and features $2,000 to $6,000
Time of payment   On publication
Expenses   Yes
Photographs   We'll take care of it.
Response time to queries   Within 2 to 3 weeks
Rights bought   *Money* holds all rights.
Kill fees   Varies

IMPORTANT QUESTIONS ANSWERED

Q: What sparks you interest in a query?
A: Good ideas.
Q: What is the key element of a good, professional query?
A: Well researched.
Q: Do you always want clips from new writers and how many do you want?
A: Yes. [We want] three to ten.
Q: What do you look for in the writer's clips?
A: Good writing and expertise.
Q: Will you look at completed manuscripts?
A: Yes
Q: Is an SASE always necessary?
A. No
Q: Are phone calls from writers OK?
A. Letters are preferred.
Q: Is it OK if writers fax or e-mail queries to you?
A: Letters are preferred.
Q: How should writers submit their work?
A: We prefer Macintosh disks with paper printout.
Q: What is the best way to break into your magazine?
A: Good story idea/manuscript. Know what we do and what we've published.
Q: What is the best thing writers can offer?
A: Clever, knowledgeable writing with helpful advice.
Q: What are the worst things writers do?
A: Underreport. Not enough quotes. Lack of analysis and point of view.

SPARE TIME

5810 West Oklahoma Avenue
Milwaukee, WI 53219

Phone number   414-543-8110
Fax number   414-543-9767

Parent company   Kipen Publishing Corporation
Circulation   307,000
Online status   Not yet
Magazine availability   Subscription/controlled only
Target audience   Males and females of all ages who run or desire to run businesses in their spare time
Magazine's history and mission   Founded in 1955 by Harvey Kipen as a quarterly sales digest. Mission is now to provide information and opportunities to help people earn extra income.
Nonfiction   100%
Percent of articles freelance-written   98%
Number of articles bought annually   30 to 35
Sections of the magazine open to freelance writers   All
Article interests and needs   Articles on business issues such as bookkeeping, sales techniques, and direct marketing methods, as well as topics on health, relationship management, time management, selecting a venture, making it work, etc.
Queries should be directed to   Robert R. Warde, Managing Editor
Length of articles   500 to 2,000 words
Payment $.15 per word
Time of payment   On publication
Expenses   Not compensated
Photographs   Accepted, fee negotiable
Response time to queries   One month
Rights bought   First North American
Kill fees   None, publish what we commit to, though edition may change
Writer's guidelines   Yes
Sample issues $2.50 postpaid

TIPS FOR WRITERS (FROM *SPARE TIME'S* WRITER'S GUIDELINES)

Include examples of people who have started businesses (if a profile) or have faced the particular challenge discussed in the article. Real life examples provide readers with hope and learning possibilities. Theory bores them and makes it difficult for them to relate it to their own situations.

Quote experts rather than write articles that read like essays. If possible, get them to share real examples that you can quote.

Have side bars with checklists, how-to's, or tips.

Children/Teen/Young Adult

AMERICAN GIRL

P.O. Box 620986
Middleton, WI 53562-0986

Phone number   608-836-4848
Fax number   608-831-7089
Parent company   Pleasant Company Publications, Inc.
Circulation   600,000
Magazine availability   Newsstands and subscription
Target audience   Girls ages 8 and up
Magazine's history   Founded in 1992. Mission: "To celebrate girls, yesterday and today."
Nonfiction   67%
Fiction   33%
Percent of articles freelance-written   5%
Number of articles bought annually   Short profiles—6 or more; Features—1 to 2
Sections of the magazine open to freelance writers   Girls Express (short profiles of girls, trends, short how-to's, and crafts), Giggle Gang (puzzles and games), Features
Article interests and needs   Contemporary girl profiles, trends, sports that have strong visual possibilities, ideas with a girl (not a woman) as the focus
Queries should be directed to   Magazine Department Assistant
Length of articles   Fiction—up to 2,300 words; Girls Express—no more than 175 words
Payment   Varies. $1 per word is a guide.
Time of payment   On acceptance
Expenses   Phone expenses paid
Response time to queries   8 to 12 weeks
Rights bought   We prefer to buy all rights
Kill fees   Varies
Writer's guidelines   Yes
Sample issues   Available in many children's bookstores or send check for $3.95 made out to *American Girl* and a 9 × 12 SASE with $1.93 in postage.

TIPS FOR WRITERS
Julie A. Finlay, Managing Editor

Queries to avoid sending: Romance, makeup, dating, ghost stories, profiles on obvious historical figures (Annie Oakley, Amelia Earhart, Laura Ingalls Wilder, Harriet Tubman, Elizabeth Blackwell, Juliet Lowe).

   Professional etiquette: Always send an SASE. Please don't call. Prefer that you not e-mail or fax queries. Do not send to specific editors but to the Magazine Department Assistant.

Angle: Make the girl the focus of your article.
Query: Prefer queries to finished pieces. Include your credential and clips.

BOYS' LIFE
1325 West Walnut Hill Lane
P.O. Box 15079
Irving, TX 75015-2079

Phone number   214-580-2366 Editorial (We do not take phone queries.)
Parent company   Boy Scouts of America
Circulation   1.3 million
Online status   Web site at http://www.bsa.scouting.org
Magazine availability   Subscription
Target audience   Boys ages 8 to 18
Magazine's history and mission   According to an interview in *Pro Speak*, October 1993, "The publication was first printed in 1911 . . . In a broad sense, our mission is to get the youth of America interested in reading. We are the magazine for all boys. Within that mission there are other missions too, one of which is to add a really positive element to a boy's Scouting experience."
Nonfiction   Almost all
Fiction   We usually do one fiction piece per issue.
Percent of articles freelance-written   70 to 80%
Article interests and needs   Articles must interest and entertain boys ages 8 to 18. Writing should be punchy, relatively short, straightforward, and should follow *The New York Times* manual of style and usage.
Queries should be directed to   The Editor
Length of articles   Major articles: 500 to 1,500 words; Columns: 300 to 750 words; Fiction: 1,000 to 1,500 words
Payment   Major articles: $400 to $1,500; Columns: $150 to $400; Fiction: $750 and up
Time of payment   On acceptance
Expenses   Yes, reasonable
Photographs   Only if assigned
Response time to queries   6 to 8 weeks
Rights bought   First-time rights for original, unpublished material
Kill fees   Yes
Writer's guidelines   Send SASE (#10 envelope).
Sample issues   Send $2.50 and 9 × 12 SASE.

AN IMPORTANT QUESTION ANSWERED

Q: How can writers break into Boys' Life?
A: Submit good ideas and persuade us that they can execute them well.

CALLIOPE

9 School Street
Peterborough, NH 03458

Phone number   603-924-7209
Fax number   603-924-7380
Parent company   Cobblestone Publishing, Inc.
Circulation   10,000
Magazine availability   Subscription
Target audience   Youth, grades 4 to 9
Magazine's history   September of 1990, *Calliope* became a world history magazine. Previously, since 1981, it had focused on the ancient Greeks and Romans.
Nonfiction   Up to 100%
Fiction   Legend or myth sometimes included in an issue.
Percent of articles freelance-written   Approximately 4 to 5 articles per issue
Number of articles bought annually   20 to 25
Sections of the magazine open to freelance writers   All
Article interests and needs   Query for themes and guidelines
Queries should be directed to   Rosalie F. Baker, Editor
Length of articles   400 to 1,000 words
Payment $.20 to $.25 per word
Time of payment   On publication
Photographs   Per photo
Response time to queries   1 to 3 months
Rights bought   We buy all rights.
Kill fees   Yes
Writer's guidelines   Send an SASE.
Sample issues   Send $4.50 per sample and SASE.

TIPS FOR WRITERS
Rosalie F. Baker, Editor

Calliope is a theme-oriented world history magazine geared to students in grades four to nine. As editor, I choose the themes and topics we want to cover in each issue. I read all queries and select those I feel: 1) show the best and most accurate research, 2) have an "alive" feeling to them, not just a regurgitation of facts, and 3) express a feeling that the author enjoyed writing and researching the piece.

Even if a query is on a completely different aspect of history than I had originally chosen, if it meets the criteria, I often choose the author and ask him or her to write on a topic I do want in the issue.

We usually have two consulting editors for each issue, both experts in the field. I also do considerable research on each issue. This allows me to be more critical.

CHILDREN'S PLAYMATE

1100 Waterway Boulevard
Indianapolis, IN 46206

Phone number   317-636-8881
Fax number   317-636-8094
Parent company   Children's Better Health Institute
Circulation   114,000
Magazine availability   Subscription
Target audience   Children ages 6 to 8
Magazine's history   First published in 1929.
Nonfiction   30 to 40%
Fiction   60 to 70%
Percent of articles freelance-written   80%
Number of articles bought annually   Hard to say—a lot
Sections of the magazine open to freelance writers   Fiction, nonfiction (some), recipes, poems, activities
Article interests and needs   Health and safety issues, holiday material, sports
Queries should be directed to   Terry Harshman, Editor
Length of articles   300 to 700 words
Payment   Up to $.17 per word
Time of payment   On publication
Photographs $15 minimum (for photo features—no single photos)
Response time to queries   3 months
Rights bought   All
Writer's guidelines   Available upon request
Sample issues $1.25 per copy

TIPS FOR WRITERS

We only care about the story you have submitted. It's OK to send up to five or six poems, but refrain from sending more than two stories at one time. The emphasis is on *short* stories—no book length manuscripts, please.

EXPLORING

1325 West Walnut Hill Lane
P.O. Box 152079
Irving, TX 75015-2079

Phone number   214-580-2365
Fax number   214-580-2079

Parent company   National Office Boy Scouts of America
Circulation   350,000
Magazine availability   Controlled circulation
Target audience   Teens, both boys and girls, ages 14 to 21. National audience. Members of BSA's Exploring program.
Magazine's history   Began 1971
Nonfiction   100%
Percent of articles freelance-written   90%
Number of articles bought annually   16
Sections of the magazine open to freelance writers   All
Article interests and needs   Outstanding Explorer post programs (careers, outdoor adventures), hobbies, movies, music, fashion, teen pop culture
Queries should be directed to   Scott Daniels, Executive Editor
Length of articles   750 to 1,600 words
Payment $300 to $1,000
Time of payment   On acceptance
Expenses   Are paid.
Photographs   Use professional freelance photographers
Response time to queries   2 weeks
Rights bought   First North American serial
Kill fees   Negotiated
Writer's guidelines and sample issues   Send SASE with $2 postage.

GIRLS' LIFE

4517 Harford Road
Baltimore, MD 21214

Phone number   410-254-9200
Fax number   410-254-0991
Parent company   Monarch Avalon
Circulation   150,000
Magazine availability   Newsstands and subscription
Target audience   7- to 14-year-old girls
Magazine's history and mission   Founded by Karen Bokram in 1994 when she couldn't find a magazine suitable for her niece, age 10.
Nonfiction   95%
Fiction   5%
Percent of articles freelance-written   Varies
Number of articles bought annually   Varies
Sections of the magazine open to freelance writers   All, except food and books, which have regular contributors
Article interests and needs   Articles to empower and raise awareness in girls
Queries should be directed to   Kelly White, Senior Editor

Length of articles   750+ words
Payment   Varies
Time of payment   On publication
Expenses   No
Response time to queries   90 days
Rights bought   First American serial
Kill fees   No
Writer's guidelines   Free with SASE
Sample issues $5

TIPS FOR WRITERS
Kelly White, Senior Editor

Short, punchy queries usually catch the eye of a *GL* editor. It is a good idea to go ahead and send a complete manuscript, on spec only, if you are confident enough that it is a finished product. We also like to see clips of other published works, plus a resume. You will not get a response unless you include an SASE. Telephone queries are completely unacceptable. The best way to angle a story for our readers is to include some light humor, and be very careful not to use a condescending tone. We are a children's publication, but we treat our girls like the intelligent human beings that they are. We are always open to new article ideas and access to stories that we would not be able to tap into ourselves (for example, an interview that might be difficult to obtain, like Chelsea Clinton).

GUIDEPOSTS FOR KIDS
P.O. Box 538A
Chesterton, IN 46304

Phone number   219-929-4429
Fax number   219-926-3839
E-mail address   WALLYT5232@AOL.COM
Parent company   Guideposts
Circulation   200,000
Magazine availability   Subscription based
Target audience   A 32-page, four-color, value-centered direct mail magazine that is *fun* to read for kids 7 to 12 years (emphasis on upper end of age bracket).
Magazine's history and mission   Originally named *Faith 'n Stuff*, the magazine's premier issue was published in January 1990. Beginning November 1994 the magazine was renamed *Guideposts for Kids* to be more closely associated with its parent company, *Guideposts*.
Nonfiction   90%
Fiction   10%
Percent of articles freelance-written   Almost all

Number of articles bought annually 60

Sections of the magazine open to freelance writers All—except Dear Wally

Article interests and needs Nonfiction: celebrity pieces, controversial issues, environmental issues, ethnic pieces, historical, holiday themes, humor, interviews/profiles, miracles, sports, think pieces, true stories, fantasy. Fiction: adventure, fantasy, frontiers, historical, humor, contemporary, mystery plays.

Queries should be directed to Nonfiction only: Dr. Sailor Metts, Associate Editor

Length of articles 300 to 1,500 words

Payment $150 to $400

Time of payment On acceptance

Expenses Negotiable

Photographs Negotiable

Response time to queries 4 to 6 weeks

Rights bought All rights

Kill fees Occasionally

Writer's guidelines Yes—upon request with an SASE (#10 envelope, $.32 postage).

Sample issues Yes—for $3.25 per copy and a 10 × 13 SASE ($1.24 postage).

HIGHLIGHTS FOR CHILDREN

803 Church Street
Honesdale, PA 18431

Phone number 717-253-1080

Circulation 3 million

Magazine availability 100% subscription

Target audience Children ages 2 to 12

Magazine's history and mission *Highlights for Children* was founded in 1946 by Garry Cleveland Myers, Ph.D., and Caroline Clark Myers, a husband-wife team of educators. The magazine's theme is "Fun with a Purpose." According to the founders, "This book of wholesome fun is dedicated to helping children grow in basic skills and knowledge, in creativeness, in ability to think and reason, in high ideals and worthy ways of living, for children are the world's most important people!"

Nonfiction 50%

Fiction 40%

Percent of articles freelance-written 98%

Number of articles bought annually Approximately 250

Sections of the magazine open to freelance writers All sections except the following: For Wee Folks, Science Corner, The Timbertoes, Goofus and Gallant, Matching, Dino Don's Dinosaur Days, Our Own Pages, Thinking, Headwork, Check . . . and Double Check

Article interests and needs We need articles that interest young readers by transferring enthusiasm for the subject to the reader. We need stories with strong female leads. We are always looking for sports, arts and music other than biographies, children in other cultures, stories with children facing contemporary issues. We are also interested in one-page nonfiction articles for very young children.

Queries should be directed to Rich Wallace, Coordinating Editor
Length of articles Feature articles: 300 to 900 words; Short pieces: 25 to 150 words
Payment $.14 per word and up
Time of payment On acceptance
Photographs We prefer to purchase all rights.
Response time to queries 4 to 6 weeks
Rights bought We acquire all rights.
Kill fees N/A
Writer's guidelines Free upon request
Sample issues Send $3.95 and large SASE.

TIPS FOR WRITERS

Please send for our guidelines and sample copies to get a feel for our style before submitting. If you write nonfiction material, query us first. Otherwise just send manuscripts. We are always interested in new topics. Avoid worn out themes. It is not necessary to send clips of writing with a manuscript.

We are looking for quality fiction and nonfiction that appeals to children, encourages them to read, and reinforces positive values. We do not want to see stories of war, crime, and violence. We would like to see more suspense stories/articles with world culture settings, sports pieces, action/adventure stories. For nonfiction we do not want to see trendy topics, fads, and violence. When submitting a nonfiction article, it is recommended to include photocopies of reference materials. We prefer an SASE with each submission. All queries on status of submissions should be in written form. Please do not call or fax us. We try to respond to manuscripts within three months.

HUMPTY DUMPTY'S MAGAZINE

P.O. Box 567
Indianapolis, IN 46206

Phone number 317-636-8881
Fax number 317-684-8094
Parent company Children's Better Health Institute
Circulation 250,000
Online status We aren't yet online.
Magazine availability Subscription only
Target audience Children aged 4 to 6
Magazine's history and mission Founded by *Parent Magazine* in 1952. Mission is to provide children with material that entertains, educates, and broadens their minds.
Nonfiction 25%

Fiction   50%
Percent of articles freelance-written   80%
Number of articles bought annually   60 to 70
Sections of the magazine open to freelance writers   All
Article interests and needs   We particularly need articles about the outdoors and nature. We are always looking for good fiction, especially fiction that presents a positive health message. Health should not be the main focus but should be subtly woven into the plot of the story.
Queries should be directed to   *Don't query!* Send complete manuscript to Sandy Grieshop, Editor.
Length of articles   150 to 500 words
Payment $.22 per word
Time of payment   On publication
Photographs   Accepted only with editorial material
Response time to manuscripts   10 to 12 weeks
Rights bought   Buy all rights. Onetime rights to photos
Kill fees   No
Writer's guidelines   Free with SASE
Sample issues $1.25

JACK AND JILL

1100 Waterway Boulevard
Box 567
Indianapolis, IN 46206

Phone number   317-636-8881
Parent company   Children's Better Health Institute
Circulation   260,000
Magazine availability   Subscription
Target audience   Children age 7 to 10
Magazine's mission   To present health, fitness, and nutrition information in a fun and interesting manner.
Nonfiction   50%
Fiction   50%
Percent of articles freelance-written   70%
Number of articles bought annually   24
Sections of the magazine open to freelance writers   All but "Ask Doctor Cory"
Length of articles   200 to 700 words
Payment $.17 per word
Time of payment   On publication
Photographs   Onetime rights

Writer's guidelines   Write with SASE.
Sample issues $1.25 each

RANGER RICK

8925 Leesburg Pike
Vienna, VA 22184

Phone number   703-790-4274
Fax number   703-442-7332
Parent company   National Wildlife Federation
Circulation   850,000
Magazine availability   *Ranger Rick* can be found on newsstands but it is acquired mostly through subscription
Target audience   Children ages 6 to12
Magazine's history and mission   *Ranger Rick* began in 1967. "We aim to inspire a greater understanding and appreciation of the natural world and our place in it."
Nonfiction   90%   (varies)
Fiction   10%   (varies)
Percent of articles freelance-written   Varies
Number of articles bought annually   Varies
Sections of the magazine open to freelance writers   All
Article interests and needs   Wildlife, nature environment, environmental themes
Queries should be directed to   Gerald Bishop, Editor
Length of articles   Up to 900 words
Payment   Up to $575
Time of payment   On acceptance
Photographs   Purchased from freelancers
Response time to queries   2 months
Rights bought   Usually buy all rights
Kill fees   Negotiated in advance
Writer's guidelines   Free with SASE
Sample issues $2.00 plus SASE

TIPS FOR WRITERS FROM *RANGER RICK WRITERS' GUIDELINES*

The only way you can write successfully for *Ranger Rick* is to know the kinds of subjects and approaches we like. And the only way you can do that is to read the magazine.

We prefer that you send us a query describing your intended subject, along with a lead or sample paragraph. Any special qualifications you may have to write on that subject would be worth mentioning. If you are not an expert on the subject, please list your main references and names of experts you will contact. Please do not query by phone or fax. Include a self-addressed, stamped envelope with all queries.

SEVENTEEN

850 Third Avenue
New York, NY 10022

Phone number   212-407-9700
E-mail address   thespin@aol.com
Parent company   K-111 Magazines
Circulation   2.1 million
Online status   On America Online
Magazine availability   Newsstands and subscription
Target audience   Females 12 to 21 years old—core readership 13 to 17
Magazine's history and mission   Founded in 1944. First mass magazine to recognize teenagers as a demographic and market.
Nonfiction   95%
Fiction   5%
Percent of articles freelance-written   50 to 60%
Number of articles bought annually   50 to 75 (including smaller pieces)
Sections of the magazine open to freelance writers   The Spin, Voice (young writers), fiction, features, EAT, entertainment
Article interests and needs   Of interest to teenage girls/young women
Queries should be directed to   Joe Bargmann, Features Editor
Length of articles   50 word items to 3,000 word features and fiction
Payment $1.00 per word
Time of payment   On acceptance
Expenses   Yes (reasonable)
Photographs   No
Response time to queries   8 to 10 weeks
Rights bought   One time North American rights
Kill fees   25%
Writer's guidelines   Available with SASE
Sample issues   Available for $4 each

TIPS FOR WRITERS
Joe Bargmann, Features Editor

Writing for teenagers, and particularly for *Seventeen,* is much more difficult than a lot of writers might assume. The challenge is to write clearly and concisely on topics that are both timely and interesting to young women, but never to "write down" to the audience. In other words, meet the reader on her level and don't underestimate her intelligence. We have a lot of success with pieces written in the second person. We feel this personalizes the magazine, which makes sense: Our readers tend to be proprietary about the magazine. They read it cover to cover and take it very seriously. I would suggest that freelancers do the same if they're interested in working for us. Read the magazine, and you'll discover that we don't deal in stereotypes, and that the magazine has changed A LOT in recent years. We get our story ideas from the news. We're not interested in 40- or 50-something writers reminiscing about "when I was a kid . . ." We want stories that are substantive and challenging. Please don't call in or fax ideas. Always include an SASE. The best way to break in, if you're not a seasoned pro with a portfolio, is with shorter pieces for The Spin section.

We accept unsolicited fiction. Stories should be 4,000 words or less. First-time authors are okay. Again, stories should be substantive and challenging.

SHOFAR MAGAZINE

43 Northcote Drive
Melville, NY 11747

Phone number   516-643-4598
Fax number   516-643-4598
Circulation   15,000
Magazine availability   Subscription
Target audience   Jewish children ages 9 to 13
Article interests and needs   Poetry, puzzles, games, cartoons. All material must be on a Jewish theme.
Queries should be directed to   Gerald H. Grayson, Managing Editor
Length of articles   600 to 1,000 words
Payment $.10 per word plus five copies
Time of payment   On publication
Photographs   Black/white, color prints purchased with manuscript at additional fee.
Response time to queries   6 to 8 weeks
Rights bought   First North American serial rights
Writer's guidelines   Yes
Sample issues   Send 9 × 12 SASE with $1.01 postage.

TURTLE MAGAZINE FOR PRESCHOOLERS

P.O. Box 567
Indianapolis, IN 46206

Phone number   317-636-8881
Fax number   317-684-8094
Parent company   Children's Better Health Institute

Circulation   400,000
Online status   Not yet
Magazine availability   Through subscription
Target audience   2 to 5 year olds. National distribution.
Magazine's mission   The mission of our magazine is to entertain and educate preschool children about good health and nutrition.
Nonfiction   50%
Fiction   50%
Percent of articles freelance-written   100%
Number of articles bought annually   8
Sections of the magazine open to freelance writers   All, except book and product reviews, poster page, cartoon feature
Article interests and needs   Short, simple stories and articles with health/nutrition focus for preschoolers
Queries should be directed to   *Turtle Magazine for Preschoolers*. Do not query. Submit best work to Children's Better Health Institute.
Length of articles   100 to 250 words max.
Payment $.22 per word on publication; varies for poems, activities
Time of payment   On publication
Expenses   No
Photographs   Will consider photo essays by professionals.
Response time to completed manuscripts   2 to 3 months
Rights bought   We buy all rights.
Kill fees   None
Writer's guidelines   On request with SASE.
Sample issues   On request with $1.25 and SASE.

TIPS FOR WRITERS

Submit your best work based on familiarity with the magazine. Study back issues. Stay focused on the preschool audience. Short, simple, easy-to-read prose will be considered. Do not send artwork. We'll review photo essays (professional quality). If submitting pencil activities or recipes/simple science experiments, check out suitability with childhood development expert.

YM

685 Third Avenue
New York, NY 10017

Phone number   212-878-8700
Fax number   212-286-0935
Parent company   Gruner and Jahr USA Publishing

Circulation   2 million
Magazine availability   Newsstands and subscription
Target audience   Young women, ages 12 to 21
Magazine's history and mission   *YM* was founded in the forties under the name *Polly Pigtails*. It became *Young Miss* in 1966, and then *Young and Modern (YM)* in 1989. Its mission is to bring readers the most up-to-date advice on relationships, fitness, fashion, beauty, celebrities, and social issues of interest to young women.
Nonfiction   100%
Percent of articles freelance-written   75%
Number of articles bought annually   Approximately 200
Sections of the magazine open to freelance writers   First person, real life, relationships, entertainment, celebrities, quizzes
Article interests and needs   Dramatic first-person stories involving teenagers
Queries should be directed to   Stephanie Dolgoff, Senior Editor
Length of articles   200 to 1,200 words
Payment $.70 to $1.00 a word
Time of payment   On acceptance
Expenses   On a case by case basis
Photographs   Assigned by magazine
Response time to queries   4 to 6 weeks
Rights bought   We buy all rights
Kill fees   25%
Writer's guidelines   Available on request
Sample issues   Not available

TIPS FOR WRITERS

The most important thing we look for in a query is tone. *YM* has a very special voice. We speak to teenagers in their own language, as a friend and not as an authority figure. The writing must be conversational and energetic, not stilted or overly formal. For first-person stories, the writer's proposal or clips must show an ability to get at the emotional heart of a piece, and to recreate events and feelings in the subject's voice.

If a writer hasn't written for us before, he or she must include clips, preferably ones that demonstrate an ability to write the kind of piece being proposed (i.e., beauty clips when pitching a beauty idea). For first-person stories, a query must include all relevant information (age of subject, date when event or events occurred) as well as any newspaper clips relating to the event.

We do not want to see a completed manuscript—if one is available, we'll ask for it if the query letter piques our interest. An SASE is also a must. We don't accept pitches by phone call, fax, or e-mail.

Here are some common pet peeves of editors at all magazines (not just *YM*):

- Writers who don't seem to have read the magazine. It's always good to be able to suggest a specific department that an idea might be right for.
- Mass-mailing queries, with the wrong magazine name in the letter.

- Queries addressed to editors who haven't worked at the magazine for a year or more. Always check the masthead before you write!
- Too many clips. We don't need to see your entire life's work—a few of your best will do.

Breaking into any magazine is a challenge. We publish very few unsolicited manuscripts, but we read and respond to all queries (if they include an SASE, that is). The best way to break into our magazine is to have strong clips combined with fresh ideas, targeted at specific areas of the magazine. It's best if a writer has a special interest in teenagers or the teen market. If you want to write for *YM*, talk to young people you know, or visit schools in your area and talk to teenagers there about their interests, concerns, and passions. The more you know about a magazine's readers, the more likely you are to come up with ideas that will interest its editors.

College Alumni Magazines

COLUMBIA MAGAZINE

P.O. Box 10027
New York, NY 10027

Phone number   212-870-2429
E-mail address   magazine@columbia.edu
Parent company   Columbia University
Circulation   160,000
Magazine availability   Subscription; free to Columbia University alumni
Target audience   Alumni of all divisions of Columbia University
Magazine's history and mission   Founded approximately in 1975 for Columbia alumni.
Nonfiction   98%
Percent of articles freelance-written   15 to 20%
Number of articles bought annually   15 to 20
Sections of the magazine open to freelance writers   Features, department items
Article interests and needs   Pertaining to alumni, faculty activities of Columbia University
Queries should be directed to   Leslie Bernstein, Editor; Patrick S. Queen, Associate Editor; Brett Forman, Assistant Editor
Length of articles   Not more than 1,500 words for a feature; 350 to 700 words for department items

Payment   Our pay scale runs from $50 for a book review to $1,000 for a feature, depending on the topic's complexity, number of people to be interviewed, etc.
Time of payment   On acceptance
Expenses   Within reason
Response time to queries   We try to reply within 3 to 4 weeks.
Rights bought   Negotiable
Kill fees   None
Writer's guidelines   Available upon request
Sample issues   Available upon request

TIPS FOR WRITERS
Leslie M. Bernstein

What sparks our interest? Anything that has to do with Columbia University alumni or faculty activities: whether a profile, some news of Columbia research projects, or any other news that affects or involves Columbia. Historical notes about Columbia and the Morningside Heights area of New York City may also be of interest.

The best way to be in touch is by telephone. Any writer who suggests graphics that might accompany a story gets an extra plus. If a story has no connection with Columbia University, we almost certainly will not publish it.

CORNELL MAGAZINE
55 Brown Road
Ithaca, NY 14850

Phone number   607-257-5133
Fax number   607-257-1782
E-mail address   cornell_magazine@cornell.edu
Parent company   The Cornell Alumni Federation
Circulation   30,000
Online status   Available online at: http://cornell-magazine.cornell.edu
Magazine availability   Subscription only
Target audience   Alumni, staff, faculty, and friends of Cornell University
Magazine's history and mission   The magazine was founded in 1899. Its mission is to report news of Cornell University and its alumni.
Nonfiction   With very rare exceptions, the magazine is entirely nonfiction.
Percent of articles freelance-written   About 50%
Number of articles bought annually   Roughly 40
Sections of the magazine open to freelance writers   Features and departments
Queries should be directed to   Beth Saulnier, Associate Editor
Length of articles   Departments: 1,000 to 1,500 words; Features: 3,000 to 5,000 words
Payment   Departments: $300; Features: $1,000

Expenses   Varies
Time of payment   On acceptance
Photographs   As the magazine has no staff photographers, most photos come from freelancers.
Response time to queries   Varies
Kill fees   Varies

HARVARD MAGAZINE

7 Ware Street
Cambridge, MA 02138

Phone number   617-495-5746
Fax number   617-495-0326
Parent company   Harvard Magazine, Inc.
Circulation   220,000 bimonthly
Magazine availability   Boston area newsstands—1,000; subscription—20,000; and controlled circulation to alumni—200,000
Online status   Web site at http://www.harvard-magazine.com
Target audience   Graduates of Harvard College and Harvard University's graduate and professional schools (law, business, medicine, divinity, education, public health, government, etc.).
Magazine's history and mission   Established in 1898 by Harvard College alumni; owned by Harvard Magazine, Inc., a self-perpetuating alumni group. Mission: to be about the University.
Nonfiction   100%
Percent of articles freelance-written   50%
Number of articles bought annually   Right Now—30; Features—10 to 15
Sections of the magazine open to freelance writers   Right Now pieces on current research assigned to local writers; features vary; Vita (900 word historical biographies)
Article interests and needs   Must be by or about Harvard or Harvard people, faculty, graduates, etc.
Queries should be directed to   John S. Rosenberg, Editor
Length of articles   Right Now: 800 words; Vita: 900 words; Features: 1,200 to 7,000 words
Payment   Right Now: $250; Vita: $350; Features: $300 to $1,000
Time of payment   On publication
Expenses   Negotiable
Photographs   Assigned by art director
Response time to queries   Immediate to 4 weeks
Rights bought   We buy first rights, onetime, although will want to put text on Web site.
Kill fees   Negotiable
Writer's guidelines   None
Sample issues   Send $5 and address for mailing.

IMPORTANT QUESTIONS ANSWERED

Q: Do you always want clips from new writers?

A: Yes. Queries must include an example of finished writing similar in scope to the piece being proposed if the author is new to the publication and editor.

Q: Will you look at completed manuscripts?

A: Yes, but there is a *very* low probability of acceptance.

Q: Is it OK if writers e-mail queries to you?

A: No

Q: Is it OK if writers fax queries to you?

A: Yes, but [we] still need clips.

Q: Are phone calls from writers OK?

A: Yes but we strongly prefer *not*.

Q: What is the best way to break into Harvard Magazine?

A: We must have some Harvard connection.

College/Careers

AMERICAN CAREERS

6701 West 64th Street, Suite 304
Overland Park, KS 66202

Phone number   913-362-7788
Fax number   913-362-4864
Parent company   Career Communications, Inc.
Circulation   500,000
Magazine availability   Subscription
Target audience   U.S., Guam, Puerto Rico, Virgin Islands, U.S. Dept. of Defense Dependent Schools in Europe
Magazine's history and mission   Founded by James P. Dick and Barbara F. Orwig in 1990 to help students explore career options, introduce them to their educational choices, including school-to-work programs, and promote career planning while still in school.
Nonfiction   100%
Percent of articles freelance-written   25%
Number of articles bought annually   10
Sections of the magazine open to freelance writers   We run feature stories on careers, take-it-yourself career interest tests, career education features, charts and other sidebars related to jobs, salaries, education needed, etc.
Article interests and needs   See above
Queries should be directed to   Mary Pitchford, Editor

Length of articles   500 words, some more and some less
Time of payment   30 days after acceptance
Expenses   Only approved ones
Photographs   Yes, we're interested in photos related to stories
Response time to queries   Approximately 30 days
Rights bought   We buy all rights or make work-for-hire assignments.
Kill fees   No
Writer's guidelines   Yes
Sample issues   Yes

TIPS FOR WRITERS

The query: It's best for new writers to ask for a copy of our writer's guidelines and sample magazines before sending a query. Too often we receive story ideas that have little to do with our audience or purpose. Before we work with a writer, we review resumes and clips. We're interested in seeing if a writer can relate to our readers. Rarely have we purchased a completed manuscript, and then we've had to ask for a rewrite suited to our audience and purpose.

Professional etiquette: We prefer written queries for information, because phone, fax, or e-mail queries are disruptive. Regarding SASEs, please send a 9 × 12 envelope with $1.70 worth of postage on it if you want samples. It's amazing! Writers will send a #10 envelope with one first-class stamp on it and ask for a sample magazine that requires a larger envelope and more postage to send. Only one prospective writer in the last two years has sent a large enough envelope with appropriate postage.

Best way to break into the magazine: Send us a story idea that's appropriate to our purpose and our readers. Send us some clips that indicate you know how to write for teens.

Best things that writers do: We appreciate writers who meet deadlines, ask questions, handle their assignments professionally, and respond to our suggestions.

Pet peeves: Don't nag us on the telephone. Don't request guidelines and samples on a torn scrap of paper in illegible handwriting.

Angles: When looking for an angle, ask yourself about what would interest a teenager and get that teenager to read the story.

LINK - THE COLLEGE MAGAZINE

110 Greene Street
New York, NY 10012

Phone number   212-966-1100
Fax number   212-966-1380
E-mail address   editor@linkmag.com
Parent company   Creative Media Generations
Circulation   1 million

Online status   Extensive Web site at http://www.linkmag.com

Magazine availability   Controlled circulation (1 million direct-mailed to students nationwide)

Target audience   College; 17 to 25; male and female

Nonfiction   100%

Percent of articles freelance-written   75%

Number of articles bought annually   45+

Sections of the magazine open to freelance writers   All

Article interests and needs   College life, issues, and entertainment

Queries should be directed to   Ty Wenger

Length of articles   600 to 900 words

Payment $100 to $200

Time of payment   On publication

Expenses   Not usually

Photographs   Varies widely

Response time to queries   2 months

Rights bought   First-time

Kill fees   Occasionally; varies

Writer's guidelines   Yes

UNIQUE OPPORTUNITIES

455 South Fourth Avenue, Suite 1236
Louisville, KY 40202

Phone number   502-589-8250

Fax number   502-587-0848

E-mail address   ULP@aol.com

Parent company   U O, Inc.

Circulation   Controlled; 80,000 physicians nationwide

Magazine availability   Only through subscription

Target audience   Physicians interested in new career opportunities in all specialties. Audience includes young physicians as well as those in career transition.

Magazine's history and mission   Founded by Bobby C. Baker, M.D., Mel Weinberger, and Barbara Barry in 1991. The mission is to guide physicians in making career decisions. Barry and Weinberger are the current publishers.

Nonfiction   100%

Percent of articles freelance-written   50 to 60%

Number of articles bought annually   12 to 15 per year

Sections of the magazine open to freelance writers   Features

Article interests and needs   We use articles on subjects of interest to physicians in career transition, including legal, economic, and personal aspects of starting, changing, or running a medical practice. This also includes trends in physician work force issues and articles on various career opportunities for physicians. Book reviews and physician profiles are also occasionally used.

Queries should be directed to   Bett Coffman, Assistant Editor

Length of articles   Features: 2,000 to 3,000 words; Profiles/book reviews: 500 words

Payment   Features: $.50 per word; Profiles/book reviews: $200 flat fee

Time of payment   30 days from acceptance

Expenses   Up to $50 per article; additional expenses are covered with prior approval.

Photographs   Usually assigned by the design editor

Response time to queries   It varies. Because we work with an editorial calendar up to a year in advance, it may take from two weeks to three months to receive a query response.

Rights bought   We purchase first North American serial rights, exclusive for 90 days from publication date.

Kill fees   To be arranged if necessary

Writer's guidelines   Send an SASE (#10 envelope).

Sample issues   For a sample issue with writers' guidelines, send a 9 × 12 envelope with $1.47 postage.

TIPS FOR WRITERS

There are always more good writers contacting us than we have assignments, but if more good writers provided all their information with their first query, more of them would get assignments. The first things we would like to see from a writer are a query or introductory letter with two or three clips. A resume is optional, but references of editors with whom the writer has worked previously are helpful. Subsequent queries via telephone, e-mail, or fax are welcome and do not require SASEs. We will respond via telephone or return letter.

We prefer not to receive completed manuscripts for several reasons. First, we will not publish work that has been previously published. Second, because our focus is narrow and our audience is specific, we prefer to guide the writer with an assignment before research and writing begin. That way the writer doesn't have to spend a lot of time reworking the article.

A good query shows us that the writer has an understanding of our audience. The clips demonstrate the writer's ability to research and compose an article. The references help us determine the writer's professionalism and reliability. If a writer demonstrates an understanding of our audience, good writing and research ability, and an ability to fulfill assignments, there is a good chance we will call that writer. If the writer who accepts an assignment delivers a well-researched article, on target with the assignment, on time, and is willing to make adjustments based on the editor's requests, we will call that writer again.

All articles written for *UO* should be directed to physicians and written in an informative, conversational tone. Interviews with physicians are always in order, regardless of the nature of the article. We request that a writer provide regular updates throughout the research and writing process. Prior to the initial submission, the writer should double check the spelling of names, titles, and companies, as well as important facts and statistics included in the article. The names, addresses, and telephone numbers of sources should be submitted with the first draft of the article so that photos and art can be assigned.

A writer can expect success writing for *UO* or any publication if he or she follows the assignment as closely as possible (notifies the editor if there is good reason to alter the assignment), provides adequate research, and delivers a clean, concise article on time.

Computers/Technology

BYTE

One Phoenix Mill Lane
Peterborough, NH 03458

Phone number   603-924-9281
Fax number   603-924-2550
E-mail address   editors@bix.com
Parent company   The McGraw-Hill Companies, Inc.
Circulation   512,000
Online status   Web site at http://www.byte.com
Magazine availability   Newsstands and subscription
Target audience   Computer technologists, advanced users
Magazine's history and mission   Founded in 1975. According to a McGraw-Hill press release, *Byte* is a multiplatform computer publication that meets "... the information needs of the computer industry's technology experts with extensive coverage of leading-edge computer technologies and products."
Nonfiction   100%
Percent of articles freelance-written   40%
Queries should be directed to   John Montgomery, 415-513-6950 (fax)
Payment   On a case-by-case basis
Expenses   On a case-by-case basis
Rights bought   Once an article is agreed upon, contract is written.
Time of payment   On publication
Writer's guidelines   Send inquiries to John Montgomery

COMPUTER GRAPHICS WORLD

10 Tara Boulevard, 5th Floor
Nashua, NH 03062

Phone number   603-891-9166
Fax number   603-891-0539
E-mail address   stevep@pennwell.com
Parent company   Penn Well Publishing
Circulation   75,000
Online status   We have a Web site that complements the magazine.
Magazine availability   Newsstands and subscription
Target audience   Professional computer graphics users involved in CAD and animation applications
Magazine's history and mission   Founded in 1978, *CGW* is the premier authority on computer graphics.
Nonfiction   100%
Percent of articles freelance-written   70%
Number of articles bought annually   60
Sections of the magazine open to freelance writers   Features, reviews, computer application stories
Article interests and needs   We need strong writers who are also technically knowledgeable about computer graphics.
Queries should be directed to   Stephen Porter, Editor
Length of articles   1,000 to 3,000 words
Payment   On acceptance
Time of payment   About $.50 per word
Expenses   Yes
Photographs   No
Response time to queries   4 weeks
Rights bought   We buy all rights
Kill fees   25%
Writer's guidelines   No

MACWORLD
501 Second Street
San Francisco, CA 94107

Phone number   415-243-0505
Fax number   415-442-0766
E-mail address   macworld@macworld.com
Parent company   International Data Group (IDG)
Circulation   625,000
Online status   America Online, and the Web (http://www.macworld.com)
Magazine availability   Newsstands and through subscription
Target audience   Active users and buyers of Macintosh software and hardware
Magazine's history and mission   Founded by David Bunnell when the Mac was launched in 1984 to serve Macintosh users.

Nonfiction   100%
Percent of articles freelance-written   40%
Number of articles bought annually   150 to 200
Sections of the magazine open to freelance writers   All but columns
Article interests and needs   Reviews of products, technology news/trends
Queries should be directed to   Reviews: Wendy Sharp, Reviews Coordinator; Features/Comparisons: Charles Piller, Features Coordinator; News: Galen Gruman, Executive Editor
Length of articles   Varies
Payment $.75 to $1.25 per word
Time of payment   On acceptance
Expenses   No
Photographs   Done in-house or through freelance pros
Response time to queries   We respond only to accepted ideas: one month
Rights bought   All
Kill fees   None for new writers; 50% thereafter in most cases
Writer's guidelines   Yes
Sample issues   No

TIPS FOR WRITERS

A good query is one that targets our audience—it's clear that the author has read our magazine and knows what we deliver to our readers, and is proposing something that will do just that. We need to see clips that show both topical expertise and ability to do the kind of article proposed; usually three or so suffices.

Most writers who want to break in don't do their homework—it's clear they have no idea what kind of stories we actually run—and thus they propose stories that have no place for us. Many other authors, especially less experienced ones, simply don't have the experience with the Macintosh or products to provide the expertise needed to write news analyses for us or to review products. If you don't have that experience, get it first; try your local user group newsletter, for example.

There's no need to send an SASE. We prefer no calls until after we've seen a proposal and clips. Similarly, e-mail is usually not helpful, because it can't transmit clips; once an author is established, e-mail and calls are great.

Good writers—those who are knowledgeable, conscientious, deadline-oriented; those who have clear organization and engaging style; those who can work with people and share the ownership of their content with the publication that will print it (in terms of its focus, conceptualization, and execution)—are hard to find. Be one of those, and you'll have no trouble getting work.

ONLINE ACCESS
900 North Franklin, #700
Chicago, IL 60610

Phone number   312-573-1700
Fax number   312-573-0520
E-mail address   editor@onlineaccess.com
Parent company   Red Flish Internet
Circulation   70,000
Online status   Web page
Magazine availability   Newsstands and subscription
Target audience   Broad consumer
Magazine's history and mission   Founded in 1986 by publisher Bob Jordan. Mission: to be the online authority.
Nonfiction   100%
Percent of articles freelance-written   70%
Number of articles bought annually   60
Sections of the magazine open to freelance writers   All
Article interests and needs   Online and Internet computing
Queries should be directed to   Kathryn McCabe, Editor-in-Chief
Length of articles   2,000 words
Payment $500
Time of payment   On acceptance
Expenses   Yes
Photographs   No
Response time to queries   2 to 3 months
Kill fees   Yes, $50
Writer's guidelines   No
Sample issues   No

PC WORLD

501 Second Street, Suite 600
San Francisco, CA 94107

Phone number   415-243-0500
Fax number   415-442-1891
E-mail address   CompuServe: go pwo; Internet:customer_service@pcworld.com; AOL: keyword pc world; Prodigy: jump pc world
Parent company   IDG
Circulation   1 million
Online status   PC World online can be reached at the above e-mail addresses and on the World Wide Web at http://www.pcworld.com
Magazine availability   Newsstands and subscription
Nonfiction   100%

POPULAR MECHANICS

224 West 57th Street
New York, NY 10019

Phone number 212-649-2000
Fax number 212-586-5562
E-mail address popularmechanics@hearst.com
Parent company The Hearst Corp.
Circulation 1.4 million subscribers; 200,000 newsstand
Online status Web page (http://popularmechanics.com)
Magazine available Newsstands and subscription
Target audience Male, ages 35–55, median income $45,000, married with children, owns his home and at least two cars, and probably works in a technically oriented profession.
Magazine's history and mission Established in 1902 and dubbed "the original men's service magazine," we try to addresss the diverse interests of today's male, while providing him with information to improve the way he lives. We cover stories from how-to, do-it-yourself projects to technological advances in aerospace, military, auto-motive, electronics, computers, telecommunications, sports, science, and so on.
Non-fiction 100%
Percent of articles freelance-written 5%
Number of articles bought annually 2
Sections of the magazine open to freelance writers Tech Update section open to free-lance writers; good way to get started writing for the magazine with longer feature articles.
Article interests and needs Our guiding principle is to help our readers better under-stand the technology of how things work in today's highly technical society. Therefore, we're interested in articles of technical nature that cover the latest developments and ad-vancements in the industries that our five departments cover—our five departments are: Automotive, Home Improvement, Science/Technology, Boating/Outdoors, Electronics/Photography.
Queries should be directed to If your query doesn't fit into any of the departments, send it to the editor-in-chief.

Dan Chaikin, Automotive
Steven Willson, Home Improvement
Brian Fenton, Electronics/Photography/Telecommunications
Jim Wilson, Science/Technology, Aerospace
Rich Taylor, Outdoors
Joe Oldham, Editor-In-Chief

Length of articles 1,000–2,000 words for Major Feature
  800–1,000 words for Short Feature
  300–500 words for News Brief
  100–400 words for Tech Update section

Payment $300–$2,500 for Major Feature
   $500–$600 for Short Feature
   $300 for News Brief
   $300 for Tech Update section
   $200 for Finder's Fee
Time of payment   On acceptance
Expenses   Negotiable
Photographs   Photographs are a plus, but not required. Send photos—slides, prints, 5×, and transparencies—with submission. No additional payment offered for photos accepted with manuscript.
Response time to queries   2 months
Rights bought   All rights purchased, including copyright, on a work-for-hire basis.
Kill fees   25%
Writer's guidelines   Available. Send SASE.
Sample issues   Not available

TIPS FOR WRITERS

The query: To spark our interest, the query should propose an article that is new to PM, one we haven't published before. A query about a subject that we already covered in one way or another shows that the writer really doesn't know our magazine and hasn't done his/her research. Before submitting a query, we suggest that writers check the *Guide to Periodical Literature* or our own indexes (available through our Reader Information Services department). The key elements in a good, professional query are active voice with a great lead flowing into an outline, well-defined description of the subject matter and how the writer intends to get the story; i.e., contacts already in place, material available for art, etc. Clips are not necessary, although a brief list of credentials and previous publications in which the writer's work has appeared helps. Completed manuscripts are generally not read through. It's better to make the proposal first before sending a completed story.

   Professional etiquette: SASE is not necessary, but considered polite and appreciated for easy and quick response time. Phone calls are okay in circumstances that involve timely material that needs to be reported on immediately or the story becomes old and published elsewhere. Faxed and e-mailed queries are always welcomed and considered.

   The best way to break into *PM* is through the Tech Update section. It's where a new writer can learn our style, what we need and want for certain subject matter, and it allows our editors to become familiar with the writer and possibly move on to bigger feature assignments.

   The key to breaking in to *PM* is to be familiar with our magazine—i.e., know who our reader is and our target audience, and, most importantly, know that we did not already cover that subject in one form or another over the past few years; unless, of course, there have been some new developments that we have yet to report on.

   The best thing writers do is stick to the line count given once a proposal has been accepted and a contract drawn up and a story assigned.

The worst thing writers do is write fluff pieces that read like press releases rather than good, unbiased reporting.

Writers can angle their stories for *PM* by referring to any of the topics our five departments (see Guidelines) cover; reading through back issues of *PM* that cover similar subjects and analyzing the approach we took in printing the stories—for example, pay attention to the layout, the types of photos used, the art illustrated.

Overall advice to writers: Know your subject, have contacts, and get the facts straight. Your writing ability is not as important as being able to back up your words with facts that are true and thoroughly researched. Writing can always be edited, but fact checking and researching information that a writer is supplying are not always available to every editor, be it for reasons of limited time or limited resources and small staffs.

WINDOWS MAGAZINE

One Jericho Plaza
Jericho, NY 11753

Phone number   516-733-8300
Fax number   516-733-8390
E-mail address   winmag@cmp.com
Parent company   CMP Publications, Inc.
Circulation   700,000
Online status   Available on America Online, CompuServe, and through Tech Web, CMP's online technology source at http://techweb.cmp.com/win/current
Magazine availability   Newsstands and subscription
Target audience   Buyers of Windows hardware and software products
Magazine's history and mission   Founded by David Nelson in 1990. Re-launched by CMP as *Windows Magazine* in February 1992.
Nonfiction   100%
Percent of articles freelance-written   About 50%
Number of articles bought annually   About 300
Sections of the magazine open to freelance writers   All sections except for opinion column
Article interests and needs   Articles on all aspects of Microsoft Windows
Queries should be directed to   Mike Elgan, Executive Editor
Length of articles   Between 500 and 5,000 words
Payment   About $1.00 per word
Time of payment   Invoice submitted for payment on acceptance
Expenses   Generally not
Photographs   No
Response time to queries   One day if query by e-mail
Rights bought   Depends
Kill fees   Usually about 50% of contracted amount

Writer's Guidelines   Will send upon request.
Sample issues   Yes, we have sample issues.

TIPS FOR WRITERS

If queries demonstrate knowledge and experience, we'll take a good look at it. Anything that demonstrates a fresh approach is good. An SASE is not necessary. E-mail is preferred over other means of communication.

The best way to start writing for *Windows Magazine* is to study the magazine and send us an article on spec that fits our magazine.

WIRED

520 Third Street, 4th Floor
San Francisco, CA 94107

Phone number   415-222-6200
Fax number   415-222-6209
E-mail address   Many
Parent company   Wired Ventures, Ltd.
Circulation   250,000
Online status   Lots
Magazine availability   Newsstands and subscription
Target audience   People interested in digital culture
Magazine's history and mission   Founded by Louis Rossetto in 1992 as a voice of the digital revolution.
Nonfiction   95%
Fiction   5%
Percent of articles freelance-written   100%
Number of articles bought annually   150 feature length
Sections of the magazine open to freelance writers   All
Article interests and needs   Digital culture
Queries should be directed to   Jesse Freund, Editorial Assistant, at submissions @wired.com
Length of articles   1,000 to 5,000 words
Payment   Depends
Time of payment   On publication
Expenses   Reasonable
Photographs   Yes
Response time to queries   2 to 3 weeks
Rights bought   Yes
Kill fees   Yes
Writer's guidelines   Yes—guidelines@wired.com
Sample issues   Available for purchase

IMPORTANT QUESTIONS ANSWERED

Q: Do you always want clips from new writers?
A: Yes
Q: Will you look at completed manuscripts?
A: Yes
Q: Is it OK if writers e-mail or fax queries to you?
A: E-mail preferred.
Q: What is the best way to break in to your magazine?
A: Good writing. Through the shorter sections.
Q: What are the best things writers do?
A: Write.
Q: How can writers angle their stories for your magazine?
A: Voice.
Q: What is your overall advice to writers who want to get published?
A: Write.

WORDPERFECT FOR WINDOWS MAGAZINE

270 West Center Street
Orem, UT 84057

Phone number   801-226-5555
Fax number   801-226-8804
E-mail address   wpwinmag@wpmag.com
Parent company   Ivy International Communications, Inc.
Circulation   200,000
Online status   Web site at http://www.wpmag.com; CompuServe—go wpmag; America Online—keyword wpmag
Magazine availability   Newsstands and subscription
Target audience   WordPerfect users who want to learn how to be more productive using WordPerfect
Magazine's history and mission   Founded in 1989 by WordPerfect Publishing. Mission: Our readers want to use WordPerfect easier, faster, and better. We show them how.
Nonfiction   100%
Percent of articles freelance-written   80%
Number of articles bought annually   60 to 80
Sections of the magazine open to freelance writers   Features (General WordPerfect how-to articles)
Article interests and needs   Tips-oriented articles that show readers how to use WordPerfect better.
Queries should be directed to   *WordPerfect for Windows Magazine*
Length of articles   1,400 to 1,600 words

Payment $400 to $700
Time of payment   On acceptance
Response time to queries   60 days
Rights bought   All articles are work for hire.
Writer's guidelines   Available on request
Sample issues   Available on request

TIPS FOR WRITERS

WordPerfect for Windows Magazine publishes articles that give useful tips and other information about how to use WordPerfect easier, better, and faster. Queries should be well organized, easy to understand, and should teach useful WordPerfect concepts. We accept queries in manuscript or outline form.

In the past, *WordPerfect for Windows Magazine* has published keystroke-oriented articles that show how to create forms, calendars, and other types of documents. We are now moving away from keystroke articles in favor of tips-oriented articles. Tips-oriented articles give independent tips about getting more out of a particular WPWin feature. These articles make it easy for readers to glean useful information without having to read the entire article while at the computer.

WORDPERFECT MAGAZINE FOR DOS

270 West Center Street
Orem, UT 84057

Phone number   801-226-5555
Fax number   801-226-8804
E-mail address   wpmag@wpmag.com
Parent company   Ivy International Communications, Inc.
Circulation   Approximately 180,000
Online status   America Online, CompuServe, WWW, AT&T Interchange
Magazine availability   Newsstands and subscription
Target audience   Those who use *WordPerfect* in the workplace or home office
Magazine's history and mission   First published in January 1989 by Howard Collett, who had the verbal support of WordPerfect Corp. founders (they were on the board of trustees). Mission: to help people use WordPerfect easier, faster, and better.
Nonfiction   100%
Percent of articles freelance-written   Approximately 80%
Number of articles bought annually   Approximately 80 to 100
Sections of the magazine open to freelance writers   All
Article interests and needs   Articles written already in our format—including necessary keystrokes in explanations.
Queries should be directed to   Lisa Bearnson, Editor-in-Chief

Length of articles   Columns and short features: 1,200 to 1,400 words preferred. Full-length features: 1,500 to 1,800 words preferred. Macros: under 50 lines preferred
Payment $400 to $700
Time of payment   On acceptance
Expenses   No
Photographs   Yes
Response time to queries   2 weeks to 1 month
Rights bought   All world rights
Kill fees   Yes
Writer's guidelines   On request—SASE
Sample issues   On request—SASE

TIPS FOR WRITERS

The query: Most important—it covers an interesting topic. An application of WordPerfect or something that can be done in WordPerfect. Especially of interest are useful macros not over (approximately) 70 lines.

Including the opening paragraph is useful—sometimes this determines whether we buy the article or buy the idea and have it written in-house. (Outline helpful also.)

Queries are not required. Manuscripts are accepted for consideration—preferable, in fact.

SASE preferred. We also *prefer* correspondence by U.S. mail or e-mail—not fax. E-mail queries are fine, as well as manuscripts.

The best things writers do: Read the magazine—get a feel for style and format. (Human interest just isn't what we publish.) We have almost a "formula" for articles—as all are technical and we want it easy to read and understand for any WordPerfect user.

The worst things writers do: Write an article full of jargon. Make it too complex. Or write about already generally known things to use WordPerfect for . . . like printing envelopes (unless there is a new slant).

Consumer Products/Services

CONSUMERS DIGEST

5705 North Lincoln Avenue
Chicago, IL 60659

Phone number   312-275-3590
Fax number   312-275-7273
Parent company   Consumers Digest, Inc.

Circulation   1.3 million

Magazine availability   Newsstands and subscription

Target audience   Median age 53 years with 50% of readers between ages 25 and 54; average income $43,000; majority own their homes; 70% married; 63% employed full- or part-time; 60% completed college; 52% female; 48% male

Magazine's history and mission   Founded in 1962 by Arthur Weber as a buying guide. That's still the main thrust, as the subtitle of the magazine proclaims: "For People Who Demand Value."

Nonfiction   100%

Percent of articles freelance-written   Approximately 70%—most often by "regulars" who specialize in different fields and write on topics we specify.

Number of articles bought annually   140 approximately (but, as noted, almost all on topics we specify)

Sections of the magazine open to freelance writers   All except departments

Article interests and needs   According to *Consumer Digest Guidelines for Writers*, the editorial concept goes beyond product-purchasing advice. "We show our readers how to obtain the best value for the services they need: doctors, lawyers, hospitals, financial advisers, and so on. We tell our readers about recent advances in medicine, medical technology, nutrition and healthcare, and how the reader can access these new developments . . . Throughout the magazine, the underlying theme is reinforced—telling the readers how they can get the most at the lowest possible cost."

Queries should be directed to   John Manos, Editor-in-Chief

Length of articles   2,000 to 2,500 words is usual length; no briefs

Payment   About $.50 per assigned word

Time of payment   On acceptance

Expenses   Usually only phone and express-mail charges

Photographs   Don't buy

Response time to queries   Usually 3 to 4 weeks

Rights bought   We prefer to buy all rights; sometimes this is negotiable.

Kill fees   One-half the price offered for satisfactory article

Writer's guidelines   Write for free copy with SASE

Sample issues   1 free

Cooking/Wine/Epicurean/Healthy Lifestyle

BEST RECIPES

1503 SW 42nd Street
Topeka, KS 66609

Phone number   913-274-4300
Fax number   913-274-4305

Circulation   200,000
Magazine availability   Newsstands and subscription
Target audience   Families with children in the home
Nonfiction   100%
Percent of articles freelance-written   10%
Number of articles bought annually   6 to 10
Sections of the magazine open to freelance writers   Food, lifestyle
Article interests and needs   Informative articles to assist families—eating healthy, food budgeting and buying, trends, etc.
Queries should be directed to   Michael Scheibach
Length of articles   1,000 to 1,500 words
Payment $.22 per word
Time of payment   On publication
Expenses   Agreed upon only
Photographs   When appropriate
Response time to queries   60 to 90 days
Rights bought   First
Kill fees   No
Writer's guidelines   No
Sample issues   Yes, $4.00

TIPS FOR WRITERS

An SASE is always necessary. Phone calls from writers are not OK nor are fax or e-mail queries.

COOKING LIGHT, THE MAGAZINE OF FOOD AND FITNESS

2100 Lakeshore Drive
Birmingham, AL 35209

Phone number   800-366-4712 or 205-877-6000
Fax number   205-877-6600
E-mail address   Cook Light@aol.com; CookingLight@msn.com
Parent company   Southern Press Corporation
Circulation   1.2 million
Online status   Yes
Magazine availability   Newsstands and through subscription
Target audience   Nearly 85% of our readers are women between 30 and 60. They are affluent, sophisticated, well-educated, professional, and interested in living a healthy lifestyle.
Magazine's history and mission   Started in 1987 by SPC, which also produces *Progressive Farmer, Southern Living, Southern Accents*, and our book division, Oxmoor House, *Cooking Light* is dedicated to helping readers eat, feel, look their best.

The magazine also explores food and nutrition news as well as fitness, health, beauty, and the indulgences that make healthy living more fun.

Nonfiction   100%

Percent of articles freelance-written   95%

Sections of the magazine open to freelance writers   All

Article interests and needs   Healthy lifestyles, fitness, food, beauty, and indulgences.

Queries should be directed to   Food—Jill Melton, Senior Food Editor; Fitness—Melissa Aspell, Fitness Editor

Length of articles   Varies from 500 to 2,000

Payment   Average of $1.00 a word

Time of payment   On acceptance

Expenses   Yes

Photographs   Sometimes

Response time to queries   Usually within about one month

Rights bought   Yes

Kill fees   Yes

Writer's guidelines   Sent upon request

Sample issues   No

TIPS FOR WRITERS

The query: All query ideas must be submitted in writing. Please enclose a paragraph or two about each idea, your resume, and, perhaps, three sample clips from other national publications. Our editors look for well-thought-out, concise ideas that include possible interviews, research/reference material, and evidence of the idea's validity and popularity with our readers.

Professional etiquette: An SASE is a must. Phone calls are strongly discouraged. Fax and e-mail queries are welcome, but we stress that resume and clips are required.

The best way to break into our magazine is with great, timely ideas—in a fashion clearly illustrating familiarity with our content. The key, basically, is to tell us why we should publish your idea.

The worst thing a writer can do is to send in an idea not suited for our magazine—an immediate giveaway that the writer has not taken the time to become familiar with our publication. Overall advice to writers who want to get published: know the magazine you are writing for.

VEGETARIAN TIMES

P.O. Box 570
Oak Park, IL 60303

Phone number   708-848-8100

Fax number   708-848-8175 or 708-848-2031 for editorial

E-mail address   74651.215@compuserve.com
Parent company   Cowles Magazines
Circulation   310,000
Online status   Magazine not online.
Magazine availability   Newsstands and subscription
Target audience   Magazine is an informative monthly, covering topics of interest to vegetarians and others seeking a healthier lifestyle.
Magazine's history   Founder: Paul Obis, 1974
Nonfiction   100%
Percent of articles freelance-written   75%
Sections of the magazine open to freelance writers   Food Departments, News, Features, Herbalist
Article interests and needs   Focus is on vegetarian cooking, nutrition, and health. We also cover environmental issues, animal rights, alternative medicine, and government policy.
Queries should be directed to   Toni Apgar, Editorial Director
Length of articles   Varies
Payment   Food articles: $200 to $600; News: $50 to $125; Nonfood features: $400 to $1,500
Time of payment   On publication
Expenses   Paid
Photographs   Art department assigns
Response time to queries   2 to 6 weeks
Rights bought   Negotiable
Kill fees   Usually half
Writer's guidelines   Send SASE.
Sample issues $4 each

Tips for Writers

We look for articles that are extensively researched and well-written and that provide fresh ideas and new information. It is crucial that articles be from a vegetarian perspective—a diet free of meat, poultry, and fish, and an outlook that is sensitive to animals and the environment. The tone should be authoritative and engaging. Though we tend to challenge conventional wisdom and mainstream practices, we strive for objectivity, which means incorporating viewpoints that may be different from our own. We strongly recommend that you read a few issues of the magazine to get a sense of our tone and focus.

We prefer queries rather than phone calls. Non-recipe queries should demonstrate that you have already done enough research to have a solid handle on the subject; an outline of your proposed story is helpful. Include two or three recent clips and an SASE.

The best way to query a recipe feature is to submit a letter telling us what subject you'd like to write about. Include your qualifications to write about that subject and supply a few recipes you'd like to include in the piece (just the title and short description will do).

If we accept your query, we will contact you by phone, so please include your phone number.

We do not accept stories on how you became a vegetarian.

Queries may be sent by mail, fax, or e-mail. Once accepted, you may submit your article by e-mail.

VEGGIE LIFE

1041 Shary Circle
Concord, CA 94518

Phone number   510-671-9852
Fax number   510-671-0692
E-mail address   VeggieEd@aol.com
Parent company   EGW Publishing
Circulation   300,000
Magazine availability   Newsstands and subscription
Target audience   80% women, median age 50, median income $62,000, 78% college-educated, 18% vegetarian, 48% partial, 60% coastal states, 40% rest of U.S. Distributed in Canada, too.
Magazine's history and mission   *VL* was founded in April 1993. It is devoted to helping people adapt healthier eating, cooking, and environmentally safe cooking techniques and preferences. It is also devoted to natural health and nutrition through plant-based foods and medicines.
Nonfiction   100%
Percent of articles freelance-written   90%
Number of articles bought annually   60 to 65
Sections of the magazine open to freelance writers   All sections
Article interests and needs   Food features, Health & Nutrition features, Gardening features, and Departments
Queries should be directed to   Veggie Life Editor
Length of articles   1,000 to 1,500 words
Payment $.25 to $.35 per word
Time of payment   On acceptance of completed manuscript
Expenses   Author's responsibility
Photographs $50 each published photo
Response time to queries   2 to 4 months
Rights bought   Simultaneous rights
Kill fees   25%
Writer's guidelines   Send SASE.
Sample issues   Send $3.95 to Back Issues, Customer Service, 1041 Shary Circle, Concord, CA 94518

TIPS FOR WRITERS
How to Get Published in *Veggie Life*
Sharon Mikkelson, Editor

Anyone can get published in *Veggie Life*. It's not that hard, provided the writer takes the time to research our magazine. I would invite any writer with an interest or experience in vegetarian cooking, organic gardening, natural health, herbs, or nutrition, to submit queries. To have your query seriously considered for publication, it certainly helps to try and do most of the following.

- **Study back issues of the magazine**—Make sure we have not already covered the same or similar topic. Also pay attention to the style and structure of the articles and departments.
- **Send an SASE for our editorial calendar and writer's guideline**s—If you can pitch a query to us for an unassigned future article topic, or can suggest an interesting twist to an upcoming topic, you'll get our attention first.
- **Pick a query topic in which you can prove you have expertise or knowledge**— Generally, we only assign food articles to food writers or chefs, nutrition articles to RDs or PhDs. But credentials aside, I always prefer to go with a good, experienced, creative writer who has specialized in one of our featured areas for some time and can send published clips backing up this expertise.
- **Always send related clips**—If you want to write about herbs, send a clip of a previously published herb article. If you have not covered this area before, prove you can now with a thoroughly researched unpublished sample. At all costs, at least send one published clip regardless of topic.
- **Get to the point fast**—I get about 5 queries a day, so I don't always read every word of them. Keep the query brief, but convincing. If you want to write about growing corn, tell me in a cover letter why you are qualified to cover this piece, then follow with a complete outline of the proposed article. I want to see what you can say about corn that other potential writers can't.
- **Please be patient**—Reading queries and responding to all of them takes time— which editors do not have a lot of. To speed up a response, send an SAS postcard with responses written on it. If all I have to do is check a box, I'm likely to do it right away and send it back to you. E-mail is another great plus. I send quick e-mail replies every day because they take no time at all. Just hold tight and wait. We usually cover all responses within three months.

Pet peeves are pretty much the opposite of the above bullet points: writers who are obviously not familiar in any way with our magazine, writers who query topics we've already covered, writers who want to write about something they have no background in and who give no indication in their letter that they can tackle the topic, and writers with no published clips who send 500 words about their grades in journalism school and who leave only one sentence for the query itself. I get torrents of "How I Became a Vegetarian," and "I Want to Write about Beets"—stories that have no particular slant, point, or originality and that are quickly followed by phone calls from writers wanting to know if I opened my mail yet.

Veggie Life magazine as a whole has a common voice, and we are looking for writers that speak with that voice. So please, take a good look at our magazine past and future editorial before your query.

Don't always go for the big story, either. Many of our regular writers began by selling cooking tips and department, short info bytes. Our writer's guidelines spell out which departments we are seeking submissions for.

Good luck.

P.S. Also, make sure you address the current editor and not someone who worked here three years ago.

WINE SPECTATOR

387 Park Avenue South
New York, NY 10016

Phone number   212-684-4224
Fax number   212-684-5424
Parent company   M. Shanken Communications
Circulation   170,000
Magazine availability   Newsstands and subscription
Target audience   National magazine appealing to food and wine lovers and members of the wine industry
Nonfiction   100%
Percent of articles freelance-written   20%
Sections of the magazine open to freelance writers   News, features
Article interests and needs   Food and wine
Queries should be directed to   Jim Gordon, Managing Editor
Payment   Varies—$250 (news story) to $1,200 (feature)
Time of payment   On publication
Expenses   Paid
Response time to queries   2 months
Rights offered   None
Kill fees   Varies
Writer's guidelines   Available
Sample issues   Available from circulation department

Diseases and the Physically Challenged

ACCENT ON LIVING

P.O. Box 700
Bloomington, IL 61702

Phone number   309-378-2961
Fax number   309-378-4420
E-mail address   Cheeverpub@aol.com
Parent company   Cheever Publishing, Inc.
Circulation   18,000
Magazine availability   Subscription only
Target audience   18 and over, disabled people, and rehab professionals, worldwide
Magazine's history and mission   Founded in 1956 by Ray Cheever. Mission: to provide a resource for those who happen to have a disability.
Nonfiction   100%
Percent of articles freelance-written   85%
Number of articles bought annually   50
Sections of the magazine open to freelance writers   All
Queries should be directed to   Betty Garee, Editor
Length of articles   1,000 maximum
Payment $.10 per word
Time of payment   On publication
Photographs   Very sharp, clear photos (B/W or color), slides
Response time to queries   3 to 6 weeks (hot items: right away)
Rights bought   We buy onetime rights
Kill fees   None
Writer's guidelines   Available
Sample issues $3.00 each

ARTHRITIS TODAY

1314 Spring Street NW
Atlanta, GA 30309

Phone number   404-872-7100
Fax number   404-872-9559
E-mail address   shorton@arthritis.org
Parent company   Arthritis Foundation
Circulation   600,000
Magazine availability   Subscription

Target audience   Written for people with arthritis, their friends and family. Average reader is a 63-year-old female with some college education.

Magazine's history and mission   Founded in 1987 by the Arthritis Foundation to provide a comprehensive and reliable source of information about arthritis research, care, and treatment for the nearly 40 million Americans who have arthritis.

Nonfiction   100%

Percent of articles freelance-written   50%

Number of articles bought annually   40 to 50 features; 40 to 50 shorts or department articles

Sections of the magazine open to freelance writers   All (with exception of As We See It, Medical Answers, Home Front)

Article interests and needs   Health/lifestyle topics; research/medical updates; physical and emotional coping strategies

Queries should be directed to   Shelly Morrow, Associate Editor

Length of articles   750 to 3,000 words

Payment   Depends on writer's experience, topic, length of article, research requirements ($.40 to $1.00 per word).

Time of payment   On acceptance

Expenses   We will reimburse any direct expenses incurred in researching articles.

Photographs   Will consider author's photos when/if appropriate to article. Payment depends on quality and extent of use.

Response time to queries   4 to 6 weeks

Rights bought   Modified first North American serial rights; exclusive rights for four months following initial publication; unlimited reprint in any Arthritis Foundation affiliated publication.

Kill fees   Yes—25% of original contract amount

Writer's guidelines   Available free upon request

Sample issues   Available free upon request

TIPS FOR WRITERS

Some basic knowledge about arthritis is helpful, but not essential. Become familiar with our magazine and the types of articles we run and query us with appropriate ideas. The majority of assignments we make to freelancers are the result of their own queries.

COUNTDOWN

Juvenile Diabetes Foundation
120 Wall Street, 19th Floor
New York, NY 10005-4007

Phone number   212-785-9500
Fax number   212-785-9595

Parent company Juvenile Diabetes Foundation International
Circulation 150,000
Online status Not yet
Magazine availability Subscription—Member benefit of JDF
Nonfiction 100%
Percent of articles freelance-written 75%
Number of articles bought annually 20 to 25
Sections of the magazine open to freelance writers Features, research news
Queries should be directed to Julie Mettenburg, Editor
Length of articles 200 to 3,000 words
Payment $200 to $1,500
Time of payment On acceptance
Photographs Yes
Response time to queries 1 to 2 weeks
Rights bought First North American serial (articles). Onetime use (photos, artwork).
Writers guidelines Yes

TIPS FOR WRITERS

We are always looking for writers who can read and understand highly technical/medical topics and interpret them for a lay audience.

Economics/Government

THE FREEMAN

30 South Broadway
Irvington, NY 10533

Phone number 914-591-7230
Fax number 914-591-8910
E-mail address freeman@westnet.com
Parent company Foundation for Economic Education
Circulation 15,000
Magazine availability Subscription
Target audience Adult, nationwide
Nonfiction 100%
Percent of articles freelance-written 85%
Number of articles bought annually 150
Sections of the magazine open to freelance writers All

Article interests and needs   Articles, book reviews—Send query first.
Queries should be directed to   Beth A. Hoffman
Length of articles   2,000 words and under
Payment $.10 per word+
Time of payment   On publication
Photographs   Max. of $50
Response time to queries   1 week
Rights bought   First North American serial rights
Kill fees   No
Writer's guidelines   On request
Sample issues   On request

TIPS FOR WRITERS

The Freeman is a well-established specialty magazine with a rather limited focus. Most writers who approach us know our stance. If they don't, it shows!

I'm always happy to hear from freelancers who have original ideas, solid prose, and a flair for adding a twist to an article. I discourage phone calls from writers as a rule, but welcome faxes.

We have always encouraged young writers—including high school students. We regard it as an investment in the future.

Environmental/Nature/Outdoor

APPALACHIAN TRAILWAY NEWS

P.O. Box 807
Harpers Ferry, WV 25443

Phone number   304-535-6331
Fax number   304-535-2667
E-mail address   Fidosmom@aol.com
Circulation   25,000
Magazine availability   Newsstands, subscription, and some backpacking stores
Target audience   Conservation/hiking community
Magazine's history and mission   Started in 1939 to keep ATC members informed of Trail project. Broadened audience appeal over years.
Nonfiction   100%
Percent of articles freelance-written   30%
Number of articles bought annually   15 to 20

Sections of the magazine open to freelance writers   30% (mostly features)

Article interests and needs   Articles about people, places, and events pertaining to the Appalachian Trail and related hiking, conservation, and environmental issues as described in writer's guidelines.

Queries should be directed to   Judith Jenner, Editor

Length of articles   750 to 1,500 words

Payment   Ranges from $25 to $300

Time of payment   On acceptance

Photographs   Yes. Query for needs. Payment $25 to $150.

Response time to queries   Usually within 4 weeks

Rights bought   First-time only

Kill fees   N/A (Pay on *acceptance*)

Writer's guidelines   Available with SASE

Sample issues   Available for $2 each (no SASE)

TIPS FOR WRITERS
Judith Jenner, Editor

SASEs are necessary for guidelines and/or queries. Clips from new writers aren't. Manuscripts speak for themselves. Queries are preferable when the story idea is questionable. Apparently because we have "Appalachian" in our title, we receive a lot of folklore kinds of stories, many of them fiction. All are inappropriate to our needs. We have so far resisted sending any freelancer a "form rejection." It's not in my nature to do so. But I do receive a large number of inappropriate freelance material.

Telephone calls are NOT desirable. We're kind of limited in what we accept. The most successful freelancers for us have already had a knowledge of the Trail project or have taken the time to learn about it. Location is also a factor—although the Trail goes through 14 states, many writers have to travel some distance to get to any part of it.

AUDUBON
700 Broadway
New York, NY 10003-9501

Phone number   212-979-3127

Fax number   212-477-9069

Parent company   National Audubon Society

Circulation   500,000

Online status   Not yet

Magazine availability   On newsstands and through subscription

Target audience   People interested in environmental matters

Magazine's history and mission   Founded February 1887, by the Society. Our mission is to conserve and restore natural ecosystems—focusing on birds, other wildlife, and their habitats—for the benefit of humanity and the earth's biological diversity.

Nonfiction   100%
Percent of articles freelance-written   95%
Number of articles bought annually   Approximately 100
Sections of the magazine open to freelance writers   All
Article interests and needs   Timely articles on wildlife, natural history, and the environment
Queries should be directed to   Mike Robbins, Editor
Length of articles   500 to 5,000 words depending on subject
Payment   Depends on subject and author and length
Time of payment   On acceptance
Expenses   Expense allowance decided by editor after discussion with author
Photographs   Magazine usually handles the assigning or obtaining of photos
Response time to queries   Variable
Rights bought   We buy First North American rights.
Kill fees   Yes, we pay kill fees.
Writer's guidelines   Provided upon request
Sample issues $5 each

TIPS FOR WRITERS

An *Audubon* editor will look at completed manuscripts as well as queries. A self-addressed, stamped envelope is always necessary. It is not OK to call. Nor is it OK to fax or e-mail queries to *Audubon*.

BASSMASTER MAGAZINE

P.O. Box 17900
Montgomery AL 36141

Phone number   334-272-9530
Fax number   334-279-7148
Parent company   B.A.S.S., Inc.
Circulation   650,000+
Online status   In progress
Magazine availability   Subscription, except for three newsstand issues per year
Target audience   Bass fishermen, amateur and professional
Magazine's history and mission   Founded in 1968 by Ray Scott. Mission is to promote the sport of bass fishing.
Nonfiction   95%
Fiction   5%
Percent of articles freelance-written   98%
Number of articles bought annually   150
Sections of the magazine open to freelance writers   Features/Short Casts, Destinations

Article interests and needs   Fishing how-to's, techniques, lures, etc.
Queries should be directed to   Dave Precht, Editor
Length of articles   Short Casts: 250 to 300 words; Destinations: 1,000 words; Features: 2,500 to 3,000 words
Payment $.25 per word
Time of payment   Upon acceptance
Expenses   Not paid
Photographs   Required with manuscripts. 4 color slides or transparencies.
Response time to queries   2 to 3 weeks
Rights bought   Buy all rights
Kill fees   No
Writer's guidelines   Available upon request
Sample issues   Available upon request

TIPS FOR WRITERS

The query should be short, focusing on the main points to be discussed, sources to be used, and points of interest. Clips are okay, but not necessary. Clips should be an example of the type of writing being offered, preferably outdoor writing samples. We will accept manuscripts, but don't prefer them.

SASEs are appreciated but not necessary. Phone calls from writers are discouraged. Fax and e-mail queries are acceptable.

The best way to break into the magazine would be to establish a solid writing style. Then research the magazine and offer ideas not yet covered by the established writers. Be familiar with the bass fishing industry and the B.A.S.S. tournament trail. Having references or previously published works is a plus.

When an idea is accepted, make sure to submit complete packages, including any photos, maps, and illustrations that may be necessary to publish the story. Photos should be of professional quality, using high-grade film and processing, and should contain a wide variety of shots and subjects.

Overall advice: Know your subject and present ideas concisely and creatively.

BIRD WATCHER'S DIGEST

P.O. Box 110
Marietta, OH 47459

Phone number   614-373-5285
E-mail address   readbwd@aol.com
Parent company   Pardson Corp.
Circulation   95,000
Online status   Forum on America Online

Magazine availability   Newsstands and subscription

Target audience   Ages 25+, male or female, all professions and geographic areas

Magazine's history and mission   Founded in 1978 by William H. and Elsa Thompson, *Bird Watcher's Digest* is North America's first popular magazine about birds and bird watching.

Nonfiction   80%

Fiction   20%

Percent of articles freelance-written   50%

Number of articles bought annually   60 to 70

Sections of the magazine open to freelance writers   Most

Article interests and needs   How-to articles for bird enthusiasts, articles focused on backyard topics that are both interesting and useful

Queries should be directed to   Bill Thompson III, Editor

Length of articles   2,500 words or less

Payment   From $100 for features, less for sidebars

Time of payment   On acceptance

Expenses   Shipping/film *if* article is assigned

Photographs   Yes

Response time to queries   8 weeks

Rights bought   First North American/onetime North American

Kill fees   Not usually

Writer's guidelines   Yes—send SASE (first class postage)

Sample issues $3.50

TIPS FOR WRITERS

The query: We send a reply letter to most queries asking the writer to submit the finished article on speculation. We get so many queries from freelancers and almost never make a decision based upon the information we can glean from a query. The exception is with queries from our regular contributors.

Professional etiquette: We always prefer to receive an SASE with a submission. Phone calls are not OK. Fax queries are also unacceptable, and e-mail queries are pretty unacceptable, too. We are best suited to responding to mailed-in inquiries and submissions.

The best ways to break in: Get familiar with the kind of material we publish, find an unusual topic, and send us a tightly written, professional article.

The best things writers do: Show familiarity with our magazine's contents, with our readership, with our editorial style. Show a working knowledge of birds and bird watching. Communicate/write clearly in both cover letter and in actual submission.

Pet peeves: Incorrect spelling of editorial names, bird names, or our magazine's title; being unfamiliar with our writer's guidelines; and calling to check on a submission one week after sending it. Also: simultaneous submissions to our competitors.

Angles: Find a topic we have not covered recently. Put yourself in the editor's shoes and ask yourself: what would you most like to receive or read?

Overall advice for writers: Be professional, be patient, be enthusiastic and persistent.

E, The Environmental Magazine

P.O. Box 5098
Westport, CT 06881

Phone number   203-854-5569
Fax number   203-866-0602
E-mail address   emagazine@prodigy.com
Parent company   Earth Action Network
Circulation   70,000
Magazine availability   Newsstands and subscription
Magazine's history and mission   *E*'s first issue hit the newsstands in January 1990. Since then, it has outlived two other start-up environmental magazines and remains a leading environmental magazine. The founder/editor/publisher is Doug Moss.
Nonfiction   100%
Percent of articles freelance-written   80%
Sections of the magazine open to freelance writers   All
Article interests and needs   Those dealing with environmental issues and currents of environmental thought and action, and articles that explore the connections between environmental and other social changes/humanitarian issues.
Queries should be directed to   Jim Motavalli, Managing Editor
Length of articles   Varies according to departments
Payment $.20 per word
Time of payment   On publication
Expenses   Negotiable
Photographs   Negotiable
Response time to queries   ASAP
Kill fees   No
Writer's guidelines   Available
Sample issues   Send $5.00 /check payable to *E Magazine*

Tips for Writers

All writers should first send a written query to *E Magazine*. Write to us about your idea, its approximate length, and what section of the magazine it seems to fit. Articles should be written in a journalistic style and easily understood by those not immersed in the environmental movement. Unfamiliar terms, scientific language, and jargon should be avoided or explained for the benefit of the lay reader. Although *E* is an "advocacy" magazine, we are not interested in strident, opinionated writing. We want a balanced tone that will not alienate the casual reader. *E*'s mission is to broaden the base of environmental understanding, not to preach to the converted. A variety of quoted sources are a must in each article.

If photos and/or artwork are available, please indicate so in your query, but do not send any art materials until they are requested. We are not responsible for unsolicited artwork. Also, please include a few sentences about who you are for the brief "author bio" included at the end of most articles.

Clips are a good idea to send along with your query, as examples of your writing experience and style. Please include an SASE with your submission so we can respond as quickly as possible. Those ideas best fit for publication in *E* are provocative, original ideas. Do not send vague ideas about "writing about the environment." It's a good idea to become familiar with past issues to see what topics we have covered and develop new and intriguing ones.

FLORIDA SPORTSMAN

5901 SW 74 Street
Miami, FL 33143

Phone number   305-661-4222
Fax number   305-284-0277
Parent company   Wickstrom Publishers
Circulation   112,000
Online status   Web site at http://www.flsportsman.com
Magazine availability   Newsstands and subscription
Target audience   Outdoors persons throughout Florida
Magazine's history   Founded 1969
Nonfiction   100%
Percent of articles freelance-written   95%
Number of articles bought annually   150
Sections of the magazine open to freelance writers   All, except Action Spotter
Article interests and needs   Fishing, salt and fresh waters in Florida (boating, diving), how-to, and where-to
Queries should be directed to   Glenn Law, Editor
Length of articles   2,000 to 3,000 words
Payment $400+
Time of payment   On acceptance
Expenses   Negotiable
Response time to queries   30 days
Rights bought   First North American serial
Kill fees   Negotiable
Writer's guidelines   Yes
Sample issues $3.95

FLORIDA WILDLIFE

620 South Meridian Street
Tallahassee, FL 32399-1600

Phone number   904-488-5563
Fax number   904-488-6988
Parent company   Florida Game and Fresh Water Fish Commission (State of Florida)
Circulation   25,500; 93% is paid circulation
Online status   Will soon be on the Internet with general magazine information. Will follow later in 1996 with summaries of selected magazine articles plus a complete index of several years of publication.
Magazine availability   *Florida Wildlife* is primarily subscription circulated.
Target audience   Residents of Florida interested in outdoor recreation, conservation, and wildlife. Many subscribers live part of each year in Florida and part of each year in another state. *Florida Wildlife* appeals to a wide age range. The magazine is not targeted to any one sex or to an urban or rural audience. Readership is higher in suburban than in urban areas.
Magazine's history and mission   *Florida Wildlife* first appeared in June of 1947. The magazine was originally published by the Game and Fresh Water Fish Commission as an educational tool to "acquaint and educate the public about the many problems connected with the immense task of conserving a natural heritage for all future generations." Early emphasis was on hunting and fishing. Currently, the content of *Florida Wildlife* blends conservation and non-consumptive interest in (non-commercial) outdoor recreation with hunting and fishing.
Nonfiction   Nearly 100%
Fiction   Currently there is almost no fiction, primarily because of space limitations. Poetry and cartoons are no longer published.
Percent of articles freelance-written   Approximately 55%
Number of articles bought annually   Approximately 40
Sections of the magazine open to freelance writers   All except Conservation UpDate
Article interests and needs   Hunting stories (Florida game species), freshwater fishing stories, articles about Florida species, camping, canoeing, wildlife management, endangered species, how-to stories, outdoor-related, hunting and boating safety, rivers, lakes, distinctive natural areas in Florida, natural history of interesting-but-little-known Florida animals and plants, "vanishing Florida" stories relating to early Florida's natural history (from a personal perspective). All stories should be Florida based or have a Florida angle.
Manuscripts should be directed to   Dick Sublette, Editor
Length of articles   800 to 1,200 words. Delicate Balance articles should be about 450 words.
Payment $50 for each printed page published. Freelance writers are sent three copies of the magazine in which their article appears.
Time of payment   On publication
Photographs   *Florida Wildlife* uses and welcomes appropriate color slides. Freelance photos (slides) account for 90% of the illustrations. The magazine does not accept for publication glossy prints or black-and-white photos. All photos receive a photo credit. Freelancers should send an SASE with slides. All slides are returned after publication. Payment for each slide used is from $35 to $75.

Rights bought   First publishing (print) rights. Reserves the right to reproduce content for promotional purposes and to use on magazine's Internet education service.
Writer's guidelines   Upon request with SASE.
Sample issues   Upon request with check to *Florida Wildlife* for $2.95.

TIPS FOR WRITERS
Dick Sublette, Editor

We accept manuscripts at *Florida Wildlife*. All manuscripts are read. Those that have a possibility of being published are logged in. We assign the manuscript a log number and contact the writer. Sometimes a manuscript may wait for up to two years before it is published.

Those manuscripts we cannot use are sent back to the freelance writer after being reviewed by the edit board. We do not need clips. We are interested only in the specific manuscript and to see if it fits into our edit mix.

SASEs are always necessary. Phone calls from freelancers are acceptable. Sometimes we will request a rewrite of the manuscript, to condense it or to expand the subject. We offer a writer's guide on our style and our approach.

Stories should be specific to Florida or have a Florida bias. Since we are published by the Game and Fresh Water Fish Commission, we welcome and encourage stories that feature fresh water recreation and fresh water fishing. We do not run salt water stories or articles about deep sea creatures.

We are often in the market for hunting stories which emphasize more than the harvest. Stories on conservation, outdoor ethics, nature appreciation, natural history, boating, hiking, camping, ecology, how-to topics, as well as wildlife photography are welcome.

We purchase onetime rights to manuscripts and photographs with the proviso that some content may be used on our Internet service.

We prefer manuscripts that are accompanied with 35 mm color slides that illustrate the story.

Articles that advertise or promote businesses, refer to alcohol or tobacco products, or use profanity are not accepted. All brand names should be omitted if possible. We try not to use blood descriptions or show scenes of carnage.

Submitting a well-thought-out manuscript is the best (and only) way to get published in *Florida Wildlife*. Manuscripts based on research and fact are far more likely to be accepted. Manuscripts must be readable, that is typed or computer generated, single-sided, double-spaced, and in the 800 to 1,200 word range. The magazine uses *The Associated Press Stylebook* as a style guide. We prefer articles that are written in the active voice, use quotes, and have full attribution.

Freelancers should take the time and trouble to review several copies of *Florida Wildlife* before submitting a manuscript. It is amazing how many inappropriate manuscripts we receive from writers that could not have seen a copy of the magazine.

Once a freelancer has had a story published in *Florida Wildlife* and it has been favorably received, that freelancer's chances of having other stories published in *FW* have increased.

MICHIGAN OUT-OF-DOORS

P.O. Box 30235
Lansing, MI 48909

Phone number   517-371-1041
Fax number   517-371-1505
Parent company   Michigan United Conservation Clubs
Circulation   120,000
Target audience   Geographic area: Michigan
Magazine's history and mission   Founded by Michigan United Conservation Clubs
in 1947 to inform the public about conservation issues.
Nonfiction   100%
Percent of articles freelance-written   50%
Number of articles bought annually   120
Sections of the magazine open to freelance writers   All
Article interests and needs   Hunting and fishing primarily. Must be based in Michigan.
Queries should be directed to   Kenneth S. Lowe, Editor
Length of articles   Eight typewritten pages as an average
Payment $75 to $150
Time of payment   On acceptance
Photographs $25 for black-and-white; $150 for cover photos
Response time to queries   One week
Writer's guidelines   Available upon request
Sample issues   Available for $2.50 per copy

TIPS FOR WRITERS

We do not need clips from new writers. An SASE is always necessary. Phone calls from
writers are OK, but we prefer query letters. Writers can fax queries.

MIDWEST OUTDOORS

111 Shore Drive
Burr Ridge, IL 60521-5885

Phone number   708-887-7722
Fax number   708- 887-1958
Parent company   MidWest Outdoors, Ltd.
Circulation   50,000+
Magazine availability   Newsstands throughout the Midwest
Target audience   We target mostly men, all ages, living in the Midwest.

Magazine's history and mission   Magazine founded in 1967 by Gene Laulunen, still the current editor and publisher. *MidWest Outdoors* strives to help people enjoy the outdoors.

Nonfiction   98%

Fiction   2%

Percent of articles freelance-written   100%

Number of articles bought annually   Roughly 650

Sections of the magazine open to freelance writers   All

Article interests and needs   First-time writers are best off sticking with articles pertaining to one specific state or area when writing. First-time writers should always request writer's guidelines before submitting.

Queries should be directed to   Gene Laulunen, Editor and Publisher; Carolyn Figge, Editor

Length of articles   750 to 1,500 words

Payment $30

Time of payment   On publication

Expenses   None

Photographs   Welcome addition to any submission

Response time to queries   1 month to 1 year

Writer's guidelines   Should be obtained by sending SASE to office before any submission is made.

Sample issues   On request

Tips for Writers

The best way to capture the attention of an editor at *MidWest Outdoors* when you are a new writer is to submit a story or story idea that specifically covers one state or one area in a state.

Writers need not send clips, but instead can send completed manuscripts. An SASE with the manuscript is always appreciated, but if we are not interested, we will send the manuscript back without an SASE.

Phone calls concerning potential stories are neither necessary nor appreciated, but new writers are encouraged to call to request our writer's guidelines *before* they have made a submission. A faxed or written request for our writer's guidelines is also fine.

The best way to break into *MidWest Outdoors* is, again, to write for a specific area or state. "How to catch cold water bass" will probably not be accepted from a first-time writer, but "How to catch cold water bass while cruising the Mississippi River/Quad Cities Area" will definitely warrant a look.

With over 150 submissions coming into this office every month, the worst thing a writer can do is follow a submission with a phone call to see what the status is. As plainly stated in our writer's guidelines, if we like your story, we will keep it for publication. It could be printed next month or next year, but it will be printed. If we decided not to consider your submission for print, we will send it back immediately.

MOTHER EARTH NEWS

40 East 21st Street, 11th Floor
New York, NY 10010

Phone number   212-260-7210
Fax number   212-260-7445
E-mail address   MEarthNews@aol.com
Parent company   Sussex Publishers, Inc.
Circulation   400,000
Magazine availability   Newsstands and subscription
Percent of articles freelance-written   85%
Number of articles bought annually   Approximately 100
Sections of the magazine open to freelance writers   News, features
Queries should be directed to   Hara Marano, Editor
Length of articles   Varies. News pieces from 250 to 500 words; Features from 2,500 to 6,000 words
Payment   Typically $.50 per word
Time of payment   On publication
Expenses   Modest expenses are reimbursed with receipts.
Photographs   Commissioned or purchased through companies
Response time to queries   Six to eight weeks
Rights bought   We negotiate with writers on either sole and exclusive rights or first-time publishing rights.
Kill fees   20 % of the contracted pay

TIPS FOR WRITERS

Concise query letters are the best, usually one paragraph. Three clips are recommended—ones that show the writer's range. Phone calls from writers are not preferred—unless they're returning our call. Faxing or e-mailing queries is fine—especially e-mail because we typically respond much faster.

The best way to break into the magazine is through news pieces. This section will get the writer groomed and the editor up to speed on what to expect from a particular writer: ideas, style, and follow-through.

SIERRA

730 Polk Street
San Francisco, CA 94109

Phone number   415-923-5622
Fax number   415-776-4868
E-mail address   sierra.letters@sierraclub.org or information@sierraclub.org

Parent company   The Sierra Club
Circulation   500,000
Online status   http://www.sierraclub.org
Magazine availability   Newsstands and subscription
Target audience   Sierra Club members, environmentally concerned readers, outdoors people
Magazine's history and mission   Began publishing in 1893 as the journal of the Sierra Club, founded by John Muir in 1892, to "explore, enjoy, and protect the wild places of the earth."
Nonfiction   100%
Percent of articles freelance-written   60%
Number of articles bought annually   Features: 18 to 20 features; Departments: 10 to 12
Sections of the magazine open to freelance writers   Features, Departments: Good Going, Hearth & Home, Way to Go
Article interests and needs   Stories on environmental and outdoor themes of interest to Sierra Club members and environmentally concerned readers
Queries should be directed to   Marc Lecard, Managing Editor
Length of articles   500 to 3,000 words
Payment $500 to $2,500
Time of payment   On acceptance
Expenses   Usually, up to 10 % of purchase price
Photographs   Query art director Martha Geering
Response time to queries   2 months
Rights bought   First North American serial/electronic
Kill fees   Negotiated
Writer's guidelines   Free with SASE
Sample issues   Yes—$2.95 plus $.50 for postage and handling

TIPS FOR WRITERS
Marc Lecard, Managing Editor

The first thing we look for in a query is whether the writer has understood the kind of story we're after. *Sierra* has very particular requirements: the most basic is that the story proposal have some significance for Sierra Club members, who are environmentalists, conservationists, and outdoorspeople. Club involvement in a story is not required (though a big plus when it can be introduced into a piece), but the story should address issues of concern to Club members. The best way to find out what those issues are, of course, is to read the magazine. We tend to like stories on forestry, sustainability, biodiversity, pollution, land use, government agencies concerned with the foregoing, environmental politics and activism, and, broadest of all, adventure travel with an environmental theme. Articles on scientific topics (like biodiversity) should be written for a nontechnical audience (though the science must be perfect). Photo essays are also well-loved, though these are nearly always commissioned.

We like to see written queries (with SASEs). Phone calls are chancy—I personally dislike them, though other editors here are more tolerant. But even if we're interested, we'll ask you to put your idea in writing before making an assignment. Faxes and e-mail are acceptable—but are still subject to our two-month average response time.

We read a writer's clips with close attention; aside from the basics of clarity and organization, they tell us whether the writer in question can tell a story and has a distinctive style. It's best to send copies of stories that relate in some way to the issues we cover, if possible.

Departments like Good Going, Way to Go, and Hearth & Home are the easiest entries for first-time freelancers. These columns have their own subrequirements, and again, the best way to understand these is to read the columns. Briefly, Good Going features personal, literate travel writing; Way to Go serves up how-to travel to wild places threatened with destruction or recently saved from it. A Club connection in the story is requisite here. Hearth & Home concerns home-front environmentalism—how to save the planet without leaving the house.

Editors are most pleased when writers' stories come in on time, and are lively, well-written, and well-researched. Perhaps the worst thing a writer can do is to turn in something insufficiently researched and that turns out to be full of holes. The second worst is to turn in a mass of unorganized material and expect us to sort it out.

WESTERN OUTDOORS

P.O. Box 2027
Newport Beach, CA 92659-1027

Phone number   714-546-4370
Fax number   714-662-3486
E-mail address   woutdoors@aol.com
Parent company   Western Outdoors Publications, Inc.
Circulation   100,000
Magazine availability   For OWAA members
Target audience   Freshwater and saltwater anglers—and private fishing boat owners—in California, Oregon, and Baja California
Magazine's history and mission   Established 1961. Mission: to provide the latest and best information about fishing in the West
Nonfiction   100%
Percent of articles freelance-written   40%
Number of articles bought annually   About 35 to 40
Sections of the magazine open to freelance writers   Features only
Article interests and needs   Strong, accurate, authoritative fishing 'how-to's
Queries should be directed to   Jack Brown, Editor
Length of articles   1,500+ words
Payment $400 to $600

Time of payment   On acceptance
Expenses   No
Photographs $50 to $100 inside, $250 cover
Response time to queries   2 to 3 weeks
Rights bought   First North American serial rights
Kill fees   No
Writer's guidelines   Yes
Sample issues $2.00; $1 for OWAA members

TIPS FOR WRITERS
Jack Brown, Editor

Western Outdoors covers freshwater and saltwater fishing like no other outdoor magazine. We are the West's leading authority on fishing techniques, tackle, and destinations, and all reports present the latest and most reliable information. Our writers must demonstrate the highest journalistic integrity and credibility, and they are responsible for the accuracy of their work.

Writers who are new to us are encouraged to submit only one query at a time, in order that we may give it full consideration. Queries should be submitted via U.S. mail; no faces or e-mail, and certainly no phone queries. And, because we consider *Western Outdoors* as being distinct from all other outdoor magazines, simultaneous queries and submissions are not considered.

Over-the-transom submissions of completed articles are discouraged. All contributions receive reasonable care, but the publisher cannot be held responsible for unsolicited manuscripts, photos, or artwork.

We look for ideas that are new or extraordinary. They must pertain strictly to fishing in the West, involving species found in the West such as salmon, steelhead, trout, largemouth, smallmouth, and striped bass—or tuna, marlin, wahoo, yellowtail, and other ocean game fish. They must be authoritative, with facts and comments attributed to persons recognized as authorities in their fields.

Submissions, including queries, should include a self-addressed envelope and sufficient postage for return. We reply in two or three weeks, or earlier. Lousy stuff goes back the day it's received.

Because we plan the following year's issues in March through May, some queries may be filed for consideration at that time. Permission to hold will be requested of the writers.

Queries and other submissions are answered with a personal letter or note from the editor; we have no form letters.

Pet peeves:

- Writers who think they are experts. We say experts are those who know the right questions to ask of the right person.
- Simultaneous queries. We can spot them, no matter how well they are disguised.
- Poor research and inaccuracies. A writer once sent readers 24,000 miles out of the way by giving instructions to turn east instead of west.
- Clichés and bromides. We gag at "gin-clear water" and "bluebird weather."

- Clueless writers. They should learn what *Western Outdoors* is all about before proposing articles.

The best thing writers can do to become *Western Outdoors* byliners is to submit professional quality packages of good writing accompanied by excellent photography. Also, they should perform 110 percent above what is expected of them by including graphs, charts, sketches, and other graphic means of improving the published appearance of their work.

The pros anticipate what is needed, and whatever else is requested is provided immediately. What's more, they meet deadlines!

Ethnic

THE B'NAI B'RITH INTERNATIONAL JEWISH MONTHLY

1640 Rhode Island Avenue, NW
Washington, D.C. 20036

Phone number   202-857-6645
Fax number   202-296-1092
E-mail address   jrubin@bnaibrith.org
Parent company   B'nai B'rith International
Circulation   200,000
Online status   Some articles available online
Magazine availability   Subscription and BBI membership
Target audience   American Jewish men and women of all classes, ages, denominations. We have several thousand international readers as well.
Magazine's history and mission   Founded in 1886, *The B'nai B'rith International* is the oldest continually published Jewish publication in the U.S. It explores today's Jewish world from a wide range of perspectives, covering politics, personalities, culture, religion, Israel, and other places Jews live, work and travel.
Nonfiction   100%
Percent of articles freelance-written   50 to 75%—varies per issue
Number of articles bought annually   20–25
Sections of the magazine open to freelance writers   All
Article interests and needs   See above
Queries should be directed to   Jeff Rubin, Executive Editor
Length of articles   1,000 to 3,000 words
Payment $200 to $500
Time of payment   On publication
Expenses   No

Photographs Yes
Response time to queries 2 weeks
Rights bought First North American
Kill fees 50%
Writer's guidelines On request
Sample issues On request

GERMAN LIFE

1 Corporate Drive
Grantsville, MD 21536

Phone number 301-895-3859
Fax number 301-895-5029
E-mail address GWWC14A@prodigy.com
Parent company Zeitgeist Publishing
Circulation 50,000
Online status On electronic newsstands only
Magazine availability Through subscriptions and newsstands, including major bookstores
Target audience *German Life* is a bimonthly, written for all interested in the diversity of German culture, past and present, and in the various ways that the United States (and North America in general) has been shaped by its German element. The magazine is dedicated to solid reporting on cultural, historical, social, and political events.
Magazine's history and mission Founded by Lisa A. Fitzpatrick (publisher) in 1993. Premiere issue July 1994.
Nonfiction 100%
Number of articles bought annually 60
Sections of the magazine open to freelance writers Besides the 4 or 5 features for each issue, the magazine's departments include: German-Americana, Profile (portrays prominent Germans, Americans, and/or German-Americans), Gallery (presents artistic shows, exhibits, film, theater, etc.), At Home (includes cuisine, home design, gardening, household topics), Library (for book, video, CD, and/or cassette reviews), And finally . . . (provides forum for essayistic opinion piece regarding Germany, German-American relations, and the like).
Article interests and needs At present, we do not accept literary submissions; however, this is subject to change by the end of 1996.
Queries should be directed to Heidi L. Whitesell, Editor
Length of articles Feature-length pieces should be 2,000 to 2,500 words. Department length ranges from 800 to 1,000 words. Book reviews should be limited to 300 to 350 words.
Payment $125 per printed page
Time of payment On publication
Expenses Paid only when article is/was solicited

Photographs Accepted and paid separately.
Response time to queries 4 to 6 weeks
Rights bought *German Life* retains the first North American rights for publication.
Kill fees Apply only for contracted writers.
Writer's guidelines Available
Sample issues Available

TIPS FOR WRITERS

Considering the number of unsolicited manuscripts *German Life* receives weekly, writers do well to submit well-written and well-thought-out proposals to catch the editor's interest. The best queries include several informative proposals. Clips and curriculum vitae are required with all queries, but no lengthy clips. Ideally, clips show a background in a German-related topic, but more importantly, a flair for telling stories on a topic. Phone calls are not encouraged. Fax and e-mail are OK.

Even though *German Life* is a special interest magazine, writers should avoid overemphasizing autobiographical experiences/stories. The majority of articles in *German Life* present a human interest angle on topics ranging from business and politics to travel, culture, and history.

The most important thing a writer can do is grab the editor/reader's interest with a strong lead. A good proposal could likely end up as a lead.

NATIVE PEOPLES MAGAZINE

5333 North Seventh Street, Suite C-224
Phoenix, AZ 85014

Phone number 602-252-2236
Fax number 602-265-3113
E-mail address native-peoples@amcolor.com
Parent company Media Concepts Group, Inc.
Circulation 125,000
Online status Web site at http://www.atiin.com/native-peoples/
Magazine availability Newsstands and subscription
Target audience Those interested in the arts and lifeways of the native peoples of the Americas. Audience mirrors U.S. population density areas, predominantly 35 to 54 in age, college grads: 29%, 77% has income of $50,000+
Magazine's history and mission Magazine was founded by Gary Avey at the Heard Museum in 1987. Taken private by Avey in 1988, it is now affiliated with 10 museums, including the National Museum of the American Indian/Smithsonian Institution. Its mission is dedicated to the sensitive portrayal of the arts and lifeways of the native peoples of the Americas.
Nonfiction 100%
Percent of articles freelance-written 100%

Number of articles bought annually   30 to 40

Sections of the magazine open to freelance writers   All

Article interests and needs   Nonfiction on native subjects, contemporary and traditional, and first person pieces included as well. Looking for the person best-positioned to tell the story. No Gonzo journalists please.

Queries should be directed to   Rebeca Withers, Editorial Coordinator

Length of articles   1,800 to 2,400 words

Payment $.25 per word

Time of payment   On publication

Expenses   No

Response time to queries   30 to 60 days

Rights bought   Onetime/original only

Kill fees   No

Writer's guidelines   Upon request

Sample issues   Upon request

IMPORTANT QUESTIONS ANSWERED

Q: What is the key element of a good, professional query?

A: One page

Q: Will you look at completed manuscripts?

A: Yes

Q: What is the best way to break into your magazine?

A: Read the magazine.

Q: What is the key to breaking in to your magazine?

A: Read the magazine.

Q: What are the worst things writers do?

A: Fail to read a copy prior to query.

REFORM JUDAISM

838 Fifth Avenue
New York, NY 10021

Phone number   212-650-4240

Fax number   212-650-4249

Parent company   Union of American Hebrew Congregations

Circulation   300,000

Magazine availability   On selected New York City newsstands as well as subscriptions.

Target audience   Members of Reform Jewish synagogues in the United States and Canada

Magazine's history and mission   *Reform Judaism* was founded more than 60 years ago and took its current title in 1972. Its Statement of Purpose explains: *"Reform Judaism*

is the official voice of the Union of American Hebrew Congregations, linking the institutions and affiliates of Reform Judaism with every Reform Jew. *RF* covers developments within our Movement while interpreting world events and Jewish tradition from a Reform perspective. *RJ* conveys the creativity, diversity, and dynamism of Reform Judaism. Members of UAHC congregations receive *RJ* as a benefit of membership."

Nonfiction   95%

Fiction   5%

Percent of articles freelance-written   60%

Number of articles bought annually   50

Sections of the magazine open to freelance writers   Features and Departments

Article interests and needs   Articles relevant to North American Reform Jews

Queries should be directed to   Joy Weinberg, Managing Editor

Length of articles   Features: 1,200 to 1,800 words; Departments: 1,200 words

Payment $.30 per word

Time of payment   On publication

Expenses   Telephone expenses covered

Photographs   Depends on story. Sometimes important.

Response time to queries   4 to 6 weeks

Rights bought   First North American serial rights

Kill fees   For commissioned manuscripts, 25% of established fee

Writer's guidelines   Available

Sample issues $3.50 payable to *Reform Judaism*

TIPS FOR WRITERS
Joy Weinberg, Managing Editor

The query: Queries should be as well-written, inventive, and thought-provoking as the finished article. They should state specifically why this story is right for our magazine and how the story will be/is tailored for our readership. Queries should include a brief biographic sketch of the writer, including previous publishing history. New writers should always enclose published clips with queries—preferably three.

Professional etiquette: Queries should be written and mailed first-class to the attention of Joy Weinberg, Managing Editor. An SASE is always necessary, unless the writer has established a publishing relationship with the magazine.

Breaking into the magazine: Familiarize yourself with our magazine before sending queries or submissions. Articles should reflect the perspective of the Reform Jewish movement.

Games

DRAGON MAGAZINE

201 Sheridan Springs Road
Lake Geneva, WI 53147

Phone number   414-248-3625
Fax number   414-248-7144
E-mail address   TSRMAGS@aol.com
Parent company   TSR, Inc.
Circulation   100,000+
Magazine availability   Newsstands and subscription
Target audience   Predominantly male, ages 12 to 40; gamers and fantasy hobbyists
Magazine's history and mission   Founded in 1974 as America's first magazine for players of *Dungeons & Dragons* and other fantasy role-playing games.
Nonfiction   Game related nonfiction is the bulk of the magazine.
Fiction   Approximately 7% (1 story per month)
Percent of articles freelance-written   Most 75%+
Number of articles bought annually   About 70
Sections of the magazine open to freelance writers   All but reviews
Article interests and needs   Game-related articles
Queries should be directed to   Anthony J. Bryant, Editor
Length of articles   1,000 to 5,000 words
Payment   Nonfiction: $.04 to $.06 per word; Fiction: $.05 to $.08
Time of payment   On acceptance
Expenses   Negotiable
Photographs   Seldom used
Response time to queries   Within 1 month. Usually 1 to 2 weeks
Rights bought   Fiction: FNASR; Game material: buys all rights
Kill fees   Usually 25%
Writer's guidelines   For SASE
Sample issues $4.00

TIPS FOR WRITERS
Anthony J. Bryant, Editor

Dragon Magazine is simply not a magazine that one can write for without first reading it. As the nation's premier magazine for enthusiasts of fantasy role-playing games (FRPGs), we have a very specific audience. Our focus, of course, is on *Advanced Dungeons & Dragons* (*AD&D*) and other TSR gaming products, but we also cover games such as *Cyberpunk, Call of Cthulhu, Shadowrun*, etc. Someone wanting to write for us should understand the mechanics of a specific gaming system and propose an article that expands or otherwise adds to it. Sample topics (from recent issues) include *AD&D* character class kits based on Indian/Mughal culture; modifying traditional castle designs to make them defensible against powerful magic and airborne assaults; and new spells, magic items, and monsters to put into the game.

The best way to break in to *Dragon Magazine* is to write something that a reader can take right to the gaming table.

We have a disclosure form that must accompany submissions or we cannot read them. The form is available with our guidelines (request them and enclose a business-sized SASE) and is available online in several locations (TSR's AOL presence, on the role-playing game forum in CompuServe, etc). As the material relates to our games, we purchase all rights. The only thing we don't buy outright is fiction; for that, we purchase first world serial rights.

A query letter is usually better than a blind manuscript submission. I get lots of manuscripts to read, and unless I've asked to see it, a manuscript that comes in goes to the bottom of the pile. Still, everything gets looked at within a week. I usually respond yea or nay fairly quickly, but sometimes something comes in that we need to think about. That can take two weeks or so, especially if I have to show it to the designers of the game system in question to make sure the article is valid.

The best thing a writer can do is show me he understands the game, has a clear idea of what he wants to do, and knows how to do it. If he can do that professionally (both in terms of execution and performance), then I'll have someone I can call when I need an article written.

The worst thing a writer can do is submit something (and I see this on cover letters far too often) with no concept of grammar or spelling. I am not going to do the writer's job for him. There are certain basics that anyone wanting to sell to a magazine simply must know. Among them are how to spell, basic grammar and syntax, and proper manuscript format. I don't even look at manuscripts that aren't typed, and may send back to be redone a single-spaced, small character, proportional font–printed manuscript without even looking at it.

If a writer expects a reply, he needs to enclose an SASE, and tell me whether the manuscript is disposable. We have a very small staff, so I generally dislike getting pitch calls or update requests from writers unless we already have a working relationship. I get enough calls from readers already who want to know if I can find "that issue about five years ago that had something about vampires . . ." and answer a question.

Gardening

FINE GARDENING

63 South Main Street
Newtown, CT 06470

Phone number   203-426-8171
Fax number   203-426-0313
Parent company   The Taunton Press

Circulation   185,000
Magazine availability   Newsstands and subscription
Target audience   Average age: 45 years average, national, 65% female
Magazine's history and mission   Founded 1988 by Jan and Paul Roman. Purpose: to provide educational literature for gardeners.
Nonfiction   99%
Fiction   1%
Percent of articles freelance-written   10%
Queries should be directed to   Carole Turner, Editor
Time of payment   One-third on acceptance.   Balance on publication.
Photographs   Yes
Kill fees   Yes
Writer's guidelines   Yes
Sample issues   Yes

FLOWER & GARDEN

700 West 47th Street, Suite 310
Kansas City, MO 64112

Phone number   816-531-5730
Fax number   816-531-3873
Parent company   KC Publishing, Inc.
Circulation   750,000
Magazine availability   Newsstands and subscription
Target audience   Home gardeners
Magazine's history and mission   Founded in 1957. Mission is to give solid gardening information to do-it-yourself gardeners.
Nonfiction   100%
Percent of articles freelance-written   75%
Number of articles bought annually   60 to 75
Sections of the magazine open to freelance writers   Most all
Article interests and needs   How-to articles for home gardeners on plants, flowers, vegetables, and landscape
Queries should be directed to   Kay Olson, Editor-in-Chief
Length of articles   1,000 words
Payment $300 to $400
Time of payment   On acceptance
Expenses   No
Photographs   Pays separately for photos
Response time to queries   4 to 6 months
Rights bought   First-time North American rights/nonexclusive reprint rights

Kill fees   No
Writer's guidelines   On request
Sample issues   On request

THE GROWING EDGE

P.O. Box 1027
Corvallis, OR 97339

Phone number   503-757-2511
Fax number   503-757-0028
E-mail address   talexan@peak.org or tcoene@peak.org
Parent company   New Moon Publishing
Circulation   20,000
Online status   Web site at http://www.teleport.com/~tomalex
Magazine availability   Newsstands and subscription
Target audience   International, mostly males from 20 to 50 years old, soil and hydro growers
Magazine's history and mission   Founded by Tom Alexander in the late 1980s to fulfill the legitimate hydroponic gardening niche.
Nonfiction   100%
Percent of articles freelance-written   70%
Number of articles bought annually   Approximately 25
Sections of the magazine open to freelance writers   Feature articles and book reviews
Article interests and needs   High-tech hydroponic articles, indoor growroom gardening, greenhouse, and pest research
Queries should be directed to   Trisha Coene, Managing Editor
Length of articles   2,500 to 3,000 words
Payment $.10 per published word
Time of payment   On publication
Expenses   Not paid
Photographs $175 for cover; $25 to $50 for interiors
Response time to queries   Within one month
Rights bought   You own work, but *Growing Edge* must be credited if piece is subsequently published elsewhere
Kill fees   N/A
Writer's guidelines   Available upon request
Sample issues   Available upon request

Gay/Lesbian/Bisexual

BEAU

P.O. Box 470
Port Chester, NY 10573

E-mail address Dianaeditr@aol.com
Parent company Sportomatic, Ltd.
Circulation 20,000
Magazine availability Newsstands and subscription
Target audience Gay males
Magazine's history and mission Founded in 1988. Mission: to reach gay males and give them entertainment.
Nonfiction All the columns
Fiction All the stories
Percent of articles freelance-written 100%
Number of articles bought annually Four columns × 8 issues per year
Sections of the magazine open to freelance writers All the hot stories and the Gay Style column. The other columns are regularly assigned to freelance writers.
Article interests and needs Need Gay Style columns on things of interest to gay men—politics especially. Also anything else such as food, home furnishings, dating mores, etc.
Queries should be directed to Diana Sheridan, Associate Editor
Length of articles 2,000 to 3,000 words
Payment $100
Time of payment On publication
Expenses No
Photographs No
Response time to queries Real fast
Rights bought Buy all rights. Will reassign book rights on request
Kill fees No
Writer's guidelines With SASE
Sample issues With SASE (5 first-class stamps) and $2.95

TIPS FOR WRITERS
Diana Sheridan, Associate Editor

The Query: Keep it brief. I'm busy. I'm not that impressed by what you have done before; I'm more interested in what you can do now. If you're good, I don't give a good G-D if you've never been published before. We all have to start someplace. Except for the Gay Style column, I'd rather see completed work than queries. Keep your query letter short, neat, correctly spelled—if you can't even spell in your query letter, or construct a sentence grammatically, I'm not going to have much confidence in your ability to handle a whole article.

If you can't convey the idea of your article in just a few sentences, I question if you can get the article itself into 2,000 to 3,000 succinct words—or maybe the subject is wrong for us. (Yes, there are exceptions, and if your article truly is one of them, I'll take that into account.)

If your query shows spark, style, verve, I'm likely to be impressed, but don't strain to be clever just to impress me; a good solid, simple professional query will impress me too! I don't put much stock in clips—I never know if they're showing me what a good writer you are or what good editors the articles landed in the hands of after you wrote them!

Though I'd rather see a completed manuscript, I recognize the value of a query insofar that it prevents a writer from writing, for us, an article that might not be salable.

I have three words to say about SASEs: Always, always, always! (OK—if you've been selling to me for a year and I never return a single story to you anymore, you're probably safe in omitting them.)

No phone calls—like many other editors today, I work at home, "telecommuting," so I'm not even *in* the office. And the office staff doesn't want to have to take messages and call me with them. Therefore no faxes either—they'd only have to re-fax to me. E-mail is always welcome and *gets an even quicker answer than "snail"*—but I'm known for responding to any manuscripts or queries quickly. No simultaneous submissions, please. Also:

The best way to break into our magazine: Send for our guidelines, so you know what we're looking for; then send good, hot stories that are carefully crafted and just as carefully proofed, that are good and hot, and that I can't resist buying. I'm really not that difficult to please. (Don't send more than one story at a time. It's asking too much of my time—I edit quite a few different magazines—and if you're off on the wrong track, you're wasting your own time.)

The best thing writers can do: Surprise me with a good, hot, well-written, different, yet believable story that is just offbeat enough to not be S.O.S. ("Same Old Stuff") and yet isn't off-the-wall. Wow, does that light up my day!

The worst things writers can do: Got an hour? Seriously, send single-spaced manuscripts laden with typos and/or "spellos" and that are totally unlike anything we'd ever buy (do they have a clue at all what our mag is about???!!)— and then not even include an SASE!

Ways writers can angle their stories for our mag: Read the guidelines, read the mag itself, get a feel for what we're looking for, and send us something tailored for us.

Overall advice for writers who want to get published: I don't believe the old maxim about having to write about what you yourself know. Do you think most mystery writers are murderers? A good imagination can carry you far. But have some *interest* in what you're writing, or at least an interest in *writing* about it.

I have straight and even female writers writing gay and male erotica. True, most of my writers are gay males. But it's not an absolute prerequisite. (Your writing does have to have the ring of authenticity, however.)

So—can you write well? Are you sure the material you're sending out is suitable for the market you've aimed it at? If you have answered yes to both questions, don't give up at your first—or twentieth—rejection. Keep at it. (But if you butt your head against a brick wall repeatedly, maybe it's time to try some other field of writing. Maybe you should be writing fiction instead of non, or vice versa. Or maybe you should be doing corporate writing—press releases or something of that ilk, rather than being a freelancer.)

OPTIONS

P.O. Box 470
Port Chester, NY 10573

E-mail address   Dianaeditr@aol.com
Parent company   AJA Publishing Corp.
Circulation   100,000
Online status   E-mail welcome
Magazine availability   Newsstands and subscription
Target audience   Bisexual men and women
Magazine's history and mission   Founded in 1981. Mission: to reach Bi's all across North America
Nonfiction   1 article, the columns
Fiction   All the rest
Percent of articles freelance-written   100%
Number of articles bought annually   10 articles, 60 stories
Sections of the magazine open to freelance writers   All but the columns, which are freelance written but regularly assigned
Article interests and needs   One article in every issue. Query or send complete article of interest to Bi's.
Queries should be directed to   Diana Sheridan, Associate Editor
Length of articles   2,000 to 3,000 words
Payment $100
Time of payment   On publication
Expenses   No
Photographs   No
Response time to queries   Real fast
Rights bought   Buy all rights. Will reassign book rights on request.
Kill fees   No
Writer's guidelines   With SASE
Sample issues   With SASE (5 stamps) and $2.95

TIPS FOR WRITERS

See entry above.

OUT

110 Greene Street, Suite 600
New York, NY 10012

Phone number   212-334-9119
Fax number   212-334-0145
E-mail address   out@aol.com
Parent company   Out Publishing, Inc.
Circulation   120,000
Online status   Web site at http://www.out.com
Magazine availability   Newsstands and subscription
Target audience   Lesbian, gay, and bisexual readers and their friends and families in the U.S. and internationally
Nonfiction   100%
Percent of articles freelance-written   80%
Number of articles bought annually   300
Sections of the magazine open to freelance writers   All
Queries should be directed to   Sarah Pettit
Length of articles   50 to 5,000 words
Payment   Rates negotiated on assignment
Time of payment   On publication
Expenses   Preapproved expenses paid
Photographs   Yes—unsolicited photos not encouraged
Response time to queries   6 weeks
Rights bought   First North American serial
Kill fees   25%
Writer's guidelines   Available upon request
Sample issues   No

General Interest

AIR & SPACE/SMITHSONIAN

901 D Street SW
Washington, DC 20024

Phone number   202-287-3733
Fax number   202-287-3163
E-mail address   airspacedt@aol.com
Parent company   Smithsonian Institution
Circulation   300,000
Online status   Web site at http://www.airspacemag.com/
Magazine availability   Newsstands and subscription

Target audience   Readers with a focused interest in aerospace but not necessarily professionally involved in the field

Magazine's history and mission   Founded in 1985 as the official magazine of the National Air and Space Museum.

Nonfiction   100%

Percent of articles freelance-written   95%

Number of articles bought annually   150

Sections of the magazine open to freelance writers   All

Article interests and needs   Aerospace with immediacy and authority

Queries should be directed to   George Larson, Linda Shiner, Pat Trenner (depts)

Length of articles   Average 3,000 words

Payment   Varies—about $2,000 for a typical feature.

Time of payment   On acceptance

Expenses   Pay with receipts.

Photographs   Assign our own.

Response time to queries   60 days

Rights bought   First North American

Kill fees   25%

Writer's guidelines   On request

Sample issues $3.50

TIPS FOR WRITERS

Excerpted from an article published in Writers Magazine *called "How to Write for Air & Space Magazine," by George C. Larson, Editor of* Air and Space *magazine.*

We prefer authors with a track record in magazines or books, but we buy good stories, not big names, and much of our best material has come from first-time writers.

We work from proposals (send clips with the first one), which can be as brief as a single page.

Stories should have enough stature to command a place in a national magazine, not just a national newspaper.

If your story offers nothing more than traditional library research and a reassembly of facts that are already well documented, your proposal probably won't sell.

It's somewhat easier to break in with a story about space (as opposed to aviation) because those stories have traditionally been harder to find and more good writers are out there competing with you in the aviation field. We also try to give new writers a first shot with a shorter piece so we can get to know each other.

Successful proposals have one quality that sets them apart: when we read them, we come away with the immediate impression that you not only know what you're talking about, but you know how to handle this as a *magazine* story. The best proposals instill an almost immediate sense of confidence that both the idea and the writer are sound, and a successful feature story will emerge from the effort.

THE AMERICAN SCHOLAR

1811 Q Street NW
Washington, DC 20009

Phone number   202-265-3808
Fax number   202-986-1601
Publisher   Phi Beta Kappa Society
Circulation   25,000
Magazine availability   Newsstands and subscription
Target audience   College-educated
Magazine's history and mission   *The American Scholar,* according to its Writer's Guidelines, ". . . is a quarterly journal published by Phi Beta Kappa for general circulation. Our intent is to have articles by scholars and experts but written in nontechnical language for an intelligent audience."
Nonfiction   100%
Percent of articles freelance-written   100%
Number of articles bought annually   100
Sections of the magazine open to freelance writers   100%
Article interests and needs   Subjects include the arts, sciences, current affairs, history, and literature.
Queries should be directed to   Joseph Epstein, Editor
Length of articles   3,500 to 4,000 words
Payment   Up to $500
Time of payment   On acceptance
Expenses   No
Photographs   No
Response time to queries   2 months
Kill fees   Half
Writer's guidelines   Yes
Sample issues   No

A TIP FOR WRITERS

See a few issues for the types of articles we publish.

THE ATLANTIC MONTHLY

77 North Washington Street
Boston, MA 02117

Phone number   617-536-9500
Fax number   617-536-3730
Circulation   500,000

Magazine availability   Newsstands and subscription

Magazine's history and mission   Founded in 1857 by Ralph Waldo Emerson, Henry David Thoreau, and others. Intended to be a magazine of the arts and public affairs.

Nonfiction   Everything, except one story per issue

Fiction   One story per issue

Percent of articles freelance-written   70%

Number of articles bought annually   200

Sections of the magazine open to freelance writers   All

Queries should be directed to   Bill Whitworth, Editor-in-Chief; Cullen Murphy, Managing Editor; C. Michael Curtis, Senior Editor; Jack Beatty, Senior Editor

Length of articles   1,000 to 10,000 words (2,000 to 6,000 ideal)

Payment   Varies ($1,000 and up)

Time of payment   On acceptance

Expenses   When agreed upon in advance

Photographs   Not required, sometimes gratefully received

Response time to queries   2 to 3 days to several months

Rights bought   First North American serial

Kill fees   Always for assigned pieces

Writer's guidelines   None

TIPS FOR WRITERS
C. Michael Curtis

We're most responsive to queries that seem proportionate to the dimensions of the piece proposed, that make clear what the writer intends to do with his/her subject, that promise original research rather than a skimming of secondary sources, that suggest the writer's competence to produce a piece that will have freshness and authority, that proposes a reasonable deadline and expenses, and which doesn't outline a piece that overlaps with either material already published in *The Atlantic* or material available in other periodicals. Clips are helpful in the case of writers whose work we don't know. Two or three clips are sufficient. What we look for is evidence of writing and reporting skills, objectivity, and a sense of authority. We will gladly look at completed manuscripts— indeed, we prefer them.

SASEs are highly recommended. Normally, we don't respond to submissions sent without them, and even queries sent without SASEs are at risk. Phone calls are ill-advised, since they seem to require an instant decision on the part of an editor whose mind is likely to be elsewhere. A written proposal is very much preferred. Once an editor and a writer have developed a personal relationship, phone calls make more sense, though they may lead, simply, to a request for a written proposal or manuscript. We would prefer not to receive queries by fax or e-mail.

The best way to break into *The Atlantic* is to send a completed and publishable manuscript. Where queries are concerned, the Reports section is the place to look. Many writers began writing for *The Atlantic* in Reports, then graduated to longer text pieces.

The keys to breaking in are not mysterious, and have everything to do with skill and sophistication as a writer, and a sense of what we do and do not publish. Reading the magazine is probably the only way to solve the puzzle. Would be *Atlantic* contributors should bear in mind, however, that our monthly deadlines discourage us from encouraging topical reporting, that we tend not to encourage or publish "police" stories, articles about celebrities, or pieces about ongoing scandals that do not have some apparent public policy implication.

Successful *Atlantic* writers normally have a point to make, and have opinions, but have learned to subordinate those views to reportage—letting the facts make the case for them. They are also sensitive, as above, to our disinclination to encourage pieces about breaking news, or to publish even "in depth" pieces about subjects widely discussed elsewhere. These writers are also attentive to punctuation, spelling, and grammar matters, and tend to be fastidious about reasonable and necessary expenses associated with their reporting for *The Atlantic.*

Among the difficulties we encounter with writers are the following: carelessness about sources, an overreliance on secondary sources, an emphasis on polemics where reporting ought to carry the day, a failure to read the magazine or to appreciate the hopelessness of projects that are wildly inappropriate for our format or sensibility, indifference to precision or organizational coherence, disingenuousness about journalistic protocol (such as submitting a piece already in print elsewhere or borrowing heavily from other public sources), quarrelsomeness about editing or fact-checking procedures . . . and so on.

How writers can redirect article ideas so as to enhance their appeal for *The Atlantic:* find or imagine the larger national or general policy implications of what might otherwise seem localized issues (for example, an air pollution battle in one industrial city can be transformed into an examination of air pollution controls nationwide, an assessment of EPA performance, or the like).

Overall advice to writers who want to get published in *The Atlantic*: read the above with care, and read six issues of the magazine with an eye for length, emphasis, organizational logic, range of subject matter, and the discrete balance between information and opinion.

All these matters aside, *The Atlantic* is a good market for freelancers, both because it is open to a great many ideas and subjects, and because it is indifferent to the celebrity of its authors. Expertise and a graceful, thoughtful writing style matter far more than public reputation.

GRIT

1503 SW 42nd Street
Topeka, KS 66609

Phone number   913 274-4300
Fax number   913-274-4305
Circulation   250,000
Magazine availability   Subscription only
Magazine's history   Founded in 1882
Nonfiction   90%

Fiction   10%
Percent of articles freelance-written   70%
Number of articles bought annually   100 to 150
Sections of the magazine open to freelance writers   All
Article interests and needs   Family lifestyle, history, and traditions
Queries should be directed to   Michael Scheibach, Editor-in-Chief
Length of articles   1,000 to 1,500 words
Payment $.22 per word
Time of payment   On publication
Expenses   Agreed upon only
Photographs   Yes
Response time to queries   60 to 90 days
Rights bought   First
Kill fees   No
Writer's guidelines   Yes
Sample issues $4.00

THE NEW YORKER

20 West 43rd Street
New York, NY 10036

Phone number   212-536-5800
Fax number   Don't fax, please!
E-mail address   Don't e-mail, please!
Parent company   Advance Publications
Circulation   850,000
Magazine availability   Newsstands and subscription
Magazine's history   *The New Yorker* was founded in 1925 by Harold Ross.
Nonfiction   80 to 90%
Fiction   5 to 10%
Percent of articles freelance-written   Very few
Sections of the magazine open to freelance writers   Goings On, Talk, Shorts, Comment
Article interests and needs   Anyone interested in submitting to *The New Yorker* should read it backwards and forwards before proposing a piece.
Queries should be directed to   Fiction editor, Nonfiction Editor, Poetry Editor, etc.
Length of articles   Varies
Payment   Varies
Time of payment   Depends
Expenses   Depends
Photographs   Very rarely

Response time to queries   1 to 3 months
Rights bought   First serial
Kill fees   Usually

TIPS FOR WRITERS

Know the magazine really, *really* well before submitting. It's incredibly annoying—not to say insulting—to get pieces sent by people who have obviously never read the magazine.

PARADE

711 Third Avenue
New York, NY 10017

Phone number   212-450-7000
Fax number   212-450-7284
Parent company   Advance Publications
Circulation   37,000,000
Magazine availability   Distributed nationally in Sunday newspapers
Target audience   General
Magazine's history   Founded in 1941 by Marshall Field.
Nonfiction   100%
Percent of articles freelance-written   Most articles are written by contributing editors and regular freelancers.
Article interests and needs   Topics with national scope or implications. According to *Parade*'s guidelines, "Many stories involve news, social issues, common health concerns, sports, community problem-solving, or extraordinary achievements of ordinary people . . . Do not propose spot news, fiction or poetry, cartoons, regular columns, nostalgia or history, quizzes, puzzles or compilations of quotes or trivia."
Queries should be directed to   Articles Correspondent
Length of articles   1,200 to 1,500 words
Payment   *Parade* discusses payment with writers upon acceptance of their proposal.
Time of payment   Upon acceptance of the story
Photographs   *Parade* does not accept unsolicited photography.
Response time to queries   4 to 6 weeks
Rights bought   *Parade* reserves all rights for seven days after publication. After that, any reprints or further use of the story require the permission of *Parade*.
Kill fees   Discussed individually
Writer's guidelines   Available upon request
Sample issues   Available upon request

IMPORTANT QUESTIONS ANSWERED

Q: Will you look at completed manuscripts?

A: *Parade* rarely accepts completed manuscripts.

Q: Are phone calls from writers OK?

A: *Parade* does not accept any proposals by phone.

Q: Is it OK if writers fax or e-mail queries to you?

A: *Parade* does not accept proposals by e-mail. Faxes are acceptable.

Q: Is an SASE always necessary?

A: An SASE is recommended.

Q: What do you look for in a writer's clips?

A: Writing samples should reveal the writer's reporting skills and the ability to write concisely, informatively, and with the appropriate style.

THE PHILADELPHIA INQUIRER MAGAZINE

Box 8263
Philadelphia, PA 19101

Phone number   215-854-4580
Fax number   215-854-5193
E-mail address   InqSunMag@Delphi.com
Parent company   Philadelphia Newspapers, Inc./Knight-Ridder Corp.
Circulation   900,000 per week
Magazine availability   Newsstands and subscription—with Sunday *Inquirer*
Target audience   All demographic groups. (Older women love us.)
Fiction   Two issues a year (eight stories) are all fiction.
Nonfiction   As a newspaper magazine, we hope all stories in the other 50 issues are nonfiction.
Percent of articles freelance-written   50%
Number of articles bought annually   150
Sections of the magazine open to freelance writers   All sections, all topics except those pertaining specifically to a reporter's beat
Article interests and needs   General interest news stories told in an intriguing, engaging, narrative structure. Or essay-type thought pieces.
Queries should be directed to   Avery Rome, Editor, *Philadeplhia Inquirer Magazine*
Length of articles   Cover: 6,000 words; second story: 4,000 words; third story: 2,000 words;
Payment   Cover: $1,500 to $3,000; second: $800 to $1,500; third story: $500 to $1,200
Time of payment   Upon publication
Expenses   Fully paid when negotiated at time of assignment
Response time to queries   Within a month
Rights bought   Nonexclusive "publication rights"
Kill fees   One-half agreed-upon payment

A Tip for Writers

Write well and fast.

Real People

950 Third Avenue, 16th floor
New York, NY 10022

Phone number   212-371-4932
Fax number   212-838-8420
Parent company   Main Street Publishing
Circulation   95,000
Magazine availability   Subscription
Target audience   Women 30 to 35; working; middle income
Magazine's history   Began in 1988 by Main Street Publishing.
Nonfiction   100%
Percent of articles freelance-written   Approximately 10 to 20% are from new writers each issue. We have a core of regular [freelancers] who do columns and features.
Number of articles bought annually   10 to 15 from writers who are not regular contributors
Sections of the magazine open to freelance writers   Features, short subjects
Article interests and needs   Entertainment
Queries should be directed to   Alex Polner, Editor—Features; Brad Hamilton, Shorts Editor; Philip Recchia— News
Length of articles   200 to 2,500 words
Payment $50 to $500
Time of payment   On publication
Expenses   Negotiable
Photographs   Discuss
Response time to queries   2 to 4 weeks
Rights bought   We buy all rights
Kill fees   One-third
Writer's guidelines   Available
Sample issues $4.00 with SASE

Remember

7002 West Butler Pike
Ambler, PA 19002

Phone number   215-643-6385
Fax number   215-540-0146

Parent company   Family Digest, Inc.

Circulation   150,000

Magazine availability   Newsstands and subscription

Target audience   Everyone, from baby boomers to WWII vets and more—college students, grandparents—everyone with an interest in movies, politics, American culture.

Magazine's history and mission   Founded in 1994 by P. M. Publications in Connecticut. The title was sold in 1995 to Family Digest, Inc. Our mission is to review "The People and News We Can't Forget" in arts, politics, and more, throughout the twentieth century.

Nonfiction   100%

Percent of articles freelance-written   75%

Sections of the magazine open to freelance writers   Feature stories, Departments

Queries should be directed to   Craig Peters, Publisher

Length of articles   Feature stories: 1,500 to 2,000 words

Payment   Varies. Feature stories are $300. Other departments pay from $75 to $150 (depending on length and particular column).

Time of payment   On publication

Expenses   No

Photographs   Not necessary, but a plus

Response time to queries   ASAP

Writer's guidelines   Send for with SASE.

Sample issues   Available for $3.00

IMPORTANT QUESTIONS ANSWERED

Q: What sparks your interest in a query?
A: Subject matter primarily—is it appropriate to my current needs?

Q: Do you always want clips from new writers?
A: Not necessary, but a plus.

Q: What do you look for in the writer's clips?
A: Clear thinking, good style.

Q: Is an SASE always necessary?
A: A plus.

Q: Are phone calls from writers OK?
A: Prefer no; I'm busy enough on the phone as it is.

Q: Is it OK if writers fax queries to you?
A: Sure!

SILVER CIRCLE

4900 Rivergrade Road
Irwindale, CA 91706

Phone number   818-814-7282
Circulation   500,000
Magazine availability   Controlled
Target audience   Ages 40 plus, male and female, middle/upper income, nationwide distribution
Magazine's history and mission   Published by Home Savings for high-balance customers
Nonfiction   100%
Percent of articles freelance-written   100%
Number of articles bought annually   Approximately 24
Sections of the magazine open to freelance writers   All
Article interests and needs   Financial planning, home, family, travel, leisure, health, hobbies
Queries should be directed to   Jay Binkly, Editor
Length of articles   800 to 3,000 words
Payment $500 to $2,000
Time of payment   On acceptance
Expenses   Phone
Photographs   Slides, transparencies
Response time to queries   2 to 3 weeks
Rights bought   First North American
Kill fees   20%
Writer's guidelines   Send SASE.
Sample issues   Send $8\frac{1}{2} \times 11$ SASE.

SOMA MAGAZINE

285 Ninth Street
San Francisco, CA 94103

Phone number   415-558-8080
Fax number   415-558-8253
Circulation   50,000
Magazine availability   Newsstands and subscription
Target audience   *SOMA* is aimed at those between the ages of 20 and 50 who are interested in popular culture. It is a national magazine with an international circulation. It is read equally by men and women.
Magazine's history   *SOMA* was founded in 1986 by A. Ghanbarian.
Nonfiction   100%
Percent of articles freelance-written   10%
Sections of the magazine open to freelance writers   All
Article interests and needs   Popular culture including film, music, fashion, technology, the arts, etc.

Queries should be directed to   Jonathan S. Keats, Editor-in-Chief
Length of articles   Dispatches: 400 to 600 words; Features: 1,000 to 3,000 words;
Reviews: 100 to 300 words
Payment $.05 per word
Time of payment   Within 30 days of publication
Expenses   Negotiable
Photographs   Negotiable
Response time to queries   4 to 6 weeks
Kill fees   Yes
Writer's guidelines   Available with SASE
Sample issues   Available on newsstands

TIPS FOR WRITERS
Jonathan S. Keats, Editor-in-Chief

Freelance writers like to talk about how difficult it is to break into magazine journalism. What they're unlikely to hear is that magazine editors have just as difficult a time finding good freelancers. There are many freelance writers out there, but the truth is that very few of them can really write. In other words, a good writer need not worry about competition; there's not a lot out there to begin with.

At *SOMA,* we tend to have our greatest success with fiction writers who have chosen to try their hand at nonfiction. These are the people who approach articles from a narrative standpoint, who pay attention to voice, rhythm, and pacing. Even if the topic on which they are reporting requires intense investigation or the explanation of complex ideas, what these writers finally produce is a *story*, a piece of nonfiction that, even were it fiction, would be well worth reading. Traditional journalists, it would appear, never learn these skills. From the standpoint of magazine writing, journalism school generally does far more damage than good.

Nevertheless, writers who have a degree in journalism should mention this in their query. The more an editor knows about a writer's background, the more likely it is he'll be able to accurately assess the potential of the query. We like to see writers who happen also to have a degree in geology or experience repairing plane engines. These are the sorts of backgrounds that can lead to unique insights, that can make a writer right for an article.

Clips are also essential to the query package, as, without them, it is impossible for the editor to determine the freelancer's writing ability. While the clips need not be topically relevant to the article proposed, it is helpful for us at least to see material in the style the writer intends to use. This, together with a cover letter, a resume, and an SASE, makes for the ideal query. An editor must be able quickly to work his way through the proposal, but at the same time must have enough information to make an educated guess as to the viability of the article idea.

One final note: It is absolutely essential that freelancers read the publication to which they intend to pitch an article before even beginning to develop story ideas. Every good magazine has a very specific scope and tone, both of which can only be fully grasped by studying back issues. We get countless queries every month which either are so generic they could be angled at any magazine on the planet (but would likely appear in none), or are so specific to the style and content of another magazine they must certainly already have been rejected by their intended target. These queries are of not use to anybody. Please do not send them.

STAR

660 White Plains Road
Tarrytown, NY 10591

Phone number   914-332-5000
Fax number   914-332-5044
Parent company   American Media, Inc.
Circulation   2,513,233
Magazine availability   Newsstands and subscription
Magazine's history   Founded February 1974
Number of articles bought annually   Approximately 500
Sections of the magazine open to freelance writers   All
Article interests and needs   Celebrity stories
Queries should be directed to   Dick Belsky, News Editor
Length of articles   Up to 1,000 words
Payment   Varies
Time of payment   On publication
Expenses   Yes
Photographs   Yes
Response time to queries   24 hours
Kill fees   Yes

TROIKA MAGAZINE

125 Main Street, Suite 360
Westport, CT 06880

Phone number   203-227-5377
Fax number   203-222-9332
E-mail address   troikamag@aol.com
Parent company   Lone Toot Publications, Inc.
Circulation   100,000+
Magazine availability   Newsstands and subscription. Distributed nationally by Time Warner. At B. Dalton, Walden Books, Barnes and Noble, et al.

Target audience   Educated, upscale men and women in the 20s to 50s age bracket seeking a balanced lifestyle: personal achievement, family commitment, community involvement
Magazine's history   Founded by Eric S. Meadow in 1993
Nonfiction   80%
Fiction   20%
Percent of articles freelance-written   80%
Number of articles bought annually   60 to 80
Sections of the magazine open to freelance writers   All—health, science, leisure, Pro Bono, music, culture, business, features, fiction
Article interests and needs   Informative, investigative, cutting edge features, high brow humor/satire
Queries should be directed to   Celie Meadow, Editor
Length of articles   Columns: 750 to 1,000 words; Features: 2,500 words (approximately)
Payment $250 to $1,000
Time of payment   On publication
Expenses   No
Photographs   Yes
Response time to queries   30 days
Rights bought   First North American
Kill fees   No kill fees
Writer's guidelines   Yes—send SASE.
Sample issues   Yes—send $5.00 postage and handling.

Health/Fitness

HEART & SOUL

733 Third Avenue, 15th floor
New York, NY 10017

Phone number   212-338-9091
Fax number   212-338-9144
Parent company   Rodale Press
Circulation   220,000
Magazine availability   Newsstands and subscription
Target audience   Black women; average age 32
Magazine's history and mission   Began as a quarterly in the summer of 1993, jointly published by Rodale Press and founder Reggie Ware's Ware Communications. Now a bimonthly published entirely by Rodale. Its mission is to provide the best health, fitness, and lifestyle information to African-American women.

Nonfiction   100%
Percent of articles freelance-written   Approximately 66%
Number of articles bought annually   Approximately 96; 16 per issue
Sections of the magazine open to freelance writers   All (front of book, well, and back of book), but especially well and back
Article interests and needs   According to *Heart & Soul*'s writer's guidelines, feature stories cover relationships, self-esteem, fitness, celebrity weight-loss and exercise, and hard health. The editors are interested in articles for sections called My Body, Interactive Sisterhood, Body, Mind, Sports Page, Eating Right, Weight Loss, and relationship features.
Queries should be directed to   Claire McIntosh, Senior Editor
Length of articles   1,000 to 2,000 words
Payment $.75 to $1.00 per word
Time of payment   On acceptance
Expenses   Yes, with prior approval and if itemized
Photographs   We negotiate photograph fees per use.
Response time to queries   6 to 8 weeks
Rights bought   Usually we require all rights (except for book excerpts, of course).
Kill fees   25%
Writer's guidelines   Yes

IMPORTANT QUESTIONS ANSWERED

Q: What do you want in a query letter?
A: A one or two page outline of your story idea with the same "feel" that your article would have, with specifics on whom you would interview, and which research sources you might refer to.
Q: Is an SASE always necessary?
A: Yes
Q: Are phone calls from writers OK?
A: No
Q: Is it OK if writers fax queries to you?
A: Preferably no.

PSYCHOLOGY TODAY

40 East 21st Street, 11th Floor
New York, NY 10010

Phone number   212-260-7210
Fax number   212-260-7445
E-mail address   PsychToday@aol.com
Parent company   Sussex Publishers, Inc.
Circulation   350,000

Magazine availability   Newsstands and subscription

Percent of articles freelance-written   85%

Number of articles bought annually   Approximately 100

Sections of the magazine open to freelance writers   PT News, columns, features

Queries should be directed to   Hara Marano, Editor

Length of articles   Varies. News pieces are from 250 to 500 words, columns are about 1,500 words, and features are 2,500 to 6,000 words.

Payment   Typically $.75 per word

Time of payment   On publication

Expenses   Expenses are reimbursed with receipts. Major expenses must be cleared with the editor first.

Photographs   Commissioned or purchased through companies

Response time to queries   Six to eight weeks

Rights bought   We negotiate with writers on either sole and exclusive rights or first-time publishing rights.

TIPS FOR WRITERS

Concise query letters are the best, usually one paragraph. Three clips are recommended that show the writer's range. Phone calls from writers are not preferred—unless they're returning our call. Faxing or e-mailing queries is fine; especially e-mail because we typically respond much faster.

The best way to break into the magazine is through news pieces. This section will get the writer groomed and the editor up to speed on what to expect from a particular writer: ideas, style, and follow-through.

SHAPE

21100 Erwin Street
Woodland Hills, CA 91367

Phone number   818-595-0593

Fax number   818-704-5734

Parent company   Weider Publications

Circulation   970,093

Magazine availability   Newsstands and subscription

Target audience   Approximately 85% women, median age 30.4, median household income $48,326

Magazine's history and mission   *Shape* was started in 1981 by Christine MacIntyre. *Shape* magazine takes women's health media forward by delivering immediately useful techniques and stimulating a deeper understanding of fitness. Top experts from diverse fields of exercise, nutrition, health, psychology, and beauty join forces with nationally known journalists to make each issue a complete how-to manual for a healthful lifestyle.

Nonfiction   100%

Percent of articles freelance-written   70%
Number of articles bought annually   180, mostly from regular contributors
Sections of the magazine open to freelance writers   Active travel, beauty, health, psychology, and some fitness
Article interests and needs   Health and fitness, including all of the above
Queries should be directed to   Peg Moline, Editorial Director
Length of articles   Columns: 600 to 800 words; Features: 1,500 to 2,500 words
Payment   Competitive
Time of payment   On acceptance
Expenses   None or on approval
Response time to queries   One to two months
Rights bought   All
Kill fees   One-third
Writer's guidelines   Available with SASE
Sample issues   Available with large-sized SASE

IMPORTANT QUESTIONS ANSWERED

Q: What sparks your interest in a freelancer writer?
A: One who has been previously published, who sends a well-written, informative query and a pertinent idea.

Q: What are the key elements of a good, professional query?
A: Intelligence, imagination, and grammar.

Q: Do you always want clips from new writers?
A: Yes

Q: How many do you want?
A: Three

Q: What do you look for in writer's clips?
A: Publication in a well-respected publication or a magazine similar to ours.

Q: Will you look at completed manuscripts?
A: No

Q: Is an SASE necessary?
A: Yes

Q: Are phone calls from writers OK?
A: Yes, but only if checking on a query that's been in for a while.

Q: Is it OK if writers e-mail or fax queries to you?
A: No

Q: What are the keys to breaking into your magazine?
A: A writer who is familiar with a topic, has been previously published, writes well, and also, staff familiarity with the writer's work.

Q: What are the best things writers do?
A: Send an idea, know the topic, and write it well.

Q: What are the worst things writers do?
A: Call a week after sending a query, call without sending a query, inappropriate ideas, and simultaneous pitches.

WHOLE LIFE TIMES

P.O. Box 1187
Malibu, CA 90265

Phone number   310-317-4200
Fax number   310-317-4200
Parent company   Whole World Communications, Inc.
Circulation   55,000
Magazine availability   Newsstands, bookstores, health food stores, health centers, and subscriptions
Target audience   Broad readership—generally our readers are 30 to 65 years, professional, personal-growth and holistic health-oriented, in the Los Angeles area
Magazine's history and mission   Founded in 1979 by Joseph Kottler. Present ownership since 1986. We are a forum for expanded life options.
Nonfiction   95%
Fiction   5%
Percent of articles freelance-written   85%
Number of articles bought annually   50
Sections of the magazine open to freelance writers   Features: Nonfiction, profiles, interiors. Departments: environment, healing, food, personal growth, etc.
Article interests and needs   Holistic health, politics, vitamins, nutrition, exercise
Queries should be directed to   Abigail Lewis, Publisher/Editor; S. T. Alcantara, Associate Editor; Kristen Pratt, Reviews Editor
Length of articles   1,000 to 2,000 words
Payment   We pay $.05 per word for *features only*. Department stories are *non-paid*.
Time of payment   Within 30 days of publication
Expenses   If story is assigned, may reimburse for long-distance calls and faxes. *Only by pre-arrangement.*
Photographs   If possible, please include, with photo credit, to support story.
Response time to queries   Generally 1 to 2 months
Kill Fees   Not available
Writer's guidelines   Available with SASE
Sample issues   Available for $3 a copy

TIPS FOR WRITERS

Query and submissions: A good query is one that provides a one to two paragraph description of a story idea. Include details: Is it an interview? Profile? Q & A? Are photographs available? Provide a "teaser" of one to two paragraphs if not sending a complete manuscript.

New writers should send at least two to three clips. The clips should include a variety of stories, such as interviews, investigative pieces, and features.

We look for clear, concise writing that addresses a sophisticated readership. Cutting-edge information presented in a practical format is always attractive, as are interviews with high-profile people in the entertainment industry who have similar interests or leaders in related fields.

We prefer to receive completed manuscripts and writers should be aware that *WLT* buys only about 50 manuscripts a year. The remaining 50 or so stories published in the magazine are *nonpaid* departments (such as health, personal growth, or horoscope).

Professional etiquette: An SASE is required for a response. We will not fax writer's guidelines if it is not a local call. If you are from out of the country, send an appropriately stamped SASE.

Do not query by phone. It is best to send or fax a query.

Currently we do not have an e-mail address, but are working on getting one in the future.

Best way to break into the magazine: Read the magazine, request writer's guidelines, and pitch story by mail or fax. Send a completed manuscript with phone number.

Become familiar with the editorial content of the magazine and realize our readership is sophisticated, affluent, and already well-educated about the healing arts. They want new information presented in a practical and palatable way.

Best things writers do: Provide stories that present cutting-edge information in an easy to read, entertaining manner. Provide several attributions to bonafide experts in the field. Book excerpts are not an equivalent to interviews with these experts.

Worst things writers do: Submit stories that are not researched adequately or are geared to a mainstream readership that is not well-informed about the health/New Age industry. Submit stories that are not proofed for obvious errors in spelling, grammar, and the like!

Also, we do not like opinion pieces.

Ways to angle story for our publication: Read the magazine. Notice that most stories are either investigative pieces or else present a familiar subject with a new angle. For example, a story on acupressure was geared to women and how to self-treat to help manage PMS symptoms.

Overall advice: Be familiar with the magazine's editorial content. Do not call to query. Send completed manuscripts and do not call us every week to check on status. Turnaround time is generally two months.

Present progressive subjects such as recycling, but with new information or with an innovative angle.

Give your story to someone to proof. The story should be "clean" upon submission. A sloppy story is quickly dropped in the recycled paper bin.

Yoga Journal

2054 University Avenue
Berkeley, CA 94704

Phone number   510-841-9200
Fax number   510-644-3101
Parent company   California Yoga Teachers Association

Circulation   85,000

Online status   Electronic newsstand, Natural Connection. Also Web site, part of Consciousnet, at http://www.yogajournal.com

Magazine availability   Newsstands and subscription

Target audience   Average age 46 years, 75% female, 51% married, majority have completed college

Magazine's history and mission   The first issue was published in May 1975. According to the magazine's formal mission statement, "*Yoga Journal* is dedicated to communicating, to as broad an audience as possible, the qualities of being that yoga exemplifies: peace, integrity, clarity, and compassion. In particular, we focus on body/mind approaches to personal and spiritual development—such as hatha yoga, holistic healing, transpersonal psychology, body work and massage, the martial arts, meditation, Eastern spirituality, and Western mysticism . . ."

Nonfiction   95 to 100%

Fiction   0 to 5%

Percent of articles freelance-written   90 to 95%

Number of articles bought annually   About 80

Sections of the magazine open to freelance writers   All

Article interests and needs   Interested in a variety of fields and disciplines devoted to enhancing human health and consciousness, while maintaining our emphasis on the practice and philosophy of yoga.

Queries should be directed to   Rick Fields, Editor-in-Chief

Length of articles   Features: 3,000 to 5,000 words; Departments: 1,000 to 2,000 words

Payment $1,200, Cover Story; $600 to $1,000, Features; $250 to $500, Departments; $75 to $100, Book Reviews

Time of payment   Within 90 days of final acceptance

Expenses   Per-case basis

Photographs   Indicate availability in query. Mark photographs with brief description and photographer's name and address.

Response time to queries   This can vary

Rights bought   Exclusive North American serial rights

Kill fees   Yes—25%

Writer's guidelines   Free with SASE

Sample issues   Free with SASE

TIPS FOR WRITERS

Potential freelancers should:

Make their queries as specific and in-depth as possible.

Include contact information in their cover letter (sometimes we have no indication—not even an address—of how to get in touch with them).

Refrain from calling to check up on the status of their query.

Double-space their manuscripts.

YOUR HEALTH & FITNESS

900 Skokie Boulevard
Northbrook, IL 60062-4028

Phone number   847-205-3000
Fax number   847-564-8197
Parent company   General Learning Communications
Circulation   500,000+
Magazine availability   Through subscription
Target audience   Adult laymen, age 21 and over; national
Magazine's history and mission   We are in the 18th year of publication with a continuing mission to educate the general reader on common health concerns and to empower readers to be savvy healthcare consumers and to take care of themselves through a healthful lifestyle.
Nonfiction   100%
Percent of articles freelance-written   80%
Number of articles bought annually   40+
Sections of the magazine open to freelance writers   Exercise & Fitness, Drug Data, Psychology, Nutrition, Safety, Disease, General Health Concerns
Article interests and needs   We determine topics. We do not cover alternative medicine topics.
Queries should be directed to   Carol Lezak, Executive Editor
Length of articles   350 to 850 words
Time of payment   After publication
Expenses   None
Photographs   None
Rights bought   We buy *all* rights.
Kill fees   50%
Writer's guidelines   Sent after we receive cover letter, resume, and writing samples
Sample issues   See above.

History/ Military

AMERICA'S CIVIL WAR

741 Miller Drive, SE, Suite D-2
Leesburg, VA 22075

Phone number   703-771-9400
Fax number   703-779-8345

Parent company   Cowles Magazines, Inc.

Circulation   125,000

Magazine availability   Newsstands and subscription

Target audience   College-educated males over age 40. Many are veterans. Throughout the U.S. and Canada, United Kingdom, and other selected countries.

Magazine's history and mission   First published: May 1988. Founders: Adam Landis and Carl Gnam. Published bimonthly, for those interested in compelling, incisive accounts of land, naval, and air warfare from early history to modern times.

Nonfiction   100%

Percent of articles freelance-written   95%

Number of articles bought annually   48 manuscripts (Feature length); 24 manuscripts (Departments)

Sections of the magazine open to freelance writers   All except Editorial

Article interests and needs   Choose stories with strong art possibilities. We would like journalistically "pure" submissions that adhere to basics, such as full name at first reference. Definition of prior or related events. Popular history, accompanied by period art.

Queries should be directed to   Roy Morris, Editor

Length of articles   Features: 4,000 words; Departments: 2,000 words

Payment   Features: $300 features; Departments: $150

Time of payment   On publication

Expenses   No

Photographs   No extra payment and should accompany the article. If no photographs, please give possible sources for photos.

Response time to queries   3 months—include an SASE

Rights bought   We buy all rights; exclusive worldwide publication rights through the 120th day after the on-sale period of the issue in which the article appears.

Kill fees   None

Writer's guidelines   Send an SASE.

Sample issues   Send $3.95 along with request for guidelines or call 800-435-9610. Outside the U.S., call 815-734-5824.

TIPS FOR WRITERS

Prospective contributors should submit a concise, self-explanatory query summarizing the article and describing its highlights. Successful queries include a description of sources of information and suggestions for color and black-and-white photography or artwork. The likelihood that an article can be effectively illustrated often determines its ultimate fate. Photocopies of suggested illustrations with sources are extremely helpful. Phone queries are not acceptable; fax queries are.

Completed manuscripts will be reviewed; however, they must be double-spaced and accompanied by an SASE. The author's name, address, telephone number, and social security number must appear on the title page. Authors should also include a brief biography, a description of their expertise in the subject matter, and suggestions for further reading along the lines of their articles. Relevant clips are also helpful. Inclusion of an IBM or Mac compatible disk copy of the manuscript increases its chances of acceptance.

The best way to break into our magazine is to write an entertaining, informative, and unusual story that grabs the reader's attention and holds it. We favor carefully researched, third-person articles or firsthand accounts that give the reader a sense of experiencing historical events. We do not publish reprints. Manuscripts with misspelled words, poor grammar, weak leads, partial names, unsupported statements, or unattributed quotes are rejected out of hand.

MILITARY HISTORY

741 Miller Drive, SE, Suite D-2
Leesburg, VA 22075

Phone number   703-771-9400
Fax number   703-779-8345
Parent company   Cowles Magazines, Inc.
Circulation   150,000
Magazine availability   Newsstands and subscription
Target audience   College-educated males over age 40. Many are veterans. Throughout the U.S. and Canada, United Kingdom, and other selected countries.
Magazine's history and mission   First published: August 1984. Founders: Adam Landis and Carl Gnam. Published bimonthly, for those interested in compelling, incisive accounts of land, naval, and air warfare from early history to modern times.
Nonfiction   100%
Percent of articles freelance-written   95%
Number of articles bought annually   18 manuscripts plus 6 interviews (Features); 24 manuscripts (Departments)
Sections of the magazine open to freelance writers   All except Editorial. Open departments are: Intrigue, Weaponry, Perspectives, Personality, Travel, and Book Reviews. Also, four Feature articles plus one Feature-Interview.
Article interests and needs   Choose stories with strong art possibilities. We would like journalistically "pure" submissions that adhere to basics, such as full name at first reference. Definition of prior or related events. Popular history, accompanied by period art.
Queries should be directed to   Jon Guttman, Editor
Length of articles   Features: 4,000 words; Departments: 2,000 words
Payment   Features: $400; Departments: $200
Time of payment   On publication
Expenses   No
Photographs   No extra payment and should accompany the article. If no photographs, please give possible sources for photos.
Response time to queries   3 months—include an SASE
Rights bought   We buy all rights; exclusive worldwide publication rights through the 120th day after the on-sale period of the issue in which the article appears.
Kill fees   None
Writer's guidelines   Send an SASE.

Sample issues   Send $3.95 along with request for guidelines or call 1-800-435-9610. Outside the U.S., call 815-734-5824.

TIPS FOR WRITERS

See entry under *America's Civil War.*

NAVAL HISTORY
118 Maryland Avenue
Annapolis, MD 21402-5035

Phone number   410-268-6110, 6114
Fax number   410-269-7940
Parent company   U.S. Naval Institute
Circulation   40,000
Magazine availability   Newsstands and subscription
Target audience   Even though we definitely would like to attract younger readers, our core audience consists mostly of retired sea service officers and history enthusiasts over 50.
Magazine's history and mission   On the heels of the tremendously successful publication of Tom Clancy's first book, *The Hunt for Red October,* the Naval Institute sought ways by which it could expand its service to members, many of whom were clamoring for more history. A solicitation of interest in a history magazine spawned 12,000 charter subscribers.
Nonfiction   100%
Percent of articles freelance-written   90%
Number of articles bought annually   Approximately 50
Sections of the magazine open to freelance writers   All, except regular columns such as Looking Back, Salty Talk, and Historic Fleets
Article interests and needs   Merchant Marine, Coast Guard, and Korean War History
Queries should be directed to   Fred L. Schultz, Editor-in-Chief
Length of articles   3,000 to 3,500 words (exceptions made occasionally)
Payment $100 to $400
Time of payment   On acceptance
Expenses   No
Photographs   Yes. Contact photo editor for current rates.
Response time to queries   2 to 3 months
Rights bought   All work for hire
Kill fees   Not standard procedure
Writer's guidelines   Yes
Sample issues   Yes—$3.50

TIPS FOR WRITERS
Fred L. Schultz, Editor-in-Chief

Freelance writers looking to be published in *Naval History* face a formidable obstacle—a huge bank of already accepted manuscripts. Professionals will appreciate that publications usually buy more manuscripts than they can possibly use, because it is always better for an editor to have too much material from which to choose than not enough. Hence, the competition is stiff for getting your manuscript accepted in the first place and equally so in having it published.

That said, a good story will invariably make it into the magazine more quickly than a "for the record" reminiscence of life at sea. Many of our correspondents have taken a good story and drained every bit of drama from it, most times because of an inability to shake a mysterious writing style that compels the author to tell the reader what he is going to say, to say it, then to repeat it for emphasis or in the interest of academic constrictions. This is not to say that we are uninterested in well-documented facts. We are simply looking for an engaging narrative to accompany them.

Queries are always the best bet before an author assembles a story. We may already have related material in the bank, the topic may have been recently exhausted, or it may simply not be right for this publication. Because of the amount of mail we receive, the query should grab the editor's attention from the start. Give away the best part of the story in the first paragraph of the query. Then delineate your qualifications for writing such a piece. And have a thick skin, because a favorable response from the editor will likely elicit only a form letter agreeing to see the manuscript on speculation, with no commitment on the publisher's part; completed manuscripts are always welcome and are evaluated in the same manner as all others.

Be patient after submitting the piece, allowing at least a few months to lapse before inquiring about the status of your manuscript. Most magazines deal with hundreds of authors at a time, so sympathize with the editors making the decisions.

Sample clips hardly ever sway an editorial decision, but they do give further indication of the query writer's ability. Evidence that the author has been published before, while not necessarily a qualification for writing naval history, does play a part in the equation.

Most editors likely will agree that freelancers should refrain from telephone queries, on both interest in a topic or the status of a manuscript under evaluation or already purchased. If all authors called editors with such questions, not much evaluating—or publishing, for that matter—would get done.

The best way to "break into" *Naval History* is first to identify a good story, with one or several of the following: drama, action, humor, irony, emotion. Then give your best shot in the lead paragraph, generally without giving away—unlike the query—the upshot of the story. The author-editor team has only seconds to draw the reader into the story. The opening needs to be sufficiently provocative or attractive as to leave the reader wanting more. Save the vital statistics of the characters or other arcane details for later in your story. In other words, do not begin with "He was born on New Year's day . . . ," unless of course that is the focus of the piece.

Most editors can tell the difference between a professional and an amateur, no matter how good the writing is. The pros allow the evaluation and editorial process to flow at its own pace. Amateurs are in too much of a hurry. Refrain from being a pest. If you must be one, at least be a courteous pest. Editors at *Naval History* would like nothing more than to accommodate and publish all their authors expeditiously. Unfortunately, it is simply an impossible goal. Be patient.

WILD WEST

741 Miller Drive, SE, Suite D-2
Leesburg, VA 22075

Phone number   703-771-9400
Fax number   703-779-8345
Parent company   Cowles Magazines, Inc.
Circulation   175,000
Magazine availability   Newsstands and subscription
Target audience   Average age 40; college-educated males throughout the U.S. and Canada, United Kingdom, and other selected countries
Magazine's history and mission   First published: June 1988. Founders: Adam Landis and Carl Gnam. Published bimonthly, for those interested in compelling, incisive accounts of land, naval, and air warfare from early history to modern times.
Nonfiction   100%
Percent of articles freelance-written   95%
Number of articles bought annually   24 manuscripts (Feature length); 16 manuscripts (Departments)
Sections of the magazine open to freelance writers   All except Editorial. Sections include: Westerners, Warriors & Chiefs, Gunfighters and Lawmen, Western Lore. Five Feature articles.
Article interests and needs   Choose stories with strong art possibilities. We would like journalistically "pure" submissions that adhere to basics, such as full name at first reference. Definition of prior or related events. Popular history, accompanied by period art.
Queries should be directed to   Gregory Lalire, Editor
Length of articles   Features: 4,000 words; Departments: 2,000 words
Payment   Features: $300; Departments: $150
Time of payment   On publication
Expenses   No
Photographs   No extra payment and should accompany the article. If no photographs, please give possible sources for photos.
Response time to queries   3 months—include an SASE
Rights bought   We buy all rights; exclusive worldwide publication rights through the 120th day after the on-sale period of the issue in which the article appears.
Kill fees   None
Writer's guidelines   Send an SASE.

Sample issues Send $3.95 along with request for guidelines or call: 800-435-9610. Outside the U.S., call: (815) 734-5824.

TIPS FOR WRITERS

See entry under *America's Civil War.*

WORLD WAR II

741 Miller Drive, SE, Suite D-2
Leesburg, VA 22075

Phone number 703-771-9400
Fax number 703-779-8345
Parent company Cowles Magazines, Inc.
Circulation 200,000
Magazine availability Newsstands and subscription
Target audience Average age 52; college-educated males, veterans. Throughout the U.S. and Canada, United Kingdom, and other selected countries.
Magazine's history and mission First published: May 1986. Founders: Adam Landis and Carl Gnam. Published bimonthly, for those interested in compelling, incisive accounts of land, naval, and air warfare from early history to modern times.
Nonfiction 100%
Percent of articles freelance-written 95%
Number of articles bought annually 24 manuscripts (Feature length); 18 manuscripts (Departments)
Sections of the magazine open to freelance writers All except Editorial. Open Departments include: Personality, Undercover, Armament, Perspectives, and Books Reviews. Also, four Feature articles.
Article interests and needs Choose stories with strong art possibilities. We would like journalistically "pure" submissions that adhere to basics, such as full name at first reference. Definition of prior or related events. Popular history, accompanied by period art.
Queries should be directed to Michael Haskew
Length of articles Features: 4,000 words; Departments: 2,000 words
Payment Features: $200; Departments: $100
Time of payment On publication
Expenses No
Photographs No extra payment and should accompany the article. If no photographs, please give possible sources for photos.
Response time to queries 3 months—include an SASE
Rights bought We buy all rights; exclusive worldwide publication rights through the 120th day after the on-sale period of the issue in which the article appears.
Kill fees None
Writer's guidelines Send an SASE.

Sample issues   Send $3.95 along with request for guidelines or call: 800-435-9610. Outside the U.S., call: 815-734-5824.

TIPS FOR WRITERS
See entry under *America's Civil War.*

Hobby/Craft/How-to

AMERICAN WOODWORKER
33 East Minor Street
Emmaus, PA 18098

Phone number   610-967-5141
Fax number   610-967-7692
E-mail address   awjules@aol.com
Parent company   Rodale Press, Inc.
Circulation   300,000
Online status   AOL affiliate
Magazine availability   Newsstands and subscription
Target audience   Woodworking hobbyists and small-shop professionals. Median age 51. Worldwide distribution
Magazine's history and mission   Founded in 1985 by Jim Jennings, Hendersonville, Tennessee. Acquired in 1987 by Rodale Press. Mission: to motivate, entertain, and challenge the woodworking enthusiast with in-depth and accessible information and ideas that will help him develop the skills he needs to become a better woodworker.
Nonfiction   100%
Percent of articles freelance-written   70%
Number of articles bought annually   60 to 70 features and short subjects
Sections of the magazine open to freelance writers   All except Finishing and Wood Facts departments
Article interests and needs   Woodworking techniques, projects, tools, and materials
Queries should be directed to   Tim Snyder, Managing Editor
Length of articles   To 3,000 words
Payment $150 per published page
Time of payment   On publication
Expenses   Case-by-case basis
Photographs   Fee included in page rate, or as negotiated. We will take photos, if needed.

Response time to queries   2 weeks
Rights bought   Prefer all rights, including electronic, reprint, and promotional
Kill fees   Negotiable
Writer's guidelines   Available
Sample issues   Available

TIPS FOR WRITERS
Tim Snyder, Managing Editor

Here are some things I look for in a prospective contributor.

1. Are you a reader of my magazine? Are you familiar with the mix of articles that goes into each issue (projects, techniques, tool articles, jigs and fixtures, etc.)? And have you noticed how we treat certain subjects, especially compared to the way other competitive magazines treat these same subjects? It's important for me to know about your familiarity with the magazine, because that tells me how much educating and orienting I'll have to do as a preamble to acquiring an article from you, the prospective author.

   What editors like to hear in a cover letter in regards to this point should go something like:

   > "I enjoyed the article on repairing antique furniture. The approach you used was a lot different than the article that ran about a year ago in *Woodwork* magazine."

2. Are you an expert in the area of your proposed article? I hope so, because I don't want to pay a non-expert to do research, unless he or she is one hell of a technical journalist. Be smart, and pitch an article dealing with something you know a lot about. You've already got the necessary information in your head.

   What editors like to hear in a cover letter in regards to this point should go something like:

   > "I've used this method to join boards for a long time. It's a real improvement over the way I used to do it."

3. Where's the lead paragraph? Your cover letter needs to "hook" me just like I'd (we'd) like to hook the reader. Get the main point of the story across quickly and concisely.

4. What visuals will go with your story? If you're a reader (see first point above), you know how important photos and drawings are in any article. Let me know that you're thinking not just in terms of a manuscript, but also in terms of ways to illustrate the article.

   What editors like to hear in a cover letter in regards to this point should go something like:

   > "I've enclosed several photos to give you a look at the unusual latch I devised for this cabinet. There's also a sketch showing how it works."

5. Have you written before? Notice that this is my fifth concern, not my first. If you've passed muster in categories 1 through 4, I'm pretty sure we can work together and make an article. If you have writing experience, that's helpful. But it's not critical.

DOLLS, THE COLLECTOR'S MAGAZINE

170 Fifth Avenue
New York, NY 10010

Phone number   212-989-8700
Fax number   212-645-8976
Parent company   Collector Communications Corp.
Circulation   130,000
Magazine availability   Newsstands and subscription
Target audience   Doll collectors—primarily adults, in the U.S. and abroad, ranging from beginning collectors to experienced professionals
Magazine's history and mission   Founded in 1982 by Robert Campbell Rowe, publisher. *Dolls* magazine was founded to provide a beautiful, informative, and exciting publication to serve doll collectors of every type of doll.
Nonfiction   100%
Percent of articles freelance-written   75%
Number of articles bought annually   50
Sections of the magazine open to freelance writers   Feature material only
Article interests and needs   We are looking for highly focused, well-researched stories on antique, collectible, and contemporary dolls, including profiles of artists and stories on museum collections.
Queries should be directed to   Stephanie Finnegan, Managing Editor
Length of articles   800 to 2,000 words
Payment $200 to $400
Time of payment   30 days after acceptance
Expenses   If arranged in advance
Photographs   Usually bought as package with manuscript.
Response time to queries   4 to 6 weeks for manuscript; 2 to 4 weeks for queries
Rights bought   First North American serial rights
Kill fees   Only for assigned pieces
Writer's guidelines   Send SASE for guidelines.
Sample issues $2

POPULAR MECHANICS

224 West 57th Street
New York, NY 10019

Phone number   212-649-2000

Fax number   212-586-5562

E-mail address   popularmechanics@hearst.com

Parent company   The Hearst Corp.

Circulation   1.4 million subscribers; 200,000 newsstand

Online status   Have Web site on the Internet called the PMZone (http://popularmechanics.com)

Magazine availability   Newsstands and subscription

Target audience   Male, ages 35 to 55, median income $45,000, married with children, owns his home and at least two cars, and probably works in a technically oriented profession.

Magazine's history and mission   Established in 1902 and dubbed "the original men's service magazine," we try to address the diverse interests of today's male, while providing him with information to improve the way he lives. We cover stories from how-to, do-it-yourself projects to technological advances in aerospace, military, automotive, electronics, computers, telecommunications, sports science, and so on.

Nonfiction   100%

Percent of articles freelance-written   5%

Number of articles bought annually   2

Sections of the magazine open to freelance writers   Tech Update section open to freelance writers; good way to get started in writing longer feature articles for the magazine.

Article interests and needs   Our guiding principle is to help our readers better understand the technology of how things work in today's highly technical society. Therefore, we're interested in articles of a technical nature that cover the latest developments and advancements in the industries that our five departments cover. Our five departments are: Automotive, Home Improvement, Science/Technology, Boating/Outdoors, and Electronics/Photography.

Queries should be directed to   If your query doesn't fit any of the departments, send it to Joe Oldham, Editor-In-Chief. Otherwise, send your query to one of the following people: Dan Chaikin, Automotive; Steven Willson, Home Improvement; Brian Fenton, Electronics/Photography/Telecommunications; Jim Wilson, Science/Technology, Aerospace; Rich Taylor, Outdoors

Length of articles   1,000 to 2,000 words for Major Feature; 800 to 1,000 words for Short Feature; 300 to 500 words for News Brief; 100 to 400 words for Tech Update section

Payment $300 to $2,500 for Major Feature; $500 to $600 for Short Feature; $300 for News Brief; $300 for Tech Update section; $200 for Finder's Fee

Time of payment   On acceptance

Expenses   Negotiable

Photographs   Photographs are a plus, but not required. Send photos—slides, prints, and transparencies—with submission. We offer no additional payment for photos accepted with manuscript.

Response time to queries   2 months

Rights bought   All rights purchased, including copyright, on a work-for-hire basis.

Kill fees   25%
Writer's guidelines   Available. Send SASE.
Sample issues   Not available

TIPS FOR WRITERS

The query: To spark our interest, the query should propose an article that is new to *PM*, one we haven't published before. A query about a subject that we already covered in one way or another shows that the writer really doesn't know our magazine and hasn't done his/her research. Before submitting a query, we suggest that writers check the *Guide to Periodical Literature* or our own indexes (available through our Reader Information Services department). The key elements in a good, professional query are active voice with a great lead flowing into an outline, a well-defined description of the subject matter, and how the writer intends to get the story—i.e., contacts already in place, material available for art, etc. Clips are not necessary, although a brief list of credentials and previous publications in which the writer's work has appeared helps. Completed manuscripts are generally not read through; it's better to make the proposal first before sending a completed story.

Professional etiquette: An SASE is not necessary, but considered polite and appreciated for an easy and quick response. Phone calls are okay in circumstances that involve timely material that needs to be reported on immediately or the story becomes old and published elsewhere. Faxed and e-mailed queries are always welcomed and considered.

The best way to break into *PM*: The best way to break in is through the Tech Update section. It's where a new writer can learn our style, and what we need and want for certain subject matter, and it allows our editors to become familiar with the writer and possibly to have them move on to bigger feature assignments.

The key to breaking in to *PM*: The key is to be familiar with our magazine—i.e., know who our reader is and our target audience, and, most importantly, know that we did not already cover that subject in one form or another over the past few years; unless, of course, there have been some new developments that we have yet to report on.

The best thing writers do: The best thing writers do is stick to the line count given once a proposal has been accepted and a contract drawn up and a story assigned.

The worst thing writers do: The worst thing writers do is write fluff pieces that read like press releases rather than good, unbiased reporting.

Writers can angle their stories for *PM*: Writers can angle stories by referring to any of the topics our five departments (see Guidelines) cover; reading through back issues of *PM* that cover similar subjects, and analyzing the approach we took in printing the stories—for example, pay attention to the layout, the types of photos used, the art illustrated.

Overall advice to writers: Know your subject, have contacts, and get the facts straight. Your writing ability is not as important as being able to back up your words with facts that are true and thoroughly researched. Writing can always be edited, but fact-checking and researching information that a writer is supplying are not always available to every editor, be it for reasons of limited time or limited resources and small staffs.

SKY & TELESCOPE

P.O. Box 9111
Belmont, MA 02178-9111

Phone number   617-864-7360
Fax number   617-864-6117
E-mail address   sky&tel@skypub.com
Parent company   Sky Publishing Corp.
Circulation   Approximately 120,000
Online status   Web site at www.skypub.com
Magazine availability   Newsstands and subscription
Target audience   Amateur astronomers and casual sky-gazers
Magazine's history   Founded in 1941 by Charles Federer
Nonfiction   100%
Percent of articles freelance-written   Approximately 10%
Number of articles bought annually   Approximately 40
Sections of the magazine open to freelance writers   Feature articles. Departments are unpaid.
Article interests and needs   Cutting edge astronomy and cosmology. Telescopes and observatories.
Queries should be directed to   Timothy Lyster, Managing Editor
Length of articles   Approximately 2,000 to 4,000 words
Payment $.10 to $.25 per word
Time of payment   On publication
Expenses   No
Photographs   Send with manuscript.
Response time to queries   Approximately 1 to 2 weeks
Rights bought   All or first serial
Kill fees   No
Writer's guidelines   Available with SASE
Sample issues   On request

TIPS FOR WRITERS

The editors are continually looking for interesting stories from the universe of astronomy. Make sure you read several past copies to get an idea of the editorial content and level of presentation. Most of our readers are amateur sky-gazers, not professionals. They appreciate the aesthetic pleasures of the night sky but also often like to be challenged on a technical level.

When writing about a subject that has appeared in *Sky & Telescope* before, read the relevant past issues. The editors have over 100 years of experience and we go to unusual lengths to ensure our material is both factually correct and consistent. A badly researched manuscript will be summarily rejected!

We do read completed manuscripts, but generally advise sending a proposal first, no more than a page in length. An SASE is not necessary, unless photographs need to be returned. Phone inquiries are OK, but fax or e-mail is preferred.

A well-researched manuscript, with good supporting illustrations, stands a favorable chance of being published.

Humor

NEW HUMOR MAGAZINE

P.O. Box 216
Lafayette Hill, PA 19444

Phone number   215-482-7673
Fax number   215-487-2640
E-mail address   Newhumor@aol.com
Parent company   Edward Savaria Jr./Suzanne Tschanz Publishers
Circulation   4,000
Online status   Just e-mail.
Magazine availability   Magazine found at scattered stores. Best to get by mail
Target audience   The magazine's target audience is 20 to afterlife. This includes subscribers mostly from the United States but some international.
Magazine's history and mission   The magazine was started in 1994 by Edward Savaria Jr. and Suzanne Tschanz. The mission is to continually supply readers with intelligent, tasteful, and, yes, funny humor in the form of stories, poems, jokes, and cartoons.
Nonfiction   20%
Fiction   90%
Percent of articles freelance-written   80%
Number of articles bought annually   About 120 pieces of humor
Sections of the magazine open to freelance writers   All areas
Article interests and needs   Poetry, cartoons, jokes, humorous stories. According to editor and publisher Edward Savaria Jr. in his guidelines for writers, ". . . we read all the mail and look for material that says *funny*. Speaking as the editor now, I like Dave Barry, the great satirist of our time. I automatically buy anything with the name *Barry* on it. If your name is just *Dave*, it doesn't count as much. If your first and last initials are D and B, respectively, then you have a pretty good chance. Although, some stories we print don't even look like *Dave*'s work. Hey, go figure."
Queries should be directed to   Edward Savaria Jr., Editor
Length of articles Keep stories to about 1,000 words or less

Payment $25 for cartoons; $35 to $100 for stories; $5 to $15 for jokes and short poems; a little more for fillers
Time of payment   On acceptance
Rights bought   We buy any rights offered.
Kill fees   Never had need for kill fee
Writer's guidelines   Available
Sample issues   Send $4.50 for a copy of the magazine.

TIPS FOR WRITERS
Edward Savaria Jr., Editor

A query is not necessary with this publication. Humor is difficult to describe in a letter. Best to just send the work in. Request a guideline sheet or pay for a sample copy to see if you want to even bother with this publication. Everyone has a different sense of humor.

An SASE is always necessary if you want the material returned. I prefer not to talk to writers on the phone because they will quickly realize that I don't have their material in front of me and can't answer their questions. Best to e-mail or write. I'm not a fax fan.

I find that a funny introduction letter will sometimes make me more upbeat about the material I'm about to read. Then again, I seem to buy just as many stories from the humorists that just give their name and the name of the story. Hey, go figure.

While reading the work, I'm looking for humor with a surprise, or an edge, perhaps. I also like zany and off-the-wall comedy. All work should be clean in a nonsexiest, non-racial, nondegrading way. You can be funny without being too insulting. Although, the interview with God piece got a few letters.

It does not matter if you have been published before. If the work is what I'm looking for, then it has a good chance for publication.

Lastly, I don't like writing anything on rejection sheets. Any dribble I write will only cause quizzical looks on the recipient's face.

Inflight

EXCURSIONS
SCG, Inc.
5110 North 44th Street, Suite 210-L
Phoenix, AZ 85018

Fax number   602-952-1170 (Writers can fax their requests for current airline destinations and pay rates to Lisa Polacheck, Editorial/Magazine Coordinator.)
Parent company   Stateswest Communications Group, Inc.

Circulation   Monthly readership of 400,000

Magazine availability   Complimentary magazine available to passengers of Reno Air, which serves Los Angeles, Albuquerque, Anchorage, Seattle, Tucson, Vancouver, and more.

Target audience   Our demographics are fairly inclusive—anyone who flies for business, vacations, and visiting is a potential reader—so topics and writing style should reflect that variety.

Nonfiction   100%

Percent of articles freelance-written   Approximately 75%

Number of articles bought annually   10

Article interests and needs   We seek destination-related features and relevant, vibrant photos. We prefer, of course, articles that are tight yet thorough, informative yet entertaining, brief yet memorable. In order to create reader-friendly magazines, we request that all features include a 200 to 300 word service sidebar listing contact information for major places or attractions listed in the article. Specialty columns span finances, cars, dining, and accommodations.

Queries should be directed to   Lisa Polacheck, Editorial/Magazine Coordinator

Length of articles   600 to 1,600 words

Payment   In general, compensation for column material (600 to 800 words) is $250. The fee for assigned features of 1,000 to 1,600 words is $350. The rate for solicited photos is $75.

Time of payment   On publication. We [also] furnish all contributors with one copy of the magazine.

Photographs   Yes. Photography and art in the form of color slides may be accepted, although we can't guarantee the return of unsolicited materials.

Response time to queries   Unfortunately, it's rather upended, although we do try to respond to SASEs and enclosed postcards within one month.

Rights bought   The fee paid by the publisher to the writer purchases the rights to publish the article one time in any or all SCG magazines.

Kill fees   We make assignments carefully and therefore do not have a kill fee structure. If a story cannot run due to unforeseen circumstances, a kill fee may be offered on a case-by-case basis.

Sample issues   Complimentary if you fly Western Pacific, Reno Air, KIWI, or Air South. Otherwise, send an SASE with $3 postage and your specific request to Stateswest Communications Group, Inc.

TIPS FOR WRITERS
Lisa Polacheck, Editorial/Magazine Coordinator

In our minds, there are two legitimate types of queries: the idea query and the "here's-my-disk, photos-upon-request" query. The first type of query is quick, concise, and doesn't take too much of either party's time. However, in a pinch, we love having a few of the second query type—we can simply call the writer for FedEx-ed visuals and start editing copy immediately.

An SASE isn't necessarily mandatory—but if you want to know whether your query arrived safely, a stamped postcard'll do the trick. Of course, if you require immediate return of rejected materials, an SASE is perfect. We're not always as timely with our acceptances/rejections as is ideal, but we do keep dauntingly full freelance files, so don't be surprised to hear from us six months after your query!

Our favorite writers, photographers, and artists are cooperative, deadline-attentive, and, well, inexpensive. Freelancers with stock materials they've assembled on independent trips are popular. And if you're a native of one of our destination cities, all the better—you can give readers the insider view of their vacation spots. Rarely do we pay expenses to send a writer on assignment far, far away.

HEMISPHERES

Pace Communications, Inc.
1301 Carolina Street
Greensboro, NC 27401

Phone number   910-378-6065
Fax number   910-378-8265
Parent company   Pace Communications, Inc.
Circulation   500,000
Magazine availability   Inflight and subscription
Target audience   41-year-old males and females, professional, managerial, household income of $88,351, college-educated
Magazine's history   Pace Communications started publishing *Hemispheres* in October 1992. Before that the United inflight magazine was *Vis a Vis*.
Nonfiction   95%
Fiction   5%
Percent of articles freelance-written   100%
Number of articles bought annually   Approximately 250 to 300
Article interests and needs   Of interest to professionals who travel frequently
Sections of the magazine open to freelance writers   All
Queries should be directed to   Kate Greer, Editor-in-Chief
Length of articles   1,200 to 1,500 words
Payment   Varies
Time of payment   On acceptance
Expenses   Reasonable and necessary documented incidental expenses, toll, phone calls, and local travel ($.20 per mile) will be reimbursed. No other expenses will be reimbursed unless authorized prior to being incurred.
Photographs   Professional photographers only
Response time to queries   Approximately 3 months
Rights bought   First North American

Kill fees   20%
Sample issues $5.00 per issue

HOT AIR

The Boathouse, Crabtree Lane
London SW6 8LU
England

Phone number   0171 470 2400
Fax number   0171 385 6946
E-mail address   alexf@johnbrown.Luk
Parent company   John Brown Publishing
Circulation   500,000 readers per issue
Target audience   Virgin Atlantic passengers—all classes
Magazine's history and mission   Founded with airline to inform and entertain passengers.
Nonfiction   90%
Fiction   10%
Percent of articles freelance-written   80%
Number of articles bought annually   35
Sections of the magazine open to freelance writers   Freelance submissions very rarely accepted.
Length of articles   1,500 to 3,000 words
Payment   By arrangement
Writer's guidelines   None

KIWI/AIR SOUTH

SCG, Inc.
5110 North 44th Street, Suite 210-L
Phoenix, AZ 85018

Fax number   602-952-1170 (Writers can fax their requests for current airline destinations and pay rates to Lisa Polacheck, Editorial/Magazine Coordinator.)
Parent company   Stateswest Communications Group, Inc.
Magazine availability   Complimentary magazine available to passengers of KIWI International Air Lines and Air South Airlines. KIWI is based in Newark and serves Chicago, Atlanta, and several Florida destinations. Air South is based in Columbia, South Carolina, and serves destinations in the Carolinas, Florida, Georgia, and more.
Target audience   Our demographics are fairly inclusive—anyone who flies for business, vacations, and visiting is a potential reader—so topics and writing style should reflect that variety.

Nonfiction   100%
Percent of articles freelance-written   Approximately 75%
Article interests and needs   We seek destination-related features and relevant, vibrant photos. We prefer, of course, articles that are tight yet thorough, informative yet entertaining, brief yet memorable. In order to create reader-friendly magazines, we request that all features include a 200 to 300 word service sidebar listing contact information for major places or attractions listed in the article. Specialty columns span trivia, self-improvement, poignant success stories, and whimsical compositions.
Queries should be directed to   Lisa Polacheck, Editorial/Magazine Coordinator
Length of articles   600 to 1,600 words
Payment   In general, compensation for column material (600 to 800 words) is $250. The fee for assigned features of 1,000 to 1,600 words is $350. The rate for solicited photos is $75.
Time of payment   On publication. We also furnish all contributors with one copy of the magazine.
Photographs   Yes. Photography and art in the form of color slides may be accepted, although we can't guarantee the return of unsolicited materials.
Response time to queries   Unfortunately, it's rather upended, although we do try to respond to SASEs and enclosed postcards within one month.
Rights bought   The fee paid by the publisher to the writer purchases the rights to publish the article one time in any or all SCG magazines.
Kill fees   We make assignments carefully and therefore do not have a kill fee structure. If a story cannot run due to unforeseen circumstances, a kill fee may be offered on a case-by-case basis.
Sample issues   Complimentary if you fly Western Pacific, Reno Air, KIWI, or Air South. Otherwise, send an SASE with $3 postage your specific request to Stateswest Communications Group, Inc.

TIPS FOR WRITERS

See entry under *Excursions*.

SAWASDEE

23/F Right Emperor Commercial Building, 122-126,
Wellington Street, Central, HONG KONG,
Hong Kong S

Phone number   852-2545-1618
Fax number   852-2805-1809
Parent company   Travel & Trade Publishing (Asia), Limited
Circulation   105,000
Magazine availability   Subscription
Target audience   Business and leisure travelers on Thai Airways International

Magazine's history and mission   Founded in 1972 by present publishers
Nonfiction   100%
Percent of articles freelance-written   85%
Number of articles bought annually   72
Sections of the magazine open to freelance writers   Features
Article interests and needs   Strong angles, unusual destinations close or within easy access of route net
Queries should be directed to   David Keen, Editor
Length of articles   Less than 1,800 words
Payment   US $.30 per word
Time of payment   On publication
Expenses   Negotiable
Photographs   Yes
Response time to queries   One month
Rights bought   No
Kill fees   No
Writer's guidelines   Yes

TIPS FOR WRITERS

Anyone submitting a query should try and familiarize themselves with *Sawasdee* before approaching the editor with story ideas. Queries should be focused angles on any Thai destination. They can involve everyday life or concentrate on an unusual angle. The more detailed the query the better: freelancers are well advised to suggest the story structure as well as the idea. Pictures are crucial. Photographers should submit pix in 35 mm format or larger or color copies or prints of trannies. We never use dupes and never use prints from negative film.

   Presentation of written work and images is very important: the better a piece looks, the more chance it has of selling.

SKY

1301 Carolina Street
Greensboro, NC 27401

Phone number   910-378-6065
Fax number   910-274-2220
E-mail address   skymag@aol.com
Parent company   Pace Communications, Inc.
Circulation   2 million readers
Target audience   Delta Air Lines passengers
Nonfiction   100%
Percent of articles freelance-written   70%
Article interests and needs   Business, sports, technology, travel, and humor

Queries should be directed to   Mickey McLean, Managing Editor
Length of articles   1,200 words
Payment $.50 to $1.00 per word depending on type of article

IMPORTANT QUESTIONS ANSWERED

Q: Will you look at completed manuscripts?
A: We prefer queries, not manuscripts.
Q: Do you wants clips?
A: New writers should send three to five clips.
Q: Are phone calls from writers OK?
A: No phone calls.
Q: Is it OK if writers fax or e-mail queries to you?
A: Faxes and e-mail are OK.

SKYVIEW

SCG, Inc.
5110 North 44th Street, Suite 210-L
Phoenix, AZ 85018

Fax number   602-952-1170 (Writers can fax their requests for current airline destinations and pay rates to Lisa Polacheck, Editorial/Magazine Coordinator.)
Parent company   Stateswest Communications Group, Inc.
Magazine availability   Complimentary magazine available to passengers of Western Pacific Airlines, whose home base is Colorado Springs. Destinations include the West Coast, Midwest, and some Texas cities.
Target audience   Our demographics are fairly inclusive—anyone who flies for business, vacations, and visiting is a potential reader—so topics and writing style should reflect that variety.
Nonfiction   100%
Percent of articles freelance-written   Approximately 75%
Article interests and needs   We seek destination-related features and relevant, vibrant photos. We prefer, of course, articles that are tight yet thorough, informative yet entertaining, brief yet memorable. In order to create reader-friendly magazines, we request that all features include a 200 to 300 word service sidebar listing contact information for major places or attractions listed in the article. Specialty columns span finances, cars, dining, and accommodations.
Queries should be directed to   Lisa Polacheck, Editorial/Magazine Coordinator
Length of articles   600 to 1,600 words
Payment   In general, compensation for column material (600 to 800 words) is $250. The fee for assigned features of 1,000 to 1,600 words is $350. The rate for solicited photos is $75.

Time of payment   On publication. We [also] furnish all contributors with one copy of the magazine.

Photographs   Yes. Photography and art in the form of color slides may be accepted, although we can't guarantee the return of unsolicited materials.

Response time to queries   Unfortunately, it's rather upended, although we do try to respond to SASEs and enclosed postcards within one month.

Rights bought   The fee paid by the publisher to the writer purchases the rights to publish the article one time in any or all SCG magazines.

Kill fees   We make assignments carefully and therefore do not have a kill fee structure. If a story cannot run due to unforeseen circumstances, a kill fee may be offered on a case-by-case basis.

Sample issues   Complimentary if you fly Western Pacific, Reno Air, KIWI, or Air South. Otherwise, send an addressed envelope with $3 postage and your specific request to Stateswest Communications Group, Inc.

TIPS FOR WRITERS

See entry under *America's Civil War.*

SWISSAIR GAZETTE

Frontpage AG
8045 Zurich
Switzerland

Phone number   411 201 78 29
Fax number   411 281 20 18
Parent company   Swissair
Circulation   200,000
Magazine availability   Aboard Swissair flights
Target audience   The *Swissair Gazette* is targeted to an international readership. (Articles appear in English, French, German, and Italian.) Business travelers are our first focus; leisure travelers are next; 60% are male; 40% female; 33% are ages 45 to 54; 31% are 35 to 44; 20% are 34 and younger; and 16% are 55 and older.
Nonfiction   80%
Fiction   20%
Percent of articles freelance-written   90%
Number of articles bought annually   70
Sections of the magazine open to freelance writers   All sections are open to freelance writers. But please note that we only take articles that we have requested and are based on the concept we are working on.
Article interests and needs   Travel (especially travel tips regarding a particular region), aviation, science, etc.

Queries should be directed to Viviane Egli, Editor-in-Chief
Length of articles 1,000 to 9,000 characters (roughly 150 to 1,300 words) depending on the editorial concept
Payment $200 to $1,500, depending on the concept
Time of payment On acceptance
Expenses Expenses are sometimes included.
Photographs High-quality photographs are always needed, as they relate to the editorial concept.
Response time to queries If a writer sends a query, we generally respond within a week. But please, please note carefully: We do not accept unsolicited manuscripts. We only request and accept material that we have ordered. Therefore, there is no point in an author sending us a query. We will accept a resume and clips. We don't generally respond to the writer regarding his work unless we find him suitable for our publication.
Rights The writer/photographer has the rights four months after the piece is published.
Kill fees As I said before, we do not accept unsolicited material. Therefore, we do not pay any type of fee for unsolicited material. If we have asked a writer to prepare something for us and have accepted the finished piece, then we will pay the full fee as agreed upon, even if in the end we do not publish the piece.
Sample issues If requested, we will send samples of the magazine.

Tips for Writers

A writer with a personal, charismatic point of view always sparks my interest. Of course, experience is a plus. If this person can think clearly and speak well, and is understandable on the phone or in correspondence, then that is a sign that readers will equally understand his article. I also look for someone who is a careful researcher and relates well to the concept. I am especially pleased when the writer feels the concept as I feel it: both the hard, factual side and the emotional side. I feel the briefing phase is very important. I like a journalist who is not complicated, but who asks good questions and shares his feelings about the topic. Above all, I like a person who is punctual and who stays in touch with us throughout the writing process.

The worst things a writer can do are to write more than we ask for, turn his story in late, fail to follow the concept guidelines, or fail to provide us with thorough or correct information.

Before contracting with a new writer, I always want to see samples of his previous work, whether it is published or unpublished/unfinished material. When I look at the clips, I look for a unique style, professionalism, a command of the language, and a charisma in the text. I prefer that a writer contact me by fax or through the mail.

The *Swissair Gazette* revolves around a different theme each month, a theme which is chosen up to a year in advance. Therefore, we do not accept unsolicited material. If a writer would like, we can send him a list of the themes we are working on and he can suggest ideas for stories. Otherwise, I suggest that the writer sends us his clips, a resume, and a detailed list of topics he can write about. That way, we will know what this writer can do, should related topics arise.

Literary

CENTURY

P.O. Box 150510
Brooklyn, NY 11215-0510

E-mail address   robkill@aol.com or rkjk@newscorp.com
Circulation   4,000 to 5,000 readers
Online status   Web site at http://www.supranet.com/century/
Magazine availability   Newsstands and subscription
Target audience   Avid readers of literary fiction and/or science fiction, fantasy, magic realism, etc.
Magazine's history and mission   Founded in 1995. We aim to blend the conceptual kick of science fiction and fantasy with the high literary standards of "mainstream" fiction.
Fiction   100%
Percent of articles freelance-written   100%
Number of articles bought annually   50
Sections of the magazine open to freelance writers   All
Article interests and needs   Just good fiction
Queries should be directed to   Robert K. J. Killheffer, Editor
Length of articles   1,000 to 10,000 words
Payment $.04 to $.06 per word
Time of payment   On acceptance
Response time   2 to 3 months for complete manuscripts
Rights bought   First world English language and nonexclusive anthology rights
Writer's guidelines   Send SASE
Sample issues $5.95 US; $6.95 Canada and overseas

TIPS FOR WRITERS
Robert K. J. Killheffer, Editor

Because *Century* publishes only fiction, I don't like to see queries at all. In my opinion, fiction can only be judged by looking at the full manuscript, so any writer who's interested in publishing in *Century* should submit the complete story. I do like cover letters; though I don't think they're absolutely necessary, they do make a submission look more thoughtful and professional, and that always counts for something, at least in the initial impression. (Nevertheless, I have bought stories that come without cover letters.) There's no need to get verbose in a cover letter—a simple "Hi. Here's my story, hope you like it, look forward to hearing from you," is fine. Include information about previous credits if you have them, and please concentrate on the *relevant* credits; that is, for my purposes, nonfiction publications (editorials in newspapers, magazine articles, etc.) don't mean much—there are plenty of people who can write nonfiction well who can't produce publishable fiction. Just as in a resume you'd highlight previous experience that bears specifically on the job you're applying for, your cover letter should emphasize the credits that might say something about your ability to write fiction.

An SASE is always necessary if the writer wants their manuscript returned, and I prefer an SASE in any case, for the ease of my response. (When you've got hundreds of manuscripts every month, typing up envelopes and adding stamps can turn out to be an awful lot of time and money.) Recently the one exception I've recognized is when the writer does not want their manuscript returned and requests a reply via e-mail; in that case, no SASE is necessary, but be sure you include your e-mail address prominently on both your cover letter and your manuscript. In general I discourage phone calls from writers, since at *Century* we have no offices, operating the magazine out of our homes; and even when I have worked at magazines with offices, I've preferred a query letter or e-mail to phone calls. Often an editor has deadlines and other pressing matters to attend to, and can't take the time to deal with inquiries exactly when they come in, so letters or e-mail provide the leeway for the editor to find the time when he or she can. Of the two, e-mail is probably the best for both writer and editor; it's almost as fast as a phone call, and it costs less than a first-class stamp.

In the end, though, there's no "key" to breaking into *Century* except writing a really fine story. And that means understanding what we mean when we talk about quality— it's not a question of how revolutionary the concept behind the story may be, nor how great a TV movie it might make, but the degree to which it inspires or evokes emotion and thought in the reader; a *Century* story should stimulate, excite, enliven, engage—it should have more going on in it than just what you've put on a page. In our view, reading is not a passive entertainment, it's a collaborative experience—so *Century* stories should not be shallow adventures which vanish from the mind as soon as they're read, but stories that somehow reflect on or refer to authentic human experience and resonate with the reader's own. That's the way in to our magazine.

The worst thing I see in writers these days is an unwillingness to revise, either before submitting a story, or, particularly, in response to my comments. I often find stories that seem almost right, and I invite writers to submit rewrites; frequently the process results in a sale with which both I and the writer are pleased (and with which our readers are as well). Revision I think is nearly essential; there are very, very few writers whose first drafts need little or no work, and the ability to recognize the failings of the first draft and correct them are vital skills for any writer, of fiction or nonfiction. And that's advice I'd give to any writer hoping to break in to a magazine market—before you submit a piece, read it over critically and see if you can't improve it somehow, and always be willing to make revisions for an editor who shows interest. This doesn't mean you should let an editor change the basic meaning or purpose of a story—you can politely decline to take their advice—but you should always consider an editor's comments very seriously, since they're not only a sample reader, but a very experienced reader, too, in most cases. Stick to your guns if you think you're right about how to handle something in a story, but don't reject constructive criticism out of hand.

Beyond that, all I would say to hopeful writers is don't give up. It's something of a cliché to point out how many world-famous writers (including Stephen King) spent years collecting rejections before finally breaking in, but being a cliché doesn't mean it's not true. In the final analysis, the quality of your story is a subjective thing, and just because one editor doesn't see it, doesn't mean the next one won't. The only way in is to keep plugging away.

THE PARIS REVIEW

541 East 72nd Street
New York, NY 10021

Phone number   212-861-0016
Fax number   212-861-4504
Circulation   20,000
Online status   Web page
Magazine availability   Newsstands and subscription
Target audience   People who read
Magazine's history and mission   Founded in 1953 by Peter Mathiesson, Harold Humes, and George Plimpton, *TPR* exists to publish the best fiction, poetry, and essays.
Nonfiction   25%
Fiction   40%
Payment   Varies
Time of payment   On publication
Writer's guidelines   With SASE
Sample issues $10 each

Maturity/Retirement

MODERN MATURITY

3200 East Carson Street
Lakewood, CA 90712

Phone number   310-496-2277
Fax number   310-496-4124
Parent company   American Association of Retired Persons
Circulation   22 million
Magazine availability   To members of AARP
Target audience   People aged 50+
Magazine's history   Started in 1958 by AARP.
Nonfiction   Currently 100%
Fiction   Very infrequent

Percent of articles freelance-written Majority
Sections of the magazine open to freelance writers All
Article interests and needs National general interest magazine for people aged 50+. Health, money, consumer, travel, food, news.
Queries should be directed to J. Henry Fenwick, Editor
Length of articles 150 to 4,000 words
Payment $1.00 per word
Time of payment On acceptance
Expenses Yes
Photographs Yes
Response time to queries 6 to 8 weeks
Rights bought First North American
Kill fees 25%
Writer's guidelines Yes
Sample issues Yes

TIPS FOR WRITERS

Know the magazine before you query. Keep query to one page. Include clips. Don't call.

SENIOR GOLFER MAGAZINE

55 Corporate Drive
Trumbull, CT 06611

Phone number 203-459-5190
Parent company Weider Publications, Inc.
Circulation 175,000
Online status Linked with 1-Golf on America Online
Magazine availability Newsstands and subscription
Target audience Generally trying to reach an upscale, professional market with the time, desire, and resources to enjoy golf and golf travel.
Magazine's history and mission It was started independently in 1992 and was bought by Weider Publishing in the summer of 1995.
Nonfiction 85%
Fiction 15%
Percent of articles freelance-written It varies, but generally about 50%
Sections of the magazine open to freelance writers All
Article interests and needs Golf instruction, golf travel, history of the game, features on professional and top amateur players, as well as equipment stories
Queries should be directed to Larry Dennis, Editor-in-Chief; David Chmiel, Executive Editor
Length of articles Varies
Payment Varies

Time of payment Varies
Expenses Generally
Photographs We assign photos—unless freelancer is a professional
Response time to queries Within a month
Rights bought Negotiated
Kill fees Negotiated
Sample issues Upon request

SENIOR HIGHLIGHTS

26081 Merit Circle, Suite 101
Laguna Hills, CA 92653

Phone number 714-367-0776
Fax number 714-367-1006
Parent company Senior Highlights, Inc.
Circulation 440,000
Magazine availability Newsstands and subscription
Target audience Age 50+; males and females; retired or planning on retirement or in second careers; Southern and Central California
Magazine's history and mission Founded by Lee S. McCannon, publisher, in 1984. Publishes lifestyles, money, and travel articles that directly pertain to target audience to inform as well as entertain.
Nonfiction 100%
Percent of articles freelance-written 30%
Number of articles bought annually Approximately 60 manuscripts a year—however, most for byline only. No compensation for unsolicited articles.
Sections of the magazine open to freelance writers All
Article interests and needs Upbeat and positive health stories; personal profiles of outstanding seniors
Queries should be directed to Editorial Department
Length of articles 800 words max.
Payment Varies (small amount—$25 to $50); however, no payment for most, especially for unsolicited articles
Time of payment On publication
Expenses No expenses paid
Photographs Welcomed; no payment—color slides/transparencies for cover—black and white prints for inside
Response time to queries Approximately 3 months
Rights bought First, second (reprint), and simultaneous rights
Kill fees N/A
Writer's guidelines Available with SASE (#10 envelope)
Sample issues $3 with 9 × 12 SASE ($1.25 postage)

IMPORTANT QUESTIONS ANSWERED

Q: What is the key element of a good query?
A: It coincides with our editorial calendar.
Q: What do you look for in a writer's clips?
A: Excellent, concise writing.
Q: Will you look at completed manuscripts?
A: Yes
Q: Is an SASE always necessary?
A: Yes
Q: Are phone calls from writers OK?
A: No
Q: Is it OK if writers fax queries to you?
A: Yes
Q: What is the best way to break in to your magazine?
A: Specialize; good writing.

SENIOR MAGAZINE

(Central Coast Edition)
3565 South Higuera
San Luis Obispo, CA 93401

Phone number   805-544-8711
Fax number   Prefer mail.
Parent company   California Senior Magazine, Inc.
Circulation   40,000
Target audience   Males and females age 45+, living between Paso Robles, California, and Santa Barbara, California.
Magazine's history and mission   Magazine has been published since June of 1981 as an information and entertainment source for those age 45 and over.
Nonfiction   90%
Fiction   10%
Percent of articles freelance-written   90%
Number of articles bought annually   300
Sections of the magazine open to freelance writers   All
Article interests and needs   Personality profiles, destination, history, movies, TV, books, and music
Queries should be directed to   Gary Suggs, Editor and Publisher
Length of articles   1,000+ words
Payment $1.50 per inch
Time of payment   On publication
Expenses   No

Photographs $25, black-and-white
Response time to queries   30 to 60 days
Rights bought   First
Kill fees   None
Writer's guidelines   Yes
Sample issues   Only with SASE

IMPORTANT QUESTION ANSWERED

Q: What is the best way to break into your magazine?
A: Write something entertaining or illuminating, but necessary!

SUCCESSFUL RETIREMENT

950 Third Avenue, 16th floor
New York, NY 10019

Parent company   Grass Roots Publishing
Circulation   100,000
Magazine availability   Subscription only
Target audience   Retirees or those preparing to retire, ages 60 to 80
Magazine's history and mission   Launched in 1992. The mission is to provide pertinent information regarding retirement. Upbeat, motivational.
Nonfiction   95%
Fiction   5%
Percent of articles freelance-written   75 to 90%
Number of articles bought annually   30 to 40
Sections of the magazine open to freelance writers   All *except* regular columns such as Money, Healthful Hints, etc.
Article interests and needs   Articles on relationships, retirement locales, finances, health, and fitness
Queries should be directed to   Marcia Vickers, Editor
Length of articles   Approximately 1,000 words
Payment $150 to $250
Time of payment   On publication
Expenses   No
Photographs   Purchase *only* occasionally—very low payment
Response time to queries   6 months
Rights bought   We buy all rights.
Kill fees   None
Writer's guidelines   Send SASE.
Sample issues   Send $3.95 plus postage.

TIPS FOR WRITERS
Marcia Vickers, Editor

What sparks my interest: I like queries that are fairly short and to the point. I want to be able to ascertain immediately by skimming a query letter what the topic is, the angle, and the approach the writer wants to take. If I get bogged down in an explanation, I get bored.

Most of the time I can tell when queries are written by writers who have never seen a copy of the magazine. They will write first-person, essay-type pieces that don't fit. We are a service-oriented publication and "What I Did on My Summer Vacation," or "My First Year of Retirement" pieces just don't cut it for us. Also, don't bore me with a page full of credentials. I just don't care. The only thing that interests me is if you've got a good idea and can write fairly well.

A good query is written by a writer who has seen the publication and has thought up a unique angle on a subject such as "Tips on Selling Your Home in Less Than Two Weeks," or "Twelve Steps for Incorporating Humor into Your Life," or "Downhill Ski Trips for Folks Over Sixty."

I like to see clips, but the most important element is the query itself. I have used several writers who've had good ideas but limited clips. Sometimes they work out, sometimes they don't. The number of clips isn't important—send me one or two good ones. In fact, it's annoying when a writer sends more than four clips. If you can write, you can show me in one or two.

Completed manuscripts are acceptable for me in a few areas: humor, travel (sometimes), and retirement locales (sometimes). Really, I'd say the only time a manuscript is *required* is for a humor piece when I really need to see the writer's style, theme, etc. I dislike receiving (yellowed, dog-eared) manuscripts that have (obviously) been sent to a plethora of editors. I generally reject them immediately.

Professional etiquette: An SASE is necessary. I prefer it. But if you've written for me several times, I don't care as much. Why? At that stage it's fairly obvious that I like the writer's work and will often file the query away for possible assignment in a future issue.

Do not call me. Riding the trend, I happen to be an independent contractor for *Successful Retirement* and am seldom at my publisher's office. And, unless I've established a relationship with a writer, I will not accept phone calls at home. If a writer's idea is good and right for the magazine, I will be getting back to the writer in time. If not, I generally send out a rejection letter immediately.

The best way to break in: The best way to break in is to send me a query letter on a fabulous, targeted idea that is right for our magazine. I get so few of these (and I receive thousands of queries a year) that I'll be sure to notice and will most definitely use the writer. (A caveat: sometimes ideas are fabulous, but we've run the same or similar article in the last year of so. I try to indicate that on the rejection letter if that's the case.)

Also, writing for our short sections is a good way to break in. We have a few, including The Retirement Life in which we profile retirees who are doing interesting things (300 words). In All Together Now we profile groups of retirees (500 words)—such as a senior big band, tap dancers, lawn bowlers, etc.

The best things writers do: I love it, again, when a writer sends me a short, succinct, pithy query letter with a targeted idea that I can use. Also, a writer's phone number and address should be on both the query letter and (if applicable) the manuscript. If a writer has read the magazine and thinks his idea will fit and tells me why, that's great. Also, we don't pay much for photographs. In fact, we try to obtain them gratis from travel bureaus, etc. Telling me you have a photographic source lined up saves me a lot of headaches. Also, we do everything on computer, so if a writer lets me know that they're computer literate and tells me what system they use that's great.

If a writer is considered a true professional, my opinion is that he or she will have entered the computer age. I get annoyed with writers who say they "just don't understand" computers. Grow up and join the real world. Word processing is simple, fast, and neat. And again, because we do everything on desktop, if I can get a diskette from a writer it makes my job a lot easier.

The worst things writers do: Oh boy, could I have a field day with this one! There are so many "worsts." I'll list some:

Forgetting or purposely not putting a phone number on a query. (You'd be surprised, I can't tell you the number of times I've had to call information in Bismark or Baton Rouge trying to track down a writer!) If a writer does this on purpose (i.e., he or she only wants to do business by mail), unless he or she is Hemingway, forget it. I don't have the time to do business this way. Wake up and join the twentieth century!

Sending original clips (not photocopies) and expecting me to return them (I usually try, but sometimes there's no SASE, etc.).

Ideas that are so generalized that an epic on the topic wouldn't suffice. Examples: "What to Experience in Retirement" or "Aging Doesn't Have to Be Bad."

Queries that have gone out (and are often still addressed) to other publications. (If a writer's sending out multiple submissions, he should be careful to get the editor's name and publication's name correct. This mistake, which I see as sloppiness and unprofessionalism, happens all the time.)

Essay-type, first person pieces that are not right for us. (You can often tell someone has been in a "writing class" and is sending us their homework.)

Those small SASE envelopes in which nothing fits. I have to send out standard, business (8.5×11) letters . . . writers, be professional and use business-size envelopes and stationery for all your freelance correspondence!

Writers who send me a thick manuscript, query, and clips and then expect me to mail everything back in a regular-size envelope with a 32-cent stamp. I've actually received nasty letters from writers who claimed that I kept their manuscripts for some devious purpose . . . such as publishing it unbeknownst to them. Give me a break! My slogan: "If it doesn't fit, in the trash can it sits."

Writers who send me their church newsletter or company brochure as examples of their writing. (This says—no, shouts—"amateur.")

Overall advice to writers who want to be published: Go out and purchase one of those "How to write query letter books." Look at samples of well-written queries and emulate their style and succinctness. Always try to get a copy (or back copies) of the magazine for which you wish to write. Study it. Act like a marketing professional (which as a freelancer, you better think like one or you'll be out of work) and propose article ideas that are somewhat unique, have a fresh angle, and are targeted to that particular publication. Send only your best one or two clips to editors.

Finally, and here's the best advice you'll ever get: Be tenacious. I can't tell you how many rejection letters I received when I first started freelancing myself. But it didn't bother me. In fact, I saved them all in a file which I still have. When I do get plum assignments these days, I glance at that thick file and experience the warm glow of contentment, knowing that I worked hard to get where I am (oh, this sounds so sappy and self-aggrandizing, but it's true).

But a caveat, unless you're doing all the right things that I've mentioned previously, simply being tenacious won't get you very far. Tenacity comes after you've gotten the tedious, professional stuff out of the way. Otherwise, you'll simply be beating your head against a wall (fingers against a keyboard . . . ?). Finally, a certain amount of luck never hurts, so good luck!

Men's Magazines

MEN'S JOURNAL
1290 Avenue of the Americas
New York, NY 10025

Phone number   212-484-1690
Fax number   212-487-6284
E-mail address   JRasmus@aol.com
Parent company   Wenner Media
Circulation   340,000
Magazine availability   Newsstands and subscription
Target audience   Middle-class men, ages 29 to 52, interested in travel, with a disposable income
Magazine's history and mission   Founded by Rolling Stone's Jann Wenner in 1992. To provide adventure and excitement and practical information for our readers.
Nonfiction   100%
Percent of articles freelance-written   50%
Sections of the magazine open to freelance writers   Notebook, Health & Fitness, Sex, Equipment
Article interests and needs   Travel, adventure, fitness, unusual destinations
Queries should be directed to   Features: Bill Beuttler; Health, Fitness: Wayne Kalyn; Sex: Jon Gluck; Equipment: Jim Kaminsky. Please send a Mac disc if submitting a manuscript and include 2 clips.

Length of articles Notebook: 900 to 12,000 words; Equipment: 1,000 to 1,500 words; Features: 4,000 to 6,000 words; Health & Fitness: 1,200 to 2,000 words
Payment $1.00 to $1.50 per word
Time of payment On acceptance
Expenses Varies, depending on the story length
Photographs No. We use our own.
Response time to queries 4 to 6 weeks
Rights bought First serial
Kill fees 25%

TIPS FOR WRITERS
Nora Isaacs

A good query is very concise, and obviously, well-written. I like the ones that start with an anecdote and then tell me how the writer will proceed with the story.

Look at the masthead or call to see to whom you should address your specific query. I can't tell you how many queries we get that are addressed to editors who do not work here anymore. Others are blatantly misspelled. We figure if you are too lazy to read the masthead or to pick up the phone, we definitely don't want you writing a story for us.

I suggest including two clips with a query. Ideally, the clips should be written in the same writing style as the proposed story. (If you're querying us with a serious piece on scuba-diving injuries, don't send us a humor column.) Don't send original materials. Make copies. Originals inevitably get lost, leading to bad feelings between the magazine and the writer.

An SASE is not necessary, but appreciated. I recommend calling to follow up after sending a query. If you don't, you run the risk of the query ending up on the bottom of the pile. If you do, most likely the query will see the light of day. Our fax room is a mess. If you send a fax, call afterwards to make sure that it is retrieved.

The best way to break into the magazine is starting out with a query for a small Notebook piece, which appears at the front of the book. Once a relationship is established, it is much easier to query larger stories. I can't remember any instances when a brand new writer was assigned a feature story.

It sounds obvious, but read the magazine! The worst thing writers do is send query letters with the name of the wrong magazine filled in where our name should be. The best thing writers do is establish a relationship with somebody, over the phone or in person, at the magazine.

PENTHOUSE

277 Park Avenue
New York, NY 10172

Phone number 212-702-6000
Fax number No queries by fax or e-mail

Parent company   General Media, Inc.
Circulation   1.1 million
Online status   Penthouse Web site at http://www.penthouse mag.com
Magazine availability   Newsstands and subscription
Target audience   Men 18 to 50, all U.S.
Magazine's history and mission   Founded in 1969 in U.S. by Bob Guccione. Features the best in men's entertainment and information.
Nonfiction   Approximately 90%
Fiction   10%
Percent of articles freelance-written   80%
Number of articles bought annually   Approximately 150
Sections of the magazine open to freelance writers   Articles and essays
Article interests and needs   Exclusive exposés and profiles
Queries should be directed to   Peter Bloch, Editor
Length of articles   1,000 to 5,000 words
Payment   We pay $3,000 and up for a major feature, depending on the amount of time needed, the subject, and the writer.
Time of payment   On acceptance
Expenses   Included in fee.
Photographs   No
Response time to queries   3 weeks
Rights bought   All
Kill fees   25%
Writer's guidelines   With self-addressed, stamped envelope
Sample issues   No

Tips for Writers

The following questions to and answers from Peter Bloch, Editor of Penthouse, are quoted from Magazine Editors Talk to Writers *by Judy Mandell, John Wiley & Sons, Publishers.*

Q: How can a first-time writer get published in Penthouse? *What must he or she present to spark your interest in an idea and his or her ability to write the article?*

A: The writer must know what *Penthouse* is. [Writers] have to read the several times to see what we do and don't do. There's no point in suggesting literary essays or poetry or other things that we don't do. Writers must think very far ahead. We have a very long lead time. The writer must offer something special. We can't repeat material that has been in *Time* magazine two or three months before.

Q: What do writers do that annoys you?

A: Phone calls from writers who don't have a good reason or who don't know me. I don't like to be oversold on an idea or an article.

Faxes. Unless it's a cutting-edge story, I hate to have my fax machine tied up by writers I have never heard of sending me endless blabber.

Q: How can writers get published in Penthouse?

A: If you have an entire article, send it in. A lot of writers write great query letters but write poor articles. Send clips that give a sense of what you want to do for *Penthouse,* what you're like as a writer. Always include an SASE.

PENTHOUSE VARIATIONS

277 Park Avenue
New York, NY 10172

Phone number   212-702-6000
Fax number   212-702-6262
E-mail address   VKMcCarty@aol.com
Parent company   General Media, Inc.
Circulation   400,000
Magazine availability   Newsstands and subscription
Target audience   Liberated lovers, couples in America
Magazine's history and mission   Began as a special issue of *Forum* in 1978 and within 10 years grew larger than its parent publication.
Fiction   100%
Percent of articles freelance-written   100%
Number of articles bought annually   50 to 60
Queries should be directed to   *Variations*
Length of articles   3,000 words
Payment   Varies. $400 for lead stories in each category
Time of payment   On acceptance
Expenses   No
Photographs   Not needed
Response time to queries   Often as much as 2 months
Rights bought   Total
Kill Fees   No
Writer's guidelines   Yes
Sample issues   No

TIPS FOR WRITERS
V. K. McCarty, V.P. Associate Publisher, Penthouse Variations

The query: While queries are not necessary, I am willing to read them. I am not interested in clips. I appreciate good professional manuscript style, with double-spacing, one-inch margins, adjacent indented paragraphs, flush left and rag right, with name and address on the first page of copy.

SASE: Necessary only if you want your material back.

Phone calls OK?: Yes, although we may not always be able to give the information desired.

Fax or e-mail OK?: Yes, although I like to think that the writer cares enough about the material to want to control the type of paper and centering and clarity of focus delivered to my desk.

The key to breaking into my book is to study it: We look for a very specific sort of material, and other preexisting erotica seldom falls successfully into our format accidentally. Our stories are squarely focused on experience and techniques and enthusiasm within one of our categories.

The best things writers can do are usually tied into their most intensely experienced observations, carefully and patiently described, using the best possible language skills. The worst things writers do seem often to be connected to an attempt to circumvent that craft of writing.

The competition is high at *Variations*, but I'm proud of any writer who goes the distance to write an acceptably excellent, highly explicit, memorably erotic category-oriented piece for us.

Mystery/Crime/Suspense

NEW MYSTERY

175 Fifth Avenue, Suite 2001
New York, NY 10010

Phone number   212-353-1582
E-mail address   nfwmyst@aol
Parent company   Friends of New Mystery
Circulation   90,000
Online status   Web site at http://mysterynew.com/mystnew
Magazine availability   Newsstands and subscription
Target audience   Ages 18 to 82—Crime fiction stories
Magazine's history and mission   Founded in 1989 by group of celebrity mystery authors
Nonfiction   10%
Fiction   90%
Number of short stories bought annually   40
Sections of the magazine open to freelance writers   All
Article interests and needs   Study an issue
Queries should be directed to   Linda Wong
Length of stories   2,000 to 5,000 words
Payment $50 to $500
Time of payment   On publication

Expenses No
Photographs Yes, $10
Response time to queries If no answer in 60 days, consider rejected
Rights bought All rights
Kill fees No
Writer's guidelines Study an issue
Sample issues Send $5 plus 9 × 12 SASE with $1.24 postage.

IMPORTANT QUESTIONS ANSWERED

Q: Is an SASE always necessary?
A: Yes
Q: Is it OK if writers fax or e-mail queries to you?
A: No
Q: How can writers angle their stories for your magazine?
A: Study an issue.

Parenting

AMERICAN BABY

249 West 17th Street
New York, NY 10011

Phone number 212-463-6543
Fax number 212-463-6410
Circulation 1,500,000 monthly
Online status On Netscape newsstand
Magazine availability Controlled circulation, limited subscriptions
Target audience Expectant and new parents, 18 to 34
Magazine's history and mission Founded in 1938 to give medical and how-to information to expectant and new parents.
Nonfiction 100%
Percent of articles freelance-written 80%
Number of articles bought annually 70 to 75
Sections of the magazine open to freelance writers All
Article interests and needs Service, medical, personal essays
Queries should be directed to Judith Nolte, Editor
Length of articles 1,000 to 2,000 words
Payment $750 to $1,200
Time of payment On acceptance

Expenses   Yes
Photographs   No
Response time to queries   4 to 6 weeks
Rights bought   First time North American serial
Kill fees   25% of article fee
Writer's guidelines   Yes, we send them.
Sample issues   Yes, we send them.

TIPS FOR WRITERS

The query must be short, concise, and show a real knowledge of our magazine. Cite sources to be used and point of view of your article.

Yes, we want clips. One or two relevant ones. We will look at a completed manuscript. An SASE is necessary. We prefer mail, not fax or e-mail.

Break into the magazine by sending us a good idea and by understanding the magazine.

The worst thing to do: call

Overall advice to writers: Read the magazine, understand who and what we are. Write an intelligent, clear query letter.

BABY TALK

301 Howard Street
San Francisco, CA 94105

Phone number   415-546-7575
Fax number   415-546-0578
Parent company   Time, Inc.
Circulation   1.1 million
Online status   Online under *Parenting* magazine's site on AOL
Magazine availability   Subscription and as a giveaway in children's departments of stores
Target audience   New and expectant parents, ages 22 to 34, nationwide
Magazine's history and mission   Founded in 1935 by Blessings Corporation as a giveaway by cotton diaper services.
Nonfiction   100%
Percent of articles freelance-written   30 to 40%
Number of articles bought annually   25 to 40
Sections of the magazine open to freelance writers   Features
Article interests and needs   Baby care, prenatal care
Queries should be directed to   Trisha Thompson, Editor-in-Chief
Length of articles   Features: 1,500 to 2,000 words; Departments: 800 to 1,000 words
Payment   From $75 to $800
Time of payment   On acceptance

Expenses   Paid
Photographs   No
Response time to queries   6 months
Rights bought   First North American serial
Writer's guidelines   Available on request
Sample issues   Available with SASE

BAY AREA PARENT MAGAZINE

401 Alberto Way, Suite A
Los Gatos, CA 95032

Phone number   408-358-1414
Fax number   408-356-4903
Parent company   Bay Area Publishing Group, Inc.
Circulation   77,000
Online status   Our Calendar sections are found on Starware
Magazine availability   Newsstands, subscription, doctor's offices, libraries, retail stores, etc.
Target audience   Parents of children (newborns to early teens)
Magazine's history and mission   Founded in 1983 by publisher Sandy Moeckel as an eight-page publication called *Kids Kids Kids*, it became *Bay Area Parent* in 1987.
Nonfiction   100%
Percent of articles freelance-written   80%
Number of articles bought annually   About 200 (includes those by regular columnists)
Sections of the magazine open to freelance writers   Features
Article interests and needs   Topics of interest to parents
Queries should be directed to   Mary Brence Martin, Managing Editor
Length of articles   1,200 to 2,000 words
Payment $.06 per word
Time of payment   On publication
Expenses   Only on assigned stories
Photographs $10 to $15
Response time to queries   Two months
Rights bought   Onetime
Kill fees   Occasionally on assigned stories
Writer's guidelines   Send SASE
Sample issues   Send $8\frac{1}{2} \times 12$ SASE with six $.32 stamps

TIPS FOR WRITERS
Mary Brence Martin, Managing Editor

What sparks interest in a query? Generally, a well-written letter with a "teaser" from the article will do the trick, especially if the story is on a topic planned for an upcoming issue and if the writer sends a few clips showing writing style and gives his or her qualifications for doing such a story. However, I usually prefer to see a cover letter and a completed manuscript. NOTE: Errors in grammar and spelling pretty much guarantee a "no thanks" reply. We are not able to respond to queries or submissions sent without an SASE.

Because we work with a number of regular columnists and feature writers, there are fewer opportunities to "break into" our publications than there were in the past. We are always on the lookout, though, for interesting, well-written articles on parenting topics, and we still publish a number of unsolicited manuscripts each year.

The information we are most likely to use is local, well-researched, and geared to our readers, who are parents of children ranging in age from newborns to early teens. We do not use poetry or fiction. Timeliness is critical, e.g., swimming in June and snow skiing in winter. We plan editorial content months ahead, so articles pertinent to a particular season should be submitted well in advance. (Halloween articles submitted in September, for example, have little chance of being published.)

In fact, receiving good articles too late to use them is one of my pet peeves. Others are: receiving manuscripts that are not targeted to our readership; receiving manuscripts with grammar errors, spelling errors, and usage errors ("She poured over the book" and ". . . the peeling bell . . ." are two recent examples); getting phone calls from writers about the status of a particular manuscript (though we do appreciate a note if the story has been sold to another publication in our readership area); and finding messages on the answering machine from a writer who has phoned long-distance to inquire about the status of a manuscript submitted without an SASE.

My overall advice to writers who want to get published: study a publication's style, subject matter, story length, etc., and tailor your submissions to the publication's needs. Send submissions along with a few clips and a snappy, error-free cover letter stating your qualifications to write a particular story and how the story would be of value to our readers. Be sure your name, address, *and* telephone number appear on the first page of the manuscript (you'd be surprised at how many writers don't do this). Enclose an SASE—and don't forget the stamp on the return envelope. Above all, don't give up easily. Sometimes an excellent manuscript is rejected only because we've recently published a story on the same topic. Submit that story to other publications, and try us again with another topic.

BIG APPLE PARENTS' PAPER *AND* QUEENS PARENTS' PAPER

36 East 12th Street, 4th floor
New York, NY 10003

Phone number   212-533-2277
Fax number   212-475-6186
Parent company   Family Communications, Inc., N.Y.C.
Circulation   102,000 per month (62,000 Manhattan edition; 40,000 Queens edition)
Online status   Our calendar of events is available online

Magazine availability   By subscription, but mainly through controlled-distribution free sites

Target audience   Our readers are predominantly well-educated, dual-income, professional couples who are also "older" parents—i.e., 35 to 55. They live in high-rise apartments, not suburban homes! Good percentage have kids in private schools.

Magazine's history and mission   Founded in November 1985, by Helen Rosengren Freedman and Rosalie Reiman Luber, following publication of Freedman's Book, *Big Apple Baby: A Resource Guide to New York for New & Expectant Parents*. Aim is to enrich the lives of NYC families with news, information, and resources.

Nonfiction   100%

Percent of articles freelance-written   95%

Number of articles bought annually   Approximately 450

Sections of the magazine open to freelance writers   All

Article interests and needs   We buy humor and essays, but these are also what we mostly receive over-the-transom. Try us—but we *need* pieces that have a newsy angle. Must be targeted to parents.

Queries should be directed to   Helen Rosengren Freedman, Managing Editor

Length of articles   1,500 maximum; average 700 to 800

Payment $35 to $50

Time of payment   On publication

Expenses   Only if agreed upon in advance

Photographs $10 per

Response time to queries   Immediate (with the exception of the summer months)

Rights bought   First NYC area

Kill fees   50% on assigned pieces

Writer's guidelines   Available (free) on request

Sample issues   Available (free) on request

TIPS FOR WRITERS
Helen Rosengren Freedman, Managing Editor

The good news: We buy *lots* of material and we treat our writers well! I've been a freelancer, so I know what it's like to wait for a reply (which often never comes) and to be driven crazy doing rewrites. We read everything carefully. We will get back to you immediately (with the exception of the summer months, mid-June to mid-September—don't send us anything then!); when we reject a piece, we'll tell you why; and when we buy a piece, that's it—no more work required. We will also send you a copy when an article appears.

The not-so-good news: We pay only $35 to $50 per article, on publication.

However, we have published many writers for the first time; and we might well be a market for a piece that you've already written (or had published elsewhere). All it takes is postage to find out! And it may give you a credit in a New York City–based publication.

What we're looking for: No poetry, fiction, or reviews. We buy humor and essays, but this is what we mostly receive over-the-transom. We are really looking for the news angle. And we like controversy! As much as possible, we need a NYC (or big-city)

angle. Our readers are city-dwellers—a lot of pieces we receive don't work because they "feel" too suburban. Celebrities are great. No obvious how-tos like: "Traveling with Your Kids"; "How to Survive the Parent-Teacher Conference"; "How to Get Baby to Sleep through the Night"; "Birthday Parties Your Kids Will Love." We've done them all. Give us an important topic and tell us what's new.

Submissions: We will always reply. If you include enough postage, we'll also return your manuscript. An SASE is courteous and appreciated.

Clips are not required; neither are complicated query letters. I don't care where you've been published before, or if you haven't. The idea, or the article, either works for us or it doesn't. Just send us the piece; or else pitch the idea—although if we don't know you, we'll have to ask you to work on spec.

Please don't call. I can't spend time on the phone. Please mail or fax—I read at home anyway, where it's quieter!

CHRISTIAN PARENTING TODAY

4050 Lee Vance View
Colorado Springs, CO 80918

Phone number   719-531-7776
Fax number   719-535-0172. Faxed queries are acceptable: however, we will not respond to queries unaccompanied by an SASE if we're not interested.
Parent company   Cook Communications Ministries, International
Circulation   225,000
Online status   Still in beginning stages
Magazine availability   Newsstands and subscription, but primarily subscription
Target audience   *CPT*'s readers, according to their writer's guidelines, are parents in traditional families, single parents, or parents in blended families who ". . . care deeply about time-tested, oral and spiritual values. They want creative, contemporary, problem-solving advice and encouragement from experts who share their Christian perspective." Ninety percent are female, 92% are married, 66% are employed, the median age is 35, 86% have attended college or graduate school. They have an average of 2 children.
Magazine's history and mission   *Christian Parenting Today* was launched in 1988 by William and Nancie Carmichael. The mission, according to the guidelines, is to ". . . bring a Christian perspective to important family issues. Our ultimate goal: to affirm parents with a biblically based, inspirational, informative, and authoritative magazine that guides them through all stages of their children's lives."
Nonfiction   100%
Percent of articles freelance-written   95%
Number of articles bought annually   10 to 20
Article interests and needs   We're especially in need of articles relating to single parents and the spiritual development of children.
Queries should be directed to   Erin Healy, Associate Editor
Length of articles   1,000 to 2,000 words

Payment   Flat rates for departments; $.15 to $.25 per published word for other articles
Time of payment   Usually on acceptance for assignments; on publication accepted unsolicited manuscripts and for departments.
Expenses   With prior approval from editor only
Photographs   Please do not send
Response time to queries   6 to 8 weeks
Rights bought   First North American serial, some reprint
Kill fees   25% of contracted amount
Writer's guidelines   Send business-size SASE.
Sample issues   Send 9 × 12 SASE bearing $3 postage.

TIPS FOR WRITERS
Erin Healy, Associate Editor

The most effective queries contain more than an excerpt from the introduction of the article. A clear statement of purpose and a detailed outline are essential. The outline minimizes misunderstandings and also gives me the opportunity to redirect a writer if I think she's close but not close enough to what we're looking for. I also appreciate it when authors itemize their qualifications for writing the article. Clips are OK but not essential.

Please do not call me to discuss a query. I tell every writer the same thing. Put it on paper and I'll get back to you. I welcome calls from writers working on assignment.

We do accept unsolicited manuscripts but prefer queries.

We do expect our writers to include SASEs in every case except when working on assignment, and I make every effort to respond in a timely manner. But if eight weeks pass and an author hasn't received a response, I encourage writers to drop me an inquiry and/or resubmit. Please be tactful when sending an inquiry. We editors are busy and imperfect people, but we do try to treat our writers respectfully. I've rejected more than one manuscript after having received an arrogant or demanding follow-up letter.

The best thing a writer can do for our magazine is to write an article that both affirms and helps parents from a positive Christian perspective. Please study our guidelines, especially the section "Do you have what we're looking for?" Articles that condescend, sermonize, or bemoan the state of today's "society" won't get far with us.

We are a Christian magazine, but some writers try too hard to force the Christian perspective when it's not necessarily appropriate to the topic (e.g., saving money for your child's education, cures for the common cold, health and fitness topics). Don't quote Scripture for the sake of it; make sure the Christian perspective is integrated, not just tacked on.

FAMILY LIFE
1633 Broadway
New York, NY 10019

Phone number   212-767-4918
Fax number   212-489-4561
E-mail address   Familylife@aol.com
Parent company   Hachette Filipacchi Magazines
Circulation   400,000
Online status   AOL as of November 30, 1995
Magazine availability   Newsstands and subscription
Target audience   Parents of above-average income with children ages 3 to 12
Magazine's history and mission   Founded in 1993 by Jann Wenner. Bought by Hachette Filipacchi Magazines in 1995
Nonfiction   100%
Fiction   An occasional short story
Percent of articles freelance-written   90%
Number of articles bought annually   120—includes FOB (front of book) and BOB (back of book)
Sections of the magazine open to freelance writers   All with exception of Editor's Letter
Article interests and needs   Computers, software, education, finance, projects
Queries should be directed to   Peter Herbst, Editor-in-Chief (no faxes or phone calls)
Length of articles   FOB: 750 to 2,000 words; Feature: 1,500 to 3,500 words
Payment   Varies with writer's experience and length of article. Generally $1.00 per word
Time of payment   On acceptance
Expenses   To be discussed before assignment
Photographs   To be discussed before assignment
Response time to queries   2 to 6 weeks
Rights bought   To be discussed before assignment
Kill fees   Yes
Writer's guidelines   By sending an SASE
Sample issues   No

LIVING WITH TEENAGERS

127 Ninth Avenue North
Nashville, TN 37234-0140

Phone number   615-251-2229
Fax number   615-251-5008
Parent company   Baptist Sunday School Board
Circulation   42,000
Magazine availability   Subscription
Target audience   Any parent of a teenager

Magazine's history and mission Founded 1978. *LWT* is a Christian monthly magazine for parents of teenagers. It focuses on the practical aspect of parenting, informing, educating, and inspiring parents to be aware of issues and understand teenagers as they grow into responsible adults.

Nonfiction 90 to 95%

Fiction 5 to 10%

Percent of articles freelance-written 50%

Number of articles bought annually 1 to 200

Article interests and needs Holiday material

Queries should be directed to Editor

Length of articles 500 to 1,800 words

Payment 500 words: $75 to $100; 800 to 1,200 words: $125; 1,300 to 1,800 words: $175; 1,800 (lead): $350

Time of payment On acceptance

Response time to queries 30 to 60 days

Rights bought All, first, onetime

Writer's guidelines Available by request with magazine-size SASE included

Sample issues Available by request with magazine-size SASE included

IMPORTANT QUESTIONS ANSWERED

Q: Will you look at completed manuscripts?

A: Yes

Q: Is an SASE always necessary?

A: Yes

Q: Are phone calls from writers OK?

A: Yes

Q: Is it OK if writers fax or e-mail queries to you?

A: Yes

Q: What is the best way to break in to your magazine?

A: Query with resume.

Q: How should writers angle their stories for your magazine?

A: To *parents*

LONG ISLAND PARENTING NEWS

P.O. Box 214
Island Park, NY 11558

Phone number 516-889-5510

Fax number 516-889-5513

Parent company RDM Publishing

Circulation 50,000

Magazine availability   Libraries, schools, after-school programs, hospitals, museums, doctor's offices, retail stores

Target audience   Parents of children expecting through teens

Magazine's history and mission   Founded in 1989. Received several awards in recent years from Parent Publications of America for excellence in editorial, design, and marketing.

Nonfiction   More than 90%

Fiction   Less than 10%

Percent of articles freelance-written   About 50% to 75%

Number of articles bought annually   30 to 50

Sections of the magazine open to freelance writers   All

Article interests and needs   Issues concerning parenting (expecting, health, sports, special needs, humor) and kids' media (books, toys, music, video, software, films) and family vacations

Queries should be directed to   Pat Simms-Elias

Length of articles   500 to 1,500 words

Payment   Yes—not much

Time of payment   On publication

Expenses   Rarely

Photographs   Yes

Response time to queries   4 to 6 weeks

Rights bought   First

Kill fees   No

Writer's guidelines   Available with SASE

Sample issues   Available with SASE

METROKIDS MAGAZINE

1080 North Delaware Avenue, Suite 702
Philadelphia, PA 19125

Phone number   215-291-5560

Fax number   215-291-5563

Parent company   Kidstuff Publications, Inc.

Circulation   75,000

Magazine availability   Controlled circulation

Target audience   Parents and families in the 8-county Philadelphia metropolitan area

Magazine's history and mission   Founded by Nancy Lisagor in 1989. She is still the publisher.

Nonfiction   95%

Fiction   5%

Percent of articles freelance-written   30%

Number of articles bought annually   35
Sections of the magazine open to freelance writers   Feature articles—especially about this region. Reviews.
Article interests and needs   Family concerns, parenting topics
Queries should be directed to   Nancy Lisagor, Editor-in-Chief
Length of articles   800 to 1,000 words
Payment $35 to $50
Time of payment   On publication
Expenses   Within certain parameters—to be discussed on assignment
Photographs   Yes, black-and-white
Response time to queries   4 to 6 months
Kill fees   No
Writer's guidelines   Available

PARENTING

301 Howard Street, 17th floor
San Francisco, CA 94105

Phone number   415-546-7515
Fax number   415-546-0578
Parent company   Time-Warner
Circulation   1,100,000
Magazine availability   Newsstands and subscription
Target audience   28 to 35, female, middle-class, nationwide
Magazine's mission   To provide parents with tips, information, and thought-provoking essays on parenting and children
Nonfiction   99%
Fiction   1%
Percent of articles freelance-written   95%
Sections of the magazine open to freelance writers   All departments
Article interests and needs   Service articles, medical updates
Queries should be directed to   Articles editor
Payment   Negotiable
Time of payment   On acceptance
Expenses   Paid
Photographs   Freelanced
Response time to queries   4 to 6 weeks
Rights bought   First North American rights
Kill fees   25%
Writer's guidelines   With SASE
Sample issues   With SASE and $5.00 check

SAN DIEGO FAMILY PRESS

P.O. Box 23960
San Diego, CA 92193

Phone number   619-685-6970
Fax number   Call first
E-mail address   Bayview@thegroup.net
Circulation   75,000
Magazine availability   Newsstands and subscription
Target audience   Mothers and fathers, ages 25 to 45, educated, San Diego County
Magazine's history and mission   Started in 1982 with the intent to inform and educate families in the Southern California area.
Nonfiction   95%
Fiction   5%
Percent of articles freelance-written   80%
Number of articles bought annually   200 to 300
Sections of the magazine open to freelance writers   All
Article interests and needs   Localized family issues
Queries should be directed to   Sharon Bay, Publisher
Length of articles   600 to 800 words
Payment $1.25 per column inch
Time of payment   On publication
Expenses   No
Photographs   No
Response time to queries   2 months
Rights bought   Yes
Writer's guidelines   Available
Sample issues   Available for $3.50 per issue with 9 × 12 envelope

TIPS FOR WRITERS

Send query with time lines.

Send for writer's guidelines—SASE.

Make articles localized if possible.

Please write articles with an educational and informative slant. We prefer to stay away from personally oriented articles.

SAN FRANCISCO PENINSULA PARENT

1480 Rollins Road
Burlingame, CA 94010

Phone number   415-342-9203
Fax number   415-342-9276
E-mail address   sfpp@aol.com
Parent company   Peninsula Parent Newspaper, Inc.
Circulation   60,000—South San Francisco to Mountain View
Magazine availability   Free. Controlled circulation. Found at stores, doctors' offices, libraries, schools, supermarkets
Target audience   Parents of children (newborn to age 12) in San Francisco–Peninsula area. Readership is generally educated and affluent.
Magazine's history and mission   Founded in 1984 by Marlene Douglas and Lisa Rosenthal (current publisher and editor). Mission is to provide comprehensible information and resources to parents in the San Francisco area.
Nonfiction   100%
Percent of articles freelance-written   70%
Number of articles bought annually   30
Article interests and needs   Profiles, travel articles, articles about child development, discipline, home, and school issues
Queries should be directed to   Lisa Rosenthal, Editor
Length of articles   1,000 words
Payment $35 to $100, depending on article length and subject; we pay less for second than for first rights.
Time of payment   On publication
Expenses   No
Photographs   Accept; will pay additional
Response time to queries   1 to 2 months
Kill fees   Generally no
Writer's guidelines   Yes
Sample issues   Yes

TIPS FOR WRITERS
Lisa Rosenthal, Editor

The query: A good query poses an interesting question or provides answers to questions that our writers have. The letter is brief and summarizes one to three story ideas. A good writer has requested and read a sample copy of our magazine before submitting a query so that she is familiar with our style. One or two clips and/or one or two articles may accompany the query.

An SASE is not mandatory although writers who submit an SASE or postcard (preferable) will receive a return response faster. A phone call to "check out" a potential story idea is OK, if it's not during deadline/production weeks (the 13th to 22nd of each month). I prefer letters to phone calls, fax, or e-mail.

The articles we are seeking give a fresh slant to old topics (i.e., travel with children, children's health, children's discipline); articles with local quotes and resources are more likely to be accepted.

The worst things writers do:

Show by their submission that they do not have a clue what our style or readership is.

Submit 5 to 10 full manuscripts with a query letter. Less is better.

Call two or three days after sending a query. It usually takes me 1 to 2 months to go through all the queries I receive and I only look at queries during the "down time" after the publication goes to press, 1 to 3 days a month. Be patient.

Submit seasonal articles close to deadline. Our articles are selected 3 to 6 months in advance.

Suggest writing a column. We're more likely to accept an occasional article rather than a column, particularly from an unknown writer.

VALLEY PARENT MAGAZINE

401 Alberto Way, Suite A
Los Gatos, CA 95032

Phone number 408-358-1414
Fax number 408-356-4903
Parent company Bay Area Publishing Group, Inc.
Circulation 55,000
Online status Our Calendar sections are found on Starware
Magazine availability Newsstands, subscription, doctor's offices, libraries, retail stores, etc.
Target audience Parents of children ages 0 to early teens
Nonfiction 100%
Percent of articles freelance-written 80%
Number of articles bought annually About 200 (includes those by regular columnists)
Sections of the magazine open to freelance writers Features
Article interests and needs Topics of interest to parents
Queries should be directed to Mary Brence Martin, Managing Editor
Length of articles 1,200 to 2,000 words
Payment $.06 per word
Time of payment On publication
Expenses Only on assigned stories
Photographs $10 to $15
Response time to queries Two months
Rights bought Onetime
Kill fees Occasionally on assigned stories
Writer's guidelines Send SASE.
Sample issues Send $8\frac{1}{2} \times 12$ SASE with six $.32 stamps.

TIPS FOR WRITERS

See entry under *Bay Area Parent Magazine.*

Politics/Culture

GEORGE

1633 Broadway, 41st Floor
New York, NY 10019

Phone number   212-767-6100
Fax number   212-767-5622
E-mail address   yeas@georgemag.com
Parent company   Hachette Filipacchi
Circulation   600,000
Online status   Yes
Magazine availability   Newsstands and subscription
Magazine's history   Founded in September 1995, by John Kennedy Jr. and Michael Berman
Nonfiction   95%
Percent of articles freelance-written   80%
Sections of the magazine open to freelance writers   All
Queries should be directed to   Articles Editor
Time of payment   On acceptance
Expenses   Yes
Photographs   Yes
Kill fees   25%

THE NATION

72 Fifth Avenue
New York, NY 10011

Phone number   212-242-8400 (after 5 P.M. 212-242-8180)
Fax number   212-463-9712
E-mail address   INFO@THENATION.COM

Parent company   Nation Co., L.P.
Circulation   93,000
Online status   Web site
Magazine availability   Newsstands
Target audience   40+, 60% men, 40% women, 83% college-educated, 50% with graduate degrees
Magazine's history and mission   According to a blurb provided by *The Nation*: *The Nation* is America's oldest weekly magazine and one of its premier journals of opinion. Established by abolitionists in 1865, *The Nation* has long been regarded as one of America's definitive journalistic voices. For more than 130 years of writing on politics, culture, books and the arts, *The Nation* has remained true to its original commitment to be the critical, independent voice in American journalism.
Nonfiction   100%
Percent of articles freelance-written   95%
Number of articles bought annually   Approximately 450
Sections of the magazine open to freelance writers   Editorials, articles, book reviews
Article interests and needs   Politically and culturally oriented
Queries should be directed to   Katrina Vanden Heuvel or Art Winslow
Length of articles   Average is 1,500 to 2,500 words.
Payment $100 per printed magazine page
Time of payment   On publication
Expenses   If worked out in advance
Photographs   Rarely
Response time to queries   1 month
Rights bought   Varies
Kill fees   For previous contributors
Sample Issues   Per request

THE WEEKLY STANDARD

1150 17th Street NW, Fifth floor
Washington, DC 20036

Phone number   202-293-4900
Fax number   202-293-4901
Parent company   News Publishing Inc. America
Circulation   Not available
Online status   Not yet online
Magazine availability   Newsstands and subscription
Target audience   Readers interested in reporting and commentary on politics and culture from a conservative point of view. National audience.
Magazine's history and mission   Magazine was founded by William Kristol, Fred Barnes, and John Podhoretz during the summer of 1995. The first issue appeared

September 18, 1995. *The Weekly Standard* was founded as the magazine for a new conservative era.

Nonfiction   100%

Percent of articles freelance-written   Approximately 50%

Sections of the magazine open to freelance writers   Freelance writers are welcome to write for all sections of the magazine.

Article interests and needs   Article interests include news pieces on politics around the country, general commentary on politics and culture, and reviews of books and movies.

Queries should be directed to   Articles Editor

Length of articles   Articles range in length, but should not exceed 3,000 words.

Time of payment   On publication

Response time to queries   Approximately 2 weeks

Writer's guidelines   Yes

Sample issues   Not available

TIPS FOR WRITERS

We have no set procedure for getting published in the magazine. Some pieces are commissioned, but we are happy to consider unsolicited manuscripts. Sending previously published clips is not helpful, but unpublished manuscripts will be given due consideration.

Public Policy/Consumer Affairs

PUBLIC CITIZEN MAGAZINE

1600 20th Street, NW
Washington, DC 20009

Phone number   202-588-1000

Fax number   202-588-7799

Parent company   Public Citizen

Circulation   100,000

Magazine availability   Mostly subscription, but also on newsstands.

Target audience   Politically concerned men and women who seek more information than what is offered in the mainstream media.

Magazine's history and mission   *Public Citizen Magazine* was founded in 1980 by Ralph Nader. Its goal is to fight for consumer rights in the marketplace, safe products, a healthy environment and workplace, fair trade, clean and safe energy sources, and corporate and government accountability.

Nonfiction   100%

Percent of articles freelance-written   Up to 15% comes from freelance writers, but mostly staff written.
Number of articles bought annually   Varies
Sections of the magazine open to freelance writers   Commentary and features
Article interests and needs   Read the publication to get a feel for our articles.
Queries should be directed to   Peter Nye, Editor
Length of articles   350 to 1,100 words
Payment   Fees negotiable
Time of payment   On acceptance
Expenses   No
Photographs   Yes
Response time to queries   Promptly
Rights bought   We buy onetime rights.
Kill fees   No
Sample issues   Yes

TIPS FOR WRITERS
Peter Nye, Editor

The best way to break into this magazine applies to most others—it begins with reading the publication regularly enough to get a grasp of the type of stories found in the magazine, the length of the articles, and the spirit of the content so that a proposed story would fit into the publication like a tile in a mosaic.

Often it is easy to emphasize writing and breaking into print. Those are indeed important issues. But I like to emphasize reading, which is, I think, crucial to a writing career but somehow gets overlooked. The level of one's reading reflects in one's writing. I feel that reading—everything from novels to nonfiction such as memoirs, autobiographies, biographies, and analytical works describing trends in popular culture, economics, or politics—is as important to a writer as training is to an athlete. Talent certainly is important, but at a certain level in the job market, everyone is talented, and talent will carry one only so far. Over a period of time, reading will help develop exposure to the sort of writing to emulate under varying circumstances.

The query: As author of four books and articles published in more than 100 newspapers and magazines, I have found that the higher up one is in the writing food chain, the more important a sharp, one-page query letter is—a query letter that includes one paragraph containing both how the article will be written (i.e., interview in person or by telephone and pertinent research) and personal writing-related highlights. The query should address this question: Why should someone read this? Allow at least a week or two for the query letter to arrive, and then telephone the editor to follow up.

Closing the deal: Writing, it is often said, rhymes with fighting, and my own experience has found that the two verbs share more than rhyming. My suggestion is for writers to really understand how to negotiate, because a writer, especially a freelancer, is actually a subcontractor. A good recommendation is Herb Cohen's book, *You Can Negotiate Anything.*

When the writer and editor agree to a story, length, and copy deadline, then negotiate the story fee, time of payment (i.e., on acceptance? on publication? And if upon publication, then when—some publications actually pay up to 90 days after publication, in which case payment may be sent out four months after the magazine first hits the newsstands), number of author's copies, and expenses (particularly telephone expenses or travel). All of these matters should be negotiated and agreed upon by both parties. The writer should follow up promptly with a business letter repeating all terms agreed to by both parties.

For writers starting out, assignments typically pay modestly at best, and writers tend to toil in long apprenticeships.

Regional

ADIRONDACK LIFE

P. O. Box 97
Jay, NY 12941

Phone number   518-946-2191—NO calls for queries!
Fax number   Don't you *dare* fax us a query!
Parent company   E. I. Media
Circulation   50,000
Magazine availability   Newsstands and subscription
Target audience   Audience is people who care about the Adirondack Park, which comprises 6 million acres in northeastern New York.
Magazine's history and mission   Founded in 1970. Mission is to celebrate the natural beauty and human history of the Adirondack Park.
Nonfiction   95%
Fiction   5%
Percent of articles freelance-written   80%
Number of articles bought annually   50+
Sections of the magazine open to freelance writers   All
Article interests and needs   Need well-researched journalism on the outdoors, profiles of important people, odd bits of history, wildlife. *Don't need* personal essays or poetry!
Queries should be directed to   Elizabeth Folwell, Editor
Length of articles   Departments: 1,200 to 2,400 words; Features: 2,500 to 5,000 words
Payment $.25 per published word
Time of payment   On acceptance
Expenses   No

Photographs   Yes
Response time to queries   45 days
Rights bought   First North American serial print rights
Writer's guidelines   Send SASE for guidelines. Also have photo needs list.

TIPS FOR WRITERS

Potential writers for *Adirondack Life* need to understand where the region is. We got lots of inappropriate queries and submissions from writers covering Connecticut, pet care, allergy relief, scuba diving, and other topics not relevant to our publication. Get a sample issue; go to a library and read back issues. Prepare!

ALBEMARLE

The Blake Center
1224 West main Street
Charlottesville, VA 22903

Phone number   804-979-4913
Fax number   804-979-4025
E-mail address   jamie_miller@cjp.ccmail.compuserve.com
Parent company   Carden Jennings Publishing, Ltd.
Circulation   10,000
Magazine availability   Newsstands and subscription
Target audience   Largest single demographic is females in their forties, but has strong male following. Magazine is targeted towards the broad-based community members of Central Virginia.
Magazine's history and mission   Joe Jennings and Bill Carden started the magazine soon after graduation from the University of Virginia. The parent company, Carden Jennings, was founded in 1985 with the initial publication, *The Charlottesville Guide*.
Nonfiction   100%
Percent of articles freelance-written   100%
Number of articles bought annually   Approximately 80
Article interests and needs   Accepts queries on all local topics. Coverage runs the gamut from sports to literature to family to business to gardening. Covers local history, writers, art, and successful professionals in many different fields.
Queries should be directed to   Jamie Miller, Editor
Length of articles   850 to 4,000 words, varying from department to feature
Payment   Ranges from $75 to $300, based on article length and writer's experience
Time of payment   On publication
Photographs   100% freelance
Response time to queries   About 2 months
Rights bought   First North American

Kill fees   Depends on circumstance
Writer's guidelines   Available with sample issue upon request

TIPS FOR WRITERS
Jamie Miller, Editor

Albemarle is always interested in writer queries on local topics, especially humorous or dramatic subjects. If you have short essays (850 to 2,000 words), send them in full manuscript form. When you query, always enclose clips—there is no way we can judge the suitability of your work without seeing writing samples. If you have not published previously, but feel you have a great story idea, send copies of school papers or business letters, anything that will demonstrate your writing proficiency. The chances are not good for unpublished writers, but everybody needs to start somewhere.

Queries should be brief and to the point. Even though we're a small magazine, we receive a good deal of correspondence and have little time to lose. Please send a self-addressed, stamped envelope for reply.

Albemarle asks that writers contact the publication only through the mail. No determinations can be made about a writer's work outside of sitting down and reading clips. Phone calls with story ideas will never yield an assignment. This is standard for most publications, where writer phone calls are only welcome when the writer has had a long-standing relationship with the magazine and works closely and frequently with the editor.

The four P's—professionalism, presentation, persistence, and patience—will give you the best bet for getting published, whether it's in *Albemarle* or most any other magazine. Sending a well-written (and well-proofed!) query along with two or three clips is the foot in the door. Then stay in touch. If the editor writes back and shows interest but doesn't offer an assignment, take that as a positive sign and send another query the next month. And don't stop. You'd be surprised at the number of writers who are published more because of their persistence and positive attitude than their actual writing ability.

Remember, most editors have been writers themselves and they know how important the initial acceptances can be. So even though editors may seem cold and cruel-hearted, there's a corner in the heart of most that seeks to help the novice writer. That can be you if you stay with it.

ALOHA, THE MAGAZINE OF HAWAII AND THE PACIFIC
P.O. Box 3260
Honolulu, HI 96801

Phone number   808-593-1191
Fax number   808-593-1327
Parent company   Davick Publications
Circulation   75,000
Magazine availability   Newsstands and subscription
Target audience   Upscale, well-educated, frequent visitors to Hawaii

Magazine's history   Founded in 1977
Nonfiction   100%
Percent of articles freelance-written   We run fiction very rarely.
Number of articles bought annually   At least 50%
Sections of the magazine open to freelance writers   Roughly 40
Article interests and needs   According to editorial guidelines, "Aloha offers a wide variety of subject matter, all of which is Hawaii-related. Categories generally covered in each issue and open to freelance writers are the arts, business, people, sports, destinations, food, interiors, history, Hawaiiana, fiction, and poetry."
Queries should be directed to   Cheryl Tsutsumi, Editorial Director
Length of articles   1,500 to 2,000 words
Payment $150 to $400
Time of payment   On publication
Expenses   Some. Prior approval from editorial director is needed.
Photographs   According to *Aloha*'s editorial guidelines, one photo essay is featured in each issue—Beautiful Hawaii, a collection of photographs that illustrate a theme. Occasionally, a second photo essay by a sole photographer on a specific theme is featured. Queries are essential for the latter.
Response time to queries   Within 4 to 6 weeks after receipt
Rights bought   First-time
Kill fees   Occasionally offered
Writer's guidelines   Yes
Sample issues   Yes

ARIZONA HIGHWAYS

2039 West Lewis Avenue
Phoenix, AZ 85009

Phone number   602-258-6641
Fax number   602-254-4505
Parent company   Arizona Department of Transportation
Circulation   400,000 international
Magazine availability   Newsstands and subscription
Target audience   Active adults interested in Arizona, travel, history, etc.
Magazine's history and mission   *Arizona Highways* was first published in April 1925. As a division of the Arizona Department of Transportation, the magazine, according to state statute, is published "for the purpose of encouraging tourist travel to and through the state." 76 percent of subscribers live outside of Arizona.
Nonfiction   100%
Percent of articles freelance-written   95%
Sections of the magazine open to freelance writers   Mostly all
Article interests and needs   Travel, adventure, history
Queries should be directed to   Richard G. Stahl, Managing Editor

Length of articles   700 to 2,000 words, depending on the section of the magazine

Payment $.35 to $.55 per word

Time of payment   On acceptance

Expenses   Covered

Photographs   Prefer large format (4×5, 8×10) transparencies, but will use $2\frac{1}{4}$ and half if exceptional quality or content. Prefer Kodachrome or Velvia in 35mm. No prints, negatives, or duplicate transparencies will be accepted.

Response time to queries   1 week to 1 month

Rights bought   We buy first rights only.

Kill fees   Treated individually

Writer's guidelines   Available

IMPORTANT QUESTIONS ANSWERED

Q: What sparks your interest a query?

A: A good story idea and a well-written query

Q: Do you always want clips from new writers?

A: Yes

Q: How many clips do you want?

A: Several, at least

Q: What do you look for in the writer's clips?

A: Writing ability and creativity

Q: Will you look at completed manuscripts?

A: No

Q: Is an SASE always necessary?

A: Yes

Q: Are phone calls from writers OK?

A: We prefer they not call unless a serious problem has arisen.

Q: Is it OK if writers fax or e-mail queries to you?

A: Yes

Q: What is the best way to break into Arizona Highways?

A: A good query letter

Q: How can writers learn to angle their stories for your magazine? What is your overall advice to writers?

A: Ask for a writer's guide.

ATLANTIC CITY

P.O. Box 2100
Pleasantville, NJ 08232

Phone number   609-272-7900

Fax number   609-272-7910

Parent company   Abarta-Metro

Circulation   40,000
Magazine availability   Newsstands and subscription
Target audience   Local tourism, no age
Nonfiction   100%
Percent of articles freelance-written   100%
Sections of the magazine open to freelance writers   All
Article interests and needs   Travel, local features
Queries should be directed to   Deb Ein, Senior Editor
Length of articles   1,000 to 2,500 words
Time of payment   On acceptance
Expenses   Some
Photographs   Some
Response time to queries   ASAP
Rights bought   First North American
Kill fees   20%
Writer's guidelines   Yes
Sample issues   Please send $4.

BLUE RIDGE COUNTRY

P.O. Box 21535
Roanoke, VA 24018

Phone number   540-989-6138
Fax number   540-989-7607
E-mail address   leisure@infi.net
Parent company   Leisure Publishing
Circulation   75,000
Magazine availability   Newsstands and subscription
Target audience   Ages 40 and up; travelers and admirers of region
Magazine's history   Founded in 1988.
Nonfiction   100%
Percent of articles freelance-written   75%
Number of articles bought annually   20 to 30
Sections of the magazine open to freelance writers   All
Article interests and needs   Travel, profiles, ecology
Queries should be directed to   Kurt Rheinheimer, Editor
Length of articles   500 to 1,200 words
Payment $25 to $250
Time of payment   On publication
Expenses   Mileage
Photographs   Yes
Response time to queries   2 to 4 months
Rights bought   First-time

Writer's guidelines   Yes. Send envelope with return postage.
Sample issues   Yes. Send six first-class stamps and a 9 × 12 envelope.

IMPORTANT QUESTIONS ANSWERED

Q: What sparks your interest in a query?
A: A specific proposal
Q: Do you always want clips from new writers?
A: No
Q: Is an SASE always necessary?
A: Yes
Q: Is it OK if writers fax or e-mail queries?
A: Yes
Q: Are phone calls from writers OK?
A: Yes, if specific department pieces
Q: What is the key to breaking into your magazine?
A: Know it.
Q: How can writers angle their stories for your magazine?
A: With travel backroads stories
Q: What is the best thing writers do?
A: Write well.

BOSTON MAGAZINE

300 Massachusetts Avenue
Boston, MA 02115

Phone number   617-262-9700
Fax number   617-262-4925
Parent company   Metrocorps
Circulation   100,000+
Online status   Web site
Magazine availability   Newsstands and subscription
Target audience   Urban, 25+, New England readers
Nonfiction   100%
Percent of articles freelance-written   25%
Number of articles bought annually   Approximately 50 to 75
Sections of the magazine open to freelance writers   All sections—Reporter (Front), Features (Well), Photo essay (Well)
Article interests and needs   Must be specific to Boston or outlying areas
Queries should be directed to   Kerry Nugent-Wells
Length of articles   500 to 2,500 words
Payment   Varies
Time of payment   On publication

Expenses   Negotiable
Photographs   Yes, we accept freelance photographs.
Response time to queries   2 weeks
Kill fees   Negotiable
Writer's guidelines   Yes—Available with SASE
Sample issues   No—$3.50 for back issue

TIPS FOR WRITERS

The best way to break into the magazine is to submit a good story—it's the key. Local investigative features and excellent clips from an established magazine will spark the editor's interest. The worst thing writers do is not reading the magazine before submitting. The best way to angle stories is to "go local!"

CAPE COD LIFE

P.O. Box 1385
Pocasset, MA 02559-1385

Phone number   508-564-4466
Fax number   508-564-4470
Parent company   Cape Cod Life, Inc.
Circulation   37,000
Online status   Web site at www.capecodlife.com
Magazine availability   Newsstands and subscription
Target audience   On Cape residents, off-Cape visitors, second home owners. People who love and appreciate the area.
Magazine's history and mission   Founded in 1979 by publisher/editor Shortsleeve. Mission: to share what is interesting and unique about Cape Cod and the Islands.
Nonfiction   100%
Percent of articles freelance-written   85%
Number of articles bought annually   25 to 35
Sections of the magazine open to freelance writers   All
Queries should be directed to   Laura Reckford, Managing Editor
Sample issues $4 and $1 postage

CAROLINA COUNTRY

P.O. Box 27306
Raleigh, NC 27611

Phone number   919-713-1367
Fax number   919-878-3970

E-mail address   75471.2247@compuserve.com
Parent company   North Carolina Association of Electric Cooperatives
Circulation   350,000
Magazine availability   Subscription and membership
Target audience   Members of North Carolina Electric Cooperatives
Magazine's history and mission   Founded in 1946
Nonfiction   100%
Percent of articles freelance-written   25%
Number of articles bought annually   12 to 20
Sections of the magazine open to freelance writers   Features
Article interests and needs   North Carolina subjects not usually covered by others
Manuscripts should be directed to   Editor
Length of articles   800 to 1,200 words
Payment $100 to $300
Time of payment   On acceptance
Expenses   No
Photographs $50 per photo or illustration published
Response time to submissions   1 month
Rights bought   Unlimited use
Writer's guidelines   Yes
Sample issues   Yes

IMPORTANT QUESTIONS ANSWERED

Q: Will you look at completed manuscripts?
A: No queries. Manuscripts only.
Q: Is an SASE always necessary?
A: Yes
Q: Are phone calls from writers OK?
A. No
Q: Is it OK if writers fax or e-mail queries to you?
A: No
Q: What do you look for in a publishable manuscript?
A: Fresh writing on North Carolina people and places. Especially in rural areas

CAROLINA STYLE

3975-B Market Street
Wilmington, NC 28403

Phone number   910-341-3033
Fax number   910-341-3011 or 3039
E-mail address   CaroStyle@aol.com

Parent company   Carolina Style, Inc.

Circulation   70,000

Online status   Electronic mail only

Magazine availability   Newsstands and subscription

Target audience   Upscale, 35+ years, mostly female, professional or business oriented, mostly in North and South Carolina with a handful across 47 states, Canada, and Hong Kong.

Magazine's history and mission   *Carolina Style* was founded by Stu Slater, former sales director of *INC.* magazine. The magazine's mission is to bring to light the rich and colorful heritage of the coastal good life on the Carolina Coasts. It covers the history, culture, events, lifestyles, heritage, and beauty of the coastal lifestyle.

Nonfiction   99%

Fiction   1%

Percent of articles freelance-written   100%

Number of articles bought annually   Approximately 150

Sections of the magazine open to freelance writers   All

Article interests and needs   Tales from Readers (letters to the editor), Beach Bag (potpourri of interesting short highlights of various items of interest), Coast Ghosts (feature on a haunted place, person, thing along the coast), Traveler's Tales (Landlubber's trips—features on trips inland to areas of interest, including Sunday drives), Taste of the Coast (restaurant features, recipes, food related articles), Nature (features on wildlife, plant life, environment, ecology of the coastal region), The Arts, Healthy Lifestyle, Lifestyles (a profile of a unique residential development or area along the coast), and more.

Queries should be directed to   Anthony S. Policastro, Editor-in-Chief

Length of articles   500 to 2,500 words

Payment $.10 per published word

Time of payment   After publication

Expenses   Sometimes paid

Photographs   Pay $25 to $300 for cover

Response time to queries   3 to 6 weeks

Rights bought   First-time North America, electronic

Kill fees   50% of original fee

Writer's guidelines   Available with SASE (#10 envelope)

Sample issues $5 each

TIPS FOR WRITERS
Anthony S. Policastro, Editor-in-Chief

The best queries are those that include a brief description of the proposed article and maybe a page or two of their proposed article. This tells me immediately if their writing style is acceptable and whether the publication uses that type of writing. In terms of writing, I accept any style as long as it works, meaning that the writing must be full of life, clear, concise, and to the point. Clips take time to read and don't really give me a clear picture of the writer's style because it has been gone over by an editor.

Credentials are only important to me if they pertain to the subject matter. For instance, we have one writer who does many food-related articles. She also has a degree in dairy science, so this makes her qualified to write about food. More importantly the writing has to be good—credentials mean nothing if the writing is bad.

An SASE is necessary if the writer wants to hear back from me. I don't have the time to obtain an envelope, address it, stamp it, and send it off. A postcard is also nice, especially if it has a place where I can check off my decision to run a particular piece.

Phone calls are welcomed from writers after they have sent in a query. E-mail queries are the best because they can be answered with very little effort and they are instantaneous. I also prefer writers to e-mail me their stories followed up by a mailed or faxed printed copy of the piece.

The best way to break into print is to request our writer's guidelines with an SASE with $.55 for postage, and then query me by mail or fax.

The best thing a writer can do is to suggest a story and provide photos. I use more stories accompanied with photos than those without. The best package I've seen from a writer included a printed hard copy, the story on a 3.5 computer disk, and slides with captions. It was the easiest to work with and the quickest to get in print.

The worst thing a writer can do is to call me directly and ask about the types of stories we publish. I hate to explain what our magazine is about over the phone. I don't have time.

My advice to writers wanting to get published is to study thoroughly the types of stories published in a particular magazine, and then query the editor with an idea.

CHICAGO LIFE

P.O. Box 11311
Chicago, IL 60611-0311

Phone number   312-528-2737
Parent company   Chicago Life, Inc.
Circulation   60,000
Magazine availability   Controlled
Target audience   Yuppie babyboomers (upscale professionals)
Magazine's history and mission   Founded in 1984 and focuses on improving quality of life.
Nonfiction   100%
Percent of articles freelance-written   95%
Number of articles bought annually   40
Article interests and needs   Health, fitness, finance
Length of articles   Open
Payment   Usually $30+
Time of payment   On acceptance and on publication
Photographs   Yes

Response time to queries   1 week
Rights bought   First-time
Kill fees   Sometimes
Sample issues   Send 9 × 12 SASE and 7 stamps

IMPORTANT QUESTIONS ANSWERED

Q: What sparks your interest in a query and/or a freelance writer?
A: Good writing
Q: Will you look at completed manuscripts?
A: Yes
Q: Is an SASE always necessary?
A: Yes
Q: Is it OK if writers fax or e-mail queries to you?
A: E-mail [is OK]. No faxes, please!
Q: What is the worst things writers do?
A: Fax

CRYSTAL CITY ETC.

2345 Crystal Drive, 10th floor
Arlington, VA 22202

Phone number   703-920-8500, Ext. 1144
Fax number   703-769-1190
Parent company   The Charles E. Smith Companies
Circulation   150,000
Magazine availability   Free publication through the mail
Target audience   Arlington, Old Town, Northern Virginia
Magazine's history and mission   Founded February 1990, by David Bruce Smith. Originally it was intended to educate people about Crystal City, but it has evolved into a general interest publication about the D.C. metropolitan area.
Nonfiction   100%
Fiction   Sometimes *CC* publishes a poem or short story.
Percent of articles freelance-written   100%
Number of articles bought annually   40 to 50
Sections of the magazine open to freelance writers   All
Article interests and needs   Book/restaurant reviews, features, business, health, theater/cinema/other performing arts, exhibitions
Queries should be directed to   David Bruce Smith
Length of articles   1,000 to 1,500 words (Etc column: approximately 500 words)
Payment $50 to $200
Time of payment   On publication

Expenses   N/A (except book reviews)
Photographs   On-staff photographer
Response time to queries   2 to 4 weeks
Rights bought   North American
Kill fees $50 to $100

IMPORTANT QUESTIONS ANSWERED

Q: What is the best way to break into Crystal City?
A: Send a query letter with an SASE.
Q: Will you look at completed manuscripts?
A: Yes. Manuscripts will be considered without a query.
Q: Do you always want clips from new writers?
A: No. We're more interested in writing style than clips.
Q: Are phone calls from writers OK?
A: Yes
Q: Is it OK if writers fax or e-mail queries to you?
A: Yes
Q: What is the worst thing that writers do?
A: Typographic mistakes

FLORIDA TREND

P.O. Box 611
St. Petersburg, FL 33731

Phone number   813-821-5800
Fax number   813-822-5083
Parent company   The St. Petersburg Times
Circulation   50,000
Magazine availability   Newsstands and subscription
Nonfiction   100%
Percent of articles freelance-written   Approximately 70%
Number of articles bought annually   Approximately 200
Sections of the magazine open to freelance writers   Features and some columns
Article interests and needs   Florida business and public policy issues and trends
Queries should be directed to   John F. Berry, Editor at *Florida Trend,* 490 First Avenue South, St. Petersburg, FL 33701
Length of articles   Varies. Features: 2,000 words; Column or items 300 to 1,100 words
Payment   Amounts vary on difficulty of material and quality of writer's prose.
Time of payment   On publication
Photographs   Yes

Response time to queries   Prompt
Kill fees   Yes

TIPS FOR WRITERS

Though a state magazine, *Florida Trend* prides itself on the quality of writing and accuracy of reporting. All stories are fact checked. Recent subjects: High speed rails coming to Florida, incompetence of Florida legislature, education crisis, Florida film industry.

HUDSON VALLEY

40 Garden Street, 2nd Floor
Poughkeepsie, NY 12601-3106

Phone number   914-485-7844
Fax number   914-485-5975
E-mail address   gmigriff@mhv.net
Parent company   Suburban Publishing, Inc.
Circulation   25,500
Magazine availability   Newsstands and subscription
Target audience   Age 35 to 50, professional and managerial readership, both sexes, household income $90,000 in a 10-county area of New York State
Magazine's history   Founded 1972 by Angelo R. Martinelli
Nonfiction   99%
Fiction   1%
Percent of articles freelance-written   95%
Number of articles bought annually   120 (approximately)
Sections of the magazine open to freelance writers   Most
Article interests and needs   Profiles, in-depth social trends articles, food writers
Queries should be directed to   Editor
Length of articles   100 to 4,500 words
Payment $25 to $700
Time of payment   On publication
Expenses   No (except restaurant reviews)
Photographs   Yes—inquiries should be directed to art director
Response time to queries   1 day to 1 year
Rights bought   The magazine retains rights. If reprint is requested, we negotiate fee and split with writer/reporter.
Kill fees   25% of negotiated fee on assignment
Writer's guidelines   Provided only to those commissioned to report/write for the magazine

TIPS FOR WRITERS

Queries:

1. If you are inquiring about freelancing, send resume, samples of recent clips demonstrating writing and reportage skills, and a brief cover letter saying what you consider to be your areas of expertise and interest.
2. If you are sending in a story suggestion, it should be specific, researched before sent to the magazine to assure it viable, and preferably no longer than 1 page in length.
3. Unsolicited manuscripts are discouraged.

Professional etiquette: SASEs are preferred, not required.

Written communication (mail, e-mail, fax) is the preferred way to communicate with the magazine until a writer is under contract; phone calls are highly discouraged.

INDIANAPOLIS MONTHLY

950 North Meridian Street, Suite 1200
Indianapolis, IN 46204

Phone number   317-237-9288
Fax number   317-237-9496
E-mail address   im-input@iquest.net
Parent company   Emmis Broadcasting Corp. (Indianapolis, Indiana)
Circulation   45,000
Online status   Home page at http://www.iquest.net/indymonthly
Magazine availability   Newsstands and subscription
Target audience   General—but average reader is 47 and female, with above-average income. Target area is Indianapolis and surrounding counties.
Magazine's history   Founded in 1977.
Nonfiction   100%
Percent of articles freelance-written   50%
Number of articles bought annually   About 120
Sections of the magazine open to freelance writers   Virtually everything, aside from regular columns or sections
Article interests and needs   We're looking for the stories of Indianapolis (and Indiana): Vivid, well-researched articles about life in Indy. Essays with an Indianapolis/Indiana slant also are welcome (1,500 to 2,500 words), as are stories with an Indiana-based celebrity angle (recent cover story: "Oprah's Indiana Home").
Queries should be directed to   Sam Stall, Editor
Length of articles   200 to 6,000 words
Payment $50 to $500
Time of payment   On publication
Expenses   Generally not
Photographs $50 to $200
Response time to queries   2 months

Rights bought   First North American serial rights. Also, onetime rights
Kill fees   50%
Writer's guidelines   With SASE
Sample issues $6.10 (including postage)

TIPS FOR WRITERS
Brian D. Smith, Senior Editor

The query: As with all magazines, it's best to read *Indianapolis Monthly* before submitting a query. Those who do so will notice that we're strictly focused on Indianapolis (and to a lesser extent, Indiana).

More than anything, we're looking for the stories of Indianapolis, with emphasis on the word "stories." In other words, specific articles about specific people stand a greater chance of publication than all-encompassing articles on general topics. (Example: While we probably wouldn't do a story on local organ donation, we recently ran a story about a 12-year-old auto accident victim whose donated organs saved four other lives.) So don't bother pitching titles such as "How to Talk to Your Teen" or "What Every Woman Should Know About Osteoporosis." If a story could appear in *any* magazine, it probably won't appear in ours.

Give us zesty writing sprinkled with anecdotes: Show, don't tell. Send a well-written, one- or two-page query letter with three to five good feature writing clips. We don't mind looking at completed manuscripts (and obviously will want to if it's an essay); also, we consider previously published articles that have appeared in noncompeting publications.

Show a flair not only for writing, but for accuracy—spell our editor's name right, and don't, for instance, refer to Indiana University as "the University of Indiana" or spell Eli Lilly & Co. (a local pharmaceutical firm) as "Eli Lily."

Professional etiquette: We prefer that writers always send SASEs with queries, and that they refrain from querying us by telephone. If the story has a timely element, feel free to fax us.

Breaking in: New writers usually find it easiest to break in by submitting an ATC (Around the Circle items) or a first-person essay (Hoosiers at Large, First Person). We're also open to queries on Midwestern travel destinations, as well as crime stories based in Indiana.

It's difficult to become a regular contributor if you don't live in the Indianapolis area (or at least in Indiana), but that doesn't preclude an occasional or onetime sale. Active freelance writers should stay alert for strong Indiana angles in the stories they sell elsewhere. For example, we once ran a story by two newspaper reporters who had examined 222,000 declassified pages of Warren Commission files (regarding the JFK assassination). Amid the voluminous verbiage was a surprising revelation: that the FBI once investigated whether Jack Ruby attended Communist Party meetings in Muncie, Indiana.

Articles fall into several categories: features (usually 2,500 to 6,000 words, $400 to $600), which contain several photos and receive the best play; departments (1,500 to 2,500 words, one photo, $250 to $350); and Around the Circle items, or ATCs— punchy, 250-word pieces about what's new or trendy in Indiana/Indianapolis ($50). We also do special section stories: department-length articles published in our Special

Advertising Section. Although ads are sold around them, these articles are not to be confused with advertorials.

THE IOWAN

108 Third Street, Suite 350
Des Moines, IA 50309

Phone number   515-282-8220
Fax number   515-282-0125
Parent company   Mid America Publishing, Co.
Circulation   20,000
Magazine availability   Newsstands and subscription
Target audience   People interested in the history, culture, and natural beauty in Iowa
Magazine's history and mission   Founded 1952 by now publisher David Archie
Nonfiction   100%
Percent of articles freelance-written   90%
Number of articles bought annually   45
Sections of the magazine open to freelance writers   All
Article interests and needs   Anything pertaining to Iowa
Queries should be directed to   Mark Ingebretsen, Managing Editor
Length of articles   300 to 3,500 words
Payment $50 to $500
Time of payment   On acceptance
Expenses   Depends
Photographs   Yes
Response time to queries   6 weeks
Rights bought   First serial
Kill fees   No
Writer's guidelines   Yes
Sample issues $4.50

LAKE SUPERIOR MAGAZINE

P.O. Box 16417
Duluth, MN 55816-0417

Phone number   218-722-5002
Fax number   218-722-4096
E-mail address   edit@lakesuperior.com
Parent company   Lake Superior Port Cities, Inc.
Circulation   20,000

Magazine availability   Newsstands and subscription
Target audience   Visitors and residents in the Lake Superior Watershed
Magazine's history   Founded in 1978
Nonfiction   90 to 95%
Fiction   1 to 3%
Percent of articles freelance-written   50 to 65%
Number of articles bought annually   25 to 30
Sections of the magazine open to freelance writers   All, except news clips
Article interests and needs   Lake Superior specific, human interest, history, sciences, fiction (minimal)
Queries should be directed to   Paul Hayden, Editor; Hugh Bishop, Managing Editor
Length of articles   1,000 to 1,500 words
Payment   Up to $400 for text and photo/art; $65 to $100 for text only
Time of payment   On publication
Expenses   Seldom assign, so generally not
Photographs $35 inside color; $20 inside black-and-white; $75 cover
Response time to queries   1 to 4 weeks
Rights bought   First-time in most cases
Kill fees   None, unless we've agreed to publish already
Writer's guidelines   Yes
Sample issues $3.95 plus postage or 5 stamps

MILWAUKEE MAGAZINE

312 East Buffalo Street
Milwaukee, WI 53202

Phone number   414-273-1101
E-mail address   milmag@qgraph.com
Parent company   Quad Graphics
Circulation   42,000
Magazine availability   Newsstands and subscription
Target audience   Wide range of city dwellers. Readers tend to be upper income professionals, split between men and women.
Magazine's history   Founded in 1982
Nonfiction   100%
Percent of articles freelance-written   40%
Number of articles bought annually   40 to 50 short; 15 to 20 medium to long
Sections of the magazine open to freelance writers   All, except commentary
Article interests and needs   Investigative, good service
Queries should be directed to   John Fennell, Editor
Length of articles   150 to 500 words (Shorts); 1,500 to 4,000 words (Features)
Payment $40 to $150 (short); $300 to $1,000 (long)
Time of payment   On publication

Expenses   Negotiated
Photographs   Rarely
Response time to queries   6 to 8 weeks
Rights bought   First-time
Kill fees   20%
Writer's guidelines   Yes
Sample issues $4.50

TIPS FOR WRITERS

Our editorial goal is to create an informative, literate, and entertaining city magazine that will challenge readers with in-depth reporting and analysis of issues of the day—to enlighten them with thoughtful essays and columns and provide useful service features. Underlying this mission is the strong desire to discover what is unique about Wisconsin and its people, to challenge conventional wisdom when necessary, criticize when warranted, to heap praise when deserved, and to season all with affection and concern for the place we call home.

Visual form and written content are inseparable in magazines. It is our mission to complement a writer's ideas and, when necessary, add to them with lively illustrations, inventive typography, and compelling photographs that help readers find meaning and purpose in the stories we publish.

MINNESOTA MONTHLY

10 South Fifth Street, Suite 1000
Minneapolis, MN 55402

Phone number   612-371-5800
Fax number   612-371-5801
Parent company   Minnesota Communications Group
Circulation   105,500
Magazine availability   Newsstands and subscription
Target audience   We write for a sophisticated, well-educated audience, living primarily in the Twin Cities. Age median is 50, 63% female.
Magazine's history and mission   Owned by Minnesota Public Radio's parent company, Minnesota Communications Group, and is committed to excellence in reporting local stories to Minnesota Public Radio members and subscribers.
Nonfiction   99%
Fiction   1% (annual writing competition winner)
Percent of articles freelance-written   75%
Sections of the magazine open to freelance writers   All
Article interests and needs   Minnesota lifestyle, art, entertainment, service pieces, features, travel pieces, profiles

Queries should be directed to   Daivd Mahoney, Editor
Length of articles   50 to 5,000 words
Payment $25 to $1,200
Time of payment   On acceptance
Expenses   Some
Photographs   We use our own freelancers for photos.
Kill fees   Yes, except for first-time writers
Writer's guidelines   Upon request—write for them.
Sample issues $3.95 each

TIPS FOR WRITERS

Send clips, no manuscripts. We only want queries. Send SASE. Please do not call. Queries are the best way to break through, when good clips accompany.

MONTANA MAGAZINE

P.O. Box 5630
Helena, MT 59604

Phone number   406-443-2842
Fax number   406-443-5480
Parent company   American & World Geographic Publishing
Circulation   75,000
Magazine availability   Newsstands and subscription
Target audience   Ages 30+, male and female, professional, Montana *only*
Magazine's history   Founded in 1970 by Rick Graetz.
Nonfiction   100%
Percent of articles freelance-written   98%
Number of articles bought annually   90
Sections of the magazine open to freelance writers   All
Article interests and needs   Travel, geology, outdoor sports, history, humor, profiles, current events
Queries should be directed to   Beverly R. Magley
Length of articles   800 to 3,000 words
Payment $.15 per word
Time of payment   On publication
Expenses   No
Photographs   Paid additional $50 to $125 each
Response time to queries   3 months
Rights bought   First-time North American
Kill fees   No
Writer's guidelines   Yes—SASE
Sample issues $5.00

IMPORTANT QUESTIONS ANSWERED

Q: What sparks your interest in a query and a freelance writer?
A: A great lead and good background information
Q: Do you always want clips from new writers?
A: Yes
Q: Is an SASE always necessary?
A: Yes
Q: Are phone calls from writers OK?
A: No
Q: Is it OK if writers fax queries to you?
A: Yes
Q: What is the key to breaking into your magazine?
A: A well researched, lively, entertaining query letter or complete manuscript
Q: What is the best thing a writer can do?
A: Write well.
Q: What is the worst thing writers do?
A: Telephone me.
Q: How should writers angle stories for your magazine?
A: Montana-related only
Q: What is your overall advice to writers who want to get published?
A: Keep at it!

NEVADA

1800 Highway 50 East, Suite 200
Carson City, NV 89710

Phone number   702-687-5416
Fax number   702-687-6159
E-mail address   newmag@aol.com
Parent company   The state of Nevada
Circulation   95,000
Magazine availability   Newsstands and subscription
Target audience   Residents and visitors of the state of Nevada
Magazine's history and mission   Founded in 1936, *Nevada* is the state's official tourism magazine.
Nonfiction   100%
Percent of articles freelance-written   About 90%
Number of articles bought annually   90 to 100
Sections of the magazine open to freelance writers   All
Article interests and needs   Nevada's people, history, recreation, entertainment, towns, and scenery.

Queries should be directed to   Carolyn Graham, Associate Editor
Length of articles   500 to 1,800 words
Payment   Ranges from $75 to $500, depending on article length
Time of payment   On publication
Expenses   No
Photographs   Payment ranges from $15 to $200, depending on size and quality. Transparencies preferred to color prints, although good color prints can be used. 8×10 black-and-white glossies preferred.
Response time to queries   4 to 6 weeks
Rights bought   First North American
Kill fees   No
Writer's guidelines   Available upon request
Sample issues   Available upon request

NEWCITY

770 North Halsted, Suite 208
Chicago, IL 60622

E-mail address   NewCity1@aol.com
Parent company   New City Communications, Inc.
Circulation   60,000
Online status   Web site at http://www.suba.com/~new city
Magazine availability   Free circulation at retail outlets in city and suburbs
Target audience   Young, hip
Magazine's history and mission   We celebrated our 10th anniversary February of 1996.
Nonfiction   100%
Percent of articles freelance-written   60%
Sections of the magazine open to freelance writers   All
Article interests and needs   Arts coverage of a preview nature; insightful, incisive short and cover features. Definitely read us before submitting for best chance of publication.
Queries should be directed to   Frank Sennett, Managing Editor
Length of articles   300 to 3,000 words
Payment $.10 per word
Time of payment   On publication
Expenses   Negotiable
Photographs   Yes
Response time to queries   ASAP
Rights bought   First
Kill fees   No
Writer's guidelines   Yes
Sample issues $3

Tips for Writers

Looking for solid reporting with "*Spy*-type" flair. *Very* Chicago oriented. Send clips and SASEs with queries. Will look at manuscripts. Indicate if simultaneous submission.

New Mexico Magazine

Lew Wallace Building
495 Old Santa Fe Trail
Santa Fe, NM 87503

Phone number   505-827-7447
Fax number   505-827-6496
Parent company   State of New Mexico Tourism Department
Circulation   130,000
Magazine availability   Newsstands and subscription
Target audience   Readership in 80 countries around the world with a keen interest in the American Southwest
Magazine's history and mission   Founded in 1923 as the *New Mexico Highway Journal.* We are an offspring of Route 66 and are dedicated to promoting travel in the Southwest and a greater understanding of the region.
Nonfiction   95%
Fiction   5%
Percent of articles freelance-written   80%
Number of articles bought annually   150 to 175
Sections of the magazine open to freelance writers   All in A Day, Así es Nuevo México, Sunspot, Southwest Bookshelf, general features
Article interests and needs   Travel, history, cuisine, nature, art, archaeology, science, profile
Queries should be directed to   Jon Bowman, Editor
Length of articles   250 to 2,000 words
Payment $.30 per word
Time of payment   On acceptance
Expenses   No
Photographs   Color slides/transparencies or black-and-white prints needed
Response time to queries   4 weeks to 2 months
Rights bought   First-time
Kill fees   25%
Writer's guideline   Yes
Sample issues   Yes, for $2.95

Tips for Writers
Jon Bowman, Editor

While we have been known to accept unsolicited manuscripts, the best route for free-lancers to break into *New Mexico Magazine* is through a succinct query proposing an idea that fires our imagination. Queries need not be elaborate. A few paragraphs will suffice, outlining the nature of the prospective story, indicating how quickly it can be produced and when it might best be run, suggesting a target length, and describing the availability of accompanying art (photographs, maps, illustrations, etc.).

Typos in a query are a turnoff. So are simultaneous, mass-produced queries or story suggestions that show a writer's lack of familiarity with the magazine's editorial focus.

Writers seeking to break into the magazine should send one or two clips of previous work that reflects the writer's style and voice. Our longer features (up to 2,000 words) are booked months in advance, so newcomers should try proposing bright and brief shorts (350 to 500 words) for our Así es Nuevo México (This is New Mexico) section.

We do ask for an SASE. Phone or fax queries sometimes work, but we're not as inclined to honor them as a written query, which reflects time and thought on the part of the writer.

What grabs out attention? Amazing stories we've never heard or new wrinkles to old topics. Our focus is entirely on New Mexico. Writers who discover something intriguing in a forgotten, out-of-the-way nook of the state have the best shot at publication. We also devote extensive coverage to the major population/tourism centers (Albuquerque, Santa Fe, Taos, Ruidoso), but we tend to get snowed under with proposals on these areas, so competition is fiercer.

NEWPORT LIFE

174 Bellevue Avenue, Suite 207
Newport, RI 02840

Phone number   401-847-4460
Fax number   401-847-5267
Circulation   10,000
Magazine availability   Newsstands and subscription. Available nationally through Barnes and Noble and Waldenbooks. Also available in Canada
Target audience   Upscale
Magazine's history and mission   Founded in 1993 by Lynne Tungett and Jeffrey Hall. *Newport Life* is a magazine about the people and places of Newport County.
Nonfiction   100%
Percent of articles freelance-written   90%
Number of articles bought annually   Approximately 50
Sections of the magazine open to freelance writers   All
Article interests and needs   Specific, lively articles. Departments include: Historical Newport, At the Helm, In Our Midst, The Garden Path, Built to Last, Arts Marquee, Food for Thought
Queries should be directed to   Susan Ryan, Senior Editor
Length of articles   Departments: 650 words (approximately); Features: 1,500 to 3,000 words
Payment $.10 per word

Time of payment   4 weeks after publication
Expenses   No
Photographs   Helpful but not necessary
Response time to queries   2 to 3 weeks
Rights bought   We buy onetime rights.
Kill fees   20%
Writer's guidelines   Sent on request with SASE

TIPS FOR WRITERS

Freelancers may submit articles or queries to *Newport Life*. Articles should be lively, specific, and concern the people or places of Newport County. Queries should be accompanied with clips that demonstrate the writer's ability to communicate clearly and effectively. Writers are advised to look at an issue of the magazine to get a feel for the magazine's style and content, especially that of the departments.

Writers should accompany articles or queries with self-addressed, stamped envelopes. As style is as important as content, writers are not advised to telephone with inquiries; it is impossible to get a sense of the writer's style except by seeing written work. Fax queries and submissions are not advisable because they are often difficult to read.

NORTHEAST MAGAZINE

285 Broad Street
Hartford, CT 06115

Phone number   203-241-3700
Fax number   203-520-6977 (Please do not fax manuscripts.)
Parent company   Hartford Courant
Circulation   320,000
Magazine availability   Newspaper subscription
Nonfiction   60%
Fiction   10%, no poetry
Percent of articles freelance-written   10%
Number of articles bought annually   6 to 8 unsolicited
Sections of the magazine open to freelance writers   Fiction, nonfiction writing
Queries should be directed to   Dona Winzler
Length of articles   500 to 2,500 words
Payment   Varies between $200 to $500
Time of payment   On acceptance
Expenses   No
Photographs   Please do not include
Response time to queries   6 to 8 weeks
Rights bought   First North American
Kill fees   No

Writer's guidelines   Include SASE for them
Sample issues   Include 11 × 17 SASE.

A TIP FOR WRITERS

Please include SASE for return of manuscript. Otherwise first page only returned to writer.

OKLAHOMA TODAY

P.O. Box 53384
Oklahoma City, OK 73152

Phone number   405-521-2496
Fax number   405-522-4588
Parent company   State of Oklahoma
Circulation   43,000
Online status   Planning to get at least a page up on the Web soon
Magazine availability   Newsstands and subscription
Target audience   Continuing learning and active males and females who are well-educated and opinion leaders, be they school children or senior citizens or Generation Xers; our greatest numbers tend to be between 40 and 60.
Magazine's history and mission   Founded 1956 by State of Oklahoma to help combat the lingering perception of the world that Oklahoma actually was how John Steinbeck described it in his classic, *The Grapes of Wrath.* Idea was that it would educate both Oklahomans and non-Oklahomans about the diversity of Oklahoma culture, people, heritage, and places.
Nonfiction   98%
Fiction   2% (We run some short stories and an annual fiction section.)
Percent of articles freelance-written   60 to 70% (We always have a strong amount of staff-written material.)
Number of articles bought annually   36 to 48
Sections of the magazine open to freelance writers   All but calendar and marketplace
Article interests and needs   Eye-opening, not-done-before or warmed-over pieces with a strong voice and/or angle on an Oklahoma topic—from gardening to ecology to travel to sports to profiles to history
Queries should be directed to   Jeanne M. Devlin, Editor-in-Chief
Length of articles   800 to 8,000 words
Payment $75 to $750
Time of payment   On publication unless it's a gem or prearranged
Expenses   Negotiable
Photographs   Yes, $50 to $200 each
Response time to queries   Acknowledgment at once; review 3 to 4 months
Rights bought   First-time with promo clause

Kill fees   When appropriate
Writer's guidelines   Yes
Sample issues $2.95—send big envelope with $1.30 postage.

TIPS FOR WRITERS
Jeanne M. Devlin, Editor-in-Chief

The query: I'm looking for fresh, original ideas with a strong angle or voice or perspective that indicates the writers are actually familiar enough with the magazine that they not only know an *OKT* story when they see one, but that they also know what section I'll probably use it in. I don't care if a query is in memo form so long as it hits 4 or 5 good intriguing points about why this story is an *OKT* story and why it should be done now.

From new writers, clips are bogus. I don't know who or how many editors have been over that copy; new writers who want to be in *OKT* should submit a manuscript that deserves to be in *OKT*—that's their best chance.

Professional etiquette: An SASE isn't always necessary (though it's nice). Phone calls are fine if you understand we're a small staff and when I'm on deadline I can't talk, and I may not be able to talk again for a few weeks. Faxes are fine, just confirm with our clerical staff that they arrived and got put in my box.

Best ways to break into *OKT*. Write me something brilliant on a topic so Oklahoman and timely and original I'll curse myself for not having thought of it myself.

Key(s) to breaking in to *OKT*: Be a great writer who can either prove to me that you can execute my story ideas on deadline or be a great writer with great original ideas of your own that you can execute on deadline. Be a promising writer who is willing to rewrite and then, when it's still not up to *OKT* standards, let us edit it without complaint, and then be willing to study the finished piece until you understand what we're looking for.

The best things writers do: Feed us good ideas—even when they don't want to write them themselves.

The worst things writers do: Bitch and moan because we haven't made a decision on a story or returned a manuscript (these are always the worst writers too), despite the fact that we've always taken their calls and tried to be frank about our wants, needs, time restraints, etc. And writers who leave you in the lurch by not producing a story as scheduled.

How writers can angle their stories for *OKT*: Make sure the nut paragraph (the paragraph with the critical timely or intriguing facts that motivated us to run this story) makes clear why this story should be read now by the reader, why we should care, and, of course, the regional angle is always paramount.

Overall advice to writers: Read the best, read the best, read the best—fiction, nonfiction, great magazines, great books. Go through your story and a story in *OKT* and underline how many hard cold facts we use in a piece and how few superficial adjectives or adverbs. Know your subject so well that you can not only entertain and inform those who know nothing about it but also surprise those who consider themselves experts on the subject. Be your own fact-checker. Have integrity. Do the research and legwork to produce something that isn't banal. Until you have your own voice or style, copy the voice or style of one of the best (just like beginning painters start by copycatting the masters). Keep up with what's going on in the world—in business, finance, the arts, Hollywood, pop culture, politics—this is how you get fresh and timely angles even on regional topics.

Final words: Trust me. Ninety to ninety-eight percent of what crosses an editor's desk is mediocre. If you have talent and the wherewithal to work hard and learn the style of the magazine you're interested in, you will be published! The brightest moment in my work is still that rare day when a great story from a new writer arrives in my morning mail—it happens only once or twice a year, but when it does it gets published. Good luck.

ORANGE COAST MAGAZINE

245-D Fischer Avenue, Suite 8
Costa Mesa, CA 92626

Phone number   714-545-1900
Fax number   714-545-1932
E-mail address   ocmag@aol.com
Parent company   Orange Coast Komunnications, Inc.
Circulation   40,000
Online status   Web site at http://orangecoast.com
Magazine availability   Newsstands and subscription
Target audience   Orange County residents, ages 30 to 50, male (40%), female (60%)
Magazine's history   Founded in 1974
Nonfiction   100%
Percent of articles freelance-written   80%
Sections of the magazine open to freelance writers   All
Queries should be directed to   Martin J. Smith
Length of articles   2,500 words for features. Others vary.
Payment $25 to $800
Time of payment   On acceptance
Expenses   No
Photographs   Yes
Response time to queries   8 weeks
Kill fees   20% of assignment
Writer's guidelines   Write for them.

OREGON COAST

P.O. 18000
Florence, OR 97439

Phone number   800-348-8401
Fax number   541-997-1124
E-mail address   Rob_Spooner@ortel.org (Send to publisher only—not to editorial department.)
Parent company   Northwest Regional Magazines
Circulation   70,000
Online status   Web site at Oregon Coast Online.www.oregon.coast.com
Magazine availability   Newsstands and subscription
Target audience   Residents of Oregon Coast and those in rest of country who like to travel here. Ages 30+, mid to upscale. Many RVers and campers
Magazine's history and mission   The first issue (May/June 1982) by Russ Heggen was for people who enjoyed the Oregon Coast. In 1988 the magazine was bought by Alicia and Rob Spooner, the current owners.
Nonfiction   100%
Percent of articles freelance-written   70%
Number of articles bought annually   60+
Sections of the magazine open to freelance writers   Features, not departments
Article interests and needs   Must relate to Oregon Coast
Queries should be directed to   Judy Fleagle, Managing Editor
Length of articles   500 to 1,500 words
Payment $65 to $250
Time of payment   After publication
Expenses   No
Photographs   Slides preferred, can use negatives (enclose print, too)
Response time to queries   1 month
Rights bought   First North American serial rights
Kill fees   One-third if assigned
Writer's guidelines   Free with SASE
Sample issues $4.50

TIPS FOR WRITERS
Judy Fleagle, Managing Editor

We prefer all stories to be queried, and the query should be limited to one page. Include what the story idea is about specifically and if you have photos to go with it—and if so, whether they will be by you or someone else. Clue us in on your writing qualifications with one paragraph about you and include a few clips. Limit query to three story ideas. Pet peeve is a long list of story topics with no one idea developed.

We look at all manuscripts. We expect to see an SASE and don't like queries over the phone or faxed unless there is some urgency. Pet peeve is no cover letter with manuscript.

The best way to break in is to try for a short feature where you provide both the edit and photos. We are pleased with clean, concise text; slides with sharp images (some horizontal and some vertical), and captions and credits for photos on a separate sheet of paper. We like to see maps and brochures when applicable. We like to see a complete package, that has up-to-date information with no typos or misspellings.

PENNSYLVANIA MAGAZINE

P.O. Box 576
Camp Hill, PA 17001-0576

Phone number   717-697-4660
Parent company   Pennsylvania Magazine Co.
Circulation   40,000
Magazine availability   Newsstands and subscription
Target audience   Adults 35 and over who are interested in Pennsylvania's history, current events, flora and fauna, recreational opportunities
Magazine's history and mission   Founded in 1981 by Publisher Albert E. Holliday to promote the wealth of the state's history and people to its residents
Nonfiction   100%
Percent of articles freelance-written   97%
Number of articles bought annually   100
Sections of the magazine open to freelance writers   All except Bed & Breakfast column, Book Reviews, Geneaology column, and Gardening column
Article interests and needs   Only Pennsylvania topics. Seasonal travel articles of Pennsylvania areas and sites, little known historical profiles
Queries should be directed to   Editor Matthew K. Holliday
Length of articles   300 to 2,000 words
Payment $.10 to $.15 per word; $15 to $25 photos (up to $100 cover)
Time of payment   On acceptance
Expenses   Seldom pay expenses, then only if preapproved
Photographs   Send 5 × 7 or larger PRINTS, or exceptional duplicate slides
Response time to queries   Personal reply to all queries within 3 weeks
Rights bought   Onetime only first preferred
Kill fees   Only to frequent contributors, 25%
Writer's guidelines   For SASE
Sample issues $2.95

TIPS FOR WRITERS

The query: Contains reasons why article is of interest to readers, where article fits in publication, how many words for finished text, when text will arrive, how and what type of illustrations will be supplied. If writer has been published before—contains where and when but does NOT include clips. If manuscript is already written, should be attached to query. The query serves as a summary of the proposed article—not a tease.

Always include an SASE for response. Send everything by mail, NOT phone or fax.

The key to breaking in: Send targeted ideas often. Frequent correspondence between me and the potential contributor usually results in a published article.

It's best if: The contributor is concise and organized, can supply photographs, subscribes (reads) the magazine, reads our guidelines.

It's bad if: Photos and text will arrive separately, contributor doesn't read publication or guidelines, sends queries infrequently. Sends multiple queries or uses more than one page to propose article, or sends queries on out-of-state topics.

PITCHWEEKLY

3535 Broadway, Suite 400
Kansas City, MO 64111

Phone number   816-561-6061
Fax number   816-756-0502
E-mail address   pitchwee@qni.com
Parent company   Pitch Publishing, Inc.
Circulation   85,000
Online status   Yes
Magazine availability   Free
Target audience   25 to 45; middle/upper income
Magazine's history and mission   Founded 1980 as a music review broadsheet
Nonfiction   95%
Fiction   5%
Percent of articles freelance-written   85%
Number of articles bought annually   100 to 200 (small and lengthy)
Sections of the magazine open to freelance writers   Small features/news and cover stories
Article interests and needs   Primarily we have a local/regional focus but do consider profiles/interviews with known political, artistic, and entertainment figures.
Queries should be directed to   Bruce Rodgers, Editor
Length of articles   Small news/features: 500 to 1,500 words; cover: 3,000 to 5,000 words
Payment   Small news/features: $25 to $125; cover: $150 to $250
Time of payment   Within 1 to 4 weeks after publication
Expenses   Phone, postage, and some travel if prior approval granted (half on kill fee)
Photographs $50 cover (color); $15 inside (black-and-white)
Response time to queries   1 to 2 months
Rights bought   Onetime
Kill fees   Half of agreed upon price
Writer's guidelines   No—query letter first on ideas
Sample issues $5 back issues

TIPS FOR WRITERS

The query: Send a brief, well written query—neatly prepared and to the point; include at least 3 clips. We don't want completed manuscripts except on special holiday themes (fiction stories, offbeat, please) such as Thanksgiving, Christmas, Valentine, April Fools. SASE always. Phones calls are OK after query letter is sent.

The best ways to break in: A good idea, discipline to follow through, listen to editorial tips and guidelines, meet the deadlines, have a developed or developing writing style and a *passion* to write and get published.

The worst things writers do: Not understanding the process of editing, not being patient, and bickering about payment price.

We look not so much to be objective in our stories, but *fair* and *factual*. Look for things not covered or *under-covered* in the mainstream press.

PITTSBURGH

4802 Fifth Avenue
Pittsburgh, PA 15213

Phone number   412-622-1360
Fax number   412-622-7066
Parent company   WQED Pittsburgh
Circulation   65,000
Magazine availability   Newsstands and subscription
Target audience   From young adult up, with special interest toward young families, but many of our current readers are older (50+). Our typical reader has a household income above $80,000, at least some graduate school, and is likely to be a professional. Most of our readers are in Pittsburgh and the immediate surrounding area, but we define our region more broadly: western Pennsylvania, eastern Ohio, northern West Virginia, and western Maryland.
Magazine's history and mission   The magazine began as a small arts magazine in 1969, and was soon acquired by our parent company, WQED, and merged with its television program guide. Around 1975, it was positioned as a city/regional magazine. To quote from our mission statement: "*Pittsburgh* presents a mosaic of Pittsburgh and Western Pennsylvania lifestyles. It presents issues, analyzes problems, presents occasional answers, gives exposure to artists and writers, and in general strives to encourage a better understanding of the community."
Nonfiction   100%
Percent of articles freelance-written   Varies. We have no staff writers, but the editors here do a lot of writing. We also depend on a regular pool of freelancers, including our various contributing editors in food, fashion, etc. Taken one way, I would say that most of our feature stories are freelance-written, i.e. not written by staff. On the other, I'd say that very few are the result of queries coming in over the transom. It's not that we don't want new freelancers, but that very few want to do the sort of stories that anybody would want to read, let alone buy. We have the front-of-the-book section (UpFront) that can be an easier route for freelancers.
Number of articles bought annually   As far as feature stories, I'd estimate that we print maybe 70 per year total. Maybe 40 are written by freelancers. There are many

more brief UpFront items (close to 200), of which maybe two dozen come from writer queries.

Sections of the magazine open to freelance writers   The feature well and UpFront are open to outside freelancers.

Article interests and needs   To quote from my standard rejection letter, "We are interested in information-intensive news and feature stories, and useful service pieces, with specific Pittsburgh-region angles. We do not run advocacy pieces, essays, poetry, fiction, reminiscences, or generalized stories without a strong local angle."

Queries should be directed to   Michelle Pilecki, Managing Editor. To quote some more from my standard rejection: "We prefer to review story proposals that include a sample lead and an outline of no more than one page, specifying the angle and the resources to be consulted. Proposals may be mailed or dropped off in person. We prefer that they not be faxed, and we do not take story proposals over the phone."

Length of articles   Article length varies according to the subject, as does payment. News and service pieces can easily be 3,500 to 5,000 words, and are negotiated according to complexity and how much we have to direct the writer.

Payment   We're in about the middle of the pack for regional magazines as far as payment, although we don't have the five-figure fees that the big nationals can afford. We do not have a specific per-word formula. Our regular "people" features (e.g. Interface) pay $100 for a 400-word piece. Destination, a short travel piece (less than 300 words) in UpFront, also pays $100, as does the lead piece for UpFront. We rarely buy "soft" people features for the main book anymore.

Time of payment   On publication

Expenses   Expenses (agreed upon in advance) are paid extra and separately.

Photographs   Negotiated and paid for separately

Response time to queries   Within 6 weeks

Rights bought   First-time North American rights. We retain rights to the finished product for reprint purposes in all media, but split 50-50 any proceeds from the sale of such above $100. The writer retains rights to his/her original material.

Kill fees   25%

Writer's guidelines   Available by sending an SASE

Sample issues   Available by sending an SASE

TIPS FOR WRITERS
Michelle Pilecki, Managing Editor

A good query should clearly tell me what the story is, why my readers would be interested in *buying* such a story, and why the letter writer is the one to write that story. Note the italics. I'm not interested in hearing about stories that "your readers might like to read." We're in the business of selling magazines, and that means we're interested in stories that will sell magazines, not in stories that somebody might pick up while waiting in the dentist's office with nothing better to do.

Brevity, clarity, and decisiveness are the signs of a good, professional query. Neatness helps. You should see some of the sloppy, badly typed letters I get—often missing a return address. I also want to see queries that look like they may possibly be of use for our market. We don't ever consider stories that don't have a strong local angle. Note that I said strong. The story has to relate somehow to Pittsburgh today. The subject must be something that affects Pittsburghers today.

Clips? Window dressing. They need to be there, and they need to be presentable. But good clips could be the sign of a good editor working with a bad writer, so we don't put a lot of stock in them. We've been burned several times by people with good clips but wouldn't know a story if dictated to them by Joseph Pulitzer. It helps, though, if the clips show that the writer has a proven area of expertise.

We want writers who have something to say when they write. One of the few successful queries written to us was from a woman specializing in telecommuting. She put together a good query that let us know that she knew the subject and how that subject was relevant to our readers. Not only was it a great idea—which she tailored to our audience by getting local people and companies who telecommuted—but it served as a centerpiece for a special issue on "The Changing Workplace," with supporting stories.

We prefer not to look at completed manuscripts, but we will. Rarely have we ever bought one. I've bought a few manuscripts and drastically edited them for UpFront.

Etiquette. SASE necessary only for return of material—and I must get one if you want your material returned. I prefer that people not send artwork unsolicited, because of the possibility of loss, damage, etc. I hate it when unsolicited writers phone and I dislike getting fax queries. It's always bad practice to put those kinds of presumptive moves on a prospective editor, boss, or customer. You're taking up my time (usually when I'm in the middle of something crucial) and my fax paper. People who phone me will be told to send me a proposal in writing. Once I look at a proposal, I'll let you know if I want you to phone me to discuss it or fax me an outline or first draft.

The best way to break in to this magazine (or any magazine) is to become acquainted with what sort of stories we publish. This will tell you what we're likely to buy. If you don't already have a level of expertise, be prepared to do a lot of research. We're not going to pay somebody who just likes to string a lot of words together. We want a lot of information crammed into each story. We have to be able to learn something from the story, whether it's how to market your kid to get into the college you want or how a controversial child welfare agency can clean up its act. (Those were among our two most successful stories; both were written by freelancers—on assignment.)

It helps if writers come up with their own ideas. Few do. We can be leery of trying new writers, and almost always insist that they make the first move by coming up with a salable story idea, which we can then mold for our market. We don't expect new writers to come up with stories that immediately meet our standards, but we insist that writers be able to take direction. We're very hands-on here, and work with writers very closely every step of the way. We prefer to start with a proposal, rather than a draft, so that we can guide the writer to produce the story we want. Writers who can follow directions get more commissions. Writers who can't get a kill fee.

The best thing writers can do is to bring new perspectives and ideas to the magazine and our readers. We want new twists on old topics, or ideas on topics we've never thought of. Go against the clichés and the expectations. For example, we worked with a writer (new to us) on the most eligible singles in Pittsburgh. The "singles scene" is not an idea that most people associate with Pittsburgh. She has a fresh perspective and a good sense of humor. And she's capable of working very closely with us (we had wonderful sessions deciding who to include. We went over outlines together, sample drafts, etc. When the finished story came in, it took little editing from us).

It's a far cry from the worst that writers can do and have done to us. Most of the mortal sins can be summed up in the phrase: they didn't follow directions. They didn't follow the outline we discussed with them. They didn't contact the sources we suggested. They took no care in getting a broader representation in geography, age, profession, price, or whatever it was that we asked for. Basically, they write the story that they want to write, or the one that was easy to write, not the one that we want to buy.

Another problem (can it just be our market?) is that many writers don't understand the structure necessary for a magazine feature. So many former newspaper writers think that a magazine feature is just an overgrown newspaper story. Few writers understand the need to establish a workable structure, supported by lots more research than they would ever need for a newspaper story. That's part of the reason why we work so closely with writers. Few understand our needs. And they all overwrite.

In terms of pet peeves relating just to queries, most of the rejections I send out are because the writer didn't have anything in mind that even remotely relates to what *Pittsburgh* magazine does. Most of the queries I get are obviously from people who either have never seen the magazine, or haven't looked at one for years. Yes, once upon a time, this was an arts magazine—but not within the memory of anyone working here. I also get irritated with query letters that are hard to read. I usually work on those letters in the evenings (it's eight o'clock now) and having to squint at tiny type or loopy script to decipher a return address is a real pain.

The stories I would like to see from freelancers are oriented toward Pittsburgh today. They must have a strong local angle. The reader must learn something from reading it. While we (like most city magazines) have an insatiable need for local service pieces, we also want stories on local issues, businesses, trends, etc. I would love to get more "true crime" stories, but they're rarely pitched (although they're usually bought—the one about the Amish man who disemboweled his wife was a real biggie, and earned the writer several more commissions even on noncrime stories). By the way, it also helps if the writer looks like she/he knows something about Pittsburgh and/or western Pennsylvania. You have no idea how many rejection letters I've sent to people pitching stories about "Amish country" under the assumption that this referred to a specific region. Amish and Mennonite communities are as far west as Indiana, and we've written about several within our coverage area.

We are less interested in stories that focus on Pittsburgh's past, especially those that imply how wonderful it was back then. And there is no market for those personal reminiscences that nobody outside the immediate family would even listen to.

As you can see, we're very demanding. But since we won the CRMA gold award for overall excellence, I would guess we're doing something right. We can always use good writers, and would like to get more.

Seattle, The Magazine for the Pacific Northwest

701 Dexter Avenue North, Suite 101
Seattle, WA 98109

Phone number   206-284-1750
Fax number   206-284-2550
Parent company   Adams Publishing of the Pacific Northwest
Circulation   70,000
Magazine availability   Newsstands and subscription
Target audience   Pacific Northwest professionals, well-educated, home owners
Magazine's history   Founded in April 1992, by Pacific Northwest Media
Nonfiction   100%
Percent of articles freelance-written   80%
Number of articles bought annually   75
Sections of the magazine open to freelance writers   All except calendar trail, dining, and home and design features
Article interests and needs   Most of our writers live in the Pacific Northwest and know the issues and personalities of interest here.
Queries should be directed to   Giselle Smith, Editor
Length of articles   Varies from approximately 300 to 2,500 words: Features: Word length 1,000 to 2,500; Columns: Word length 600 to 1,400; Front Lines: Word length 150 to 600
Payment   Features: Word length 1,000 to 2,500—$250 or more; Columns: Word length 600 to 1,400—Payment begins at $150; Front Lines: Word length 150 to 600—Payment $50 to $150
Time of payment   On publication
Expenses   Not unless agreed to in the contract
Photographs   Not required
Response time to queries   8 to 12 weeks
Rights bought   First
Kill fees   Yes
Writer's guidelines   Yes
Sample issues $295 plus postage

Important Questions Answered

Q: Is an SASE always necessary?
A: No
Q: Are phone calls from writers OK?
A: Yes, but not encouraged. Usually best to send proposal and follow with a phone call.
Q: Is it OK if writers fax queries to you?
A: Yes

Tips for Writers (according to Seattle's Editorial Guidelines)

All queries should be in writing. Short outlines of story ideas are preferred over fully written manuscripts. First-time writers should submit a resume and sample clips. We do not accept multiple submissions.

Good queries generally suggest how and when the proposed article will best fit into the magazine, and compelling reasons why the story is right for *Seattle*. In addition, they should show that the writer has read the magazine and understands its content and readership.

Seattle Weekly

1008 Western Avenue, Suite 300
Seattle, WA 98104

Phone number   206-623-0500 (main reception); 206-467-4370 (editorial)
Fax number   206-467-4377 (editorial)
E-mail address   seaweekly@aol.com
Parent company   Quickfish Media, Inc.
Circulation   62,000 (Circulation is steadily increasing because the paper went to free distribution November 1, 1995.)
Magazine availability   Newsstands (free)
Magazine's history and mission   *Seattle Weekly* was established in 1976 for a local and regional perspective on politics and art.
Nonfiction   99%
Fiction   Only back page (humor)
Percent of articles freelance-written   Varies
Sections of the magazine open to freelance writers   All
Article interests and needs   We could use more humor submissions for the At Large section.
Queries should be directed to   Katherine Koberg, Managing Editor
Payment $25 to $800 depending on the subject and length of article
Time of payment   On publication
Response time to queries   4 to 6 weeks
Writer's guidelines   Yes
Sample issues   With $2 fee. Contact circulation.

A Tip from the Editor

It's best to mail or fax submissions.

Sunday

The Plain Dealer
1801 Superior Avenue
Cleveland, OH 44114

Phone number   216-999-4546
Fax number   216-999-6374
Circulation   Over 500,000
Magazine availability   Magazine found inside *The Plain Dealer* on both newsstands and through subscription.
Target audience   All ages, sexes, professions
Magazine's history and mission   *Sunday*'s mission is to cover the people, places, and issues of Northeastern Ohio. *Sunday* covers Greater Cleveland with feature stories ranging from in-depth profiles on movers and shakers in business, the arts, and sports to trend stories such as bioethics in medicine and the role of martial arts in the lives of children. Weekly departments include Openers (featuring short articles about Clevelanders), cartoons, I Say, essays by our readers on everything from the weather to windmills; Food, mouth-watering, kitchen-tested recipes weekly; and the Puzzle.
Nonfiction   99.9%
Percent of articles freelance-written   25%
Number of articles bought annually   Around 150
Sections of the magazine open to freelance writers   I Say essays
Article interests and needs   Any pertaining to Northeastern Ohio, from interest, etc.
Queries should be directed to   Anne Gordon
Length of articles   800 words (sometimes more)
Payment   Varies
Time of payment   On publication only
Response time to queries   Approximately 2 to 3 weeks
Sample issues   Available for $1.00 with stamped, return-addressed, 8 × 11 envelope

Texas Parks & Wildlife

3000 I. H. 35-South, Suite 120
Austin, TX 78704

Phone number   512-912-7000
Fax number   512-707-1913
E-mail address   magazine@tpwd.state.tx.us
Parent company   Texas Parks and Wildlife Department
Circulation   150,000
Magazine availability   Newsstands and subscription
Target audience   Hunters, fishermen, campers, state park visitors

Magazine's history and mission   Founded in 1943 as hunting and fishing magazine; role has expanded to cover most outdoor recreation activities.

Nonfiction   95%

Fiction   5%

Percent of articles freelance-written   90%

Number of articles bought annually   60 to 75

Sections of the magazine open to freelance writers   Features and departments

Article interests and needs   Hunting and fishing, and state-park-related pieces

Queries should be directed to   Jim Cox, Senior Editor

Length of articles   Features: 1,500 to 2,500 words; Departments: 1,000 words

Payment   Varies

Time of payment   On acceptance and approval

Expenses   Included in payment

Photographs   Varies, depending on size and placement

Response time to queries   2 weeks

Rights bought   Onetime

Kill fees   No

Writer's guidelines   On request

Sample issues   On request

TIPS FOR WRITERS
Jim Cox, Senior Editor

The most common problem with query topics or unsolicited manuscripts is that the author often is unfamiliar with the material we seek. Aspiring contributors who are unfamiliar with our magazine should request a sample copy, freelance guidelines, and story schedule. We're more impressed with a fresh story idea in a well-written query than published clips. Faxes are fine, as are phone calls, and SASE is not required.

TWIN CITIES READER

10 South Fifth Street, Suite 200
Minneapolis, MN 55402

Phone number   612-321-7300

Fax number   612-321-7333

E-mail address   71632.214@compuserve.com (E-mail address is for preassigned articles only.)

Parent company   CityMedia, Inc.

Circulation   100,000

Online status   Soon we will have a home page under CityMedia.

Magazine availability   Newsstands (free) and subscription (paid)

Target audience   Minneapolis and St. Paul and surrounding suburbs, ages 18 to 54, average age: 36, 57% male, 68% single, 57% college-educated, 20% professional, 22% managerial, 29% technical/clerical/sales. People who enjoy cultural events and live entertainment, are politically aware, and sensitive to cultural diversity

Magazine's editorial focus: Local news, profiles, human interest, political analysis, and arts and entertainment (local bands, live music, galleries, museums, readings, local authors, performance art, sports and happenings)

Nonfiction   100%

Percent of articles freelance-written   30%

Sections of the magazine open to freelance writers   All

Article interests and needs   Local news and politics, gallery and museum, modern dance, sports writing

Queries should be directed to   Claude Peck, Editor

Payment   Depends on section and length of item: $6 to $40 for shorter items, less than 400 words; $125 to $200 for longer news stories and features. Cover stories prices individually

Time of payment   Upon publication

Expenses   Not reimbursed

Photographs   Send queries to David Steinlicht, art director

Response time to queries   3 to 4 weeks

Rights bought   First serial

Kill fees   25%

TIPS FOR WRITERS

The query: The most impressive queries come from writers who have read our paper, and know its editorial content and style. A good query is correctly addressed to our editor, states the focus of the article, explains why we should publish it, and tells why you are the best person to write it. When dealing with an unknown writer, we always ask for clips, but don't send more than five. The clips should show the writer's personal style, knowledge of the proposed subject matter, and reporting skills. We will look at completed manuscripts only if we feel it fits our editorial content.

Professional etiquette: Phone calls from writers are appropriate after the query is sent and if he/she has not heard from us after two weeks, or if the article being proposed is extremely timely. SASEs are not necessary, unless clips are to be returned (otherwise they are kept on file for at least one year). Faxed queries are fine, but we will probably call and ask for clips. Please do not e-mail queries.

The best way to break into our publication is to have a specific area of interest (politics, galleries, jazz, etc.). We will then assign according to that interest, or come to us with an idea once we have established a relationship. Book reviews are often written by freelancers, as are film shorts, but all are preassigned. The key to breaking in is to show that you are a strong writer, or have an unbeatable news story and proven track record.

The best thing a writer can do is to have confidence in their own expertise and writing and know about our paper. The worst thing a writer can do is to pester us with too many follow-up calls. Do not send us an obviously mass-mailed query or manuscript. Also, be receptive of edits and rewrites (we're critical, but not mean).

The best way to angle a story for our paper is to read our paper, get to know the style and attitude of each section. We work closely with our writers, so you're never left wondering what is expected of you.

VERMONT MAGAZINE

2 Maple Street, Suite 400
Middlebury, VT 05758

Phone number   802-388-8480
Fax number   802-388-8485
E-mail address   vtmag.aol.com
Circulation   35,000
Magazine availability   Newsstands and subscription
Target audience   Both Vermonters and out-of-staters, professionals and retirees
Magazine's history and mission   Founded in 1989 by David Skeper to explore contemporary Vermont.
Nonfiction   100%
Percent of articles freelance-written   60%, more or less
Number of articles bought annually   15 to 20
Sections of the magazine open to freelance writers   Features, politics
Article interests and needs   Profiles of Vermont personalities, issue pieces of interest to Vermonters, some Vermont travel pieces, service pieces
Queries should be directed to   Julie Kirgo, Managing Editor
Length of articles   1,000 to 2,500 words
Payment   Variable, depending on writer's experience and length of piece
Time of payment   On publication
Expenses   Yes, within reason
Photographs   Yes
Response time to queries   1 to 2 weeks
Writer's guidelines   Yes
Sample issues   Yes

IMPORTANT QUESTIONS ANSWERED

Q: What sparks you interest in a query and/or a freelance writer?
A: Style, imagination, professionalism
Q: What are the key elements of a good professional query?
A: Make it short and sweet and on-topic.
Q: Do you always want clips from new writers?
A: Yes
Q: How many clips do you want?

A: Three to four

Q: *What do you look for in the writer's clips?*

A: Style and economy

Q: *Will you look at completed manuscripts?*

A: Yes

Q: *Are phone calls from writers OK?*

A: No

Q: *Is it OK if writers fax or e-mail queries to you?*

A: Yes

Q: *What is the best way to break into your magazine?*

A: A good, solid query

Q: *What is the best thing writers do?*

A: Keep things simple.

Q: *What are the worst things writers do?*

A: Calling or worse, showing up unannounced

Q: *How should writers angle their stories for your magazine?*

A: Vermont, Vermont, Vermont

VIRGINIA MAGAZINE

24 North Buckmarsh Street
P.O. Box 798
Berryville, VA 22611

Phone number   540-955-1298

Fax number   540-955-2321

Parent company   The Country Publishers, Incorporated

Circulation   52,000

Magazine availability   Newsstands and subscription

Target audience   Generally 40+ professionals, both sexes

Magazine's history and mission   Founded in 1978 by Garrison Ellis. Mission is to enthrall the residents of Virginia with politics, education, history, art, and the environment.

Nonfiction   Approximately 80%

Fiction   Approximately 20%

Percent of articles freelance-written   75 to 100%

Number of articles bought annually   20 to 30

Sections of the magazine open to freelance writers   All

Article interests and needs   Sharp, reflective writing

Queries should be directed to   Mark Schulte, Managing Editor

Length of articles   We can talk about that.

Payment   Negotiable

Time of payment   Within 30 days of publication

Expenses   Negotiable

Photographs   Good black-and-white

Response time to queries   Several months at most
Kill fees   Negotiable

TIPS FOR WRITERS

Query: Good writing sparks interest. Completed manuscripts preferred.

   Professional etiquette: SASE necessary. Phone calls OK. Fax inquiries OK.

   Worst things writers do: Equate regional general interest magazine with vehicle for drab, hackneyed, unoriginal writing.

   Overall advice: Don't be afraid to take a chance, do not assume we are like most other publications you have seen.

THE WASHINGTONIAN

1828 L Street, NW
Washington, DC 20036

Phone number   202-296-3600
E-mail address   washmag@aol.com
Parent company   Capital Communications
Circulation   155,000
Online status   via InfiNet and AOL's "Digital City"
Magazine availability   Newsstands and subscription
Target audience   Top 10% of Washingtonians in terms of income, education, and influence
Magazine's history and mission   Begun in 1965 . . . magazine seeks to help Washingtonians make choices (restaurants, doctors, vacation spots, etc.) and to understand the region and how power in Washington works.
Nonfiction   100%
Percent of articles freelance-written   25 to 35%
Number of articles bought annually   Perhaps 40 to 55
Sections of the magazine open to freelance writers   Any section except food and wine
Article interests and needs   We're always interested in stirring first-person accounts set hard and fast in Washington area, articles that offer special insight or expertise and are geared to and are useful for our readers.
Queries should be directed to   Courtney Denby, Assistant to the Editor
Length of articles   Depends
Payment   Depends
Time of payment   On publication
Expenses   Reasonable ones, yes
Photographs   Rarely
Response time to queries   1 to 3 months
Rights bought   Yes
Kill fees   Yes

Writer's guidelines   Yes
Sample issues   No

TIPS FOR WRITERS
Howard Means, Senior Editor

Don't send a shopping list of three to seven articles you would like to write. It suggests you don't care particularly deeply about any of them. What catches our eye for center-of-the-book pieces are truly unique experiences with a hard Washington setting and subjects about which the writer clearly feels passion.

WEST MAGAZINE
750 Ridder Park Drive
San Jose, CA 95190

Phone number   408-920-5796
Fax number   408-271-3618
E-mail address   westmail@aol.com
Parent company   Knight-Ridder
Circulation   340,000
Magazine availability   Newsstands and subscription
Target audience   Readers in the San Francisco Bay Area
Nonfiction   100%
Percent of articles freelance-written   66%
Number of articles bought annually   100
Sections of the magazine open to freelance writers   All
Article interests and needs   Subjects related to life in the San Francisco Bay Area
Queries should be directed to   Fran Smith, Editor
Length of articles   Various
Payment   Negotiable
Time of payment   On acceptance
Expenses   Negotiable
Response time to queries   One week
Rights bought   Negotiable
Kill fees   One-fourth
Writer's guidelines   No
Sample issues   Yes

WHERE MAGAZINES
70 The Esplanade
Toronto, Ontario, Canada M5E 1R2

Parent company　Key Publishers of Toronto
Circulation　Varies from city to city. We publish in sixteen U.S. cities. Total circulation is slightly less than a million and a half currently.
Magazines available　*Where* magazines are distributed solely through hotels and tourist bureaus. They are not sold on newsstands, though we do have subscribers.
Target audience　The traveler who stays in upmarket hotels
Magazine's history and mission　The chain was founded in 1936 in Detroit, and was acquired by Key Publishers of Toronto in 1985. The mandate of *Where* is to provide timely, useful, accurate information to visitors in the cities in which they are published.
Nonfiction　100%
Number of articles bought annually　It varies from city to city.
Article interests and needs　There is no editorial information that is published in more than one *Where*. All our material is locally derived.
Queries should be directed to　All queries and editorial material should be addressed to the local editors in 36 cities including: New York, Chicago; Washington, D.C.; Boston, San Francisco, Atlanta, Los Angeles, St. Louis, Kansas City, Twin Cities, Seattle, New Orleans, Philadelphia, Baltimore, Toronto, Vancouver, Ottawa, Calgary, Edmonton, Winnipeg, Victoria, Halifax, and Banff/Jasper.

YANKEE

P.O. Box 520
Dublin, NH 03444

Phone number　603-563-8111
Fax number　603-563-8252
E-mail address　Queries@YankeePub.com
Parent company　Yankee Publishing Incorporated
Circulation　700,000
Magazine availability　Newsstands and subscription
Target audience　Anyone who loves New England
Magazine's history and mission　Founded in 1935 by Robb Sagendorph "to express and, perhaps indirectly, preserve" the culture of New England.
Nonfiction　95%+
Fiction　Less than 5%
Percent of articles freelance-written　60 to 70%
Number of articles bought annually　100 to 120
Sections of the magazine open to freelance writers　Feature well, Traveler's Journal, New England Sampler, Great New England Cooking, I Remember, Last Page, poetry—really everything except House For Sale, book reviews, and Plain Talk
Article interests and needs　Anything to do with New England. The hardest material to find is good enterprising journalism. Everyone wants to write personal essays.

Queries should be directed to   Don Weafer, Assistant Editor
Length of articles   Anywhere from 200 to 4,000 words
Payment   Depends on where it appears and how badly we want it—no set rate
Time of payment   On acceptance
Expenses   For assigned work
Photographs   We assign our own
Response time to queries   2 to 4 weeks
Rights bought   First magazine
Kill fees   We try to avoid them with established or familiar writers (i.e., we pay full fee). With untested writers, occasionally we will offer a kill fee in lieu of full payment.
Writer's guidelines   Yes
Sample issues   No

TIPS FOR WRITERS
Tim Clark

We have been publishing *Yankee* for 60 years and see about 100 queries or manuscripts per week, so there's very little about New England history and lore that we haven't seen before. The successful query or manuscript presents an idea in a surprising way. For example, the story of Hannah Dustin, a colonial woman kidnapped by Indians who turned on her captors, killed and scalped nine of them, and escaped back to the settlements, is an old chestnut. But one writer began her story with a literally hair-raising description of the anatomical details of scalping. That caught our attention.

Surprising us will overcome most other problems. Yes, we want clips, but only clips that show us the style of writing we're looking for—strong narrative, powerful emotions, a clean, straightforward style that doesn't get in between the reader and the story. We look at all manuscripts we receive, and though only one in a thousand is published—that one is a gem. An SASE is always welcome. We'll ask you for a written query anyway (fax and e-mail are OK), so don't waste our time and yours with phone calls. An exception might be made for stories that are happening *right now*—but we have a five-month to one-year lead time, so we're generally not all that interested in breaking stories. However, we are looking for contemporary journalism, not just history and nostalgia. We get more of that than we can possibly use.

The best way to break into *Yankee* is with short pieces for Sampler, Traveler's Journal, I Remember, or the last page. We average only three or four feature-length stories per issue, and we're not likely to assign a newcomer one of those unless it's truly remarkable. Send lots of ideas, and don't censor yourself: probably the worst mistake writers make is to say to themselves, "*Yankee* would never be interested in that." Remember: we *want* to be surprised.

Religious/Inspirational

CATHOLIC DIGEST

P.O. Box 64090
St. Paul, MN 55164

Phone number   612-962-6725
Fax number   612-962-6755
Editorial department e-mail address   CDigest@stthomas.edu
Parent company   University of St. Thomas
Circulation   523,000
Online status   Library of files on CompuServe's Catholic Online Forum; Web site expected up by April 1996.
Magazine availability   Subscription; church sales; expected newsstand sales April 1996
Magazine's history and mission   *Catholic Digest* is a 60-year-old national magazine published by the University of St. Thomas in St. Paul, Minnesota. Each month, we provide 3 million readers of all ages with the tools and motivation to lead happier, more successful, more fulfilling lives.

Catholic Digest cares for the bodies, minds, and souls of its readers with features and advice on topics ranging from health, psychology, humor, adventure, and family to ethics, spirituality, and Catholic heritage. Profiles of "successful" Catholics, from saints through the ages to modern-day heroes, inspire and motivate readers to lead lives of courage and faith, to better themselves—as individuals, as partners and parents, as believers.

Readers look to *Catholic Digest* for the most helpful, most relevant reading its editors can cull from hundreds of secular and religious periodicals, as well as inspiring articles that originate with the magazine. The result is a magazine that readers of all ages love and trust, and read from cover to cover.

Nonfiction   100%
Percent of articles freelance-written   30%
Number of articles bought annually   250
Sections of the magazine open to freelance writers *Catholic Digest* features six regular fillers each month: Open Door: statements of true incidents through which people are brought into the Church (200 to 500 words, $50); People Are Like That: original accounts of true incidents that illustrate the instinctive goodness of human nature (200 to 500 words, $50); The Perfect Assist: original accounts of gracious or tactful remarks or actions (20 to 500 words, $50); Hearts Are Trumps: original accounts of true cases of unseeking kindness (200 to 500 words, $50); Signs of the times: amusing or significant signs (give exact source) ($4); In Our Parish: stories of parish life (50 to 300 words, $20). *Catholic Digest* also uses other types of fillers: jokes, short anecdotes, quizzes, and informational paragraphs (1-liners to 500 words, payment by length up to $50).
Article interests and needs   Most articles we use are reprinted—they have in another periodical or newspaper. But we also consider all original submissions. We don't consider fiction, poetry, or simultaneous submissions. We use nonfiction articles on almost

any topic. Our readers have a wide range of interests—religion, family, science, health, human relationships, nostalgia, good works, and more.

Queries should be directed to   CDigest@stthomas.edu. If electronic submission is not possible, be sure to include a self-addressed, stamped envelope (SASE) with snail mail. Send regular-post submissions to: Articles Editor, *Catholic Digest,* P.O. Box 64090, St. Paul, MN 55164-0090.

Length of articles   1,000 to 3,500 words

Payment $100 for reprints, $200 to $400 for originals. For reuse in electronic form, we pay half of all traceable revenue derived from electronic use to owner/author.

Response time to queries   Up to 3 months

TIPS FOR WRITERS

We favor the anecdotal approach. Stories submitted must be strongly focused on a definitive topic. This topic is to be illustrated for the reader by way of a well-developed series of true-life, interconnected vignettes.

Before you submit a manuscript, study *Catholic Digest* for article tone and style.

Include your name, address, and telephone number should we need to contact you with questions or send payment.

If you are submitting an article for reprint consideration, you must include the name, address, and editor of the original source, the copyright line from the original source, and the page number and date of original publication.

FOURSQUARE WORLD ADVANCE

P.O. Box 26902
1910 West Sunset Boulevard, Suite 200
Los Angeles, CA 90026-0176

Phone number   213-484-2400, Ext. 309

Fax number   213-413-3824

E-mail address   com@foursquare.org

Parent company   International Church of the Foursquare Gospel

Circulation   100,000

Online status   Web site at http://www.foursquare.org

Magazine availability   Subscription

Target audience   Foursquare Church members and believers in Jesus Christ and those seeking Biblical Truth

Magazine's history and mission   Founded September 1917, under the name *Bridal Call* by Aimee Semple McPherson, who was also founder of The International Church of the Foursquare Gospel.

Nonfiction   Usually 100%

Fiction   Usually 0%

Percent of articles freelance-written   25% (varies)

Number of articles bought annually   60 approximately
Sections of the magazine open to freelance writers   Missions or testimonies (varies)
Queries should be directed to   Ron Williams, Editor
Length of articles   1,000 words or less
Payment $75
Time of payment   On publication
Photographs   Can be submitted with article; author pictures are generally not used.
Response time to queries   1 month approximately
Writer's guidelines   Yes
Sample issues   Yes

TIPS FOR WRITERS

All inquiries and submissions must be done through written form; mail, e-mail, or fax. Every submission will be read and considered. Articles selected for publication are generally those which are a testimony or an exposition of Biblical principles. We rarely use illustrations. Poems are used infrequently. An SASE is not required.

A submission will either be returned with a letter informing the writer that we cannot use their article, or we will retain the manuscript and keep it as a "story on hold." A promise will not be given as to when it will be used. In fact, the story may never be used at all.

Because of the nature of our magazine and the type of article used, references may be necessary to verify the writer's authenticity as a valid source for a testimony or "qualifications" to administer Biblical teaching.

GUIDEPOSTS

16 East 34th Street
New York, NY 10016

Phone number   212-251-8100
Fax number   212-684-0679
Parent company   Guideposts
Circulation   4 million
Magazine availability   Subscription
Target audience   General audience, national
Magazine's history and mission   Founded in 1945 by Dr. Norman Vincent Peale as an interfaith, inspirational magazine publishing first-person stories of people who have overcome difficulties in life through faith in God.
Nonfiction   100%
Percent of articles freelance-written   60%
Number of articles bought annually   70 to 80
Sections of the magazine open to freelance writers   All

Article interests and needs   True first-person stories telling in dramatic form how people have overcome difficulties, gained courage, or developed positive attitudes through faith in God.

Queries should be directed to   The editor, but prefer to see the finished manuscript from new writers

Length of articles   750 to 1,500 words

Payment $200 to $400, sometimes more

Time of payment   On acceptance

Expenses   Yes, if on assignment by editor

Photographs   Yes

Response time to queries   4 weeks

Rights bought   We buy all rights

Kill fees   25% on assigned stories

Writer's guidelines   Yes

Sample issues   Yes

TIPS FOR WRITERS

At first glance, a writer might feel that *Guideposts* is a simple magazine, and that writing for it would be simple. It is anything but. *Guideposts* stories are carefully crafted to present true, first-person stories showing how ordinary people have overcome troubles, gained courage, and developed positive attitudes through faith in God. The stories must be told in dramatic fashion, using the same techniques as a writer of fiction, showing through scene and character development how faith and God are at work. Each story must have conflict and resolution, in which a person's life is changed, and a "take-away," a spiritual lesson the reader can "take away" and apply to his or her own life. And each story must be within the framework of the Judeo-Christian understanding of God and the Bible.

We prefer to see completed manuscripts, accompanied by an SASE, rather than queries from first-time writers, therefore we discourage queries in any form. However, please understand that we receive some 4,000 manuscripts per month (and read them all) and buy perhaps eight or nine. It is easier to break into the magazine with shorter pieces of 500 words or less, or in one of our departments, such as His Mysterious Ways or What Prayer Can Do. Make sure you do not preach, but tell a good story.

HOME LIFE
127 Ninth Avenue, North
Nashville, TN 37234-0140

Phone number   615-251-5721
Fax number   615-251-5008
Parent company   Baptist Sunday School Board
Circulation   546,000

Magazine availability   Bulk orders to churches and subscription

Target audience   Primarily women, ages 25 to 45, national circulations, some foreign countries

Magazine's history and mission   Began publishing in 1947. *Home Life's* mission is to enrich marriage and family life.

Nonfiction   All articles and departments

Fiction   1 short story

Percent of articles freelance-written   75%

Sections of the magazine open to freelance writers   All, except departments that feature experts

Article interests and needs   Marriage enrichment, parenting, family life, inspirational

Queries should be directed to   Leigh Neely, Managing Editor

Length of articles   600 to 1,800 words

Payment $75 to $275

Time of payment   On acceptance

Expenses   Negotiated on assignments only

Photographs   Through art director

Response time to queries   2 to 4 weeks

Rights bought   All, onetime, first (when writer requests)

Kill fees   No

Writer's guidelines   Yes

Sample issues   SASE, 9 × 12, with $.98 postage *affixed*

TIPS FOR WRITERS
Leigh Neely, Managing Editor, Home Life

Persons interested in writing for *Home Life* should study multiple copies. This is a magazine that concentrates on marriage and family enrichment from a Christian perspective. We do not consider anything in conflict with those values and beliefs. Writers should understand this particular market.

A good query will give me everything I need to make a judgment about the article's suitability for our publication. What is your purpose in writing this particular article? Who is the target? Do you know the thesis statement? Beware that you don't pick a subject that is too broad. For example, don't send me a query about teenage sex. Instead, pick one aspect, like the rise of venereal disease among teens or a look at the statistics of Christian teenagers who practice premarital sex. Clips from previously published material help somewhat, but really don't let me know what you can do with that particular subject.

An SASE is always necessary. In fact, your material will not be returned without one. We have a total of eight magazines in this particular department and simply do not have a budget big enough to pay postage on returned items. Faxed queries are acceptable.

The easiest way to get published in *Home Life* is to contribute a short article for the FamilyTime department. We also like brief 600-word articles that give practical tips and advice to married couples and parents.

The key to breaking into print in *Home Life* is to be professional. Submit your best work. Make sure it is neat and easy to read. It should be double-spaced, with one-inch margins around the page—which gives the writer approximately 250 words per page. Do *not* submit an article like you would a term paper or a college essay. Read *Writer's Digest* or *The Writer* and learn the proper way to do magazine submissions. All you need is a cover letter and your article. Make sure your name is on each page.

The worst thing writers do is start a letter, "I know you said you don't accept this, but . . ." If we said we don't accept that kind of material, we don't. And we will not read further in your cover letter. We will simply reject the manuscript. We do not appreciate writers who indicate nothing should be edited. No material is published without editing. In actuality, an editor enhances your work.

If you want to get published, do what the editor requests. Be professional and stay informed about markets.

LIVE

1445 Boonville
Springfield, MO 65802

Phone number   417-862-2781
Fax number   417-862-6059
Parent company   General Council of the Assemblies of God
Circulation   130,000
Magazine availability   Subscription/local churches (Assembly of God)
Target audience   Adults (18 through senior adult) throughout the U.S. and Canada, all English-speaking ethnic groups
Magazine's history and mission   *Live* (under another name) was begun in 1928 by the Sunday School Department of the Assemblies of God. It was begun to encourage Christians in living for God through stories which apply biblical principles to everyday problems.
Nonfiction   About 50%
Fiction   About 50%
Percent of articles freelance-written   100%
Number of articles bought annually   Approximately 100 to 120
Sections of the magazine open to freelance writers   All
Article interests and needs   Fiction or true stories that encourage or inspire readers in becoming all they can be as Christians. We use humor, adventure, and address issues of current interest in the Christian world. We particularly like stories that encourage family life and reaching out to others. No preaching!
Queries should be directed to   Paul W. Smith, Adult Editor
Length of articles   General: 500 to 1,700 words; Fillers: 200 to 500 words
Payment $.03 per word for reprint rights; $.05 per word for first rights
Time of payment   On acceptance

Photographs   We do use photos in our publication and pay according to our photo payment schedule for those we choose to use.

Response time to queries   We do not answer query letters. But we do respond to submissions within 6 weeks.

Kill fees   No kill fees

Writer's guidelines   Yes (Send SASE and $.32.)

Sample issues   Yes (No charge.)

IMPORTANT QUESTIONS ANSWERED

Q: What is the best way to break into your magazine?

A: Send well-written articles according to our guidelines. We don't have any other criteria.

Q: What is the best thing writers do?

A: Give good material.

Q: What is the worst thing writers do?

A: Preach, too wordy, fail to send SASE, or send too many manuscripts at once (limit two).

Q: What overall advice would you give writers who want to get published?

A: Write well!!! Know your audience.

REFORM JUDAISM

838 Fifth Avenue
New York, NY 10021

Phone number   212-650-4240

Fax number   212-650-4249

Parent company   Union of American Hebrew Congregations

Circulation   300,000

Magazine available   On selected New York City newsstands as well as subscriptions

Target audience   Members of Reform Jewish synagogues in the United States and Canada

Magazine's history and mission   *Reform Judaism* was founded more than 60 years ago and took its current title in 1972. Its Statement of Purpose: "*Reform Judaism* is the official voice of the Union of American Hebrew Congregations, linking the institutions and affiliates of Reform Judaism with every Reform Jew. *RJ* covers developments within our Movement while interpreting world events and Jewish tradition from a Reform perspective. Shared by 290,000 member households, *RJ* conveys the creativity, diversity, and dynamism of Reform Judaism. Members of UAHC congregations receive *RJ* as a benefit of membership."

Nonfiction   95%

Fiction   5%
Percent of articles freelance-written   60%
Number of articles bought annually   50

SIGNS OF THE TIMES

P.O. Box 5353
Nampa, ID 83653-5353

Phone number   208-465-2577
Fax number   208-465-2531
Parent company   Pacific Press Publishing Assoc.
Circulation   250,000
Magazine availability   Subscription
Target audience   Ages 35 and up
Magazine's history and mission   Continuously published since 1874. Mission: to present Jesus as the all-sufficient Savior
Nonfiction   100%
Percent of articles freelance-written   30%
Number of articles bought annually   100
Article interests and needs   First person stories, people helping people
Queries should be directed to   Marvin Moore, Editor
Length of articles   700 to 2,000 words
Payment $.25 per word
Time of payment   Once edited
Expenses   No
Photographs   Yes, if requested by designer
Response time to queries   3 weeks
Rights bought   One time
Writer's guidelines   Available free with 9 × 12 SASE.
Sample issues   Yes, free with envelope above.

AN IMPORTANT QUESTION ANSWERED

Q: What is the worst thing writers do?
A: Be unfamiliar with a magazine.

ST. ANTHONY MESSENGER

1615 Republic Street
Cincinnati, OH 45210-1298

Phone number   513-241-5615
Fax number   513-241-0399
Parent company   Franciscan Friars, St. John the Baptist Province
Circulation   324,318
Magazine availability   Subscription, church racks, some bookstores
Target audience   A national publication, family oriented, more women readers than men, age 30+
Magazine's history and mission   *St. Anthony Messenger* is a religious publication for Roman Catholics. It was founded in 1893. The first editor was Rev. Ambrose Sanning, O.F.M. He described the magazine as a messenger of love and a herald of peace. It was directed to members of the Third Order and Holy Family Association. It applied Catholic teaching to daily life.
Nonfiction   90%
Fiction   10%
Percent of articles freelance-written   80%
Number of articles bought annually   50 to 55
Sections of the magazine open to freelance writers   Articles and fiction
Article interests and needs   Catholic teaching, implications for daily living, Catholic personalities, interviews, social questions, scripture, prayer, family matters, inspiration, etc.
Queries should be directed to   The editor (Fr. Norman Perry, O.F.M.)
Length of articles   2,500 to 3,000 words
Payment $.14 a word
Time of payment   On acceptance
Expenses   Only if commissioned and agreed on beforehand
Photographs $25 for black-and-whites used and submitted with an article
Response time to queries   4 to 6 weeks
Rights bought   First North American serial rights
Kill fees   Unless commissioned, all articles are submitted on speculation
Writer's guidelines   Writer's guidelines are available on request.
Sample issues $2.00

TIPS FOR WRITERS

Queries should be brief and to the point. They should not leave the editors guessing at what the writer proposes to do. Queries should clearly state the subject of the proposed article and offer a working title. The author should show some familiarity with the magazine and its style and usual content. We are not interested in travel articles or cooking features. Incorrect grammar, bad spelling, and messy queries are warning signs of what to expect in the finished article.

Every manuscript sent "over the transom" gets at least one reader unless it is scrawled in pencil or shows no signs of any professionalism.

We do expect a self-addressed, stamped envelope for both query and manuscript returns.

Both queries and manuscripts that have some hope of purchase are evaluated by six to eight readers. That takes some time. As much as six to eight weeks. Telephone calls force the editor to make the rounds of the other editors to find who has the manuscript in question at the moment and its status. That invites immediate rejection to avoid more telephone calls.

The best way to break into the magazine is to write an interesting article or story that fits the style and content of *St. Anthony Magazine*. We like articles with practical examples from real life. Live, new quotes from real life people and experts are important. We don't want articles based on book research. Articles based on interviews with experts or experiences help. Seasonal material should be sent six months or more in advance.

We expect articles written for *St. Anthony Messenger* to have some particular appeal to our readership. They need some religious and Catholic slant. Vocabulary, terminology, people quoted should fit our readership. Theology and religious teaching should conform to Catholic belief and Church teaching.

Submitting articles well beyond our preferred word length is a waste of time. And we do not serialize articles. Editors do not want to work with articles typed single space. And they are irritated by manuscripts barely legible because of overused ribbons or weak printouts.

WORLD MAGAZINE

25 Beacon Street
Boston, MA 02108

Phone number   617-742-2100
Fax number   617-367-3237
E-mail address   worldmag@uua.org
Parent company   Unitarian Universalist Association
Circulation   115,000
Magazine availability   Controlled circulation
Target audience   Members of Unitarian Universalist churches
Magazine's history and mission   Published in current format since 1987. Mission is to articulate UU values, spirituality, purposes, and history.
Nonfiction   100%
Percent of articles freelance-written   25%
Number of articles bought annually   10
Sections of the magazine open to freelance writers   Features, commentary
Article interests and needs   We only accept articles with a clear Unitarian Universalist angle—query first.
Queries should be directed to   Linda Beyer McHugh, Editor-in-Chief
Length of articles   2,000 words
Payment $700
Time of payment   On acceptance

Expenses   Phone, travel
Response time to queries   3 months
Rights bought   First-time North American print and electronic rights
Kill fees   One-third of fee
Writer's guidelines   Yes
Sample issues $4.00 each

Romance

MODERN ROMANCES

233 Park Avenue South
New York, NY 10003

Phone number   212-979-4894
Fax number   212-979-7342
Parent company   The Sterling/Macfadden Partnership
Circulation   200,000
Magazine availability   Newsstands and subscription
Target audience   Working women/mothers, ages 25 to 40
Magazine's history and mission   Founded in 1929. Mission to share true-life experiences for and about women all over the country.
Nonfiction   100%
Percent of articles freelance-written   100%
Number of articles bought annually   120
Sections of the magazine open to freelance writers   All Stories, My Corner of The Country (Feature), Poetry, Readers' Corner, Pet Pals
Article interests and needs   Looking for true-life experiences about women. Romantically oriented. Interested in stories under 9,000 words
Completed manuscripts (no queries accepted) should be directed to   Eileen Fitzmaurice, Editor
Length of articles   2,000 to 9,000 words
Payment $.05 per word
Time of payment   On publication
Photographs   We do not accept outside photos—except for Pets.
Response time to queries   9 to 11 months
Rights bought   We buy all rights.
Kill fees   None
Writer's guidelines   Available. Please send SASE.
Sample issues   Available. Please send $2.00 check.

TIPS FOR WRITERS

We do not require query letters, and would rather read a completed manuscript. But if a query letter is strong enough to pique our interest, we may contact the author for the full story. Clips are also not a requirement, but if an author wishes to send them, they will be read. However, it does not guarantee a quicker reply or acceptance.

An SASE is encouraged; we will not reply without one, and the manuscript will not be returned. Phone calls are accepted by authors inquiring about their manuscripts, but we ask that authors *be patient!* We receive a number of manuscripts, and since we read everything that comes in, reply times may often be as long as a year. If a writer wishes to send their story to another publication—especially another Sterling/Macfadden publication—we ask that the author contact the editor currently holding the story and explain their situation.

The best way to break in to the confession/romance market is to know the target audience. The best way to learn this is by reading a few issues of the magazine. Find a topic we haven't covered yet and your chances for publication are greater. Also, the more specific the plot, the better. Nothing is worse than reading the same old story over and over (reunion stories, unhappy wife decides to have an affair, kidnapping and stalker stories, etc.)

The worst things writers can do is to write a story in the third person. All of our stories are written in first person, as if you were telling your story to a friend. Another pet peeve is to send the same story to a few of our publications.

TRUE LOVE

233 Park Avenue South, 7th Floor
New York, NY 10003

Phone number   212-979-4800
Fax number   212-979-7342
Parent company   Sterling/Macfadden Partnership
Circulation   210,000
Magazine availability   Newsstands and subscription
Target audience   Women ages 16 and over. Most are working mothers, but many stay home. They are from all over the country, but primarily the South and Midwest.
Magazine's history and mission   First printed in 1924 by Bernarr Macfadden. Mission is to share true-life experiences with women all over the country.
Nonfiction   100%
Percent of articles freelance-written   98%
Number of articles bought annually   120
Sections of the magazine open to freelance writers   All
Article interests and needs   We need stories that are up to 8,000 words, and are about the real experiences of women all over the country.

Queries should be directed to   Kristina Kracht, Editor
Length of articles   Up to 8,000 words
Payment $.03 a word
Time of payment   On publication
Expenses   We do not pay any expenses.
Photographs   We do not accept outside photography except on There Comes The Bride feature
Response time to queries   Up to 8 months
Rights bought   We buy *all* rights.
Kill fees   We do not pay kill fees.
Writer's guidelines   Available. Please send SASE.
Sample issues   Available. Please send $2.00 check.

TIPS FOR WRITERS

In our case, it's best not to send a query. We'd rather read a completed manuscript, but if a writer wishes to send a query, we'll consider it. Queries should be short and give us an outline of the story. To spark our interest, the story has to be well-written and have the possibility to be a great cover line. For ideas, please pick up an issue. We don't require clips, but if authors would like to send some, they may. It doesn't mean they will have a better chance at publication, though.

An SASE is always necessary if the writers want their story back, and if they want a mailed response. If we do not get an SASE, we will not reply by mail. Phone calls from writers are fine, but we cannot accept a story based on a favorable phone call. We welcome the opportunity to speak with writers about story ideas. Writers may fax queries, but we have no e-mail address.

The best way to get published in *True Love* is to buy a few issues and get a feel for what we accept. Obviously, we look for excellent writers and true stories that appeal to all age groups. It may take a while for us to get back to you, but eventually we read everything that comes in. Unusual topics are a great way to get your story read. If you can find an original topic we haven't covered, your story will have a great shot at being published.

In our experience, the best thing a writer can do is be patient. It takes us a while to read stories, but we do that to give every story a fair chance. Knowing the market is also the best thing a writer can do. If you know what kinds of stories get published, you can get published, too.

The worst thing a writer can do is send in simultaneous submissions to the magazines in the Sterling/Macfadden Women's Group!

Writers can angle their stories to appeal to women from sixteen and up. Our readers are high school educated, and some may have gone to a trade school. Most are mothers or grandmothers and have many responsibilities in the home. Overall, the best way to get published is to write a short, well-written story about the real-life experiences of women from all over the country. Writers can spin stories of love lost and found, family crises, sexual harassment, children, disease, or obsession.

Satirical Pop Culture

SPY

40 East 21st Street, 11th Floor
New York, NY 10010

Phone number   212-260-7210
Fax number   212-260-7445
E-mail address   Spy Magaz@aol.com
Parent company   Spy Magazine, L.P.
Circulation   160,000
Magazine availability   Newsstands and subscription
Magazine's history   Founded by Kurt Andersen, Graydon, Carter, Thomas L. Phillips Jr. in 1985.
Percent of articles freelance-written   85%
Number of articles bought annually   Approximately 100
Queries should be directed to   Lance Gould, Senior Editor
Length of articles   Varies. Naked City pieces are from 100 to 500 words, columns 1,500 words, and features 2,500 to 6,000 words.
Payment   Typically $.75 to $1.00 per word
Time of payment   On publication
Expenses   Modest expenses are reimbursed with receipts.
Photographs   Commissioned or purchased through companies
Response time to queries   Six to eight weeks
Rights bought   We negotiate with writers on either sole and exclusive rights or first-time publishing rights.
Kill fees   20% of the contracted pay

TIPS FOR WRITERS

Concise query letters are best, usually one paragraph. Three clips are recommended that show the writer's range. Just because we're a slapstick magazine doesn't mean we have to fall out of our seats from a writer's clips, resume, or query. Phone calls from writers are not preferred—unless they're returning our call. Faxing or e-mailing queries is fine—especially e-mail because we typically respond much faster.

The best way to break into the magazine is through Naked City pieces. This section will get the writer groomed and the editor up to speed on what to expect from a particular writer: ideas, style, and follow-through.

Science Fiction/Movie/TV/Pop Culture

ANALOG SCIENCE FICTION AND FACT

1540 Broadway
New York, NY 10036

Phone number   212-782-8532
Fax number   212-782-8309
E-mail address   71154.662@compuserve.com
Parent company   Penny Press
Circulation   70,000
Online status   Active
Magazine availability   Newsstands and subscription
Target audience   All ages, both sexes, all professions and geographic areas
Magazine's history   Founded in 1930
Nonfiction   25%
Fiction   75%
Percent of articles freelance-written   95%
Number of articles and stories bought annually   65 to 85
Sections of the magazine open to freelance writers   All
Article interests and needs   Science fiction stories and fact articles
Queries should be directed to   Stanley Schmidt, Editor
Length of articles   Stories: up to 20,000 words; serials: 20,000 to 40,000 words; fact articles: about 4,000 words
Payment $.06 per word
Time of payment   On acceptance
Response time to queries   1 to 3 months (Query first on serials and fact articles only; for short fiction submit complete manuscript.)

TIPS FOR WRITERS

According to *Analog Science Fiction and Fact* writer's guidelines, the magazine is eager to develop new, capable writers. Editor Stanley Schmidt says, "We have no hard-and-fast editorial guidelines, because science fiction is such a broad field that I don't want to inhibit a new writer's thinking by imposing Thou Shalt Nots. Besides, a really good story can make an editor swallow his preconceived taboos." He adds, "In writing for *Analog* readers, it is essential to keep in mind that they are, in general, very intelligent and technically knowledgeable, but represent a very wide diversity of backgrounds. Thus, specialized jargon and mathematical detail should be kept to a necessary minimum. Our readers are reading this magazine largely for entertainment, and a suitable style for our articles is considerably more informal than that in many professional journals."

ASIMOV'S SCIENCE FICTION

1540 Broadway
New York, NY 10036

Phone number   212-782-8532
E-mail address   71154.662@compuserve.com (Please don't e-mail any submissions.)
Parent company   Dell Magazines
Circulation   80,000
Online status   Active
Magazine availability   Newsstands and subscription
Target audience   Teen and adult market
Magazine's mission   To publish the best science fiction
Nonfiction   20%
Fiction   80%
Percent of stories freelance-written   100%
Number of stories bought annually   About 90
Queries should be directed to   Gardner Dozois, Editor
Sections of the magazine open to freelance writers   Over 80%
Article interests and needs   Science fiction or fantasy
Length of articles   Up to 20,000 words
Payment $.05 to $.08 per word
Time of payment   On acceptance
Response time to queries   No queries on fiction
Rights bought   First English language rights
Writer's guidelines   Yes
Sample issues $3.00

SCIENCE FICTION CHRONICLE

P.O. Box 022730
Brooklyn, NY 11202-0056

Phone number   718-643-9011
Fax number   Same
E-mail address   A.Porter2@Genie.com
Circulation   6,000
Magazine availability   Newsstands and subscription
Target audience   Science fiction and fantasy professionals and readers
Magazine's history   Founded in 1979 by Andrew Porter
Nonfiction   100%
Percent of articles freelance-written   5%
Number of articles bought annually   5 to 10
Sections of the magazine open to freelance writers   News, interviews

Article interests and needs   Short news items, interviews, some obituaries
Queries should be directed to   Andrew Porter, Editor
Length of articles   Short items: 100 to 500 words; Interviews 2,500 to 4,000 words
Payment $.035 per word
Time of payment   On publication
Response time to queries   ASAP
Writer's guidelines   Yes
Sample issues   Send 9 × 12 SASE with $1.24 postage.

STARLOG

475 Park Avenue South, 8th Floor
New York, NY 10016

Phone number   212-689-2830 (We do *not* accept queries by phone and we will *not* return phone calls.)
Fax number   212-889-7933
E-mail address   Communications@starloggroup.com
Parent company   Starlog Press
Circulation   Largest circulation science fiction media magazine on Earth
Online status   Part of Microsoft Network; another Web page pending
Magazine availability   Newsstands, bookstores, and subscription
Target audience   Science fiction enthusiasts of all ages who have an interest in science fiction films, TV shows, literature, etc.
Magazine's history and mission   *Starlog* began in 1976. It chronicles the science-fiction universe (movies, TV shows, literature) through interviews with the people who create science fiction and fantasy (authors, actors, directors, special FX technicians, etc.).
Nonfiction   100%
Fiction   Zero. We NEVER publish fiction.
Percent of articles freelance-written   95%
Number of articles bought annually   160
Sections of the magazine open to freelance writers   All
Article interests and needs   Interviews with science fiction actors, writers, artists
Queries should be directed to   David McDonnell, Editor
Length of articles   1,500 to 3,000 words
Payment $125 and up
Time of payment   On publication
Expenses   Infrequently
Photographs   We pay for photos taken by writer or photographer, *NOT* movie or TV show stills.
Response time to queries   6 to 8 weeks

Rights bought   We buy all rights. We pay an additional standard reprint fee for any reprints we do.
Kill fees   25%
Writer's guidelines   Yes, for SASE
Sample issues   For SASE and $5

IMPORTANT QUESTIONS ANSWERED

Q: What sparks your interest in a query and/or a freelance writer?
A: Can out think us—suggest something we haven't thought of.

Can out race us—do something before we get around to it.

Can out-and-out read our minds—do something we planned to do.

Q: What are the key elements of a good, professional query?
A: Brevity. If it takes more than a page (or 4 to 5 paragraphs), it isn't an idea. It's a thesis.

Typed.

Must include SASE (surprisingly, *many* queries do not include SASEs).

Q: Do you always want clips from new writers and how many do you want?
A: Yes, if possible. One to three clips are nice.
Q: What do you look for in the writer's clips?
A: Coherence. Word play. Accuracy.
Q: Will you look at completed manuscripts?
A: Yes.
Q: Is an SASE always necessary?
A: Absolutely!
Q: Are phone calls from writers OK?
A: *NEVER EVER EVER* are phone calls OK. New writers always call when *they* think it's important and they *interrupt* work at the office. I don't want to know how you talk but how you write. Write a query (or a cover letter!).
Q: Is it OK if writers fax queries to you?
A: Rarely, but I'll put up with it.
Q: Is it OK if writers e-mail queries to you?
A: OK. But if writers start to abuse this avenue—a possibility we see in the future—it won't be.
Q: What are the worst things writers do?
A: Send fiction: We *never* publish it. It's an automatic UNREAD rejection. Why send it?

Call—when we specifically ask they not.

Miss deadlines.

Expect *Premiere*-size ($1 a word) rates from our smaller magazine.

Misspell words in query letters. (Boy, *that* gives us a sense of security!)

Forget to send SASEs.

Don't take "NO" for an answer. (If I turn down the story, why are you querying the same piece again 3 weeks later to me?)

Q: What is your overall advice to writers who want to get published?

A: Read the magazine they want to sell to. Freelancers should READ the entries in any writer's guides carefully. They misinterpret them all the time—to judge from submissions to us. Frankly, after *15 years* in this business, I am *a lot less eager* to work with newcomer writers than I was in the past. I no longer suffer fools gladly and writers who ignore our policies or fail to use common sense and ask me more than they should. Still, we remain committed to working with new writers, always hopeful the next writer will be great *and* easy to deal with. It could happen.

Science and Technology

POPULAR SCIENCE

2 Park Avenue
New York, NY 10016

Phone number   212-779-5000
Fax number   212-481-8062
E-mail address   Editors have individual mailboxes.
Parent company   Times Mirror Magazines
Circulation   1.8 million
Online status   Web site at http://www.popsci.com. AOL area coming soon
Magazine availability   Newsstands and subscription
Target audience   Audience is 85% male, median age 41, professional/technical, more than 60% have attended college
Magazine's history and mission   Founded in 1872. According to the *Popular Science* writers' guidelines: "*Popular Science* covers new and emerging technology in the areas of science, automobiles, the environment, recreation, electronics, the home, photography, aviation and space, and computers and software. Our mission is to provide service to our readers by reporting on how these technologies work and what difference they will make in our readers' lives. Our readers are well-educated professionals who are vitally interested in the technologies we cover."
Nonfiction   100%
Percent of articles freelance-written   70%
Number of articles bought annually   50 to 60 features, 100 to 150 news briefs, 50 to 60 product briefs, 30 to 40 Q & As

Sections of the magazine open to freelance writers   All
Article interests and needs   As stated in the *Popular Science* writers' guidelines: "We seek stories that are up-to-the minute in information and accuracy . . . We publish stories ranging from hands-on product reviews to investigative feature stories, on everything from black holes to black-budget airplanes."
Queries should be directed to   Science Features: Dawn Stover, Science Editor; Tech Features: Frank Vizard, Technology Editor; Science News and New Products: Mariette DiChristina, News Editor; Computer & Software news: Chris O'Malley, Senior Contributing Editor; Home Tech News: Judith Anne Gunther, Contibuting Editor
Length of articles   50 to 3,500 words
Payment   Roughly $1 per word depending on assignment
Time of payment   On acceptance
Expenses   Yes, for feature articles
Photographs   Depends on assignment. We have a staff photographer.
Response time to queries   2 weeks
Rights bought   First North American serial
Kill fees   Yes, 25 to 100% depending on circumstances
Writer's guidelines   Available with SASE—also on Web site
Sample issues   Not available

TIPS FOR WRITERS
(as stated in Popular Science *Writers' Guidelines)*

"We respond promptly to queries, which should be a single page or less. The writer should submit a tight summary of the proposed article and provide some indication of the plan of execution. Samples of the writer's past work and clips concerning the emerging story are helpful." Please include SASE.

Special Interest

AMERICAN IRON MAGAZINE
1010 Summer Street
Stamford, CT 06497

Phone number   203-425-8777
Fax number   203-425-8775
E-mail address   76710,1103@compuserve.com
Parent company   Tam Communications
Circulation   65,000

Magazine availability   Newsstands and subscription

Target audience   Men and women who love Harley-Davidsons. We are the best-selling, clean Harley magazine. We cater to a family clientele who all share the joys of riding Harleys. Primarily the U.S. and Canada, but we cover the world.

Magazine's history and mission   Founded in 1989. Started by Custom Chrome, Inc., and then purchased by Tam Communications after 1 1/2 years. We bring a no-nonsense attitude to all things Harley. Our target is the motorcycle and people who ride them.

Nonfiction   100%

Percent of articles freelance-written   80%

Number of articles bought annually   72

Sections of the magazine open to freelance writers   Tour articles, profiles, how-to, history, bike features (features comprise most of magazine)

Article interests and needs   See above, especially tech and how-to illustrated with a lot of quality black-and-white photos (step-by-step).

Queries should be directed to   Jonathan Gourlay, Editor

Length of articles   1,000 to 2,500 words

Payment   Depends on piece and length. From $150 to $350.

Time of payment   On publication, sorry.

Expenses   Nope

Photographs   Love 'em. Color transparencies, black-and-white prints

Response time to queries   1 month in most cases

Rights bought   First

Kill fees   Half of agreed payment when story is *assigned and killed* by editor

TIPS FOR WRITERS
Jonathan Gourlay, Editor

Clear, concise writing always appeals to me. The simple and direct approach in pitches and articles will always beat out the overblown.

New writers should provide a couple of clips or send a completed piece on spec. Completed articles will always be read, but a completed article without accompanying photography has a very slim chance of being printed.

At a minimum, supply an SASE! No SASE, no serious consideration. This is a pet peeve. When I get a letter from a prospective new writer without an SASE, I assume that person doesn't consider him or herself a pro.

The best thing a writer can do is send a completed manuscript (both hard copy and disk) with a nice assortment of pro-quality photos illustrating the article. Of course, you'd have to know the magazine pretty well in order to be sure your subject hasn't been done in the past couple of years.

The writer's guidelines should explain everything else.

Don't send "Why I Like Harleys" pieces unless they are *different!* I'm always on the lookout for new approaches and twists. "My Favorite Road" pieces are good unless they don't say anything inspiring. Most of all, know your subject. And don't send poetry or poetry disguised as prose.

CASINO REVIEW
635 Chicago Avenue, #250
Evanston, IL 60202

Parent company   Hyde Park Media
Circulation   40,000
Target audience   Chicago/NW Indiana area
Magazine's history   Launched July 1994.
Nonfiction   100%
Percent of articles freelance-written   50 to 75%
Number of articles bought annually   30 to 40
Article interests and needs   Casino gambling, how-to's, humor, first-person experiences, anything of interest to people who gamble
Queries should be directed to   Editor
Length of articles   750 to 2,000 words
Payment   Varies
Time of payment   On publication
Photographs   Paid extra—if used
Response time to queries   1 month
Rights bought   First-time and reprint purchased
Writer's guidelines   None

A TIP FOR WRITERS

Review publication, send copy with SASE, and wait for reply. That's it.

HOOF BEATS
750 Michigan Avenue
Columbus, OH 43215

Phone number   614-224-2291
Fax number   614-222-6791
Parent company   U.S. Trotting Association
Circulation   17,000
Magazine availability   Subscription
Target audience   International feature harness racing publication
Nonfiction   100%
Percent of articles freelance-written   40%
Number of articles bought annually   40 to 50
Sections of the magazine open to freelance writers   All
Article interests and needs   Features on harness racing
Queries should be directed to   Dean A. Hoffman, Executive Editor

Length of articles   1,000 words and up
Payment $100 to $400
Time of payment   On publication
Expenses   Sometimes
Photographs   Color and black and white
Response time to queries   1 week
Rights bought   Negotiable
Kill fees   Negotiable
Writer's guidelines   Available upon request
Sample issues   Available upon request

IMPORTANT QUESTIONS ANSWERED

Q: Is an SASE always necessary?
A: No

Q: Are phone calls from writers OK?
A: Yes

Q: Is it OK if writers fax or e-mail queries to you?
A: Yes

Q: What are the keys to breaking in to your magazine?
A: Know the readers. Know our needs. Good query letters.

Q: What are the worst things writers do?
A: Simultaneous submissions; missed deadlines

Q: What is your overall advice to writers who want to get published?
A: Think like an editor.

Sports

ADVENTURE CYCLIST

P.O. Box 8308
Missoula, MT 59801

Phone number   406-721-1776
Fax number   406-721-8754
E-mail address   acabike@aol.com
Parent company   Adventure Cycling Association
Circulation   30,000
Magazine availability   Subscription

Nonfiction   100%
Percent of articles freelance-written   90%
Number of articles bought annually   20 to 30
Article interests and needs   Bicycle travel, on and off road
Queries should be directed to   Dan D'Ambrosio
Length of articles   1,500 to 2,500 words
Payment   Negotiable
Time of payment   On publication
Expenses   No
Photographs   33 mm color
Response time to queries   3 weeks
Rights offered   Onetime
Kill Fees   No
Writer's guidelines   Yes
Sample issues   9 × 12 SASE with $1 postage

BICYCLING

135 North Sixth Street
Emmaus, PA 18098

Phone number   610-967-8205
Fax number   610-967-8960
E-mail address   bicmagmail@aol.com
Parent company   Rodale Press
Circulation   330,000
Online status   Our magazine appears on America Online
Magazine availability   Newsstands and subscription
Target audience   Recreational road and mountain bikers
Magazine's history and mission   Founded in 1961. Nation's oldest and world's largest cycling publication. Our goal is to inform, entertain, and motivate people who love cycling.
Nonfiction   100%
Percent of articles freelance-written   25%
Number of articles bought annually   50 to 60
Sections of the magazine open to freelance writers   Features, columns, shorts
Article interests and needs   High-quality writing that expresses a passion and expert's knowledge of cycling
Queries should be directed to   Ed Pavelka, Executive Editor
Length of articles   200 to 2,500 words
Payment $25 to $1,000
Time of payment   Depends
Expenses   Paid (receipts required)

Photographs   Paid for separately
Response time to queries   4 to 6 weeks
Rights bought   We buy all rights.
Kill fees   25% of full fee
Writer's guidelines   Send SASE.
Sample issues   Send SASE.

IMPORTANT QUESTIONS ANSWERED

Q: What is key to a good query?
A: Get to the point.
Q: Do you always want clips from new writers?
A: Yes
Q: How many clips do you want?
A: Two
Q: What do you look for in the writer's clips?
A: Style and flow
Q: Will you look at completed manuscripts?
A: Yes
Q: Is an SASE always necessary?
A: Yes
Q: Are phone calls from writers OK?
A: No
Q: Is it OK if writers fax or e-mail queries to you?
A: Yes
Q: What is the best way to break into your magazine?
A: Have a new idea.
Q: What is the key to breaking in?
A: Know the topic you're writing about.
Q: What is the best thing writers do?
A: Write to length.
Q: What is the worst thing writers do?
A: Don't know the magazine.
Q: How can writers angle their stories to Bicycling?
A: Entertainment counts.
Q: What overall advice would you give writers who want to get published?
A: Don't write first person.

BOWLING MAGAZINE

5301 South 76th Street
Greendale, WI 53129

Phone number   414-423-3232
Fax number   414-421-7977
Parent company   America Bowling Congress
Circulation   140,000
Magazine availability   Newsstands and subscription—very limited newsstand
Target audience   Adult league bowlers, predominantly male, average age 42
Magazine's history and mission   Started in 1938 as ABC newsletter to serve bowling association leaders and volunteers. Converted to consumer-focused magazine in 1988.
Nonfiction   100%
Percent of articles freelance-written   30 to 40%
Number of articles bought annually   50 to 60
Sections of the magazine open to freelance writers   Feature stories
Article interests and needs   Unique, unusual bowling-oriented stories with color photo support
Queries should be directed to   Bill Vint, Editor
Length of articles   600 to 1,500 words
Payment $100 to $250
Time of payment   On acceptance
Expenses   No unless preapproved
Photographs   Critical in most cases
Response time to queries   30 to 60 days
Rights bought   All
Kill fees   None
Writer's guidelines   Available upon request
Sample issues   Available upon request

HANDGUNS

6420 Wilshire Blvd.
Los Angeles, CA 90210

Phone number   213-782-2868
Fax number   213-782-2477
Parent company   Petersen Publishing, Co.
Circulation   Approximately 160,000
Magazine availability   Newsstands and subscription
Target audience   Outdoor and gun enthusiasts. Interest in sport shooting or concerned with self/home defense
Magazine's history   Founded by Petersen Publishing Company in 1987
Nonfiction   100%
Percent of articles freelance-written   65% of major features
Number of articles bought annually   72
Sections of the magazine open to freelance writers   Feature articles

Article interests and needs   Stories relating to handguns, shooting and defensive techniques, etc.
Queries should be directed to   Jan Libourel, Editor
Length of articles   1,500 to 3,000 words
Payment $300 to $500
Time of payment   On acceptance
Expenses   No
Photographs   Black-and-white glossies and color transparencies
Kill fees   No
Writer's guidelines   We have them
Sample issues   Yes

JOURNAL OF ASIAN MARTIAL ARTS

Via Media Publishing Co.
821 West 24th Street
Erie, PA 16502

Phone number   814-455-9517
Fax number   814-838-7811
Circulation   7,000
Magazine availability   Bookstores, subscription
Target audience   College-educated. Anyone having a special interest in Asian history and culture, particularly martial arts
Magazine's history and mission   Founded in 1992 by Via Media Publishing Company to present Asian martial arts in a comprehensive, scholarly format
Nonfiction   95%
Fiction   5%
Percent of articles freelance-written   95%
Number of articles bought annually   20 to 25
Sections of the magazine open to freelance writers   All
Article interests and needs   Technical pieces by authorities, interviews, museum and book reviews, other well-researched topics
Queries should be directed to   Michael A. DeMarco, Publisher
Length of articles   2,000 to 10,000 words for feature articles
Payment $150 to $500
Time of payment   On publication
Expenses   No
Photographs   Negotiable according to need and with article package
Response time to queries   1 to 2 months
Rights bought   First world rights and reprint rights
Kill fees   None
Writer's guidelines   Available
Sample issues   For $10

TIPS FOR WRITERS
Michael A. DeMarco, Publisher

As a martial arts publication, we are unique in the field. We seek manuscripts that approach the topic in a classical fashion, rather than with a "hype and Hollywood" slant. We publish three types of materials: 1) scholarly articles based on primary research in recognized scholarly disciplines, e.g., cultural anthropology, health and physical education, psychology, criticism, etc.; 2) more informal, but nevertheless substantial interviews (with scholars, master practitioners, etc.) and reports on particular genres, techniques, etc.; and 3) reviews of books, museums, and audiovisual materials dealing with martial arts.

Writers should have at least some martial arts experience and be familiar with Asian culture. Query letters should tell of the writer's qualifications, provide a clear outline of the intended article, and state if illustrations are available. We pull our hair out when submissions arrive that simply rehash old material or are geared to the wrong audience! Articles are published for knowledgeable readers and must offer special information and insights not available elsewhere.

It is not necessary to provide clips, but an SASE is appreciated. A complete manuscript submission is fine. We like to work with writers and are happy to provide suggestions on how to improve any materials that do not meet all criteria the first time through our office door. If you decide to submit a manuscript, have a martial artist and/or Asian scholar critique it first. Of course, the best guide for suitability is the journal itself.

KARATE/KUNG FU ILLUSTRATED

P.O. Box 918
Santa Clarita, CA 91380

Phone number   805-257-4066
Fax number   805-257-3028
Parent company   Rainbow Publications
Circulation   35,000
Online status   Yes—on the World Wide Web.
Magazine availability   Newsstands and subscription
Target audience   All ages, male and female
Magazine's history and mission   Founded in 1969. Mission: to provide martial artists with factual, historical, philosophical, and how-to stories
Nonfiction   100%
Percent of articles freelance-written   70%
Number of articles bought annually   35
Sections of the magazine open to freelance writers   All
Article interests and needs   How-to articles, historical, travel, research. No poetry, no fiction
Queries should be directed to   Robert Young, Executive Editor
Length of articles   1,000 to 3,000 words

Payment $100 to $200
Time of payment   On publication
Expenses   No
Photographs   No additional payment. Black-and-white or color
Response time to queries   3 weeks
Rights bought   We buy all rights.
Kill fees   No
Writer's guidelines   Send SASE.
Sample issues   Send 9 × 12 SASE.

A TIP FOR WRITERS

Write about a subject you know well.

MARLIN MAGAZINE

P.O. Box 2456
Winter Park, FL 32790

Phone number   407-628-4802
Fax number   407-628-7061
E-mail address   marlin@worldzine.com
Parent company   World Publications
Magazine availability   Subscription, most bookstores, tackle shops, and other select newsstand agencies
Circulation   40,000
Target audience   45-year-old male, owns boat 35 to 50 feet in length, $300,000+ a year, and fishes offshore extensively
Magazine's history   Founded in 1991. Sold to World Publications in 1992
Nonfiction   100%
Percent of articles freelance-written   50%
Number of articles bought annually   50
Sections of the magazine open to freelance writers   All
Article interests and needs   Travel, fishing techniques, fishing personalities
Queries should be directed to   David Ritchie, Editor
Length of articles   Features 2,000 to 3,500 words
Payment $300 to $500
Time of payment   On acceptance
Expenses   No
Photographs   Additional payment for photos used
Response time to queries   1 month
Rights bought   First North American
Kill fees   One-fourth

Writer's guidelines   Yes
Sample issues   With $3.00 to cover postage

MARTIAL ARTS TRAINING

24715 Avenue Rockefeller
Valencia, CA 91355

Phone number   805-257-4066
Fax number   805-257-3028
E-mail address   iczer/@anime-central.com
Parent company   Rainbow Publications
Circulation   35,000
Online status   www.blackbeltmag.com
Magazine availability   Newsstands and subscription
Target audience   Ages 10 to 90, male and female, all professions, U.S. and abroad
Nonfiction   100%
Percent of articles freelance-written   75%
Number of articles bought annually   100
Sections of the magazine open to freelance writers   All
Article interests and needs   All training, but special interest in speed training, power training, traditional training, advanced training
Queries should be directed to   Doug Jeffrey, Executive Editor
Length of articles   750 to 2,000 words
Payment $100 to $175
Time of payment   On publication
Photographs   Color
Response time to queries   1 month
Rights Offered   U.S. North American rights
Kill Fees   No
Writer's guidelines   Available
Sample issues   Yes

TIPS FOR WRITERS
Doug Jeffrey, Executive Editor

Queries should be well-written and look professional. A writer's background is not as important as his idea. If he/she has a good idea, I want to see the story. Unique training ideas are always good. Clips are important.

Yes, I welcome calls, and I welcome SASEs, though I rarely see them.

The best way to break in to the magazine? A great idea. Or an old idea with a new slant. I like comprehensive, well-researched stories.

NEW YORK SPORTSCENE

990 Motor Parkway
Central Islip, NY 11722

Phone number   516-435-8890
Fax number   516-435-8925
Circulation   125,000
Magazine availability   Newsstands and subscription
Target audience   90% male, median age 30, Eastern U.S., income $65,000, college educated 83%
Magazine's history and mission   In May of 1995, *New York Sportscene* was launched to provide full sports coverage to the sports capital of the world—New York.
Nonfiction   100%
Percent of articles freelance-written   60%
Number of articles bought annually   60
Sections of the magazine open to freelance writers   Features, Penalty Box, Foul Shots, Scene Around, Business Story, Health & Fitness
Article interests and needs   Sports photos from early New York events
Queries should be directed to   Keith Loria, Editor-in-Chief
Length of articles   1,200 to 1,800 words
Payment $25 to $200
Time of payment   On publication
Expenses   No
Photographs   Yes
Response time to queries   Approximately 3 weeks
Rights bought   Varies
Kill fees   No
Writer's guidelines   Send for them.
Sample issues   Send for them.

TIPS FOR WRITERS
Keith Loria, Editor-in-Chief

As an editor, often the thing asked most of me by writers is, "What do you look for in a letter query?" The obvious would be grammar and creativity, but what I have been most impressed with, and probably more influenced by, is a writer who presents his material in a special way. For instance, rather than just put your resume and clips in an envelope, design a folder for your work with a clever cover or laminate your clips in a scrap book. A clean, well organized presentation will give the impression of a good, well organized writer.

At *New York Sportscene*, I am a great believer in giving a beginner a chance. Tips for achieving success:

1. In your cover letter, give me an idea of a story rather than request an assignment.
2. Don't go for the obvious and offer me a professional sports feature such as a Knick or Met; instead, come to me with a business or media idea and eventually you will break into the main sports.
3. Don't take on an assignment you don't think you can handle. If you want to start in the business and aren't sure, be willing to gather quotes at a game or cover a local sport. People willing to attend news conferences have a great chance to grow with the magazine.

OFFSHORE

220-9 Reservoir Street
Needham, MA 02194

Phone number   617-449-6204
Fax number   617-449-9702
E-mail address   oshore@aol.com
Parent company   Offshore Publications, Inc.
Circulation   35,000
Magazine availability   Newsstands and subscription
Target audience   Boat owners in the Northeast (predominantly power)
Magazine's history and mission   Since 1976, serving an eclectic mix information and entertainment.
Nonfiction   90%
Fiction   10%
Percent of articles freelance-written   80%
Number of articles bought annually   50
Sections of the magazine open to freelance writers   All
Article interests and needs   Harbors and waterways between Maine and New Jersey. Also unusual boats and boating people.
Queries should be directed to   Peter Serratore, Editor
Length of articles   1,500 to 2,500 words
Payment   Negotiable ($250 to $500)
Time of payment   On acceptance
Expenses   Negotiable
Photographs   Required
Response time to queries   One week
Rights bought   First North American
Kill fees $100
Writer's guidelines   Send SASE to receive.

IMPORTANT QUESTIONS ANSWERED

Q: What sparks your interest in a query?
A: Knowledge of subject matter and a lively style. A working title helps.

Q: Do you always want clips from new writers?
A: Yes

Q: Is an SASE always necessary?
A: Yes

Q: Are phone calls from writers OK?
A: No

Q: Will you look at completed manuscripts?
A: Why not?

Q: How can writers angle their stories for your magazine?
A: [With a] Northeast regional hook.

POWER & MOTORYACHT

245 West 17th Street
New York, NY 10011

Phone number   212-463-6427
Fax number   212-463-6436
Parent company   K-III Magazines
Circulation   Approximately 157,000
Magazine availability   Newsstands and subscription
Target audience   Generally age 50+, male, middle to upper-middle class, predominately U.S., but international too
Nonfiction   100%
Percent of articles freelance-written   10%
Number of articles bought annually   Varies
Sections of the magazine open to freelance writers   Most columns and features
Article interests and needs   Clear, accurate boat tests; cruising stories
Queries should be directed to   Diane M. Byrne, Associate Editor
Length of articles   1,500 to 2,000 words
Payment $500 to $1,000, depending on article length
Time of payment   On acceptance
Expenses   Yes
Photographs   *Color* 35 mm slides (if assigned as part of a story)
Response time to queries   Within one month
Rights bought   First-time rights purchased
Kill fees   One-third of agreed-upon assignment fee
Writer's guidelines   With proper SASE
Sample issues   With proper SASE

TIPS FOR WRITERS
Diane M. Byrne, Associate Editor

The query: A query catches our attention when the story idea is targeted directly to our readers' desires and needs. Our readers are longtime (in some cases, lifetime) boaters, so they don't need or appreciate being talked "down" to. The query often reveals how knowledgeable the writer is about boating, but we still want to know exactly how long he or she has been involved in and writing about boating. *Important: we do not accept unsolicited manuscripts.* We want to give the writer some direction first so that we know he or she will be on the right track.

While we don't always get clips from freelancers, we prefer receiving them. Two or three stories are sufficient, and we like to see the clips focus on those aspects of boating which the freelancer considers his or her strengths (fishing, cruising, humor, mechanical, etc.).

Professional etiquette: An SASE is a must! However, we do not return unsolicited manuscripts, even if an SASE is enclosed; the same holds true for unsolicited photography. We don't accept queries by phone; faxed queries are fine, and once we're back on the Internet, we'll accept e-mailed queries as well.

Best ways to break into our magazine: 1) Be a knowledgeable boater, and be a good writer. Write with authority, and do it in a clear, concise way. Unfortunately, these two factors don't always go hand in hand—we've found people who know boating inside and out, yet can't write to save their lives. 2) Include your best clips. These help "sell" the writer. They tell me "Hey, I know what I'm talking about, and your readers will want to hear what I have to say." 3) Familiarize yourself with our magazine. Get inside our readers' minds. For example, since they perform a lot of their own maintenance, we run a lot of do-it-yourself stories. Our readers also enjoy cruising, so destination pieces are popular ("here's where you should go, here's how to get there, here's what you can do while you're there").

The worst things writers do: *Not proofread their own work*! I've been an editor for nearly seven years, and I can't begin to tell you how many queries and manuscripts I've received that contain typos! And I'm not just talking about common misspellings; once I actually received a query with the word "no" used instead of the word "know." How can writers expect me to hire them if they don't take the time to proofread?

Overall advice to writers wanting to get published: 1) Don't give up when you get a rejection letter. It doesn't necessarily mean the magazine dislikes you; it may just mean your idea didn't hit the mark. (I've sent rejection letters to some of my best writers.) 2) Find a niche, and serve it well. There are lots of general-interest writers out there, and while it's good to be published in a variety of magazines, you might get more pleasure out of a specialty market. You'll certainly make a name for yourself.

RACQUETBALL MAGAZINE
1685 West Uintah
Colorado Springs, CO 80904

Phone number   719-635-5396
Fax number   719-635-0685
E-mail address   rbzine@interserv.com
Parent company   American Amateur Racquetball Association
Circulation   40,000
Magazine availability   Subscription/membership
Target audience   Members of the AARA and racquetball players, manufacturers
Magazine's history and mission   Founded in 1989 by AARA to information, instruction, and product information to members
Nonfiction   90%
Fiction   10%
Percent of articles freelance-written   10%
Number of articles bought annually   Average 3 to 4
Sections of the magazine open to freelance writers   Features, humor, instruction
Queries should be directed to   Linda Mojer, Editor
Length of articles   200 to 2,000 words
Payment $100 to $200 per article, negotiated by assignment
Time of payment   On publication
Expenses   Telephone (interviews)
Photographs   Preferably to accompany work
Response time to queries   4 to 6 weeks
Writer's Guidelines   Available
Sample issues   Available on request

SAIL

275 Washington Street
Newton, MA 02158

Phone number   617-964-3030
Fax number   617-630-3737
Parent company   K-III
Circulation   185,000
Online status   E-mail only
Magazine availability   Newsstands and subscription
Target audience   Sailors, experienced and inexperienced, of any age, sex, and location
Magazine's history and mission   Founded in 1970. Mission is to teach, to enhance and encourage interest in and enthusiasm for sailing as a sport and a lifestyle
Nonfiction   100%
Percent of articles freelance-written   60%
Number of articles bought annually   150 to 200
Sections of the magazine open to freelance writers   Almost all

Article interests and needs   Destinations, personal sailing experiences, how-to techniques, racing and cruising, technical subjects, opinion, news
Queries should be directed to   Amy Ullrich, Managing Editor
Length of articles   From filler to 3,000 words, depending on section
Payment $50 to $800
Time of payment   On acceptance
Expenses   Sometimes
Photographs   Yes, necessary in many cases
Response time to queries   6 weeks
Rights bought   First North American
Kill fees   Sometimes
Writer's guidelines   Yes, write with SASE
Sample issues   Yes, $3.00

TIPS FOR WRITERS

Because most of our articles are written by sailors for sailors, we are more concerned with what the writer's experience is and what he or she may be able to communicate than with professionalism per se. We often work with a writer who has the requisite knowledge/experience to produce a publishable story. Therefore, it's the content of the query, rather than the presentation, that may be the most important element. I find queries most helpful for eliminating unsuitable ideas immediately. I do read clips to get an idea of the writer's style and depth, but many of our potential writers don't have clips. We do—at least eventually—encourage the writer to send a manuscript.

We accept queries by phone, fax, e-mail, and so on, though in most cases the query eventually ends up on paper from the potential author, so it can be reviewed by other editors. We ask for an SASE, though we won't automatically discard a submission without one; we do automatically discard simultaneous submissions.

For this magazine at least, a would-be writer can save him/herself and the editors a good deal of time and effort by reading a couple of issues before writing a proposal or a manuscript. The best way to break into the magazine is to come up with a unique topic that is within the magazine's purview; "I notice you haven't covered for a while . . . " doesn't work to the author's advantage if that very subject has just appeared (see above).

We appreciate good writers. But we're also good editors. We can work with good ideas and material from nonprofessionals who are active, enthusiastic, observant, and knowledgeable sailors.

SAILING WORLD
P.O. Box 3400
Newport, RI 02840-0992

Fax number   401-848-5048
E-mail address   70672,2725@compuserve.com
Parent company   New York Times
Circulation   65,000
Online status   Excerpts in Microsoft Network under @play
Magazine availability   Newsstands and subscription
Target audience   Performance oriented sailors of all ages
Nonfiction   100%
Percent of articles freelance-written   50%
Number of articles bought annually   12+
Sections of the magazine open to freelance writers   All. Written requests/inquiries *only*
Queries should be directed to   Kristan McClintock, Managing Editor
Time of payment   On publication
Response time to queries   3 or more months for unsolicited
Writer's guidelines   Yes
Sample issues   No

TIPS FOR WRITERS

Sailing World publishes technical articles by knowledgeable, performance-oriented sailors. Experienced sailors who are exceptional writers are also considered. Written queries (outlines) with sailing resume are preferred. The best way to "break in" is to write race reports for "Finish Line" section of the magazine. Again, written queries only in advance of event are considered.

SKYDIVING

1725 North Lexington Avenue
DeLand, FL 32724

Phone number   904-736-4793
Fax number   904-736-9786
E-mail address   skydiving@interserv.com
Parent company   AeroGraphics
Circulation   12,800
Magazine availability   Primarily paid subscriptions. Limited newsstand sales.
Target audience   Active sport parachutists and those with an interest in the sport or the industry it supports.
Magazine's history and mission   Founded in 1979 by the publisher. Mission: to provide accurate and timely news and information about the techniques, equipment, events, people, and places of sport parachuting.
Nonfiction   100%
Percent of articles freelance-written   40%

Number of articles bought annually   50
Sections of the magazine open to freelance writers   All
Article interests and needs   Author must have an insider's view of sport parachuting.
Queries should be directed to   Sue Clifton, Editor
Length of articles   Up to 3,000 words
Payment   Depends
Time of payment   On publication
Expenses   No
Photographs   Yes
Response time to queries   1 month
Rights bought   Onetime serial
Kill fees   No
Writer's guidelines   On request with SASE
Sample issues $5.00 each

SNOW COUNTRY

5520 Park Avenue
Trumbull, CT 06611

Phone number   203-373-7000
Fax number   203-373-7111
E-mail address   snowcountry@msn.com
Parent company   New York Times
Circulation   465,000
Online status   Currently available via Microsoft Network
Magazine availability   Newsstands and subscription
Target audience   *Snow Country* readers are primarily 35- to 50-year-old professionals and managers. They are affluent. Our readers are well-traveled and are active, participating in a broad range of sports including skiing, biking, and hiking.
Magazine's history and mission   *Snow Country* debuted in March of 1988. Founded by John Fry (a former editor-in-chief of *Ski Magazine*) and the New York Times Co., the magazine covers year-round sports and lifestyle issues in the mountains. Its current editor is Roger Toll.
Nonfiction   100%
Percent of articles freelance-written   85%
Number of articles bought annually   140
Sections of the magazine open to freelance writers   Mountain Living, Datebook, Featurettes, Features, Does It Work, Armchair Mountaineer
Article interests and needs   *Snow Country* would be interested in well-written adventure travel pieces, mountain life style and issue pieces, unique mountain architecture ideas, people profiles, and summer mountain activity pieces.

Queries should be directed to   Kathleen Ring, Senior Editor (Features, profiles); Debbie Frieze, Associate Editor (Sports instruction); Greg Trinker, Senior Editor (Resorts and travel)
Length of articles   From 750 to 1,500 words
Payment   Varies
Time of payment   On acceptance
Response time to queries   1 to 2 months
Rights bought   First-time all world
Writer's guidelines   Available upon request
Sample issues   Sample costs $3

TIPS FOR WRITERS

Snow Country, published eight times a year, is geared to the person who lives in or travels frequently to the mountains. With that in mind, freelance writers wishing to break into the magazine should supply a well-written query, preferably no longer than a page. The query will explain the story's unique angle and will give details on what will be included and how the writer will go about getting the story. Completed manuscripts are also reviewed.

At *Snow Country*, queries that turn into assignments, above all, offer unique story ideas. We are deluged with obvious destination-resort queries and therefore are looking for ideas on undiscovered travel adventures, interesting people who've impacted a mountain town or sport, how-tos on making mountain life easier, environmental issues and architecture. Fresh takes on mountain sports—skiing, snowboarding, biking, hiking, in-line skating, camping—are also welcome.

Snow Country appreciates writers whose stories deliver what they promise. Adherence to deadlines is important. Writers should expect to work closely with the story editor and, when necessary, handle rewrites in a timely manner.

Five to ten clips are required of new writers. Clips will be reviewed for writing style, story content, sentence structure, and grammar. An SASE is necessary. Phone calls are discouraged, unless normal query-response time will render the story obsolete. Fax and e-mail queries are accepted.

T'AI CHI

P.O. Box 26156
Los Angeles, CA 90026

Phone number   213-665-7773
Fax number   213-665-1627
E-mail address   taichi@tai-chi.com
Parent company   Wayfarer Publications
Circulation   40,000

Online status   Web site at http://www.tai-chi.com
Magazine availability   Newsstands and subscription
Target audience   Persons interested in t'ai chi chuan, Chinese health systems
Magazine's history and mission   Founded by Marvin Smalheiser in 1977, *T'ai Chi* provides inspiration and information for people who practice t'ai chi chuan, gigong, internal martial arts, and Chinese health disciplines.
Nonfiction   100%
Percent of articles freelance-written   90%
Number of articles bought annually   75
Sections of the magazine open to freelance writers   Feature articles
Article interests and needs   Articles about the practice of t'ai chi chuan. Uses of t'ai chi chuan and gigong and internal martial arts.
Queries should be directed to   Marvin Smalheiser, Editor/Publisher
Length of articles   1,200 to 4,000 words
Payment $75 to $500
Time of payment   On publication
Photographs   Included in payment
Response time to queries   2 weeks to 1 month
Writer's guidelines   Yes
Sample issues   No. $3.50 per copy

TIPS FOR WRITERS
Marvin Smalheiser, Editor/Publisher

The query should show that the writer knows the subject material and show how it will be useful for readers of the magazine. Most queries are too general and tentative. It should make clear that the article has good content and will not serve as publicity for someone or some organization.

An SASE is necessary. Phone calls tend to be not well-thought-out. If a writer has written something, it is more likely to be thought out and not off the top of the head. A fax is okay. E-mail can go astray. A phone call should follow fax or e-mail.

Writers should read a copy of the magazine and know what kind of articles it publishes. *T'ai Chi* has a very specialized kind of material.

Please avoid promotional material or publicity or gee whiz material.

WESTERN OUTDOORS
P.O. Box 2027
Newport Beach, CA 92659-1029

Phone number   714-546-4370
Fax number   714-662-3486
E-mail address   woutdoors@aol.com

Parent company Western Outdoors Publications, Inc.

Circulation 100,000

Magazine availability Subscription and selected newsstands

Target audience Freshwater and saltwater anglers and private fishing boat owners in California, Oregon, and Baja California

Magazine's history and mission *Western Outdoors* was founded in 1961 by Burt Twilegar, publisher of the weekly *Western Outdoor News*.

Nonfiction 100%

Percent of articles freelance-written 40%

Number of articles bought annually 35 to 40

Sections of the magazine open to freelance writers Features only

Article interests and needs Strong, accurate, authoritative fishing how-to's

Queries should be directed to Jack Brown, Editor

Length of articles 1,500+ words

Payment $400 up to $600

Time of payment On acceptance

Expenses No

Photographs $50 to $100 inside, $250 cover

Response time to queries 2 to 3 weeks

Rights bought First North American serial rights

Kill fees No

Writer's guidelines Yes

Sample issues $2.00; $1.00 to OWAA members only

TIPS FOR WRITERS
Jack Brown, Editor

Western Outdoors covers freshwater and saltwater fishing like no other outdoor magazine. We are the West's leading authority on fishing techniques, tackle, and destinations, and all reports present the latest and most reliable information. Our writers must demonstrate the highest journalistic integrity and credibility, and are responsible for the accuracy of their work.

Writers who are new to us are encouraged to submit only one query at a time, in order that we may give it full consideration. Queries should be submitted via U.S. mail; no fax or e-mail, and certainly no phone queries. And, because we consider *Western Outdoors* as being distinct from all other outdoor magazines, simultaneous queries and submissions are not considered.

Over-the-transom submissions of completed articles are discouraged. All contributions receive reasonable care, but the publisher cannot be held responsible for unsolicited manuscripts, photos, or artwork.

We look for ideas that are new or extraordinary. They must pertain strictly to fishing in the West, involving species found in the West such as salmon, steelhead, trout, largemouth, smallmouth, and striped bass or tuna, marlin, wahoo, yellowtail, and other ocean game fish. They must be authoritative, with facts and comments attributed to persons recognized as authorities in their fields.

Submissions, including queries, should include an addressed envelope and sufficient postage for return. We reply in two or three weeks, or earlier. Lousy stuff goes back the day it's received.

Because we plan the following year's issues in March through May, some queries may be filed for consideration at that time. Permission to hold will be requested of the writers.

Queries and other submissions are answered with a personal letter or note from the editor; we have no form letters.

Pet peeves:

Writers who think they are experts. We say experts are those who know the right questions to ask of the right person.

Simultaneous queries. We can spot them, no matter how well they are disguised.

Poor research and inaccuracies. A writer once sent readers 24,000 miles out of the way by giving instructions to turn east instead of west.

Clichés and bromides. We gag at "gin-clear water" and "bluebird weather."

Clueless writers. They should learn what *Western Outdoors* is all about before proposing articles.

The best thing writers can do to become *Western Outdoors* byliners is to submit professional quality packages of good writing accompanied by excellent photography. Also, they should perform 110% above what is expected of them by including graphs, charts, sketches, and other graphic means of improving the published appearance of their work.

The pros anticipate what is needed, and whatever else is requested is provided immediately. What's more, they meet deadlines.

WINDY CITY SPORTS

1450 West Randolph
Chicago, IL 60607

Phone number   312-421-1551
Fax number   312-421-2060
E-mail address   wcpublish@aol.com
Parent company   Windy City Publishing
Circulation   100,000
Magazine availability   We are a free publication distributed to sporting goods stores, health clubs, and sports events, as well as some Chicago buildings and street boxes. We also offer subscriptions for those who would like the magazine delivered to them.
Target audience   22 to 45 age group, 50/50 men/women, active, participate in sports themselves, live in the Chicago area

Magazine's history and mission   Founded in 1987 by Mary Thorne. *Windy City Sports* serves as a resource to the amateur community in Chicago.
Nonfiction   100%
Percent of articles freelance-written   60%
Number of articles bought annually   100
Sections of the magazine open to freelance writers   All
Article interests and needs   Stories concerning the amateur sports we cover: running, cycling, triathlon, volleyball, health clubs, outdoor sports, skiing, and snowboarding
Queries should be directed to   Jeff Banowetz, Editor
Length of articles   Approximately 1,000 words
Payment $100 to $150
Time of payment   On publication
Expenses   Yes
Photographs   Will pay for those that accompany a story.
Response time to queries   1 to 2 months
Rights bought   First-time
Kill fees   Yes
Writer's guidelines   Yes
Sample issues   Yes, for $3

TIPS FOR WRITERS
Jeff Banowetz, Editor

Windy City Sports looks for interesting story ideas on the subjects that we cover—participatory sports in Chicago and the Midwest. We don't cover professional or college sports. Writers should send written queries of story ideas with a list of other publications they have written for and two writing samples. Please submit all queries in writing, either through the mail, fax, or e-mail.

The best way to write for *Windy City Sports* is to become familiar with the magazine and the sports we cover. We are a regional magazine, so most stories have a Chicago or Midwest connection. But we do publish some first-person stories, mostly concerning adventure travel trips and outdoor sports, that go outside of our region.

We value creativity as highly as experience. Writers should do their best to stand out among the submissions. We especially like writers with a light touch and a good sense of humor.

YACHTING

2 Park Avenue
New York, NY 10016

Phone number   212-779-5300
Fax number   212-725-1035

E-mail address   71230.1446@compuserve.com
Parent company   Times Mirror
Circulation   130,000
Online status   Web site at http://www.gsn.com/yachting.net
Magazine availability   Newsstands and subscription
Target audience   Experienced sailors and powerboaters
Magazine's history and mission   Founded in 1907. An upscale for experienced yachtsmen
Nonfiction   100%
Percent of articles freelance-written   75%
Number of articles bought annually   120
Sections of the magazine open to freelance writers   All
Article interests and needs   Firsthand experiences, how-to
Queries should be directed to   Charles Barthold, Editor
Length of articles   100 to 1,500 words
Payment   Varies
Time of payment   On acceptance
Expenses   No
Response time to queries   1 month
Rights bought   First North American
Kill fees   No
Writer's guidelines   Yes
Sample issues   Yes

Travel

BUON GIORNO

777 Arthur Godfrey Road, Suite 300
Miami Beach, FL 33140

Phone number   305-673-0400
Fax number   305-674-9396
Publisher   Onboard Media
Circulation   69,950
Magazine availability   As the port magazine of Costa Cruises, it is found in the passenger cabins of each ship of the Costa Cruise fleet.
Target audience   Passengers of Costa Cruises

Nonfiction   100%

Percent of articles freelance-written   90%

Number of articles bought annually   8 to 10 features; 80 to 100 "fillers"

Article interests and needs   According to Editorial Guidelines, ". . . anything from boat making, bush teas, and butterflies to local legends, literature, and pirate lore. Nonfiction subjects of interest include: architecture, the arts, astronomy, ecology, native food, geology, marine life, language, legends, literature, nature, and current themes such as hit recordings, hot writers, and celebrity hideaways."

Queries should be directed to   Lynn Ulivieri, Managing Editor

Length of articles   Features: 2,000 to 2,500 words; fillers: 75 to 300 words; other articles: 800 to 1,500 words

Payment $.40 per word for features and articles; $20 for a filler

Time of payment   Half on execution of agreement. Half 15 to 30 days after acceptance

Expenses   We don't send writers on assignment.

Photographs   State availability. Guidelines provided upon request.

Response time to queries   30 days

Rights bought   Exclusive worldwide first periodical rights

Kill fees   Yes

Writer's guidelines   Sent upon written request.

Sample issues   11 × 14 SAE with 5 first-class stamps

TIPS FOR WRITERS
Lynn Ulivieri, Managing Editor

Subject matter: Keep in mind that the type of writing we want has less of a travel bent than a feature bent. Do not send first person travel accounts or generic overviews of port destinations. Do not send an editorial that promotes retail/dining establishments or resorts.

Focus on unique aspects of regional culture, interesting local personalities, and new twists on the themes of ecology/wildlife, food, folklore, history, and the like.

Breaking in: Know our magazines. Know the port destinations that we cover. Demonstrate your voice in your query letter. When reviewing queries, we look for writers who can clearly identify the topic, give a synopsis paragraph on the angle, and recommend a working title. Send a selection of published writing samples that reveal your range. A big plus is to include a list of geographical regions and subjects of expertise. Send a self-addressed, stamped #10 envelope for Editorial Guidelines, 11 × 14 self-addressed envelope with 5 first-class stamps for a sample magazine.

The three essential things we look for when reviewing queries or manuscripts are an intimate knowledge of the subject matter; original, well-researched material; and a smart, crisp writing style. ("This beautiful spot offers spectacular views that shouldn't be missed" is usually a clear indication that the writer doesn't know his/her stuff.) Clever presentation of material is also appealing.

Writers should always mail or fax queries. Don't call.

CARIBBEAN TRAVEL AND LIFE

8403 Colesville Road, Suite 830
Silver Spring, MD 20910

Phone number   301-588-2300
Fax number   301-588-2256
Parent company   Caribbean Travel and Life, Inc.
Circulation   130,000
Online status   Not online yet
Magazine availability   On newsstands and through subscription
Target audience   The audience is national, though concentrated in the Northeast. We target affluent, sophisticated individuals who travel frequently.
Magazine's history and mission   The magazine celebrates its 10-year anniversary in early 1996. The only publication exclusively devoted to the Caribbean, Bahamas, and Bermuda, *CTL*'s goal is to spotlight the region, its travel and cultural offerings, its history and people, as well as general destinations.
Nonfiction   100%
Percent of articles freelance-written   80%
Number of articles bought annually   15 to 20 features; 50 to 75 shorter articles
Sections of the magazine open to freelance writers   All sections
Article interests and needs   General destination pieces, cultural/history, adventure, sports, food, shopping, budget travel, personality profiles, water sports, resort reviews, etc.
Queries should be directed to   Veronica Gould Stoddart, Editor-in-Chief
Length of articles   Features: 2,000 to 2,500 words; Departments: 1,200 to 1,500 words; Shorts: 400 to 600 words
Payment   Features: $550; Departments: $200; Shorts: $75 to $100
Time of payment   On publication
Expenses   Not covered
Photographs   Paid separately. Full page: $150; $\frac{3}{4}$ page: $125; $\frac{1}{2}$ page: $100; $\frac{1}{4}$ page: $75
Response time to queries   1 to 2 months
Rights bought   First North American serial rights
Kill fees   25%
Writer's guidelines   Yes
Sample issues   With SASE ($2.50)

TIPS FOR WRITERS

We prefer stories that provide an insider's view of the Caribbean with information and expert advice not readily available elsewhere. We seek stories with a personal touch or point of view that are evocative of a place and with a good insight into the people and culture. Queries, of course, should reflect this.

One of our greatest pet peeves is when a writer telephones and says he's going to Island X and what can he do for us? Writers should have an idea in mind and be familiar enough with the magazine to know whether or not it's been done recently. A writer should study the magazine and know what will and won't be suitable to our audience. We are not looking for vague, unfocused, overly general articles about someone's trip to an island. Writers must have a strong, insider's focus on their subject matter. We cover the in-depth Caribbean—not just hotels and beaches. A unique angle or subject helps get a story published; for example, the Jewish heritage in the Caribbean, river-rafting in Jamaica, the best places for afternoon tea in the islands.

When submitting a query, writers must send along an SASE and several published clips. We do not accept phone queries or queries by fax or e-mail from writers who we've never worked with in the past.

CROWN & ANCHOR

777 Arthur Godfrey Road, Suite 300
Miami Beach, FL 33140

Phone number   305-673-0400
Fax number   305-674-9396
Publisher   Onboard Media
Circulation   792,000
Magazine availability   As the port magazine of the Royal Caribbean Cruise Line, it is found in the passenger cabins of each ship of the RCCL fleet.
Target audience   Cruise passengers of Royal Caribbean Cruise Line
Nonfiction   100%
Percent of articles freelance-written   90%
Number of articles bought annually   8 to 10 features; 80 to 100 "fillers"
Article interests and needs   According to Editorial Guidelines, ". . . anything from boat making, bush teas, and butterflies to local legends, literature, and pirate lore. Nonfiction subjects of interest include: architecture, the arts, astronomy, ecology, native food, geology, marine life, language, legends, literature, nature, and current themes such as hit recordings, hot writers, and celebrity hideaways."
Queries should be directed to   Lynn Ulivieri, Managing Editor
Length of articles   Features: 2,000 to 2,500 words; fillers: 75 to 300 words; other articles: 800 to 1,500 words
Payment $.40 per word for features and articles; $20 for a filler
Time of payment   Half on execution of agreement. Half 15 to 30 days after acceptance
Expenses   We don't send writers on assignment.
Photographs   State availability. Guidelines provided upon request.
Response time to queries   30 days
Rights bought   Exclusive worldwide first periodical rights
Kill fees   Yes

Writer's guidelines   Sent upon written request.
Sample issues   11 × 14 SASE with five first-class stamps

TIPS FOR WRITERS

See entry under *Buon Giorno.*

CRUISING IN STYLE

777 Arthur Godfrey Road, Suite 300
Miami Beach, FL 33140

Phone number   305-673-0400
Fax number   305-674-9396
Publisher   Onboard Media
Circulation   16,500
Magazine availability   As the port magazine of Crystal Cruises, it is found in the passenger cabins of each ship of the Crystal Cruise fleet.
Target audience   Passengers of Crystal Cruises.
Nonfiction   100%
Percent of articles freelance-written   90%
Number of articles bought annually   8 to 10 features; 80 to 100 "fillers"
Article interests and needs   According to Editorial Guidelines, ". . . anything from boat making, bush teas, and butterflies to local legends, literature, and pirate lore. Nonfiction subjects of interest include: architecture, the arts, astronomy, ecology, native food, geology, marine life, language, legends, literature, nature, and current themes such as hit recordings, hot writers, and celebrity hideaways."
Queries should be directed to   Lynn Ulivieri, Managing Editor
Length of articles   Features: 2,000 to 2,500 words; fillers: 75 to 300 words; other articles: 800 to 1,500 words
Payment $.40 per word for features and articles; $20 for a filler
Time of payment   Half on execution of agreement. Half 15 to 30 days after acceptance
Expenses   We don't send writers on assignment.
Photographs   State availability. Guidelines provided upon request.
Response time to queries   30 days
Rights bought   Exclusive worldwide first periodical rights
Kill fees   Yes
Writer's guidelines   Sent upon written request.
Sample issues   11 × 14 SASE with five first-class stamps

TIPS FOR WRITERS

See entry under *Buon Giorno.*

DESTINATIONS

777 Arthur Godfrey Road, Suite 300
Miami Beach, FL 33140

Phone number   305-673-0400
Fax number   305-674-9396
Publisher   Onboard Media
Circulation   260,000
Magazine availability   As the port magazine of Celebrity Cruises, it is found in the passenger cabins of each ship of the Celebrity Cruise fleet.
Target audience   Passengers of Celebrity Cruises.
Nonfiction   100%
Percent of articles freelance-written   90%
Number of articles bought annually   8 to 10 features; 80 to 100 "fillers"
Article interests and needs   According to Editorial Guidelines, ". . . anything from boat making, bush teas, and butterflies to local legends, literature, and pirate lore. Nonfiction subjects of interest include: architecture, the arts, astronomy, ecology, native food, geology, marine life, language, legends, literature, nature, and current themes such as hit recordings, hot writers, and celebrity hideaways."
Queries should be directed to   Lynn Ulivieri, Managing Editor
Length of articles   Features: 2,000 to 2,500 words; fillers: 75 to 300 words; other articles: 800 to 1,500 words
Payment $.40 per word for features and articles; $20 for a filler
Time of payment   Half on execution of agreement. Half 15 to 30 days after acceptance
Expenses   We don't send writers on assignment.
Photographs   State availability. Guidelines provided upon request.
Response time to queries   30 days
Rights bought   Exclusive worldwide first periodical rights
Kill fees   Yes
Writer's guidelines   Sent upon written request.
Sample issues   11 × 14 SASE with five first-class stamps

TIPS FOR WRITERS

See entry under *Buon Giorno.*

ECOTRAVELER

2535 NW Upshur Street
Portland, OR 07210

Phone number   503-224-9080
Fax number   503-224-4266

E-mail address   ecotrav@aol.com
Circulation   100,000
Magazine availability   Newsstands and subscription
Target audience   *EcoTraveler*'s audience is comprised of well-educated, active, and affluent men and women who are top professionals in their field. Median age: 42; 51% male, 49% female; 46% married
Magazine's history and mission   Founded by Lisa Tabb in 1990 under the name *just Go!* Became *EcoTraveler* in March of 1994. It is an adventure travel magazine with an environmental conscience.
Nonfiction   100%
Percent of articles freelance-written   80%
Sections of the magazine open to freelance writers   All
Queries should be directed to   Lisa Tabb
Length of articles   400 to 3,000 words
Payment   Variable
Time of payment   30 days after
Expenses   No
Photographs   Yes
Response time to queries   6 weeks to 2 months
Rights bought   First-time
Kill fees   Yes
Writer's guidelines   Yes
Sample issues   Yes

A TIP FOR WRITERS

Do not fax or e-mail queries to *EcoTraveler*.

ENDLESS VACATION

3502 Woodview Trace
Indianapolis, IN 46268

Phone number   317-871-9500
Fax number   317-871-9507
Parent company   Resort Condominiums International
Circulation   975,000
Magazine availability   Subscription only
Target audience   Family travelers who own a timeshare
Magazine's history and mission   *Endless Vacation*'s parent company, Resort Condominiums International, [is] a timeshare exchange company. *Endless Vacation* goes to their members.
Nonfiction   100%
Percent of articles freelance-written   70%

Number of articles bought annually   Approximately 70 to 80
Sections of the magazine open to freelance writers   Features and departments
Article interests and needs   Family and destination travel
Queries should be directed to   Elizabeth LaPlante, Senior Editor
Length of articles   700 to 2,000 words
Payment   Approximately $1.00 per word
Time of payment   On acceptance
Expenses   Some
Photographs   Photo editor uses stock and assigns photographers.
Response time to queries   1 month
Rights bought   First North American serial rights
Kill fees   25%
Writer's guidelines   Yes
Sample issues $5.00 per issue

TIPS FOR WRITERS

Queries should be addressed to the correct person and should concisely present an idea that has been well researched and obviously fits with the editorial style of *Endless Vacation*. Queries should include three clips, preferably in the style in which the writer proposes to write for *Endless Vacation* (essay or service). We will look at manuscripts on spec. An SASE is requested. Phone calls are discouraged; queries should be presented in writing, either by mail or fax.

ISLANDS

3886 State Street
Santa Barbara, CA 93105

Phone number   805-682-7177
Fax number   805-569-0349
E-mail address   islands@islandsmag.com
Parent company   Islands Publishing, Co.
Circulation   200,000
Online status   Web site at www.islands@islandsmag.com
Magazine availability   Newsstands and subscription
Target audience   Average age 47, 2/3 male, 2/3 professional, average household income to $100,000
Magazine's history and mission   Founded in 1981 in Santa Barbara. Mission: to be the best magazine for island travelers and dreamers.
Nonfiction   100%

Percent of articles freelance-written   90%
Number of articles bought annually   25 features, 50 shorter pieces
Sections of the magazine open to freelance writers   All but Readings, Caribbean Beat, Postcards From Hawaii
Article interests and needs   Most interest in Department pieces—profiles, backpage essays, Logbooks (briefs).
Queries should be directed to   Joan Tapper. Ask for guidelines.
Length of articles   Features: 2,000 to 4,000 words; Departments: 750 to 1,500 words; Briefs: 500 to 750 words
Payment $.50 per word and up
Time of payment   On acceptance
Expenses   For features
Photographs   Pay separately
Response time to queries   6 to 8 weeks
Rights bought   Buys all rights
Kill fees   25%
Writer's guidelines   Yes, on request with SASE
Sample issues $6.00

TIPS FOR WRITERS
Joan Tapper, Editor-in-Chief

There's one piece of advice for a freelance writer that overrides all others: if you want to write for a magazine, read several issues cover to cover. No matter what the guidelines—or the editors—say, it's the magazine itself that tells you what the style, tone, topics, and audience really are.

Having said that, there are some other tidbits of information that may be helpful. I'm always interested in queries with clips. I want to see not just a writer's idea, but his or her style and approach. This is particularly important for travel magazines, where a story about a place may be proposed by many people and style makes all the difference in getting an assignment.

I look for queries that make me want to read the story. If it doesn't make sense, or it puts me to sleep, there's not much hope that the story itself will be coherent and lively. If a writer doesn't have many clips or is just starting out, we're happy to look at a story on spec. But I recommend taking on a department piece or a Logbook, rather than a lengthy feature.

We do like to have an SASE with a query, though we'll accept queries by fax or e-mail. I prefer not to take queries by phone—and laundry lists of ideas are not helpful. Instead, a single page—outlining the thrust of the story, including details and information that show a writer can handle our experiential, anecdotal, personal style, and why he or she is the right person to do this piece—is all that's necessary.

The best way to break into *Islands* is with a department piece. Our feature assignments are reserved for writers who've worked with us before, or who have a great deal of experience. Because of the photo requirements and our need to schedule far in advance for features, we're more likely to take a chance on shorter, lower-risk pieces.

I expect our writers to be accurate, on time, imaginative, and talented. I expect them to provide sources for fact-checking. And above all, I expect them to know about *Islands* because they've read the magazine.

MEXICO EVENTS & DESTINATIONS
Box 188037
Carlsbad, CA 92009

Phone number   619-433-0090
Fax number   619-433-0197
Parent company   Travel Mexico Multimedia Group
Circulation   100,000 quarterly
Magazine availability   Newsstands and subscription—best by subscription
Target audience   Potential travelers to Mexico or Mexico's enthusiasts
Magazine's mission   To promote travel to Mexico and the appreciation of this country's biodiversity and cultural legacy
Nonfiction   100%
Percent of articles freelance-written   90%
Number of articles bought annually   25
Sections of the magazine open to freelance writers   All
Article interests and needs   Culture, foods, travel, photos, crafts, etc.
Queries should be directed to   Gabriela Flores, Group Editor
Length of articles   Between 300 to 1,200 words
Payment   Ranges from $.25 to $.40 per published word, depending on research needed
Time of payment   On publication
Expenses   No
Photographs   Yes
Response time to queries   1 month
Rights bought   One time
Kill fees   No
Writer's guidelines   Yes
Sample issues   Yes, with a $4.50 check or money order

TIPS FOR WRITERS

I like refreshing styles that talk from personal experience. Articles must be well researched and original, noncommercial subjects about travel. Best to send a one page query with topic and sample of style. Always include an SASE and please send before hand for the writer's and photographer's guidelines. Phone calls are not OK. Fax is OK. Only suggestion is to look for what is not easy to see for someone not from the area. What do locals do? Where do they go? What do they eat? How do you feel?

Michigan Living

One Auto Club Drive
Dearborn, MI 48126

Phone number   313-336-1330
Fax number   313-336-1344
Parent company   Automobile Club of Michigan
Circulation   1.1 million
Magazine availability   Subscription only
Target audience   Adults who like to travel
Magazine's history and mission   Founded in 1917 by the Detroit Auto Club, now AAA Michigan. Mission is to bring information to club members and other subscribers about travel opportunities and other information of interest to motorists.
Nonfiction   100%
Percent of articles freelance-written   25% to 30%
Number of articles bought annually   20 to 30
Sections of the magazine open to freelance writers   Features and items on interesting travel destinations and attractions for tourists
Article interests and needs   Best places to break in: "ShortStops" section and one-to two-column stories on topics in Michigan and surrounding states that are listed in the annual Editorial Calendar. Call for a copy.
Queries should be directed to   Larry Keller, Managing Editor
Length of articles   250 to 1,200 words
Payment $55 to $500
Time of payment   On acceptance
Expenses   Only by prior arrangement
Photographs   4 color slides or transparencies
Response time to queries   Within 30 days
Kill fees   25% of contract
Writer's guidelines   Yes
Sample issues   Yes

Important Questions Answered

Q: What is the best way to break into your magazine?
A: Query
Q: What are the keys to breaking in?
A: Know our format and editorial calendar.
Q: What is the best thing writers do?
A: Meet deadline.
Q: What is the worst thing writers do?
A: Send unsolicited manuscript.

Q: How can writers angle their stories for your magazine?
A: Read our editorial calendar.
Q: What is your overall advice to writers who want to get published?
A: Be flexible.

MOTOR HOME

2575 Vista Del Mar Drive
Ventura, CA 93001

Phone number   805-667-4100
Fax number   805-667-4484
Parent company   Affinity Group, Inc
Circulation   150,000
Magazine availability   Newsstands and subscription
Nonfiction   100%
Percent of articles freelance-written   About 50%
Time of payment   On acceptance
Response time to queries   4 to 6 weeks
Rights bought   First North American
Writer's guidelines   Yes with SASE
Sample issues   With SASE

NORTHWEST TRAVEL

P.O. Box 18000
Florence, OR 97439

Phone number   800-348-8401
Fax number   541-947-1124
E-mail address   Rob_Spooner@ortel.org (To publisher—not to editorial dept.)
Parent company   Northwest Regional Magazines
Circulation   50,000
Online status   Web site at www.harborside.com/nwtcr/nwtcr.htm
Magazine availability   Newsstands and subscription
Target audience   Residents and travelers to the Northwest, 30+, mid to upscale income. RVers, campers, and those going to resorts.
Nonfiction   100%
Percent of articles freelance-written   70%
Number of articles bought annually   48+
Sections of the magazine open to freelance writers   Features and Worth-a-Stop department
Article interests and needs   Must relate to Northwest
Queries should be directed to   Judy Fleagle, Managing Editor

Length of articles   300 to 500 (Worth-a-Stop); 500 to 2,000 (Features)
Payment $50 (Worth-a-Stop); $65 to $350 (Features)
Time of payment   After publication
Expenses   No
Photographs   Slides preferred, can use negatives (enclose prints, too)
Response time to queries   1 month
Kill Fees   One-third, if assigned
Writer's guidelines   Free with SASE
Sample issues $4.50

TIPS FOR WRITERS
Judy Fleagle, Managing Editor

We prefer all stories to be queried, and the query should be limited to one page. Include what the story idea is about specifically and if you have photos to go with it—and if so, whether they will be by you or someone else. Clue us in on your writing qualifications with one paragraph about you and include a few clips. Limit query to three story ideas. Pet peeve is a long list of story topics with no one idea developed.

We look at all manuscripts. We expect to see an SASE and don't like queries over the phone or faxed unless there is some urgency. Pet peeve is no cover letter with manuscript.

The best way to break in is to try for a short feature where you provide both the edit and photos. (In *Northwest Travel* that would be the Worth a Stop department.) We are pleased with clean, concise text; slides with sharp images (some horizontal and some vertical), and captions and credits for photos on a separate sheet of paper. We like to see maps and brochures when applicable. We like to see a complete package that has up-to-date information with no typos or misspellings.

OREGON OUTSIDE
P.O. Box 18000
Florence, OR 97439

Phone number   800-348-8401
Fax number   541-947-1124
E-mail address   Rob_Spooner@ortel.org (To publisher—not to editorial dept.)
Parent company   Northwest Regional Magazines
Circulation   30,000
Online status   Pending
Magazine availability   Newsstands and subscription
Target audience   20+, men and women, throughout Oregon and country, all income levels, families too
Magazine's history and mission   Started as *Oregon Parks* in May/June 1993 and changed to more of an activity focus in August/September 1995.

Nonfiction   100%
Percent of articles freelance-written   80%
Number of articles bought annually   40
Sections of the magazine open to freelance writers   Features and sometimes product reviews
Article interests and needs   Must relate to outdoors and Oregon
Queries should be directed to   Judy Fleagle, Managing Editor
Length of articles   500 to 1,500 words
Payment $65 to $350
Time of payment   After publication
Expenses   No
Photographs   Slides preferred, can use negatives (enclose prints, too)
Response time to queries   1 month
Rights bought   First North American serial rights
Kill fees   One-third, if assigned
Writer's guidelines   Free with SASE
Sample issues $4.50

TIPS FOR WRITERS

See entry under *Northwest Travel*.

OUTDOOR TRAVELER, MID-ATLANTIC

P.O. Box 2748
Charlottesville, VA 22902

Phone number   804-984-0655
Fax number   804-984-0656
Parent company   WMS Publications, Inc.
Circulation   30,000
Magazine availability   Newsstands and subscription
Target audience   Ages: 24 to 50. Male/female ratio: 50/50. Magazine is targeted to "active, well-educated adults who are residents or visitors to New York, Pennsylvania, New Jersey, Maryland, Delaware, Washington, D.C., West Virginia, Virginia, and North Carolina."
Magazine's history   Founded in 1993 by Marianne Marks
Nonfiction   100%
Percent of articles freelance-written   90%
Sections of the magazine open to freelance writers   Features and departments including travel, personal experience, photo essays, nature, book excerpts, technical articles, destinations, lodging, essays, and book reviews

Article interests and needs   ". . . articles about outdoor recreation, travel, and places in the Mid-Atlantic region that offer active readers timely and comprehensive information on what to do, where to go, and how to get there."
Queries should be directed to   Marianne Marks, Publisher/Editor
Length of articles   750 to 2,000 words
Time of payment   On publication
Kill fees   25% on acceptable articles that we solicit and do not use
Writer's guidelines   Yes
Sample issues   Available for $4

ROAD SMART

30400 Van Dyke Avenue
Warren, MI 48093

Phone number   810-558-7265
Fax number   810-558-5897
Parent company   Amoco Motor Club
Circulation   1.1 million
Magazine availability   Member-subscription
Nonfiction   100%
Percent of articles freelance-written   60%
Number of articles bought annually   28 to 35
Sections of the magazine open to freelance writers   Travel, safety
Article interests and needs   Safety
Queries should be directed to   Greg Nelson, Editor
Length of articles   1,200 to 1,500 words
Payment   Varies
Time of payment   On acceptance
Expenses   Varies
Photographs   Yes
Response time to queries   2 weeks or less
Writer's guidelines   Supplied on request
Sample issues   Supplied on request

RV WEST

3000 Northup Way, Suite 200
Bellevue, WA 98004

Phone number   206-827-9900; 800-700-6962
Fax number   206-822-9372

Parent company   Vernon Publications, Inc.

Circulation   40,000

Magazine availability   Subscriptions plus a variety of distributors (campgrounds, dealerships, RV shows) and newsstands

Target audience   RVers

Magazine's history and mission   *RV West* began in 1976 as *California Camper*, a four-fold newspaper with its niche in outdoor activities (hiking and camping). After a change in ownership and a couple of name changes, the scope of the magazine was expanded to cover the Western states. In the late 1980s, the name of the magazine was changed to *RV West*, and the format changed to newsprint magazine. The magazine went to a glossy stock in 1992. Vernon Publications, Inc., purchased *RV West* in late 1994. *RV West* is edited for those who own or are about to purchase an RV and use it for pleasure. The magazine provides comprehensive information on where to go and what to do while RV'ing in the West.

Nonfiction   100%

Percent of articles freelance-written   95%

Number of articles bought annually   Around 50

Sections of the magazine open to freelance writers / Article interests

1. Destination stories (focusing on destinations in the 13 Western states, western Canada, or northern Mexico).
2. Event stories (focusing on events in our region—see above—that would be of interest to RVers).
3. Quizzes
4. Jokes, limericks, humorous anecdotes
5. RV model reviews

Queries should be directed to   Sandi Becker, Editor

Length of articles   700 to 1,400 words

Payment $1.50 per column inch; $5 per photo

Time of payment   Month following publication

Expenses   We do not pay expenses

Photographs   Prefer both black-and-white and color photos (slides or prints).

Response time to queries   1 to 3 months

Rights bought   We acquire exclusive, first-time North American serial rights, full rights to historical/reprint/recap/archival *RV West*–related use; and full but nonexclusive rights for current or future electronic, digital, or optical use, including online use.

Writer's guidelines   Send SASE

Sample issues $3.50 per copy (includes shipping and handling)

TIPS FOR WRITERS
Sandi Becker, Editor

We look for stories about destinations in the 13 Western states, and activities and events to enjoy while RV'ing in this region. Because our audience members are RVers, it's crucial to provide information relevant to RV'ing: detailed campground information (name, address, and phone number of campgrounds; fees; number of RV sites; amenities, such as pool, laundry, golf course, boat ramps, etc.; hookups, length restrictions), road restrictions, availability of parking, nearby RV-repair centers, and name and number of organization to contact for more information.

For destination stories, include things to see and do at that destination—hikes, fishing spots, boat rentals, horseback riding, festivals, museums, etc.—with detailed information, such as fees, hours, parking, phone number, and address. A simple, clear map showing the spot in relation to major highways is helpful. Also, indicate the best time of the year to run the story.

If writing about an event, it's a good idea to include information on other things to see and do while in the area.

We're also looking for photo features, covering either a destination or event. Submit color photo(s) with copy (about 400 words). Detailed campground information is not necessary for photo features, but do provide names and numbers of a few campgrounds in the area, as well as a "for more information" number.

We also accept activity stories, such as quizzes, and humorous anecdotes, jokes, limericks, poetry, and cartoons specific to RVing. (Please be tasteful.)

Written queries are preferred. Send completed manuscripts (clips not necessary) and photos (slides or prints) with SASE. If a story is accepted, we ask for both black-and-white and color photos, but it's not necessary to send both with queries. SASE is necessary for response/return of materials.

TEXAS HIGHWAYS

P.O. Box 141009
Austin, TX 78714-1009

Phone number   512-483-3675
Fax number   512-483-3672
Parent company   Texas Department of Transportation
Circulation   400,000
Magazine availability   Newsstands and subscription
Target audience   Anyone interested in Texas travel and Texana
Magazine's history and mission   *Texas Highways* started as an employee publication for the Texas Highway Department in 1953. In May 1974, it became a travel magazine. As the official travel magazine of Texas, it encourages recreational travel to and within the state.
Nonfiction   100%
Percent of articles freelance-written   80%
Number of articles bought annually   75 features, 50 short pieces
Sections of the magazine open to freelance writers   All. However, the "For the Road" department is usually staff-written and carries no bylines.
Article interests and needs   All subject matter must be related to Texas. We cover destinations, history, major events, personalities, and general Texana of interest to travelers. No natural disasters or politics, please. We're trying to get people to travel in Texas. We

want to let our readers understand the people and the land; we want to tell them about things to do, where to find great food, where to hear great music, and where to have fun.

Queries should be directed to   Jack Lowry, Editor, or Jill Lawless, Managing Editor. Queries for the "Speaking of Texas" department should be directed to Ann Gallaway, Senior Editor.

Length of articles   Features 1,200 to 2,000 words

Payment $.40 to $.50 per word

Time of payment   On acceptance

Expenses   Negotiable

Photographs   We generally assign a photographer.

Response time to queries   About 4 to 6 weeks

Rights bought   First serial rights

Kill fees   Generally $100 to $150

Writer's guidelines   Available upon request. Send SASE.

Sample issues   Available upon request. Send SASE.

TIPS FOR WRITERS
by Jack Lowry, Editor

The first thing we think of when we review a query is our readership: is the proposed subject of interest to our readers? Familiarize yourself with the magazine, with the kinds of stories we publish, and with the topics we have covered recently.

Work on your writing. We like strong leads that draw in the reader immediately. We look for writing that is accurate, clear, and concise. Think about ways to tighten your writing. For example, use adjectives and adverbs sparingly; opt for nouns instead. Favor the concrete over the abstract. Get to the point. Specify. Avoid passive constructions and the "to be" form as much as possible. When appropriate, use anecdotes, quotes, wordplay, examples, and contrast. In general, your writing should help information and ideas flow smoothly for the reader.

Keep our production cycle in mind. Queries frequently arrive too late for us to consider. For most features, we must work at least a year in advance, primarily because we schedule seasonal photography one year for publication the following year.

Expect anything you send us to be edited and possibly returned (at least once) for a rewrite.

What we do *not* want? Avoid superlatives that sound like advertising copy. Don't use words whose meanings you don't really understand. Avoid words whose meanings have become distorted through general (over) usage: "Unique" is perhaps the most common example in travel writing.

Don't forget the basics—who, what, when, where, why, and how.

Put everything in writing, please! We assume that if you can't articulate your thoughts in writing, we don't want to hear them. Even if we don't want to see your story right away, we may change our minds. A memorable query may mean we'll call in the future to see if you're still interested in pursuing your story idea. Phone or drop in after you get to know us, after we have given you the go-ahead on a story, or after we have accepted your story. Then we'll have something of mutual interest to discuss.

Remember, follow the instructions in our Guidelines for Writers. They're clear, specific, and easy to understand.

In summary, to break into *Texas Highways* it helps to have talent, be willing to work at your writing, come up with topics we want to cover, and have the ability to follow through—and make sure you can deliver what your query promises. Of course, timing and good fortune factor into the formula as well. Good luck!

WASHINGTON FLYER

1707 L Street, NW
Washington, DC 20036

Phone number   202-331-9393
Fax number   202-331-7311
Circulation   180,000+
Magazine availability   Free in airports and hotels. Only in-airport publication of its kind.
Target audience   25 to 65; business professionals and tourists
Magazine's history and mission   Founded by Metropolitan Washington Airport Authority 1989 to reach business flyers and promote business and travel in Washington.
Nonfiction   100%
Percent of articles freelance-written   60%
Sections of the magazine open to freelance writers   All
Article interests and needs   Travel, business, technology, shopping, restaurant critiques
Queries should be directed to   Heidi Daniel, Editor
Response time to queries   6 to 8 months

Women's Magazines

ESSENCE

1500 Broadway
New York, NY 10036

Phone number   212-642-0600
Fax number   212-921-5173
E-mail address   ESSENCEonline@nyo.com
Parent company   ESSENCE Communications, Inc.
Circulation   1 million

Magazine availability   Newsstands and subscription
Target audience   Black women
Article interests and needs   Topics for African-American women on relationships, celebrity profiles, essays on personal and political issues, and how-to's on working, money, health, electronics, etiquette, and cars.
Queries should be directed to   The Editors
Time of payment   On acceptance

FAMILY CIRCLE

110 Fifth Avenue
New York, NY 10011

Phone number   212-463-1000
Fax number   212-463-1808
Parent company   Gruner & Jahr USA Publishing
Circulation   5 million
Magazine availability   Newsstands, subscription, and supermarket checkouts
Target audience   American women
Magazine's history and mission   Founded 65 years ago as a grocery-store giveaway. Mission: to improve the quality of women's lives
Nonfiction   100%
Percent of articles freelance-written   75%
Number of articles bought annually   140
Sections of the magazine open to freelance writers   Women Who Make a Difference; dramatic, real-life stories; health; consumer/money; opinion essays; humor
Article interests and needs   See above
Queries should be directed to   Attn: Deputy Editor or Senior Editors (Writers are advised to look at the masthead and select a specific editor.)
Length of articles   1,500 to 2,000 words
Payment $1.00 plus per word
Time of payment   On acceptance
Expenses   If agreed to in advance
Photographs   We usually take our own.
Response time to queries   4 to 6 weeks
Rights bought   All print rights or onetime print rights
Kill fees   20%
Writer's guidelines   Send SASE with request: Attn: Writer's Guidelines.
Sample issues   Not available

TIPS FOR WRITERS

Writers should familiarize themselves with *Family Circle*, then come up with article ideas that are suitable for the publication.

Queries should lead with a "hook" that commands an editor's attention—perhaps the lead of the proposed stories. It should include the basic outline of the piece, experts/participants to be interviewed. We do look at complete manuscripts submitted on spec, but we only consider complete manuscripts in the humor and personal essay categories.

Two or three clips should be attached by new writers to show a professional track record.

GLAMOUR

350 Madison Avenue, 11th Floor
New York, NY 10017

Phone number   212-880-8062
Fax number   212-880-6922
E-mail address   Letters@glamour.com
Parent company   Conde Nast Publications, Inc.
Circulation   2.3 million
Magazine availability   Newsstands and subscription
Target audience   Women, 18 to 35, career-oriented, national
Magazine's history and mission   Founded in 1939
Nonfiction   100%
Percent of articles freelance-written   40%
Sections of the magazine open to freelance writers   We accept submissions for Viewpoint, His/Hers columns.
Queries should be directed to   Pamela Erens, Articles Editor
Length of articles   Viewpoint: approximately 1,000 words; other articles: 2,000 or more words
Payment   Viewpoint: $1000; articles of 2,000 or more words: $1,500 and up
Time of payment   On publication
Response time to queries   4 to 6 weeks

TIPS FOR WRITERS

Glamour will review manuscripts but prefers to see a brief proposal first. All manuscripts should be typed, double-spaced, and accompanied by an SASE.

LADIES' HOME JOURNAL

125 Park Avenue
New York, NY 10017

Phone number   212-557-6600
Fax number   212-455-1010

Parent company   Meredith Corporation
Circulation   4.5 million
Online status   Web site at http://www.lhj.com
Magazine availability   Newsstands and subscription
Target audience   Women, ages 30 to 49, married with children. Majority of subscribers have jobs outside the home.
Magazine's history and mission   First published in December 1883 by Curtis Publishing Company, Philadelphia. First U.S. magazine to reach circulation of 1 million (1903). Popular then, as now, because of its broad appeal to American women. *LHJ* at the turn-of-the-century featured stories of international interest, fashion, and items related to the home.
Nonfiction   95%
Fiction   5%
Percent of articles freelance-written   50% (most, however, are written by professional journalists, who are frequent contributors).
Number of articles bought annually   Varies
Sections of the magazine open to freelance writers   "A Woman Today," general features, human interest
Editorial interests and needs   Read one year of back issues to get a good idea for basic editorial content.
Queries should be directed to   For "A Woman Today," send to Box WT. For all other queries, read masthead and send to appropriate editor.
Length of articles   2,000 words
Sample issues   Readily available nationwide on newsstands

MARIE CLAIRE

250 West 55th Street, 5th Floor
New York, NY 10019

Phone number   212-649-4450
Fax number   212-541-4295
E-mail address   marieclaire@hearst.com
Parent company   Hearst Corporation
Circulation   500,000
Magazine availability   Newsstands and subscription
Target audience   Professional women, ages 25 to 45, nationwide, college-educated, who earn about $45,000
Magazine's history and mission   The premier edition of American *Marie Claire* was launched by Editor-in-Chief Bonnie Fuller in September of 1994. There are currently 22 other international editions of *Marie Claire*. The magazine, in the words of our Editor-in-Chief, aims to provide "a great read on everything from world issues to intimate advice, fashion, beauty, and service."

Nonfiction   100%
Percent of articles freelance-written   Approximately 20 to 25%
Sections of the magazine open to freelance writers   Features, some beauty
Article interests and needs   According to Writer's Guidelines:

Women of the World: Lead feature in every edition—a story with an international perspective.

First Person: Written from the female subject's point-of-view as told the reporter.

True Lives: Similar content to First Person but may be written in first or third person, male or female perspective.

Emotional Issues: Relationship/sex related stories

Working: Helps working women with career issues at work, home, or in relationships.

Love Life: Deals with any facet of love, sex, marriage, and dating (or not dating).

Queries should be directed to   Catherine Romano, Features Editor
Length of articles   1,500 to 3,000 words
Payment   Approximately $1,00 to $1.50 per word
Time of payment   On acceptance
Expenses   We will pay writer's expenses.
Photographs   Depends on story
Response time to queries   3 to 4 weeks
Rights bought   Contract-for-hire
Kill fees   25%
Writer's guidelines   Yes

TIPS FOR WRITERS

The feature stories we like should have one or more of the following: First, entertainment value—does the story shock or provoke the reader? Second, news value—is there something new about this article, a new study or a new trend that we're letting the reader know about? Third, does the story have emotional content? Does it push some emotional button, whether it be sadness, pity, or excitement? Fourth, can the reader relate her own life to this story? And fifth, is the story a service piece, providing valuable information and self help to our readers?

One of the best ways to get an assignment from *Marie Claire* is to send us great clips coupled with a great story idea. If you send us first-rate clips, there is a chance that we will assign you an idea that we've come up with, but you're much more likely to get work if you pitch the idea. Regardless of whether the story is your idea or ours, we have a pretty strong idea of what we want out of our articles. We write up a very detailed assignment letter, specifying exactly what we want from you. Despite that, our writers usually have to go through at least one rewrite, and then extensive editing, since we do have a very strong editorial voice. The good news is that we kill very few pieces, so if you've gotten this far in the writing process, you're almost guaranteed a published article.

TIPS FOR WRITERS

1. Never send a query without clips, unless you have a working relationship with *Marie Claire* or are certain that the magazine has your clips on file.
2. In each query, let the editors know that you've studied the magazine, and even suggest what department your article would fit into (e.g., Women of the World, First Person, Emotional Issues, etc.).
3. Don't send more than two ideas at a time.
4. Don't send in a manuscript unless your query has been approved by our editors.
5. Don't query over the phone—put it in writing, or, if you have extreme time constraints, fax your proposal and then follow up immediately with a phone call.
6. We don't accept fiction or personal essays.

MCCALL'S

110 Fifth Avenue
New York, NY 10011

Phone number   212-463-1462
Fax number   212-463-1403
Parent company   Gruner & Jahr USA Publishing
Circulation   4,200,000
Magazine availability   Newsstands and subscription
Target audience   Women, 25 to 45, who have families and work or have worked
Magazine's history   McCall's is 120 years old.
Nonfiction   100%
Percent of articles freelance-written   Roughly 75%
Number of articles bought annually   Approximately 260
Sections of the magazine open to freelance writers   Health, celebrity, reporting, parenting, consumer news, relationships
Article interests and needs   First-person accounts, health, male-female relationships, parenting
Queries should be directed to   Cathy Cavender, Executive Editor
Length of articles   800 to 2,000 words
Payment $1.00 per word
Time of payment   On acceptance
Expenses   If approved in advance
Photographs   No
Response time to queries   Six weeks
Rights bought   First-time world rights
Kill fees   20%
Writer's guidelines   With self-addressed, stamped envelope
Sample issues   No

IMPORTANT QUESTIONS ANSWERED

Q: What sparks your interest in a query?
A: An original idea with mass appeal

Q: Do you always want clips from new writers?
A: Yes. Two to three on a related topic.

Q: What do you look for in the writer's clips?
A: Depth and tone appropriate to *McCall's*

Q: Will you look at completed manuscripts?
A: Yes

Q: Is an SASE always necessary?
A: Yes

Q: Are phone calls from writers OK?
A: No

Q: Is it OK to fax or e-mail queries to you?
A: Not necessary

Q: What are the worst things writer do?
A: Call

Q: What is the best way to break into your magazine?
A: An original, irresistible story. A brief query with clips

MS. MAGAZINE

230 Park Avenue
New York, NY 10169

Phone number   212-551-9595
Fax number   212-551-9384
E-mail address   ms@echonyc.com
Parent company   Lang Communications
Circulation   200,000
Magazine availability   Newsstands and subscription
Target audience   Women primarily, international, all ages and professions
Magazine's history and mission   The magazine premiered in *New York* on December 20, 1971. It was founded by Gloria Steinem, Patricia Carbine, Joanne Edgar, Nina Finkelstein, Mary Peacock, and Letty Cottin Pogrebin.
Nonfiction   95%
Fiction   5%
Percent of articles freelance-written   75%
Number of articles bought annually   Varies
Sections of the magazine open to freelance writers   All
Article interests and needs   We are interested in articles that have a feminist perspective.
Queries should be directed to   Manuscripts Editor

Length of articles   2000 words
Payment   Depends
Time of payment   On publication
Expenses   Covered
Photographs   Covered
Response time to queries   12 weeks
Rights bought   Depending on contracts
Kill fees   20%
Sample issues   Depends

TIPS FOR WRITERS

A query should demonstrate the freelance writer's knowledge of *Ms. Magazine*. We always want clips from writers and an SASE shows professionalism on the part of the writer. They should know we are a feminist magazine and angle their stories and queries in that manner.

NEW WOMAN

215 Lexington Avenue
New York, NY 10016

Phone number   212-251-1500
Fax number   212-251-1590
E-mail address   To come
Parent company   K-III Magazines Corp.
Circulation   1.3 million
Online status   To come
Magazine availability   50/50 newsstands and subscription
Target audience   Women ages 25 to 49, more than half college educated, 72% employed full-time
Magazine's history and mission   The first edition of *New Woman* was published in 1970. According to its editorial director, Jeannette Benny, *New Woman* is edited for contemporary women who are eager to reach for new goals and to balance their personal and professional lives.
Nonfiction   90%
Fiction   10%
Percent of articles freelance-written   75%
Article interests and needs   Relationship, inspirational, self-development.
Queries should be directed to   *New Woman*, Manuscripts and Proposals
Length of articles   1,000 to 3,500 words
Payment $1.00+ per word—varies dependent upon depth and research for the article
Time of payment   On *finalized* acceptance—byline given
Expenses   On occasion and with Editor's prior approval

Photographs   Majority of articles' graphics produced and/or acquired by *New Woman.*
Response time to queries   Approximately 3 to 4 weeks turnaround
Rights bought   Buys first North American serial rights, second serial, onetime
Kill fees   25%
Writer's guidelines   Available upon written request—include SASE
Sample issues   *NO*

REDBOOK

224 West 57th Street
New York, NY 10019

Phone number   212-619-3450
Fax number   212-581-8114
Parent company   Hearst Corporation
Online status   We are on the World Wide Web.
Magazine availability   Newsstands and subscription
Target audience   Married women, 25 to 44, with young children, generally work outside the home
Queries should be directed to   Articles Dept. or Fiction Dept.
Length of articles   Varies
Payment   Varies
Time of payment   On acceptance
Expenses   Telephone, supplies, research, etc. All expenses paid—amounts vary.
Response time to queries   4 to 10 weeks
Rights bought   First North American, all rights, onetime rights
Kill fees   One-fourth of contract fee
Writer's guidelines   Please send a stamped, self-addressed envelope.
Sample issues   We do not provide sample issues.

SELF

350 Madison Avenue
New York, NY 10017

Phone number   212-880-8800
Fax number   212-880-7704 or 880-8110
E-mail address   Comments@SELF.com (also, e-mail addresses by department, such as Nutrition@SELF.com, Fitness@SELF.com, etc.).
Parent company   The Conde Nast Publications, Inc.
Circulation   1,211,024 (as of December 1995)
Magazine availability   Newsstands and subscription

Target audience   Educated, active, professional women; nationwide, young (about 20s to 40s), interested in issues related to health, fitness, and nutrition, as well as beauty, fashion, and body/mind topics

Magazine's history   *Self* was founded in 1979; Phyllis Starr Wilson was its founding editor.

Nonfiction   100%

Percent of articles freelance-written   70%, approximately

Sections of the magazine open to freelance writers   The Body/Mind Journal, Medical Journal, and Nutrition Journal are good places for a new writer to break into the magazine. Experienced writers can submit ideas for these sections of the magazine, or for the feature well.

Article interests and needs   Articles on body/mind, nutrition, fitness and women's health issues

Queries should be directed to   (See masthead for complete list) Nutrition and food: Ellie McGrath, Nutrition and Articles Editor; Body/Mind: Beth Howard, Senior Editor; Fitness: Pamela Miller, Fitness Editor

Length of articles   300 to 6,000 words

Payment $1.00 per word; more for very experienced writers

Time of payment   On acceptance

Expenses   Reimbursed

Response time to queries   4 to 6 weeks

Rights bought   Conde Nast buys onetime rights to publish, but retains electronic rights worldwide.

Kill fees   25%

Writer's guidelines   Send SASE with request.

Sample issues   No

TIPS FOR WRITERS
Judith Daniels, Executive Editor

My interest is piqued by a writer who has taken the time to familiarize him or herself with the magazine, what we've done, the voice of the magazine, etc. I realize it's very difficult, if not impossible, for a writer to really understand all or even most of the magazines out there, but it's insulting to get a query for a story we would never do (e.g. celebrity pieces), or is identical to one we did six months ago.

A good, professional query isn't written on cheesy stationery, doesn't use my first name if the writer doesn't know me, has my name spelled correctly. It's succinct, engaging, and timely. The front of the magazine is probably the best place for new writers (or writers new to *Self*) to break in with shorter items. We welcome queries that do a good job of explaining how the writer will report and focus on the latest news in health, nutrition, and fitness information for our readers.

I think an SASE with a query is a nice courtesy but not absolutely necessary. As for clips, I like to see at least a couple, particularly any that are on a topic related to the query. I'd prefer not to get a phone call from a writer I've never worked with before; I do my best to answer all queries in a timely manner.

The best way to break into the magazine is via the front of the book, our various Journal sections—Nutrition, Medical, Fitness. (The Beauty and Style Journals may be tougher to get into, since they are staff-written in large part.)

The best thing a writer can do is to become familiar with the magazine and truly interested in and informed about the subjects it covers. Few editors have time to start at square one, explaining who the reader is, etc. Which is not to say that a good editor minds helping a writer understand better what the story's mission is and what sources and experts are appropriate. Editors tend to try new writers when they see signs of freshness, focus, flair; editors give repeat assignments when the writer has delivered a solid article in a prompt, professional manner. At its best, the process is always a true collaboration.

VOGUE

350 Madison Avenue
New York, NY 10017

Phone number   212-880-8800
Fax number   212-880-8169 (Editorial fax)
E-mail address   VOGUE-mail@aol.com (For reader mail only)
Parent company   Conde Nast Publications, Inc.
Circulation   1,136,171
Magazine availability   Newsstands and subscription
Target audience   Broad-based, well-educated audience
Nonfiction   100%
Fiction   We do not publish fiction or poetry
Percent of articles freelance-written   70%
Number of articles bought annually   120 (approximately)
Sections of the magazine open to freelance writers   Varies
Queries should be directed to   Laurie Jones, Managing Editor, or Susan Morrison, Features Director
Length of articles   500 to 2,500 words
Payment $1.00 to $1.50 per word
Time of payment   On acceptance
Expenses   Reimbursed
Response time to queries   Within one month
Kill fees   25%
Writer's guidelines   Available

THE WOMEN'S REVIEW OF BOOKS

Wellesley College
Wellesley, MA 02181

Phone number   617-283-2555
Fax number   617-283-3645
Circulation   15,000
Magazine availability   Newsstands and subscription
Target audience   Feminist book readers worldwide
Magazine's history   Founded 1983 by editor Linda Gardiner. Publishes in-depth reviews of recent books by and about women in all fields, from trade, academic, and small presses.
Nonfiction   100%
Percent of articles freelance-written   100%
Number of articles bought annually   250
Sections of the magazine open to freelance writers   All
Article interests and needs   Book reviews
Queries should be directed to   Linda Gardiner, Editor
Length of articles   Negotiated
Payment   Negotiated. $75 to $350 depending on length.
Time of payment   On publication
Expenses   No
Photographs   No
Response time to queries   2 to 8 weeks
Rights bought   First serial
Kill fees   No
Writer's guidelines   Only after an assignment is offered
Sample issues   Yes

TIPS FOR WRITERS
Linda Gardiner, Editor

Know how to write well. Know how to think. Have something to say. Make me want to read past line two. If you don't know how to do all these things already, don't waste my time; I'm not running a writing program.

The query should have the qualities just listed. Queries with bad grammar or punctuation, misspellings, or typos land in the wastebasket. So do letters impregnated with cigarette smoke.

Always send clips *but only* if their subject, length, and general approach are fairly similar to what we publish; if you don't have anything close enough, don't query until you have. One clip is enough if it's good enough. What I look for in clips: Would I have published this piece? If not, then you won't hear from me.

We don't look at unsolicited manuscript submissions.

Professional etiquette: An SASE is always necessary (but rarely included); a reply may be quicker if you send an SASE, especially if the answer is No. Phone calls permissible only from writers we've worked with in the past; otherwise, send query with clips as above. No faxes or e-mail EVER.

Worst things writers do: Lack qualities listed above. Also, in no particular order: Undated letters; handwritten letters; letters more than a page in length; proposals so vague that I don't know what they are; SASE with insufficient postage; obvious ignorance of our publication; unsolicited submissions, especially when accompanied by a request for critique even if we won't publish it; calling for a decision three days after you've sent the query letter; multiple submissions; etc.

Any other topic: How about some reality checks? We and every other magazine I know of get a substantial amount of unsolicited material that is just dreadful by any standards. These people are kidding themselves that they can write, and they're wasting editors' limited time. I realize they swell the circulation of writer's magazines, but what those magazines teach them is that some collection of gimmicks will enable them to "break in," as if talent, originality, hard work, and intelligence were irrelevant. Do the same people think that an advice book will get them into professional baseball, a symphony orchestra, piloting a plane, or a job in nuclear physics research? Unlikely. They should throw away these so-called "Insider's Guides" and start reading some real books.

WORKING MOTHER

230 Park Avenue
New York, NY 10169

Phone number   212-551-9500
Fax number   212-599-9757
E-mail address   JCulbreth@womweb.com
Parent company   Lang Communications
Circulation   925,000
Magazine availability   Newsstands and subscription
Nonfiction   100%
Response time to queries   4 to 6 weeks
Kill fees   20%
Sample issues $2.95

WORKING WOMAN

230 Park Avenue
New York, NY 10169

Phone number   212-551-9500
Fax number   212-599-4763
E-mail address   wwedit@womweb.com
Parent company   Lang Communications
Circulation   750,000
Online status   Web site
Magazine availability   Newsstands and subscription

Target audience   The only national magazine aimed at female professionals at a managerial, executive level. Also aimed at female entrepreneurs. Age range: 25 to 65.

Magazine's history and mission   Founded in November 1976 to serve women flooding into the job market. Refocused by Lynn Povich in 1991 to cover managerial, executive-level women.

Nonfiction   100%

Percent of articles freelance-written   85%

Number of articles bought annually   70

Section of the magazine open to freelance writers   Biz Buzz

Article interests and needs   News-related items pertaining to the executive-level woman

Queries to   Call to find editor who handles subject or section. Otherwise: Lynn Povich, Editor

Length of articles   Buzz: 300 to 500 words; Features: 2,500 to 3,500 words

Payment   Approximately $1.00 per word

Time of payment   On acceptance

Expenses   Yes

Photographs   No

Response time to queries   Six weeks

Rights bought   Usually, the magazine retains all rights.

Kill fees   20%

Writer's guidelines   Yes, with an SASE

Sample issues   No

TIPS FOR WRITERS
Melissa Schorr

Working Woman is looking for freelancers who have experience writing business stories for a national market. A good query for this magazine is news or trend related, with a strong tie to issues that affect executive women in the workplace.

Writers should be aware of the magazine's five to six month lead time. Writers should always have a clearly thought-out and researched idea with a timely peg, and suggestions of candidates to be interviewed.

The best way to break into the magazine is by pitching articles to our front of the book Biz Buzz section, which focuses on news, people, trends, studies, etc. Full-length features are usually assigned to writers who have previously written for the magazine.

Common mistakes writers make include sending a sloppy, hand written query, or suggesting a piece that has no place to fit into the magazine (poetry, first-person narratives, etc.). Other mistakes include pitching an idea at a level too basic for our readership, or pitching a subject that we frequently cover without a new angle to make it fresh.

Trade Magazines

ABA JOURNAL

750 North Lake Shore Drive
Chicago, IL 60611

Phone number   312-988-6018
Fax number   312-988-6014
E-mail address   abajournal@attmail.com
Parent company   American Bar Association
Circulation   400,000
Online status   Articles in back issues are on Lexis, in the ABA library, in the ABA-JNL file on WESTLAW, in the ABAJ database.
Magazine availability   Subscription
Target audience   Attorneys nationwide
Magazine's history and mission   Founded in 1915 by the American Bar Association. One objective of the *ABA Journal* is to be a forum for the free expression and interchange of ideas. Another is to report objectively on current events in law and on ideas that will help lawyers to practice better and more efficiently. Finally, articles should emphasize practical, rather than theoretical or esoteric material.
Nonfiction   100%
Percent of articles freelance-written   75%
Number of articles bought annually   180
Sections of the magazine open to freelance writers   News and features
Article interests and needs   Substantive law
Queries should be directed to   Kerry Klumpe, Managing Editor
Length of articles   3,000 words
Payment $300 to $2,000
Time of payment   On acceptance
Expenses   Reasonable
Photographs   Freelance photographers
Response time to queries   2 weeks
Rights bought   *ABA Journal* retains all
Kill fees   20%
Writer's guidelines   Free
Sample issues   Cost $7.50

TIPS FOR WRITERS

The *ABA Journal* buys only on spec. No query letters. Because of the specialized nature of the magazine, writers should have law degrees or extensive experience in legal journalism; the *ABA Journal* is very selective.

ABERDEEN'S CONCRETE CONSTRUCTION

426 South Westgate Street
Addison, IL 60101

Phone number   708-543-0870
Fax number   708-543-3112
Parent company   The Aberdeen Group
Circulation   76,000
Magazine availability   Subscription
Target audience   Concrete contractors, architects, and engineers
Magazine's history and mission   Established in 1956 to provide technical information about working with concrete as well as information about the equipment used to do the work.
Nonfiction   100%
Percent of articles freelance-written   15%
Number of articles bought annually   10
Sections of the magazine open to freelance writers   Feature articles
Article interests and needs   See mission statement
Queries should be directed to   Ward Malisch, Editorial Director
Length of articles   1,600 words
Payment $250+ (depending on article length)
Time of payment   On acceptance
Expenses   If preapproved
Photographs   Yes
Response time to queries   2 weeks
Kill fees   No
Sample issues   Yes

IMPORTANT QUESTIONS ANSWERED

Q: What do you look for in a query?
A: Prefer telephone queries.
Q: Is an SASE always necessary?
A: No
Q: Are phone calls from writers OK?
A: Yes
Q: What is the key to breaking into your magazine?

A: Background in concrete construction
Q: What types of articles do you want?
A: How-to stories preferred

ADVERTISING AGE

740 Rush Street
Chicago, IL 60611

Phone number   312-649-5200
Fax number   312-649-5331
E-mail address   76135,3513@compuserv.com
Parent company   Crain Communications
Circulation   80,000
Online status   Web site and on eWorld
Magazine availability   Newsstands and subscription
Target audience   Marketing executives at agencies, media and consumer goods marketers
Nonfiction   100%
Percent of articles freelance-written   15%
Interests and needs   Strong background in business/marketing reporting
Queries should be directed to   Melanie Rigney, Managing Editor
Length of articles   Typically 300 to 600 words
Payment   Typically $200 to $400
Time of payment   On publication
Expenses   Yes
Photographs   Yes
Rights bought   We buy all rights.
Kill fees   Some
Writer's guidelines   No
Sample issues   No

AMERICAN FITNESS

15250 Ventura Boulevard, Suite 200
Sherman Oaks, CA 91403

Phone number   818-905-0040, Ext. 200
Fax number   818-990-5468
Parent company   Aerobics and Fitness Association of America (AFAA)
Circulation   31,000
Magazine availability   Membership to AFAA or subscription

Target audience   18 to 34 female, college-educated, AFAA-certified professionals/fitness enthusiasts

Magazine's history and mission   Founded in 1983, *American Fitness* presents the latest research and trends in exercise, health, and recreational fitness. The content is enlivened with lifestyle oriented pieces for entertainment as well.

Nonfiction   100%

Percent of articles freelance-written   80%

Number of articles bought annually   60

Sections of the magazine open to freelance writers   Alternative Paths, Clubscene, Clip 'n' Post, Trends, Strength, Adventure, Men's Health and Research

Article interests and needs   Youth, senior, family, and disabled fitness

Queries should be directed to   Peg Jordan, R.N., editor-at-large

Length of articles   1,000 to 1,200 words

Payment $150

Time of payment   Four weeks after publication date

Expenses   Need to be approved by editor

Photographs   We often purchase photos from authors ($50 per slide).

Response time to queries   4 to 6 weeks

Rights bought   We buy all rights.

Kill fees   Must be approved by editor

Writer's guidelines   Available with an SASE

Sample issues   Available with an SASE

TIPS FOR WRITERS

We need timely, in-depth, informative articles on health, fitness, aerobic exercise, sports nutrition, sports medicine, and physiology. Cover a unique fitness angle, provide accurate and interesting findings, and write in a lively, intelligent manner.

We are looking for new health and fitness reporters and writers. *American Fitness* is a good place for first-time authors or regularly published authors who want to sell spin-offs or reprints. No articles on unsound nutritional practices or unsafe exercise gimmicks.

THE ARTIST'S MAGAZINE

1507 Dana Avenue
Cincinnati, OH 45207

Phone number   513-531-2690, Ext. 467

Fax number   513-531-2902

Parent company   F & W Publications

Circulation   275,000

Magazine availability   Newsstands and subscription

Target audience   Artists of all ages, professional levels, across America and abroad

Nonfiction   99%
Fiction   1%
Percent of articles freelance-written   80%
Number of articles bought annually   Approximately 160
Sections of the magazine open to freelance writers   Features and columns
Article interests and needs   Articles should focus on the technical aspects of making art. We are a "how-to" magazine. We also need marketing and business articles—how to make it as an artist.
Queries should be directed to   Art making articles to: Greg Schaber, Senior Editor. Business topics to: Ann Emmert Abbott, Managing Editor.
Length of articles   1,000 to 3,000 words
Payment $100 for short essays, $225 to $250 for columns, $350 to $400 for features, $500 for special section—depends on length and whether author assists with illustrations, etc.
Time of payment   On acceptance
Expenses   Include in payment
Photographs   We use only reproductions of art (prefer slides/transparencies and illustrations).
Response time to queries   6 weeks
Rights bought   We buy only first-time North American rights
Kill fees   20% of proposed payments
Writer's guidelines   Send an SASE to: Writer's Guidelines *The Artist's Magazine.*
Sample issues   Send $2.75 to Back Issues Manager, *The Artist's Magazine.*

TIPS FOR WRITERS

The query: What sparks my interest is a solid query from someone who knows what they're talking about. In our case that's making art (many of our writers are artists, too), or the business of promoting and selling art (this is more open to business writers with marketing knowledge).

Professional etiquette: SASEs are necessary if you want your submission returned. Phone calls are OK, but don't expect to engage an editor in a long conversation—I'd rather you mail me a query and I'll tell you this when you call. Writers may also fax queries.

The best way to break into the magazine is to query us with some information that our readers can really use. Read the magazine, get a feel for it, and decide if you have something to contribute. We try to look at everything, even if it takes a while. Be patient—if you don't hear from us right away, it may mean we're passing your query back and forth.

Best things writers do: The best things that writers can do for me is be very professional. Understand the time constraints we're under. Offer your ideas in easy-to-read queries, and then wait for our reply. Don't take rejection personally. Don't call every day wanting to know why you were rejected. We'll call you if we think you can contribute more.

Worst things writers do: The worst things writers do is present poorly written, poorly planned out queries and information packets—especially if it's obvious they have no idea about what we do!

Writers should angle their stories towards the working artist.

ASU Travel Guide

1525 Francisco Boulevard East
San Rafael, CA 94901

Phone number   415-459-0300
Fax number   415-459-0494
E-mail address   ASUguide.com
Circulation   60,000
Online status   CompuServe Online edition
Magazine availability   Subscription only
Target audience   Airline employees, their parents, and retired airline employees. Mostly U.S.; some Canada; a bit overseas.
Magazine's history and mission   Founded by a United Airlines employee in 1970. He recognized the need for a compilation of discounts airline employees receive worldwide.
Nonfiction   100%
Percent of articles freelance-written   95%
Number of articles bought annually   16
Sections of the magazine open to freelance writers   Destination travel articles. Four per quarterly issue
Article interests and needs   Geared to airline employees
Queries should be directed to   Christopher Gil, Managing Editor
Length of articles   1,800 words
Payment $200
Time of payment   On acceptance
Expenses   Can sometimes set up for trips to the destination.
Photographs   None purchased. They come from tourist boards.
Response time to queries   1 week.
Rights bought   First North American
Kill fees $50
Writer's guidelines   Yes, if SASE is sent
Sample issues   Yes, if sent $9\frac{1}{2} \times 6$ envelope with $1.41 affixed.

Tips for Writers

Writers should not call. It is best to mail or fax a list of destinations about which you can write, along with a sample of your published writing. All are kept on file.

Always send an SASE for a response. Articles must be geared to airline employees, who travel frequently, often taking shorter trips. They get free airfare, so trips are often taken.

Do not use descriptions about a place that could be used for most places. Tell why a place is unique.

BARTENDER MAGAZINE

P.O. Box 158
Liberty Corner, NJ 07938

Phone number   908-766-6006
Fax number   908-766-6607
Parent company   Foley Publishing
Circulation   144,622
Magazine availability   Newsstands and through subscription
Target audience   All those 21 years of age or older who are involved in the restaurant/bar/tavern/lounge/hotel industry dealing with alcoholic beverages.
Magazine's history and mission   *Bartender* magazine was founded in 1979 by bartender and general manager, Raymond P. Foley.
Nonfiction   90%
Fiction   10%
Percent of articles freelance-written   10%
Number of articles bought annually   6
Sections of the magazine open to freelance writers   Varies from issue to issue
Article interests and needs   Relating to industry
Queries should be directed to   Jaclyn W. Foley, Editor
Length of articles   1 to 2 pages
Payment $50 to $200
Time of payment   On publication
Expenses   No
Photographs   Yes
Response time to queries   2 months
Rights bought   First time
Kill fees   None
Writer's guidelines   No
Sample issues   Yes

TIPS FOR WRITERS

Our interest and attention will be gained by queries and writings related to the field. We would like an SASE included for response. Faxed queries are welcome; phone calls, however, are not.

ByLine

P.O. Box 130596
Edmond, OR 73013

Phone number   405-348-5591
Fax number   Same (no fax submissions or queries)
E-mail address   Byline MP@aol.com (no e-mail submissions or queries)
Circulation   3,500+
Magazine availability   Subscription only
Target audience   Writers of any age or description
Magazine's history and mission   *ByLine* was established in 1901 as a source of motivation, support, and information for freelance writers and poets.
Nonfiction   85% nonfiction and poetry
Fiction   Approximately 15% (varies: we publish one short story per issue.)
Articles freelance-written   All features and departments are freelanced. Only specific columns are staff-written.
Number of articles bought annually   Varies. Buy approximately 5 features per issue, plus maybe 5 to 10 short pieces
Sections of the magazine open to freelance writers   Features; End Piece; Only When I Laugh; First Sale; The Poetic Life
Article interests and needs   All articles must deal with how to write better, sell more, or stay motivated, etc.
Queries should be directed to   Kathryn Fanning, Managing Editor
Length of articles   Features: 1,500 to 1,800 words; End Piece: 750 words;
Payment   Features: $50; Short Story: $100; Other depts. vary
Time of payment   On acceptance
Response time to queries   1 month
Rights bought   First North American
Kill fees   No
Writer's guidelines   For SASE (#10 envelope)
Sample issues $4.00 postpaid

Compressed Air

253 East Washington Avenue
Washington, NJ 07882

Phone number   908-850-7818
Fax number   908-689-5576
Parent company   Ingersoll-Rand Company
Circulation   130,000
Magazine availability   Subscription
Target audience   Middle to upper level managers in all industries

Magazine's history and mission   Founded in 1895 by William Saunders, president of Ingersoll-Sergeant. Editorial mission: present a diverse menu of subjects to help our readers apply technology to their everyday efforts, both on the job and off.

Nonfiction   100%

Percent of articles freelance-written   100%

Number of articles bought annually   70

Sections of the magazine open to freelance writers   All

Article interests and needs   Arts, history, science, materials, construction, mining

Queries should be directed to   Tom McAloon, Editor

Length of articles   2,000 words

Payment $900

Time of payment   On acceptance

Expenses $100

Response time to queries   2 months

Rights bought   No

Kill fees   No

Writer's guidelines   Available

Sample issues   Available

IMPORTANT QUESTIONS ANSWERED

Q: Do you always want clips from new writers?

A: Yes

Q: How many do you want?

A: Two to three

Q: What do you look for in the writer's clips?

A: Is it interesting/well done?

Q: Will you look at completed manuscripts?

A: If not too long.

Q: Are phone calls from writers OK?

A: No

Q: Is it OK if writers fax or e-mail queries to you?

A: Yes

Q: What is the key to breaking in to your magazine?

A: Send me wonderful ideas for stories.

Q: What is the best thing a writer can do?

A: Send me a one paragraph outline.

Q: How can writers angle their stories for your magazine?

A: Tell readers why, not how.

THE CONSTRUCTION SPECIFIER

601 Madison Street
Alexandria, VA 22314

Fax number   703-684-0465
E-mail address   CompuServe: 72113, 1665
Parent company   Construction Specifications Institute
Circulation   19,500
Magazine availability   Membership and subscription
Target audience   Construction professionals who deal with commercial, institution, industrial, and renovation building projects
Magazine's history and mission   Founded in 1951 for the advancement of construction technology through communication (see essay).
Nonfiction   100%
Percent of articles freelance-written   99%
Number of articles bought annually   120
Sections of the magazine open to freelance writers   All
Article interests and needs   Technical articles on new construction technologies or practices
Queries should be directed to   Jack Reeder, Publisher/Editor; Anne Scott, Senior Editor
Length of articles   1,500 to 3,000 words
Payment $.15 per word
Time of payment   On publication
Expenses   Phone
Photographs   Yes
Rights bought   We take first-time rights
Kill fees   No
Writer's guidelines   Yes
Sample issues   Yes

TIPS FOR WRITERS

The Construction Specifier is a monthly magazine for construction professionals who deal with commercial, industrial, and renovation building projects. Our readers include architects, engineers, specifiers, contractors, and product manufacturers.

Freelance writers for *The Construction Specifier* must be experts in some area of construction. Our writers usually are architects, engineers, specifiers, contractors, etc.

Freelance writers interested in submitting work should request a copy of our editorial calendar and then send or fax a letter of inquiry with an outline of their proposed article. Two or three clips are always helpful in determining a writer's style and level of technical expertise. If we are interested in the writer's story proposal, we will contact him or her and work out deadlines, payment, etc.

We are not interested in case studies. Authors are expected to submit technical articles on new construction technologies or practices.

ELECTRONICS NOW
500 Bi Country Boulevard
Farmingdale, NY 11735-3931

Phone number   516-293-3000
Fax number   516-293-3115
Parent company   Gernsback Publications, Inc.
Circulation   123,000
Magazine availability   Newsstands and subscription
Target audience   Electronics professionals
Magazine's history and mission   Founded by Hugo Bernsback in 1920s. Previous titles: *Radio Craft, Radio-Electronics.*
Nonfiction   100%
Percent of articles freelance-written   80%
Number of articles bought annually   80
Sections of the magazine open to freelance writers   All
Article interests and needs   Electronics construction, technology
Queries should be directed to   Brian Fenton, Editor
Length of articles   5,000 words
Payment $50 to $500
Time of payment   On acceptance
Response time to queries   2 months
Rights bought   All
Kill fees   None
Writer's guidelines   Free for the asking
Sample issues   Free for the asking

IMPORTANT QUESTIONS ANSWERED

Q: Is an SASE always necessary?
A: No
Q: Are phone calls from writers OK?
A: Yes
Q: What is your overall advice to writers who want to get published?
A: Read and understand the magazine. A writer without an electronics background is unlikely to be published.

HISPANIC BUSINESS

360 South Hope Avenue, Suite 300C
Santa Barbara, CA 93105

Phone number   805-682-5843
Fax number   805-563-1239
E-mail address   Internet at info@hbinc.com
Parent company   Hispanic Business, Inc.
Circulation   200,000
Online status   Debut set for spring 1996.

Magazine availability   Through subscription and at Barnes and Noble book stores and affiliated chains

Target audience   Affluent Hispanic business owners across the United States; English dominant.

Magazine's history and mission   *HB* was founded by editor and publisher Jesus Chavarria in 1979 to cover the U.S. Hispanic business economy.

Nonfiction   100%

Percent of articles freelance-written   35%

Number of articles bought annually   50

Sections of the magazine open to freelance writers   News pages, features

Article interests and needs   Items and stories on successful Hispanic entrepreneurs and executives; companies must be at least 51% U.S. Hispanic-owned.

Queries should be directed to   Hector D. Cantu, Managing Editor

Length of articles   200 to 1,400 words

Payment $.25 per word

Time of payment   Within four weeks of publication

Expenses   Documented long-distance telephone calls

Photographs   Yes

Response time to queries   Up to four weeks

Rights bought   We purchase all rights.

Kill fees   Negotiable for stories killed by editors

Writer's guidelines   Free

Sample issues $3

TIPS FOR WRITERS
Hector D. Cantu, Managing Editor

There's one thing I immediately look for in any query from a freelancer: does the writer understand our audience and does he or she understand the goal of editorial? Familiarity with these editorial factors tells me a lot about the writer's skills as a journalist.

Too often, I receive queries from writers who do not take the time to become familiar with our magazine. Who do we write about? What do we write about? What are the scheduled cover stories? And what stories became cliché a year after we began publishing? For example, would a successful freelancer who's done even a tiny bit of magazine background research send a query letter to an established parenting magazine offering a story on why vaccinations are great for babies? Of course not. At the same time, *Hispanic Business* magazine long ago stopped writing stories about mom-and-pop Mexican food restaurants and immigrants who "came to America with nothing but a dollar in their pocket and the clothes on their back." *Yawn.*

These types of queries immediately tell me two things: you don't know the magazine's mission, and, judging by your query—which is the primary sample of writing and reporting an editor can judge—your story probably won't be researched any better. Rejection letter signed, sealed, and delivered. Remember: as a writer and reporter, you need to show me that your job of submitting a well-researched piece begins with the first sentence of your query.

One last note on research: it shouldn't be limited to stories. I've received query letters addressed to editors who haven't worked at the magazine in five years. This failure to verify simple information (*pick up the phone!*) makes your query DOA.

To summarize: Target a magazine that matches your writing interests. Request an editorial calendar and a sample issue. Better yet, subscribe. To learn about the magazine's readers, request a media kit from the ad department (*industry secret:* most are mailed free and include a sample issue, editorial calendar, and reader demographics). Become familiar with the type of stories published (*no secret here:* editors hate being pitched a story they ran two months ago!). Now you're prepared to send a query that an editor will *appreciate.*

THE HOLLYWOOD REPORTER

5055 Wilshire Boulevard
Los Angeles, CA 90036-4396

Phone number   213-525-2000
Fax number   213-525-2390
E-mail address   THRScott@aol.com
Parent company   BPI Communications, Inc.
Circulation   23,328 Daily edition; 33,357 Tuesday International Edition
Online status   Soon to launch on World Wide Web.
Magazine availability   Newsstands and subscription
Target audience   Anyone working in any area of the entertainment industry worldwide. Paper is business-oriented, covering film, TV, music, theater, production, exhibition, cable, interactive technology, film markets, and more.
Magazine's history and mission   Founded in 1930 by William R. Wilkerson. Paper is dedicated to covering the business side of the entire entertainment industry, from deals and mergers to new technology, legal and governmental issues, new production, reviews, international locations, film and TV markets, music, executives, studios, etc.
Nonfiction   100%
Percent of articles freelance-written   70% of Special Issues
Number of articles bought annually   200 to 300 in Special Issues Dept.
Sections of the magazine open to freelance writers   Special Issues, which produces over 100 issues yearly on a broad range of industry topics.
Article interests and needs   Must relate to a specific theme of a given issue, e.g., comedy, special effects, independent production, animation. We DO NOT seek general queries—we develop an outline on a given subject and then assign writers.
Queries should be directed to   Matthew King, Managing Editor, Special Issues
Length of articles   1,200 words average
Payment   Standard rate for average article is $400 to $500.
Time of payment   On publication
Expenses   Transportation, phone, and fax
Photographs   Writer must help to gather.

Rights bought *The Hollywood Reporter* reserves all rights.
Kill fees 50% if article killed
Writer's guidelines Yes

TIPS FOR WRITERS
Matthew King, Managing Editor

Freelance writers who want to develop a relationship with the Special Issues section of *The Hollywood Reporter* should send a letter of introduction with a resume and 3 to 5 clips. It is important that freelancers understand the audience we serve: we are an entertainment *trade* publication. We cover the business of film, TV, and music; we are not interested in star profiles. Freelancers should have previous experience in entertainment trade journalism. We seek writers with well-placed contacts and an energetic, concise style.

Because we publish over 100 issues a year on a wide range of subjects, freelancers should tell us what specific elements of the business they consider their specialty, e.g., animation, comedy, independent film. They should follow up with a phone call and ask for a copy of our editorial calendar, which details the issues we will be assembling in the coming year. At that point, they can tailor specific pitches for specific issues.

When we find a prospective writer, we'll usually start him or her off with a smaller project. If both parties are satisfied, we move onto larger assignments.

HOME BUSINESS NEWS
4505 South Wasatch Boulevard
Salt Lake City, UT 84124

Phone number 801-273-5301
Fax number 801-273-5422
Parent company American Home Business Association
Circulation 35,000
Magazine availability Subscription
Target audience Anyone who is running a business from their home or contemplating starting one.
Magazine's history and mission Founded January 1994 American Home Business Association
Nonfiction 100%
Percent of articles freelance-written 15%
Number of articles bought annually 48
Sections of the magazine open to freelance writers All
Article interests and needs Success stories of home business owners. Anything pertaining to home-based business ownership.
Queries should be directed to Carolyn Tice, Executive Editor

Length of articles   1,500 words
Payment $.10 per published word or negotiable
Time of payment   On publication
Expenses   Phone
Photographs   Yes, if applicable
Response time to queries   2 weeks
Rights bought   First rights and revert back to author after publication
Kill fees   No
Writer's guidelines   Yes
Sample issues   Yes

THE HORN BOOK GUIDE TO CHILDREN'S AND YOUNG ADULT BOOKS

11 Beacon Street, Suite 1000
Boston, MA 02108

Phone number   617-227-1555
Fax number   617-523-0299
E-mail address   hornbook@aol.com
Parent company   The Horn Book, Inc.
Circulation   5,000
Magazine availability   Newsstands and subscription
Target audience   Teachers, librarians, parents, professors, students, children's booksellers
Magazine's history and mission   Started in 1924 by Bertha Mahoney Miller. Dedicated to promoting good literature for young people
Nonfiction   100%
Article interests and needs   Articles about using books in the classroom, trends in children's literature, illustration, publishing—or of a critical nature on some aspect of children's literature
Queries should be directed to   Lauren Adams, Managing Editor
Length of articles   No longer than 2,800 words
Time of payment   On publication
Response time to queries   4 months
Sample issues   Call

THE HORN BOOK MAGAZINE

11 Beacon Street, Suite 1000
Boston, MA 02108

Phone number   617-227-1555
Fax number   617-523-0299
E-mail address   hornbook@aol.com
Parent company   The Horn Book, Inc.
Circulation   22,000
Magazine availability   Newsstands and subscription
Target audience   Teachers, librarians, parents, professors, students, children's booksellers
Magazine's history and mission   Started in 1924 by Bertha Mahoney Miller. Dedicated to promoting good literature for young people.
Nonfiction   100%
Article interests and needs   Articles about using books in the classroom, trends in children's literature, illustration, publishing—or of a critical nature on some aspect of children's literature
Queries should be directed to   Lauren Adams, Managing Editor
Length of articles   No longer than 2,800 words
Time of payment   On publication
Response time to queries   4 months
Sample issues   Call

HOW

1507 Dana Avenue
Cincinnati, OH 45207

Phone number   513-531-2690
Fax number   513-531-2902
E-mail address   HOWEDIT@aol.com
Parent company   F & W Publications, Inc.
Circulation   38,000
Online status   Exploring Web site development.
Magazine availability   Newsstands and subscription
Target audience   Graphic design professionals
Magazine's history and mission   Founded in 1985, *HOW* magazine provides readers with business information, features cutting-edge technological advances, profiles renowned and up-and-coming designers, and provides creative, how-to information about noteworthy projects.
Nonfiction   100%
Percent of articles freelance-written   90%
Number of articles bought annually   Approximately 80
Sections of the magazine open to freelance writers   All—columns and features
Article interests and needs   Profiles, business, and legal issues for designers, software, technology
Queries should be directed to   Kathleen Reinmann, Editor

Length of articles   1,000 to 1,500 words

Payment   Ranges from $200 to $700 depending on complexity of the assignment and the writer's experience.

Time of payment   On acceptance

Expenses   Will pay phone and mail expenses

Photographs   Usually don't hire photographers; artwork is responsibility of firms profiled

Response time to queries   4 to 6 weeks

Rights bought   First North American serial rights for onetime use, first foreign serial rights for foreign editions, and right to use the material on electronic or computer-based information services.

Kill fees   20%

Writer's guidelines   Available. Send SASE.

Sample issues   Available—include cover price plus $1.50 for shipping.

TIPS FOR WRITERS
Kathleen Reinmann, Editor

When you query *HOW*, make sure you're familiar with the magazine and that you pitch a specific idea for an article. And if your story idea pertains to business information, new technology, renowned or up-and-coming designers, noteworthy design projects, new markets for graphic designers, or pressing industry issues, you'll probably catch one of our editors' attention. You'll receive a response to your query four to six weeks after sending your material to *HOW*.

For 10 years, *HOW* has been providing graphic designers the business information they need to compete in their field. The magazine stays on top for our readers by printing 1,000 to 1,500-word articles that are well-researched, entertaining, accurate and concise, and written by both new and experienced writers. Don't forget *HOW* works at least five months in advance.

Here are some things to remember: send clips of published work with your query; include an SASE; submit work on Macintosh or IBM compatible $3\frac{1}{2}$-inch disk or by e-mail, along with a double-spaced printout; and submit well-labeled samples, slides, or transparencies that illustrate your story idea. (Do not send original artwork.)

HRMAGAZINE
606 North Washington Street
Alexandria, VA 22314

Phone number   703-548-3440
Fax number   703-836-0367
E-mail address   hrmag@shrm.org
Parent company   Society for Human Resource Management
Circulation   74,000

Magazine availability   Subscription and membership

Target audience   Human resource professionals

Magazine's history and mission   *HRMagazine* is the flagship publication of the Society for Human Resource Management. *HRMagazine*'s mission is to challenge readers with new approaches to their work by examining the best practices in all areas of HR management. Articles may provoke thoughtful consideration or offer practical solutions to current workplace problems.

Nonfiction   100%

Percent of articles freelance-written   30%

Number of articles bought annually   Approximately 20

Sections of the magazine open to freelance writers   All

Queries should be directed to   Michelle Martinez, Editor

Length of articles   Approximately 1,500 words

Payment   If article is assigned

Time of payment   On publication

Expenses   Phone, if article is assigned.

Response time to queries   4 to 6 weeks

Rights bought   We request all or first serial rights.

Writer's guidelines   Available upon request

Sample issues   Available for $10 per issue

TIPS FOR WRITERS

We accept queries and unsolicited manuscripts. Response time to queries is about four to six weeks, three to four months for manuscripts. Clips with a query letter or outline are appreciated. We ask for clips and credentials if a writer is looking to be hired as a freelance writer on assigned articles. Faxed and e-mailed queries are acceptable as long as the proposed article is clearly defined.

When submitting manuscripts, please send an original and three copies, typed and double-spaced, with margins no less than one inch wide. *Single-spaced or desktop formatted copies are not acceptable.* If the article is available on IBM-compatible, 3.5" disk, please send the disk, indicating the name of the file and word processing software used, with one printed copy. We also need the name, address, and telephone number of the author(s) and a short biography.

Articles should be directed toward our audience of human resource professionals and should deal with a problem, issue, or condition that is of concern to people in the HR profession. Typical articles fall in the basic functional areas of compensation benefits, labor relations, employer/employee rights, work and family, training, organizational development, and management. International HR angles are also welcomed.

MANAGING OFFICE TECHNOLOGY

1100 Superior Avenue
Cleveland, OH 44114

Phone number   216-696-7000
Fax number   216-696-7648
E-mail address   motstaff@aol.com
Parent company   Penton Publishing
Circulation   110,000
Magazine availability   Subscription and controlled circulation
Target audience   Office management professionals
Magazine's history   Founded in 1956.
Nonfiction   100%
Percent of articles freelance-written   30%
Number of articles bought annually   25 to 30
Sections of the magazine open to freelance writers   All
Article interests and needs   Articles under the headings of: Management/Human Resources (e.g., Employee Loyalty), Facilities/Ergonomics (e.g., Repetitive Stress, Ergonomics, and Exercise), Information Technology (e.g., Magnetic Media), Document Management (e.g., State of Workflow, Barcode File Tracking), Business Communication (e.g., Network Etiquette, Phone Accessories), Office Equipment (e.g., Desktop Organizers, Shredders), Product Resource Guide (e.g., Mailroom Equipment)
Queries should be directed to   Lura Romei, Editor
Length of articles   Negotiated individually
Payment   Negotiated individually
Time of payment   On acceptance
Expenses   Negotiated individually
Photographs   Negotiated individually
Response time to queries   2 months
Rights bought   First-time North American
Kill fees   None
Writer's guidelines   On request

Sample issues   On request

NAILS

2512 Artesia Boulevard
Redondo Beach, CA 90278

Phone number   310-376-8788
Fax number   310-376-9043
E-mail address   bobitpub@aol.com
Parent company   Bobit Publishing
Circulation   52,000
Magazine availability   Subscription only
Target audience   Nail technicians and salon owners, mostly female (approximately 95%), national and Canadian circulation. Age range approximately 18 to 55.

Magazine's history and mission   Founded in 1983 by Peter Grimes. Purchased in 1987 by Bobit. We strive to provide education, information, and inspiration to nail professionals.
Nonfiction   100%
Percent of articles freelance-written   40$
Number of articles bought annually   Approximately 50
Sections of the magazine open to freelance writers   Profiles, news stories, research features
Article interests and needs   Health topics, successful salon owners, business advice, tax advice, new trends in nail fashion/nail care
Queries should be directed to   Erika Kotite, Managing Editor
Length of articles   1,200 to 2,000 words
Payment $250 to $500
Time of payment   On acceptance
Expenses   Phone calls, film
Photographs   Yes—color slides or prints
Response time to queries   2 weeks to 3 months
Rights bought   We buy all rights
Kill fees   None

Tips for Writers

If a query contains an idea that will provide something valuable to readers, it will capture our attention. It should be easy to read, with the central idea in the first (short) paragraph. Further details should indicate where the writer will go for his or her information (interviews, books, self-expertise, etc.). If the writer can provide photographs, it is a big plus.

Send no more than one or two of your best clips. Include the names of other publications you've written for in your query letter. An SASE is nice, but not necessary. Writers may call if they haven't heard from us within six weeks of sending their query. Faxed queries are acceptable; e-mail is acceptable, but it is not monitored as frequently.

Writers who have some knowledge and/or experience in our industry will have an advantage. However, a newsworthy subject pitched by a good writer will certainly get serious consideration. We are not able to place stories immediately; consequently, the waiting period can sometimes be long. Be patient, but feel free to call if you want to make sure something arrived, or have additional ideas to add to your query.

Network Professional Journal

c/o Niche Associates
9710 South 700 East, Suite 206-A
Sandy, UT 84070

Phone number   801-572-7436
Fax number   801-571-8645
E-mail address   niche@xmission.com

Parent company   Network Professional Association (NPA)

Circulation   About 25,000

Magazine availability   Subscription only

Target audience   Network professionals (e.g., LAN managers, IS and IT staff, value-added resellers, system designers, etc.) in the United States between the ages of 25 and 45.

Nonfiction   100%

Articles freelance-written   1 column (Last Look)

Number of articles bought annually   Purchase 12 articles yearly for the Last Look column.

Sections of the magazine open to freelance writers   Last Look column. The articles should be technically oriented and written by someone who is obviously well-versed in networking industry language.

Article interests and needs   Basically, I am looking for articles that meet two criteria: they're funny and they're about computing, especially networking. Although I like editorials that make our readers think, I am far more interested in editorials that make them laugh. The articles should be technically oriented, written by someone who is obviously well-versed in the language of the networking industry.

Queries should be directed to   Linda Boyer, Acquisitions Editor

Length of articles   600 to 800 words

Payment $.30 a word.

Time of payment   On acceptance of a completed manuscript. We pay for the word count generated after we have edited the manuscript. We then bill the contracting company (NPA) on acceptance and pay you within 10 working days of receiving payment from them. Generally, you will receive payment 3 to 5 weeks after we accept your completed article. We do not return manuscripts.

Photographs   We usually request a photograph of a new writer and sometimes have our artist create a cartoon based on that photograph. However, you need not send a photograph with your manuscript; we will request one when and if we want one.

Response time to queries   After you have sent a manuscript, you can expect to hear from us within 4 weeks.

Rights bought   We buy all rights

TIPS FOR WRITERS

The *Network Professional Journal* is desperately seeking new material for our humorous-editorial column, Last Look.

Getting published in our journal is easy: Write a piece about the network world that makes me (and a few others in the office) laugh, and you're in. So, basically, I lied: getting published isn't easy because it isn't easy to write something funny, let alone to write something funny about local area networks (LANs), or Ethernet, or TCP/IP, or client-server and mainframe environments. I know it isn't easy, because I get so few submissions that I feel compelled to look at twice before sending another letter reading, "Although your article is funny, it is not quite technical enough to suit our audience."

So how do you know if you would be able to produce a piece that will make me look twice? Well, if your only acquaintance with computing is using a word processor or sending e-mail over the Internet, you don't have the background necessary to write an article suited for our audience. On the other hand, if you've ever written articles, manuals, or marketing materials about computing and networking, or if you've actually managed, designed, or implemented a LAN; or if you've been using a network operating system such as NetWare long enough to know what's funny about it—then you can write a publishable piece. We need articles that obviously demonstrate the writer's knowledge of the networking industry. In fact, I'd be more inclined to work with a poorly written piece that was appropriately technical, than I would be to work with a beautifully written piece that was not at all technical.

If you still don't feel you have a sense of what we are looking for, give me a call, or fax or e-mail me something. E-mail, fax, or snail-mail me an idea, and I'll tell you what I think. Send me a completed manuscript, and I'll respond within a few weeks. I'm always looking for new writers, new ideas, and genuinely funny articles for the *Network Professional Journal.*

THE NEW PHYSICIAN

1902 Association Drive
Reston, VA 22091

Phone number   703-620-6600
Fax number   703-620-5873
E-mail address   amsatnp@aol.com
Parent company   American Medical Student Association (AMSA)
Circulation   27,000
Magazine availability   Newsstands and subscription (in addition to going to members of AMSA)
Target audience   Medical students, residents, medical educators, and policymakers
Magazine's history   Founded in 1960 by AMSA
Nonfiction   100%
Percent of articles freelance-written   30%
Number of articles bought annually   Approximately 20
Sections of the magazine open to freelance writers   Feature well, news department, profile section
Article interests and needs   Medical education and healthcare
Queries should be directed to   Laura Milani
Length of articles   750 to 3,500 words
Payment   Negotiated individually
Time of payment   On acceptance
Expenses   Yes
Photographs   Yes
Response time to queries   6 to 8 weeks
Rights bought   First North American serial rights, and thereafter a nonexclusive license, including reprint and reproduction rights and electronic medium rights.

Kill fees   Yes: 20%
Writer's guidelines   SASE
Sample issues $6

TIPS FOR WRITERS

Queries should be professionally presented and well-written, giving some flavor of the article the writer is proposing as well as outlining some of the sources to be tapped. Including a couple of clips and an SASE is essential. For writers we haven't worked with before, the best way to break into the magazine is to send a completed manuscript for our review. Offering photos, etc., is also helpful.

One of our biggest pet peeves is when writers pitch a story without having any idea of what we typically cover or our tone and style. The magazine is available in most medical school libraries and in many major public libraries. Given our primary audience—med students—our articles are most often directly related to surviving and improving medical education, and our tone is casual and conversational.

OVERDRIVE

P.O. Box 3187
Tuscaloosa, AL 35403

Phone number   205-349-2990
Fax number   205-750-8070
E-mail address   dlatovd@aol.com
Parent company   Randall Publishing
Circulation   150,000
Online status   Web site at http://www.overdriveonline.com
Magazine availability   Controlled/subscription; some sales at truck stops
Target audience   Commercial truck owner-operators, small fleet owners, and company truck drivers. Primarily male, broad range of education levels, typically older (30 to 50).
Nonfiction   100%
Percent of articles freelance-written   Magazine is one-quarter to one-third freelance written, but that is mostly from regular contributing editors.
Sections of the magazine open to freelance writers   Areas most open to freelance writers are profiles of interesting truckers.
Queries should be directed to   G. C. Skipper, Editorial Director
Length of articles   Article length depends on topic.
Payment   Pay ranges from $100 to $1,000, depending on length, difficulty of assignment, quality, and art supplied.
Time of payment   Upon acceptance
Expenses   Sometimes covered by prior arrangement
Photographs   We prefer photos supplied with stories.

Response time to queries   4 to 8 weeks
Rights bought   We buy all rights, including electronic, unless otherwise negotiated.
Kill fees   Negotiable
Writer's guidelines   Available by sending SASE (#10 envelope)
Sample issues   Available by sending 9 × 12 SASE

TIPS FOR WRITERS

We're looking for good writing on topics of interest to the professional trucker. We accept both queries and completed manuscripts. Queries can be by e-mail or fax. Phone calls are discouraged. Pet peeves: illegible manuscripts and manuscripts sent without a cover letter. Good photos are a definite plus. No fiction or poetry, please. The best thing to do is write for a copy of our writer's guidelines and a copy of the magazine.

PHARMACARE ECONOMICS

7500 Old Oak Boulevard
Cleveland, OH 44130

Phone number   216-891-3150
Fax number   216-891-2683
Parent company   Advanstar
Circulation   20,000
Magazine availability   Subscription
Target audience   Managed care pharmacy directors, medical directors, administrators, P & T committee members
Magazine's history   *PCE* began as a bimonthly supplement to *Managed Healthcare*.
Nonfiction   100%
Percent of articles freelance-written   75%
Number of articles bought annually   35
Sections of the magazine open to freelance writers   Feature
Article interests and needs   Business-oriented (not consumer) articles about pharmaceutical payment and delivery systems
Queries should be directed to   Cindy Grahl, Editor
Length of articles   1,000 to 2,000 words
Payment $300 to $1,000
Time of payment   On acceptance
Expenses   Travel, phone
Photographs   Purchase first rights and reprints
Response time to queries   2 months
Rights bought   First rights and reprints
Kill fees   25%
Writer's guidelines   No
Sample issues   Yes

TIPS FOR WRITERS
Cindy Grahl, Editor

We need stories that are topical and relevant and that address industry clinical, management, and regulatory issues that are fresh and new. You must know the industry well and be specific—many stories are pitched that we have already covered, and the biggest problem is that they are too broad and general. I am as hooked on a good lead as the reader would be. SASEs are necessary, and mailed queries are preferred to calls, unless the contributor is a long-standing one. Worst things a writer can do are to be on a soapbox, to be late with copy, and to turn in an assignment that is not in line with the query, unless he/she has consulted with the editor about the direction the story is taking.

PIZZA & PASTA MAGAZINE
20 North Wacker Drive, Suite 3230
Chicago, IL 60606

Phone number   312-849-2220
Fax number   312-849-2174
Parent company   Talcott Communications Corporation
Circulation   30,000
Magazine availability   Subscription only
Target audience   Magazine is targeted at owners and operators of Italian food service establishments—upscale restaurants to pizzerias. Nationally distributed.
Magazine's history and mission   *Pizza & Pasta* has been in existence since 1989. Its mission is to inform operators of Italian food service and help them improve their restaurants.
Nonfiction   100%
Percent of articles freelance-written   10%
Number of articles bought annually   20
Sections of the magazine open to freelance writers   Features and profiles of operations
Article interests and needs   Informative how-to type stories that can help operators keep workers, satisfy customers, and produce innovative techniques to keep people coming back to their restaurant.
Queries should be directed to   Joseph Declan Moran, Editor
Length of articles   800 to 1,000 words
Payment $200 per story plus phone and other expenses
Time of payment   On publication
Expenses   We usually pay for phone expenses and travel expenses, if any, incurred in the course of the story.
Photographs   We pay expenses for photos taken, if the photos are used in the story.
Rights bought   We allow for onetime publication of story.
Kill fees   None
Sample issues   Available

TIPS FOR WRITERS
Joseph Declan Moran, Editor

My interest is sparked when I get a call from a freelancer who has thought out his or her story idea with options and suggestions as to who can be called. Also, it helps if the writer knows something about the operator/operation firsthand so that they can go right to the source.

The biggest problem I have is with writers who simply go ahead and write a story assuming that because it is so good we are going to take it. In a lot of these cases we have already run that type of story.

Also, the writer should already know something about the magazine, especially if he or she has requested a media kit. But please call me first to discuss the idea.

If a writer is serious, he or she should send relevant clips to my attention—previously published stories that have something to do with the type of pieces we publish, so that we can get a good idea of how the writer handles the material. Also, don't send more than three clips. A resume and three clips will suffice.

When I do receive a resume and clips from a prospective freelancer, I will call that person to let them know I received the information.

PLANNING

122 South Michigan Avenue, Suite 1600
Chicago, IL 60603-6106

Phone number   312-431-9100
Fax number   312-431-9985
Parent company   American Planning Association
Circulation   32,000
Online status   Available online through UMI and EBSCO
Magazine availability   Through membership in American Planning Association or through subscription
Target audience   Nationwide audience (plus small circulation in Canada and overseas); aimed at city planners, architects, developers, and others interested in land development. Audience also includes college students—majority in city planning.
Magazine's history and mission   Magazine founded in 1972 by American Society of Planning Officials, a predecessor of the American Planning Association. Mission is to report on trends and news of American communities and city planning profession.
Nonfiction   100%
Percent of articles freelance-written   25 to 50% written by paid freelancers
Number of articles bought annually   One dozen news stories and two dozen feature stories
Sections of the magazine open to freelance writers   News, features, Viewpoint (editorials)

Article interests and needs   Focus is on city planning and development trends. Subtopics include transportation, downtown and neighborhood development, environment, housing, zoning, and use of computers (especially geographic information systems) in government agencies.

Queries should be directed to   Sylvia Lewis, Editor and Associate Publisher

Length of articles   News articles: 200 to 500 words; features: 1,500 to 3,000 words

Payment $.30 per word

Time of payment   On publication

Expenses   Phone expenses, if documented

Photographs   Black-and-white or color transparencies; payment depends on amount of space the photo takes on the page.

Response time to queries   One month

Rights bought   We prefer to retain copyright, especially for stories that we initiate.

Kill fees   25%

Writer's guidelines   Available upon request

Sample issues   Available upon request

TIPS FOR WRITERS
Sylvia Lewis, Editor and Associate Publisher

We'll consider story proposals from anyone who writes a cogent query letter. But, as with other specialty publications, it's hard for freelancers to break in. We advise studying the publication before sending a query letter. The December issue carries an annual index of stories published during the preceding year, so that's a good place to start. It's also smart to ask for an editorial calendar—a list of major stories scheduled for the current year. Most of the stories are assigned to authors we already know, but there are some slots for new people. In general, it's easiest to sell us on short pieces—news stories that focus on one locale (although the topic must interest a nationwide audience), or short features describing trends (one example is a November 1995 story on recycling landfills).

Freelancers are requested to send story proposals by mail, not to call or fax them in. Clips are helpful, and we always welcome information about the writer's qualifications for writing the story in question. No SASE is required.

PROFESSIONAL PILOT

3014 Colvin Street
Alexandria, VA 22314

Phone number   703-370-0606

Fax number   703-370-7082

Parent company   Queensmith Communications Corp.

Circulation   32,000 controlled (nonpaid qualified)

Magazine availability   Subscription

Target audience   Professional pilots in corporate and regional segments of aviation. Mostly male, 20 to 55 years old

Magazine's history and mission   Magazine was started January 1967 by Murray Smith as a trading post of information for professional corporate pilots. It later branched into regional/commuter as well.

Nonfiction   100%

Percent of articles freelance-written   70%

Number of articles bought annually   60

Sections of the magazine open to freelance writers   Features on avionics, aircraft, flying techniques

Article interests and needs   Always interested in pilot-authored articles on managing flight departments, special techniques.

Queries should be directed to   Mary Silitch, Managing Editor, or Murray Smith, Publisher

Length of articles   1,200 to 3,000 words

Payment   Features start at $500

Time of payment   On acceptance

Expenses   We pay expenses on a contract article.

Photographs   We buy photos

Response time to queries   Within 7 days

Rights bought   We buy full rights.

Kill fees   50%

Writer's guidelines   We don't have a style guide. We just send the magazine.

Sample issues   Sent on request

TIPS FOR WRITERS
Murray Smith, Publisher

We're looking for pilots writing for other pilots or for articles from scientists, educators, manufacturers. In short, we're looking for writers with credentials. If someone has those credentials and is interested in writing for us, he can call or fax us.

REFEREE

P.O. Box 161
Franksville, WI 53126

Phone number   414-632-8855

Fax number   414-632-5460

Parent company   Referee Enterprises, Inc.

Circulation   35,000

Magazine availability   Subscription only

Target audience   Mostly males, ages 30 to 60, all professions, all geographic areas. Common ground: Amateur or pro officials/umpires/referees/judges, etc.

Magazine's history and mission   First issue was published in January 1976, and the magazine has been published continuously, 80 pages every month, since then. January 1996 issue was the 20th anniversary edition.

Nonfiction   100%

Percent of articles freelance-written   An estimated 30 to 65%

Number of articles bought annually   Hundreds

Sections of the magazine open to freelance writers   Virtually all

Article interests and needs   Must be related to sports officiating

Queries should be directed to   Scott Ehret, Editor

Length of articles   Varies: 250 to 3,500 words

Payment   Varies based on length

Time of payment   On acceptance with contract issued

Expenses   Some

Photographs   Helpful

Response time to queries   2 to 3 weeks

Rights bought   Usually buy all rights

Kill fees   Sometimes

Writer's guidelines   Available—send SASE.

Sample issues   Available—send SASE with 8 first-class stamps affixed.

Restaurants USA

1200 17th Street, NW
Washington, DC 20036

Phone number   202-331-5900

Fax number   202-331-2429

E-mail address   restusa@aol.com

Parent company   National Restaurant Association

Circulation   37,000

Online status   Capable of receiving queries and manuscripts online.

Magazine availability   Subscription

Target audience   Food service professionals, students, food enthusiasts. A nationwide magazine. Reaches all demographics from fast-food corporations to mom-and-pop operations.

Magazine's history and mission   Established in 1981 by the National Restaurant Association to help Association members conduct their businesses more effectively and keep them updated on new trends in the food service industry. Originally titled *NRA News*.

Nonfiction   98%

Fiction   2%

Percent of articles freelance-written   30 to 40%

Number of articles bought annually   40 to 50
Sections of the magazine open to freelance writers   Features section
Article interests and needs   Management topics, food trends, new restaurant concepts, money-saving techniques, promotions (marketing), no-nonsense, how-to articles
Queries should be directed to   Jennifer Batty, Editor
Length of articles   800 to 2,000 words
Payment   Varies by topic, length of article, and research involved. Payment can range from $50 to $900.
Time of payment   On acceptance
Expenses   Generally not paid
Photographs   Gladly accepted, more apt to consider story idea if photos are included
Response time to queries   2 to 3 months
Rights bought   Article becomes property of *Restaurants USA*
Kill fees   None. If article is rejected, author does not receive the fee.
Writer's guidelines   Available upon request with SASE
Sample issues   Sent if story is assigned or query idea is accepted.

Tips for Writers

The query: Prefer writers with food service background/experience or who specialize—a writer with management expertise giving advice on how to motivate employees, a design consultant offering restaurant redesign suggestions, etc. Initial queries should be accompanied by resume, clips, and SASE. Completed manuscripts are rarely considered for publication and will not be returned without SASE. It is preferable for freelancers to submit queries by mail. Phone calls are discouraged.

SunWorld Online

501 Second Street
San Francisco, CA 94107

Phone number   415-243-4188
Fax number   415-267-1732
E-mail address   mark.cappell@sunworld.com
Online status   Web site at http://www.sun.com/sunworldonline/
Parent company   International Data Group (IDG)
Circulation   Approximately 50,000, though circulation is increasing as more readers use the Internet.
Magazine availability   On the World Wide Web exclusively
Target audience   *SunWorld Online* is targeted at SPARC and Solaris users. Since it is available on the World Wide Web and has "mirror" sites in place or planned around the world, our magazine has no geographic border.
Magazine's history and mission   *SunWorld Online* is an online-only monthly magazine—it has no printed counterpart. The team behind *SunWorld Online* was responsible

for *Advanced* magazine, a print-based monthly that ceased publishing following the May 1995 issue. *Advanced Systems* was geared for workstation users and buyers—the very audience that first embraced the Internet and World Wide Web. The management team and editors decided to try an electronic-only magazine targeted to serve the technical needs of SPARC and Solaris (Sun Microsystems) users and buyers. A test issue of *SunWorld Online* went live in June 1995. The first issue became available in July 1995.

Nonfiction   100%

Percent of articles freelance-written   75%

Number of articles bought annually   130

Sections of the magazine open to freelance writers   No area is restricted from freelancers.

Article interests and needs   *SunWorld Online* seeks technological writers who understand the workstation market and its products in general, and UNIX in particular.

Queries should be directed to   Mark Cappel at mark.cappel@sunworld.com

Length of articles   Since *SunWorld Online* is an electronic magazine, its editors

Payment   Varies with the experience and expertise of the author, and the technical content of the article, but ranges from $250 to $2,000.

Time of payment   On acceptance

Photographs   *SunWorld Online*'s readers appreciate other artwork, including sound bites and video.

Rights bought   First rights. Interested authors should read *SunWorld Online*'s author's agreement for details.

Kill fees   Yes

Writer's guidelines   A writer's guide is available online as are all back issues of *SunWorld Online*.

TIPS FOR WRITERS
Mark Cappel, Executive Editor

The best advice we can offer writers new to *SunWorld Online* is this:

1. If you don't know what "UNIX" is, don't come a callin'. Most of our writers have a perverse technical streak that makes them curious about technical computers and related issues that most humans find boring.
2. Read our current and a few of our back issues before you propose a story idea.
3. The editors at *SunWorld Online* use e-mail more often than fax or telephone, and work with all freelancers via e-mail.

TEA & COFFEE TRADE JOURNAL
130 West 42nd Street
New York, NY 10036

Phone number   212-391-2060
Fax number   212-827-0945
Parent company   Lockwood Trade Journal Co., Inc.
Circulation   International; 10,000
Magazine availability   Only subscription
Target audience   Coffee and tea industry professionals—age 20 and up, international audience
Magazine's history and mission   Founded in 1901 by William H. Ukers. Mission is to educate and inform tea and coffee industry, and gourmet shops about tea and coffee.
Nonfiction   100%
Percent of articles freelance-written   75%
Number of articles bought annually   80
Sections of the magazine open to freelance writers   Features
Queries should be directed to   Jane McCabe, Editor
Length of articles   1,200 to 1,600 words
Payment $5.50 per published inch of copy
Time of payment   2 months after publication
Expenses   No special trips, some reimbursement for telephone
Photographs $5.50 per published inch
Response time to queries   Immediately
Rights bought   Onetime. Exclusive
Kill fees   None
Sample issues   We'll send 1 issue.

Important Questions Answered

Q: Is an SASE always necessary?
A: No
Q: Is it OK if writers fax or e-mail queries to you?
A: Yes
Q: Are phone calls from writers OK?
A: Yes
Q: Under what circumstances?
A: When I'm in a good mood.

Teaching Tolerance

400 Washington Avenue
Montgomery, AL 36104

Phone number   334-264-0286
Fax number   334-264-3121
Parent company   Southern Poverty Law Center

Circulation   200,000

Magazine availability   Free upon written request to teachers and other educators

Target audience   Teachers and other educators at all levels in public and private schools and universities in the U.S. and Canada

Magazine's history and mission   Founded in 1991 by the Southern Poverty Law Center to provide teachers with ideas and strategies to promote interracial and intercultural harmony

Nonfiction   100%

Percent of articles freelance-written   80%

Number of articles bought annually   16 to 20, including shorts

Sections of the magazine open to freelance writers   Feature articles; Departments: Idea Exchange, Between the Lines; Teacher essays

Article interests and needs   According to writer's guidelines: Features: should have strong classroom focus and national perspective where appropriate; Essays: can be a personal reflection, description of school program, community-school program, classroom activity, how-to; Idea Exchange: includes brief descriptions of classroom lesson plans, special projects, or other school activities that promote tolerance; Student Writing: includes poems and short essays dealing with diversity, tolerance, and justice.

Queries should be directed to   Sara Ballard, Editor

Length of articles   Features: 1,000 to 3,000 words; Essays: 400 to 800 words; Idea Exchange: 250 to 500 words

Payment   Features: Range from $500 to $3,000, depending on length and complexity; Essays: Range from $300 to $800; Idea Exchange: $100; Student Writing: $50

Time of payment   Features: on acceptance; Essays: upon publication; Idea Exchange: upon publication; Student Writing: upon publication

Expenses   Yes

Photographs   Idea Exchange includes photos, if available; otherwise we assign

Response time to queries   6 to 8 weeks

Rights bought   All, including copyright

Kill fees   Yes, in some cases

Writer's guidelines   Yes, upon request

Sample issues   Yes, upon request

IMPORTANT QUESTIONS ANSWERED

Q: What are the key elements of a good, professional query?

A: We want specific, practical ideas for classroom use focusing on themes of diversity, antibias, social justice, peace, etc. Clear, concise, simple writing—no rhetoric or academic writing.

Q: Do you always want clips from new writers?

A: Yes

Q: Will you look at completed manuscripts?

A: Yes

Q: Is an SASE always necessary?

A: No

Q: Are phone calls from writers OK?
A: Yes
Q: Under what circumstances are phone calls OK?
A: After we know them and their work.
Q: Is it OK if writers fax or e-mail queries to you?
A: Fax OK, no e-mail.

WOMAN PILOT

P.O. Box 485
Arlington, Heights, IL 60006-0485

Phone number   708-797-0170
Fax number   708-797-0161 (editorial fax only)
Parent company   Aviatrix Publishing, Inc.
Circulation   5,000
Online status   Soon
Magazine availability   Newsstands and subscription
Target audience   Women and men who are interested in aviation
Magazine's history and mission   Founded in 1993 by Bobbi Roe, a pilot and publisher.
Nonfiction   95%
Percent of articles freelance-written   90%
Number of articles bought annually   50
Sections of the magazine open to freelance writers   All
Article interests and needs   Features about women who fly, technical articles, historical articles about women in aviation
Queries should be directed to   Bobbi Roe, Publisher
Length of articles   500 to 3,000 words with photographs or graphics
Time of payment   On publication
Photographs   Yes
Response time to queries   3 to 6 months
Rights bought   North American first
Writer's guidelines   Free
Sample issues $3.00

IMPORTANT QUESTIONS ANSWERED

Q: How can writers break into your magazine?
A: With interesting and different articles, good writing, and great photos
Q: What is your number one pet peeve about writers?
A: Poor writing skills

WRITER'S DIGEST

1507 Dana Avenue
Cincinnati, OH 45207

Phone number   513-531-2690, Ext. 297
Fax number   513-531-1843
E-mail address   WritersDig@eWorld.com
Parent company   F & W Publications
Circulation   250,000
Online status   We are a content provider for eWorld; some articles are posted in our forum, but not the entire magazine.
Magazine availability   Newsstands and subscription
Magazine's history and mission   Founded in 1920, *Writer's Digest* seeks to be a magazine of ideas, inspiration, and information for writers of all types—nonfiction, fiction, poetry, or scripts. Our articles show writers how to produce and sell high-quality manuscripts.
Nonfiction   100%
Percent of articles freelance-written   90%
Number of articles bought annually   90 to 100 features
Sections of the magazine open to freelance writers   All are open—most break in via Writing Life, Tip Sheet, or Chronicle.
Queries should be directed to   Paul Singer, Associate Editor
Length of articles   Varies
Payment   Varies
Time of payment   On acceptance
Expenses   Sometimes paid for writers on assignment
Photographs   Used only with profiles
Response time to queries   4 to 8 weeks
Rights bought   First North American serial rights for onetime editorial use, possible electronic posting, microfilm/microfiche use, and magazine promotional use
Kill fees   20%
Writer's guidelines   Free for SASE (#10 envelope)
Sample issues $3.50, $3.70 in Ohio

TIPS FOR WRITERS

Writers interested in our philosophy should send for the guidelines, which cover all areas of the magazine in detail.

Association Magazines

COAST TO COAST MAGAZINE

2575 Vista del Mar
Ventura, CA 93001

Phone number   805-667-4100
Parent company   Affinity Group Inc. (AGI)
Circulation   300,000
Magazine availability   Membership only
Target audience   Members of Coast to Coast Resorts
Magazine's history and mission   Founded in 1982. Mission: to entertain, enlighten, and inform our members.
Nonfiction   100%
Percent of articles freelance-written   70%
Number of articles bought annually   50
Sections of the magazine open to freelance writers   Features
Article interests and needs   Destination travel features
Length of articles   2,000 to 2,500 words
Payment $400 to $600
Time of payment   Acceptance
Expenses   Phone expenses
Photographs   ASMP rates unless otherwise negotiated
Response time to queries   3 months or less
Rights bought   First North American
Kill fees   One-third

GOLF TRAVELER

2575 Vista del Mar
Ventura, CA 93001

Phone number   805-667-4100
Parent company   Affinity Group Inc. (AGI)

Circulation   130,000
Magazine availability   Membership only
Target audience   Members of Golf Card International
Magazine's history and mission   Founded in 1974. Mission: to entertain, enlighten, and inform our members
Nonfiction   100%
Percent of articles freelance-written   80%
Number of articles bought annually   20
Sections of the magazine open to freelance writers   Features
Article interests and needs   Destination golf features
Length of articles   2,000 to 2,500 words
Payment $400 to $600
Time of payment   Acceptance
Expenses   Phone expenses
Photographs   ASMP rates unless otherwise negotiated
Response time to queries   3 months or less
Rights bought   First North American
Kill fees   One-third

THE LION

300 22nd Street
Oak Brook, IL 60521

Phone number   708-571-5466
Fax number   708-571-8890
Parent company   The International Association of Lions Clubs
Circulation   600,000
Magazine availability   Subscription only
Target audience   Members of Lions Clubs primarily in the United States, western Canada, and other English-speaking areas of the world.
Magazine's history and mission   First published in November 1918 by association's founder, Melvin Jones. Its mission: to inform all members of the growth and activities of Lions Clubs everywhere.
Nonfiction   100%, except for joke page and short humor stories run on occasion.
Percent of articles freelance-written   About 20% per issue
Number of articles bought annually   Approximately 50
Sections of the magazine open to freelance writers   Feature section
Article interests and needs   Articles relating to the service and fundraising projects of Lions Clubs worldwide or general interest pieces of benefit to community minded individuals
Queries should be directed to   Robert Kleinfelder, Senior Editor
Length of articles   500 to 2,000 words

Payment $200 to $750 depending upon length, photos, and overall quality
Time of payment   On acceptance
Expenses   Limited. Meals and lodging, but usually not travel
Photographs   Generally a necessity, especially for stories on Lions Club projects. Photos should be in color (prints or slides).
Response time to queries   2 to 4 weeks
Rights bought   All
Kill fees   50%
Writer's guidelines   Yes, along with a free sample copy of *The Lion*

TIPS FOR WRITERS
Robert Kleinfelder, Senior Editor

What are the key elements of a good query? Obviously, the more succinct, the better. If a general interest story is proposed, it should tell the importance of the subject matter and why knowledge of it will benefit our readers. *The Lion*, remember, serves a broadly based readership, not only representative of many professions and age groups, but also international. If the query concerns a Lions Club project, it should describe the activity, tell how it serves the community or particular people in need, and, if it is a fund-raiser, how much money is raised and where it is allocated. Any Lions Club project must be of a rather large scale and not one which is common among clubs such as pancake breakfasts, food booths at festivals, donations of reading material to blind individuals, etc. These items are generally staff written. The query should also indicate whether photos can be secured. We are more inclined to assign a story where photo-taking opportunities are available.

Clips are not necessary. We do accept phone queries, since we prefer them in writing. Please, do not send completed manuscripts. An SASE is not required, but definitely welcomed. Also, do not fax a story or query.

The best way to break into *The Lion* is to understand what is published, the general style of writing, length, and what not to submit. To help potential contributors achieve this, we are happy to send sample copies of *The Lion* and writer's guidelines upon request. The worst thing for a writer to do is to submit a completed manuscript that doesn't come close to meeting our editorial needs. Also, the magazine doesn't do profiles on individual members, survey pieces on club activities over a number of years, or stories of ceremonial occasions (installation nights, club anniversary celebrations, charter nights . . .).

Any article on a Lions Club project must contain as many details as possible as to how the activity was carried out and the names of those Lions instrumental in its success.

MUZZLE BLASTS
P.O. Box 67
Friendship, IN 47021

Phone number   812-667-5131
Fax number   812-667-5137
Parent company   National Muzzle Loading Rifle Association
Circulation   27,000
Magazine availability   Through membership in NMLRA and some dealers
Target audience   People from all walks of life. We have members from all states and several different countries. Some are lawyers, doctors, and others are farmers or factory workers. The main interest is muzzleloading.
Magazine's history   Founded September 1939
Nonfiction   Most—our magazine mainly deals with facts
Fiction   An occasional article—humor
Percent of articles freelance-written   95%—we do not assign stories to individuals. We have a small staff. We have association materials included with each magazine that certain staff members write. We also have regular columnists—but we don't assign them a particular story. We will, on occasion, assign a review to a writer.
Number of articles bought annually   Between 150 to 200, including columns
Sections of the magazine open to freelance writers   30%
Article interests and needs   Articles on muzzleloading, firearms, accoutrements, historical period data, reenactments, muzzleloading, hunting, etc.
Queries should be directed to   Robert H. Wallace, Director of Publications
Length of articles   500 to 1,500 words
Payment   Depends on article. Normally between $50 and $400. Short reviews: $50 to $150; Good technical articles: $150 to $400.
Time of payment   On publication
Expenses   No
Photographs   Some—but usually included with article purchase. We do pay $300 for cover art work.
Response time to queries   2 to 4 weeks
Rights bought   We pay for first North American rights that extend for one year after accepted contract returns to us.
Writer's guidelines   We will send upon request.
Sample issues   Sent upon request.

TIPS FOR WRITERS
Terri Trowbridge, Assistant to the Editor

A writer should know his subject. We have technical advisors that try and spot potential problems. We are dealing with black powder arms so we have to try and ensure the writer isn't suggesting too heavy a proof load or unsafe practices. This also holds true with photographs. Sometimes we'll get a great looking shot—clear, good color, good content—but the hammer is cocked or the muzzle of the gun is pointing in an unsafe manner—or the shooters aren't wearing eye or ear protection—so we can't use the photo. We have a responsibility to our readers to present information correctly so that they won't do something "we suggested" through an article or photo that harms them or others.

We will look at completed manuscripts. A potential writer may write or fax us about an article they are thinking about to see if we would be interested. If they are new to us, it helps to include a clip or two or their previous work.

Please include an SASE if you want your materials back. We do try to send everything back anyway, but it's not guaranteed. Most magazines don't send back unsolicited materials without an SASE. We do accept phone and fax queries. Phone calls are OK if a potential writer has plans to submit the article elsewhere and needs to know the status of the article. Generally these calls are directed to me—and I get the information, then phone them back. Our Director of Publications is usually very busy and it's hard to gather information while on the phone.

The worst thing a writer can do is to write about something they have no knowledge of. For the most part, it shows. It is dangerous in the case of firearms—especially black powder—to write with no knowledge of the subject matter.

We send out acknowledgments to let the writer know we've received their work. If it has been several weeks and you still haven't heard anything, then a phone call is in order.

THE OPTIMIST

4494 Lindell Boulevard
St. Louis, MO 63108

Phone number   314-371-6000
Fax number   314-371-6006
Parent company   Optimist International
Circulation   153,000
Magazine availability   Subscription
Target audience   All members of 4200 Optimist Clubs worldwide
Magazine's history   First issue—October 1920.
Nonfiction   100%
Percent of articles freelance-written   10 to 20%
Number of articles bought annually   10 to 15
Sections of the magazine open to freelance writers   Articles only
Article interests and needs   Articles about activities of local Optimist Clubs, club members who have distinguished themselves. Also need short (200 to 400 word) articles on self-improvement or a philosophy of optimism. *No* personal stories.
Queries should be directed to   Dennis R. Osterwisch, Editor
Length of articles   500 to 1,000 words
Payment $75 to $400
Time of payment   On acceptance
Expenses   Yes, if agreed upon first
Photographs   Will purchase photos if related to an article

Response time to queries 1 to 3 days
Rights bought Onetime
Kill fees Yes
Writer's guidelines Yes
Sample issues Yes with $9\frac{1}{2} \times 11$ SASE

TIPS FOR WRITERS
The editor of The Optimist

The query: A good query will be very specific about the content and tone of the proposed article. It will allow me to make a judgment as to whether I want to pursue this idea. If there isn't enough information there, I don't have time to seek it out.

Clips are always good, but not mandatory.

I will look at completed manuscripts, but most that I receive are rejected because they are totally out of the range of what we publish.

Professional etiquette: An SASE is *always* necessary. If you query with a fantastic article idea I'm more likely to forgive this professional gaffe, but let's face it, as a writer, you are trying to sell a product. How many other businesses expect the potential customer to help pay for the sales presentation?

I prefer not to get phone calls from writers because I don't have time for them. Faxed queries are okay.

The best way to break into *The Optimist*: Send me an idea for an article about some really unusual Optimist Club activity. Or, a completed manuscript about the power of an optimistic philosophy of life.

The best things writers do: Delivering an article that exceeds my expectations.

The worst things writers do: It's the age-old problem all editors face: getting manuscripts that don't even come close to resembling anything we normally publish.

Overall advice to writers: Be sure you know exactly the kind of article the magazine publishes and know the style they use. This will save you time and money and will improve your chances of gaining an acceptance. As a freelancer myself, before becoming an editor, I don't think I really understood how important that is. Now that I've been editing a magazine for sixteen years, I realize it is the key to getting published.

RECREATION NEWS

P.O. Box 32335
Washington, DC 20007

Phone number 202-965-6960
E-mail address Recreationnews@mcmail.com
Parent company Icarus Publishers, Inc.
Circulation 104,000

Online status   MCI Mail (See address above)
Magazine availability   Controlled circulation
Target audience   Government employees in the greater Washington, D.C., area
Magazine's history and mission   Founded in 1982 by The League of Federal Recreation Associations, Inc. It is the official federal government recreation newspaper.
Nonfiction   100%
Percent of articles freelance-written   80%
Number of articles bought annually   40 to 50
Sections of the magazine open to freelance writers   Features
Article interests and needs   Travel, sports, leisure, entertainment
Queries should be directed to   Jeff Ghannam, Editor
Length of articles   900 to 2,000 words
Payment $50 to $300
Time of payment   On publication
Expenses   Up to $20—must be preapproved
Photographs $25 for published black-and-white prints; $120 for color slides
Response time to queries   2 to 3 months
Rights bought   First time
Kill fees $20 after first 3 published *Rec News* articles
Writer's guidelines   With SASE (#10 envelope)
Sample issues   With 9 × 12 envelope and $1.25 postage

Safari Magazine

Safari Club International
4800 West Gates Pass Road
Tucson, AZ 85745

Phone number   520-620-1220
Fax number   520-622-1205
Parent company   Safari Club International (SCI)
Circulation   To all members, approximately 23,000
Magazine availability   Membership in SCI
Target audience   Individuals and/or organizations interested in hunting, wildlife and habitat conservation, guns/ammunition suitable for hunting, protection of endangered or threatened species, hunting rights, etc.
Magazine's history and mission   First published in 1974 as the official journal of Safari Club International, a membership organization; mission is to inform members and other readers, on hunting, conservation, and related issues
Nonfiction   100%
Percent of articles freelance-written   75%
Number of articles bought annually   60 to 80

Article interests and needs   True stories of hunting experiences around the world; stories about hunting or weapons of historical significance; stories regarding endangered/threatened species and/or conservation measures. No bird hunting or fishing, except as a part of big game hunting story.

Queries should be directed to   Elaine Cummings, Manuscripts Editor; William R. Quimby, Director of Publications

Length of articles   2,500 words approximate

Payment $200, plus pay for onetime photo use (varies)

Time of payment   Upon publication of story

Expenses   Negotiable

Photographs   Payment to professionals for photos published, onetime use only (black-and-white: $45; four-color: $50 to $100)

Response time to queries   4 to 6 weeks for review of submission (story and pictures)

Rights bought   We buy first rights of manuscripts and extended rights to reprint in SCI collective works publications or electronic media prep.

Kill fees   Negotiable

Writer's guidelines   Yes

Sample issues $4.00 current issue; $5.00 back issue

TIPS FOR WRITERS
Elaine Cummings, Manuscripts Editor

All queries should share these points of information: the author's name, address, daytime telephone/fax numbers, status as a professional (list of titles or magazines where published), and two or three short paragraphs that either give the essence of the story and/or are a part of completed manuscript. Clips should be limited to one sample, if submitted, but are not necessary. Description of animals, especially clips, should illustrate the writer's style used in telling a story.

An SASE is preferred. Telephone calls are discouraged regarding queries, and either a short written query or a fax are preferred. We also accept on speculation manuscripts already completed and accompanied by photographs, slides, or transparencies; please include SASE. Allow 4 to 6 weeks for review process and response.

Breaking in to our magazine requires a story with an interesting or unusual approach (not just an ordinary hunt or description), that is accompanied by quality illustrative material. Of course, there are instances when photos are not available or necessary; and we do have an extensive file of wildlife photographs and slides from some of the most prestigious wildlife photographers in the world, which we use to supplement materials submitted by authors.

A pet peeve, for me, is always the manuscript that does not include all information and bio or pro background, if any, of the submitting author. A close second would be a hand-corrected manuscript or one that obviously never met a spell-check on the computer!

We receive hundreds of manuscripts annually from both our members (of SCI) and from professional outdoor writers, or specialty writers. Since we are a bimonthly magazine, there can be quite a wait between acceptance and publication, especially if the accepted story is in a North American or African setting. (Those stories, of all submissions, need to be the "different" ones.) Stories of hunts in less accessible venues often stand a chance of quicker publication.

THE TOASTMASTER

P.O. Box 9052
Mission Viejo, CA 92690

Phone number 714-858-8255
Fax number 714-858-1207
E-mail address sfrey@toastmasters.org
Parent company Toastmasters International
Circulation 180,000
Magazine availability Association members
Target audience Toastmasters members are typically 30 to 49 years old, college graduates, earning on average $35,000 a year.
Magazine's history and mission Founded in 1933 to aid Toastmasters members in their self-development efforts in communication and leadership skills, with an emphasis in public speaking
Nonfiction 100%
Percent of articles freelance-written 90%
Article interests and needs Educational or "how-to" articles relating to effective speaking and leadership skills, analytical thinking and listening skills, and Toastmasters programs
Queries should be directed to Suzanne Frey, Editor
Length of articles 1,000 to 2,000 words
Payment $100 to $250 for professional writers
Time of payment On acceptance
Expenses Sometimes paid
Response time to queries Usually two weeks
Rights bought All rights, first rights, onetime rights
Writer's guidelines On request
Sample issues On request

TIPS FOR WRITERS
Beth Curtis, Associate Editor

We prefer straightforward queries that include specific information about what the article will cover. Include a sentence or two describing your writing experience. Clips and an SASE are not required, but both are appreciated.

Completed manuscripts and faxed or e-mailed submissions are fine. Phone calls are not recommended because of the added work of having to track down articles, which most likely are still in the review process. (All articles are acknowledged upon receipt, and all queries and manuscripts are responded to usually within two months.)

The best way to break in to *The Toastmaster* is to submit well-written articles on topics that relate to our mission. While the same topics tend to be covered again and again, we like to see them approached from unique, sometimes humorous, angles.

Try to make editors' jobs as easy as possible. Follow the writer's guidelines and write clearly and succinctly. Always include a cover letter with the working title of the article and a short bit of information about your experience. *Always, always* include your name and address on the cover letter and on at least the first page of your manuscript.

Canadian Magazines

Aruba Nights

1831 Rene Levesque Boulevard West
Montreal, Quebec, H3H 1R4
Canada

Phone number 514-931-1987
Fax number 514-931-6273
Parent company Nights Publications, Inc.
Category Travel and Lifestyle
Circulation 200,000
Magazine availability Distributed free at hotels, airports, cruise ship departure points, retail outlets, etc.
Target audience 30- to 60-year old tourists, male and female, upper income
Magazine's history and mission Founded in 1988 by Douglass Markus, Publisher. Mission is to focus on lifestyle aspect of the destination.
Nonfiction 100%
Percent of articles freelance-written 95%
Number of articles bought annually 5 to 10
Sections of the magazine open to freelance writers Features, how-to articles, first person experiences
Article interests and needs Personality profiles, activities, art and entertainment, gambling
Queries should be directed to Stephen Trotter, Editor
Length of articles 250 to 1,000 words
Payment $50 to $400
Time of payment On acceptance
Expenses No
Photographs $25 to $100 per slide
Response time to queries 2 weeks
Rights bought First North American and Caribbean rights
Kill fees 15% on assigned manuscripts only
Writer's guidelines Yes, free
Sample issues $5 (U.S.) per copy

TIPS FOR WRITERS
Stephen Trotter, Editor

The query: Demonstrate your voice in your query. Be descriptive. Bring all the senses into play. Give me a taste of what I can expect. I also consider completed manuscripts. Clips are a plus, but not necessary. The quality of your query and actual copy carries far more weight. New writers welcome.

Professional etiquette: SASE only required if writer wants material returned. Phone calls welcome. No collect calls, please. Queries and manuscripts can be faxed.

Best way to break into our magazine: Submit entertaining, flowing, descriptive copy that stands out from the crowd of cliché copy. Length should not exceed 1,000 words.

Pet peeves: Writers who do not honor deadlines.

Subject matter: I am always in the market for fresh angles on topics that would appeal to tourists who are already on the island. We do not target off-island tourists. Forget generic pieces. Stories must focus on the island's unique lifestyle. I am looking for features (600 to 1,000 words) as well as shorts (50 to 250 words).

BONAIRE NIGHTS
1831 Rene Levesque Boulevard West
Montreal, Quebec, H3H 1R4
Canada

Phone number   514-931-1987
Fax number   514-931-6273
Parent company   Nights Publications, Inc.
Category   Travel and Lifestyle
Circulation   60,000
Magazine availability   Distributed free at hotels, airports, cruise ship departure points, retail outlets, etc.
Target audience   30- to 60-year-old tourists, male and female, upper income
Magazine's history and mission   Founded in 1993 by Douglas Markus, Publisher. Mission is to focus on lifestyle aspect of the destination.
Nonfiction   100%
Percent of articles freelance-written   95%
Number of articles bought annually   5 to 10
Sections of the magazine open to freelance writers   Features, how-to articles, first person experiences
Article interests and needs   Personality profiles, activities, art and entertainment, gambling
Queries should be directed to   Stephen Trotter, Editor
Length of articles   250 to 1,000 words

Payment $50 to $400
Time of payment   On acceptance
Expenses   No
Photographs $25 to $100 per slide
Response time to queries   2 weeks
Rights bought   First North American and Caribbean rights
Kill fees   15% on assigned manuscripts only
Writer's guidelines   Yes, free
Sample issues $5 (U.S.) per copy

TIPS FOR WRITERS

See previous entry.

CANADIAN GARDENING

130 Spy Court
Markham, Ontario, L3R OW5
Canada

Phone number   905-475-8440
Fax number   905-475-9560
Parent company   Camar Publications
Category   Consumer/Gardening
Circulation   130,000
Magazine availability   Newsstands and subscription
Target audience   Avid home gardeners in Canada
Magazine's history and mission   Founded in 1989. The magazine's mission is "to be inspirational, educational, down to earth. An indispensable magazine for Canadians who love to garden."
Nonfiction   100%
Percent of articles freelance-written   90%
Sections of the magazine open to freelance writers   Most sections
Queries should be directed to   Liz Primeau, Editor
Length of articles   Depends
Payment   Depends—$75 to $700 (Canadian dollars)
Time of payment   On acceptance
Expenses   Negotiated
Photographs   Photos assigned
Response time to queries   One month, sometimes longer
Rights bought   Depends, usually first North American
Kill fees   Yes, negotiated, usually 25 to 50%

Writer's guidelines   Yes
Sample issues   No

TIPS FOR WRITERS

Strong Canadian angle—read most recent issues of magazine (at least the last four). Please, *no* unsolicited manuscripts, send samples. Queries/outlines are best. An SASE is not always necessary. Phone calls from writers are not OK. Faxes are OK.

CANADIAN WORKSHOP MAGAZINE

130 Spy Court
Markham, Ontario, L3R OW5
Canada

Phone number   905-475-8440
Fax number   905-475-9560
Parent company   Camar Publications
Circulation   115,000
Magazine availability   Newsstands and subscription
Target audience   Do-it-yourself home hobbyists, ages 25 to 65
Magazine's history   Founded in 1977.
Nonfiction   100%
Percent of articles freelance-written   70%
Sections of the magazine open to freelance writers   Features, service pieces, woodworking technique, etc.
Queries should be directed to   Hugh McBride
Length of articles   Query letter first
Time of payment   On publication
Photographs   Not required / We arrange photography
Response time to queries   Varies greatly from a month to 2 to 3 months
Kill fees   Yes

IMPORTANT QUESTIONS ANSWERED

Q: Is an SASE always necessary?
A: Yes
Q: Are phone calls from writers OK?
A: No. Query letters first
Q: Is it OK if writers fax or e-mail queries to you?
A: Yes

CANCUN NIGHTS

1831 Rene Levesque Boulevard West
Montreal, Quebec, H3H 1R4
Canada

Phone number   514-931-1987
Fax number   514-931-6273
Parent company   Nights Publications, Inc.
Category   Travel and Lifestyle
Circulation   550,000
Magazine availability   Distributed free at hotels, airports, cruise ship departure points, retail outlets, etc.
Target audience   30- to 60-year-old tourists, male and female, upper income
Magazine's history and mission   Founded in 1992 by Douglas Markus, Publisher. Mission is to focus on lifestyle aspect of the destination.
Nonfiction   100%
Percent of articles freelance-written   95%
Number of articles bought annually   5 to 10
Sections of the magazine open to freelance writers   Features, how-to articles, first person experiences
Article interests and needs   Personality profiles, activities, art and entertainment, gambling
Queries should be directed to   Stephen Trotter, Editor
Length of articles   250 to 1,000 words
Payment $50 to $400
Time of payment   On acceptance
Expenses   No
Photographs $25 to $100 per slide
Response time to queries   2 weeks
Rights bought   First North American and Caribbean rights
Kill fees   15% on assigned manuscripts only
Writer's guidelines   Yes, free
Sample issues $5 (U.S.) per copy

TIPS FOR WRITERS

See entry under *Aruba Nights*.

CURACAO NIGHTS

1831 Rene Levesque Boulevard West
Montreal, Quebec, H3H 1R4
Canada

Phone number 514-931-1987
Fax number 514-931-6273
Parent company Nights Publications, Inc.
Category Travel and Lifestyle
Circulation 155,000
Magazine availability Distributed free at hotels, airports, cruise ship departure points, retail outlets, etc.
Target audience 30- to 60-year-old tourists, male and female, upper income
Magazine's history and mission Founded in 1990 by Douglas Markus, Publisher. Mission is to focus on lifestyle aspect of the destination.
Nonfiction 100%
Percent of articles freelance-written 95%
Number of articles bought annually 5 to 10
Sections of the magazine open to freelance writers Features, how-to articles, first person experiences
Article interests and needs Personality profiles, activities, art and entertainment, gambling
Queries should be directed to Stephen Trotter, Editor
Length of articles 250 to 1,000 words
Payment $50 to $400
Time of payment On acceptance
Expenses No
Photographs $25 to $100 per slide
Response time to queries 2 weeks
Rights bought First North American and Caribbean rights
Kill fees 15% on assigned manuscripts only
Writer's guidelines Yes, free
Sample issues $5 (U.S.) per copy

TIPS FOR WRITERS

See entry under *Aruba Nights*.

DETECTIVE FILES GROUP

1350 Sherbrooke Street West
Montreal, Quebec, H3G 2T4
Canada

Parent company Globe Publishing Corp.
Category True crime
Circulation 100,000
Magazine availability Newsstands and subscription
Nonfiction 100%

Percent of articles freelance-written   100%
Number of articles bought annually   200
Queries should be directed to   Dominick A. Merle, Editor-in-Chief
Length of articles   3,000 to 6,000 words
Payment $250 to $350
Time of payment   On acceptance
Expenses   No
Photographs   Included in payment
Response time to queries   1 month
Rights bought   All rights
Kill fees   No
Writer's guidelines   Available with SASE and IRCs (International Response Coupons —available at post offices)

FLARE MAGAZINE

777 Bay Street, 7th Floor
Toronto, Ontario, M5W 1A7
Canada

Phone number   416-596-5452
Fax number   416-596-5184
E-mail address   editors@flare.com
Parent company   Maclean Hunter Publishing, Ltd.
Category   Fashion, beauty, health and fitness
Circulation   188,873
Magazine availability   Newsstands and subscription
Target audience   18 to 34, Canadian working women, National distribution
Magazine's history and mission   1979—Founded as *Flare*, by Maclean Hunter (First publisher: Donna Scott)
Sections of the magazine open to freelance writers   Features
Article interests and needs   Fashion, beauty, health, fitness, careers (finance), sex
Queries should be directed to   Bonnie Brooks: Editor-in-Chief; Suzanne Boyd: Associate Editor; Liza Finlay: Managing Editor; Jan Hulton: Fashion Editor
Writer's guidelines   Available upon request
Sample issues   Available upon request

MARQUEE ENTERTAINMENT MAGAZINE

77 Mount Avenue, Suite 621
Toronto, Ontario
Canada

Phone number   416-538-1000, Ext. 235
Fax number   416-538-0201
Category   Entertainment—movies/music
Circulation   700,000
Magazine availability   Subscription—insert in 6 daily newspapers
Magazine's history and mission   Founded in 1975. Originally an in-theater publication
Nonfiction   100%
Percent of articles freelance-written   80%
Number of articles bought annually   100 to 125
Sections of the magazine open to freelance writers   All
Article interests and needs   On Location, Personality Profiles
Queries should be directed to   Jack Gardner, Editor
Length of articles   500 to 750 words
Payment $200 U.S.
Time of payment   On publication
Expenses   No
Photographs   No
Kill fees   Yes—half

OUTDOOR CANADA

703 Evans Avenue, Suite 202
Toronto, Ontario, M9C 5E9
Canada

Phone number   416-695-0311
Fax number   416-695-0381
Category   Consumer
Parent company   Canadian National Sportsmen's Shows
Circulation   93,000
Magazine availability   Newsstands and subscription
Target audience   Ages 18 to 49, 75% male, within Canada
Magazine's history and mission   Founded in 1972 by Ron and Sheila Kaighin, purchased by Canadian National Sportsmen's Shows in 1986—a nonprofit organization encouraging Canadians to appreciate, enjoy, and protect Canada's outdoors
Nonfiction   99%
Fiction   1%
Percent of articles freelance-written   90%
Number of articles bought annually   35 to 40, usually with photos
Sections of the magazine open to freelance writers   Features & Sportsman's Journal
Article interests and needs   Fishing, camping, canoeing, hiking, hunting, snowmobiling, cross-country skiing, wilderness adventure, and wildlife

Queries should be directed to   James Little, Editor
Length of articles   1,000 to 2,500 words
Payment $100 and up
Time of payment   On publication
Expenses   Reimbursement for telephone expense only
Photographs   35 mm transparencies. Captions and model releases required. Pays $35 and up, $400 for cover.
Response time to queries   Within 3 weeks
Rights bought   First North American rights
Kill fees   Full payment when story is commissioned and accepted, but not used
Writer's guidelines   Available upon request
Sample issues   Available for $2 per copy

REPORT ON BUSINESS MAGAZINE

444 Front Street West
Toronto, Ontario, M5V 259
Canada

Phone number   416-585-5000
Fax number   416-585-5705
E-mail address   robmag@GlobeAndMail.ca
Parent company   The Globe and Mail
Category   Consumer/business
Circulation   550,000
Online status   Online via InfoGlobe (Globe Information Services)
Magazine availability   Subscription to *Globe and Mail* newspaper only or single copy purchase of *Globe* newspaper
Target audience   Managers, professionals, owners, entrepreneurs, national distribution in Canada
Magazine's history and mission   Established 1984 by *The Globe and Mail.*
Nonfiction   100%
Percent of articles freelance-written   70%
Number of articles bought annually   150 to 200
Sections of the magazine open to freelance writers   All
Article interests and needs   General business issues, public policy
Queries should be directed to   David Olive, Editor
Length of articles   150 to 6,000 words
Payment $1.00 per word (Canadian)
Time of payment   On acceptance
Expenses   Approximately 10% of story fee
Response time to queries   2 weeks
Kill fees   50% of story fee

Writer's guidelines   Not available
Sample issues   Available on request

St. Maarten Nights

1831 Rene Levesque Boulevard West
Montreal, Quebec, H3H 1R4
Canada

Phone number   514-931-1987
Fax number   514-931-6273
Parent company   Nights Publications, Inc.
Magazine Category   Travel and Lifestyle
Circulation   225,000
Magazine availability   Distributed free at hotels, airports, cruise ship departure points, retail outlets, etc.
Target audience   30- to 60-year-old tourists, male and female, upper income
Magazine's history and mission   Founded in 1984 by Douglas Markus, Publisher. Mission is to focus on lifestyle aspect of the destination.
Nonfiction   100%
Percent of articles freelance-written   95%
Sections of the magazine open to freelance writers   Features, how-to articles, first person experiences
Article interests and needs   Personality profiles, activities, art and entertainment, gambling
Queries should be directed to   Stephen Trotter, Editor
Length of articles   250 to 1,000 words
Payment $50 to $400
Time of payment   On acceptance
Expenses   No
Photographs $25 to $100 per slide
Response time to queries   2 weeks
Rights bought   First North American and Caribbean rights
Kill fees   15% on assigned manuscripts only
Writer's guidelines   Yes, free
Sample issues $5 (U.S.) per copy

Tips for Writers
Stephen Trotter, Editor

See entry under *Aruba Nights*.

TODAY'S BRIDE

37 Hanna Avenue
Toronto, Ontario, M6K 1X1
Canada

Phone number   416-537-2604
Fax number   416-538-1794
Parent company   Family Communications
Magazine category   Bridal/consumer
Circulation   150,000
Magazine availability   Newsstands
Target audience   Engaged couples (usually in early to mid-20s) across Canada who are planning their wedding.
Magazine's history   *Today's Bride* was founded in 1978 and purchased by Family Communications in 1986.
Nonfiction   100%
Percent of articles freelance-written   Very small—1 or 2 articles per issue; mostly written in-house
Number of articles bought annually   Approximately 4 to 6
Sections of the magazine open to freelance writers   Standard planning pieces (i.e., choosing music, flowers, D.J., etc) and all travel articles *are written in-house*, so anecdotal "lifestyle" types of articles are usually what we buy from freelancers.
Queries should be directed to   Shirley-Anne Ohannessian, Assistant Editor
Length of articles   Approximately 1,200 words
Payment $250 to $300 (Canadian dollars)
Time of payment   On acceptance
Expenses   Negotiable
Photographs   Negotiable
Response time to queries   Usually within 6 weeks
Writer's guidelines   No
Sample issues   No

TIPS FOR WRITERS

An original idea is what sparks my interest. I like queries to be as brief and to-the-point as possible. Clips are helpful but not necessary—two or three are enough. We will look at completed manuscripts. An SASE is appreciated but we will respond to queries without an SASE. Fax queries are fine. We don't have e-mail.

The best way to break into *Today's Bride* is to catch our attention with a unique idea. (If you can provide good quality photos, that's definitely a plus, too.) One of the best things a writer can do is *look at* the magazine before sending a query (it's quite easy to tell who has and who hasn't!). The worst thing a writer can do is telephone and say "Have you had a chance to look at my query?" or "Do you want to buy my article?" This is definitely a case of don't call me, I'll call you . . . if we want to buy it. Otherwise you'll be notified by mail.

YOU

37 Hanna Avenue, Suite #1
Toronto, Ontario
Canada

Phone number 416-537-2604
Fax number 416-538-1794
Parent company Family Communications
Circulation 226,000
Magazine availability Newsstands and subscription
Target audience Canadian women, 18 to 49
Magazine's history Founded in 1982. Purchased by Family Communications in 1984
Nonfiction 100%
Percent of articles freelance-written 10% (approximately)
Number of articles bought annually 20 (approximately)—don't always run that year, can be held over.
Sections of the magazine open to freelance writers Lifestyle, nutrition
Article interests and needs Lifestyle, nutrition
Queries should be directed to Shirley-Anne Ohannessian, Assistant Editor
Length of articles 800 to 1,200 words
Payment $250 (Canadian)
Time of payment On acceptance
Expenses Long distance phone charges can be negotiated.
Photographs Helpful
Response time to queries Usually within 8 weeks
Rights bought Onetime first North American rights
Writer's guidelines On request
Sample issues On request

IMPORTANT QUESTIONS ANSWERED

Q: Do you always want clips from new writers?
A: Clips are not necessary but helpful.
Q: Will you look at completed manuscripts?
A: We will look at completed manuscripts.
Q: Is it OK if writers fax or e-mail queries to you?
A: Query by fax or mail [is OK], but not phone.
Q: What is the best way to break into your magazine?
A: Pick up a copy. Get to know our style.
Q: Is an SASE always necessary?
A: A self-addressed envelope is great but don't put a stamp on it. [A U.S. stamp is] not much good to the Canadian post office.
Q: What is the worst thing writers do?
A: Submit "personal experience" stories.
Q: How can writers angle their stories for your magazine?
A: Self-help; upbeat tone.

Glossary

NORA ISAACS
Assistant Editor, *American Photo*

Nora Isaacs graduated from Columbia Graduate School of Journalism in 1995, where she majored in magazines and wrote her master's project on performance poetry. After graduation, she worked at Men's Journal *magazine, a monthly men's adventure magazine published by Wenner Media in New York, the publishers of* Rolling Stone *and* Us. *Nora moved to* American Photo, *a bimonthly consumer magazine for serious photographers, owned by Hachette Filipacci.*

A

angle   Focus a writer chooses to concentrate on for a story.

AP (style)   Following the *Associated Press* stylebook. See style.

assignment   Agreement between a writer and an editor to proceed with an article. It usually involves a written contract in which the angle of the story, the fee, the kill fee, and expenses for that story are clearly delineated.

B

blurb   Also deck or subhead. Words appearing under a headline that give an accurate indication of what follows in the text.

book   Another word for magazine. Example: fitness articles always appear in the front of the book.

byline   The line that gives the writer's name.

C

Chicago (style)   Following the *Chicago Manual of Style* stylebook. See style.

circulation   Number of copies a magazine distributes, including newsstand and subscription sales.

clips   Copies or originals of previous articles published. Clips demonstrate to an editor your writing ability and should be sent along with a query letter.

consumer magazines   Magazines found on the newsstand.

contract   Legal document between author and publisher that states agreement on copyright, fees, expenses, and ownership of published material.

controlled circulation   Complimentary subscriptions, also known as comp subs. Sent to places like doctor's offices or other magazines.

copyediting   Improving a manuscript by paying close attention to detail and style. Most common copyediting changes involve proper word usage, punctuation, consistency of capitalization, spelling, agreement of verbs and subjects and other syntax, quotation marks, and parentheses. Copyeditors should have a thorough knowledge of what to look for in these areas as well as the ability to make quick and logical decisions, and refer either to the *Chicago Manual of Style* or the *Associated Press* stylebook, as well as to the house stylesheet for reference.

cover line   Text that appears on the front cover of a magazine.

D

deadline   Due date of an article.

E

editor   Person who alters, adapts, and refines an author's work. The amount of editing necessary depends on the nature of the material, the audience, and the author's skill in preparing the story.

e-mail, electronic mail   A means of communicating rapidly over the Internet; a fast mode of communicating via computer. Authors can now send manuscripts via e-mail, which saves everybody time.

editorial calendar   A month-by-month schedule of a magazine's content.

etiquette   The unwritten rules. Sending an SASE with a query, for example, is good etiquette.

F

freelance writer   A writer with no long-term contractual commitment to any one publication. Freelancers get paid on a story to story basis.

H

hard copy   Paper printout of a manuscript.

head   Headline.

house style   The set of style rules adopted by a particular magazine. These override the rules of a particular stylebook.

I

in-house writers   Writers on staff. Paid on salary rather than by individual article.

Internet   A series of interconnected computers that allow remote users to access information and communicate. A great research tool for writers.

K

kill fee   Payment for an article that does not appear in a magazine; usually a percentage of the fee agreed upon in the contract.

L

lead   The first sentence or paragraph of a story. Also spelled lede.

lead time   The lapse of time between the magazine's production and the magazine's sale. For example, working the first week in May for an issue that appears the first week in August leaves a two-month lead time.

lineup   The contents of an issue and the number of pages allotted to each article.

literary fiction   Narrative technique that focuses on style rather than plot and a strong voice of the writer.

literary nonfiction   Narrative technique that includes the voice of the writer, but also retains high standards of accuracy.

M

magazine's mission   A statement orchestrated upon the birth of a magazine describing the goals the magazine wishes to accomplish and the purpose of the publication.

manuscript   Hard copy of a story. Frequently abbreviated as "ms."

map   Visual display of each page of a magazine, including advertisements.

masthead   The page of a magazine where staff names, subscription information, and contact numbers appear. The masthead serves as a place to identify appropriate contacts, but make sure to check the most recent one before sending anything to a specific editor.

multiple submissions   Manuscripts sent to more than one magazine at a time. It is always good to indicate a multiple submission in a cover letter to avoid any complications and to nudge the editor into making a decision.

O

online The act of using the Internet, whether it be e-mail or traveling to a Web site. Also, the act of simply being on a computer.

over the transom Anything received unsolicited. Unsolicited manuscripts arrive over the transom.

P

paid circulation Paid subscriptions.

parent company The larger group to which a magazine belongs, usually a publisher.

payment on publication When a writer agrees to get paid after the story is published.

photo credits Identification of the name of the individual or organization responsible for photos. Make sure to send credits with manuscripts.

pitch Idea for a story that is presented to an editor. Who or what is the story about? Where and when will it take place? How will the writer go about reporting and writing it? Why should the magazine be interested? Same as a query.

profiles Article chronicling the actions of an individual.

Q

query What an editor asks an author about a manuscript. Usually written in the margins of a manuscript or on slips of paper attached to manuscript. The author should respond to all editor queries.

query letter Letter to an editor regarding a story idea. See pitch. Sometimes referred to as the query.

R

revising The process of reorganizing or suggesting other ways to present material. Altering an article based on an editor's changes after an assigned story is submitted.

rewriting Also called substantive editing.

S

sample issues Issues sent to prospective writers so they can inspect the style of the magazine.

SASE Self-addressed, stamped envelope. Often sent with a query to make it easier to reply. It's good etiquette.

service stories Articles providing information to a reader.

shop a story   The process of trying to sell an article to several magazines at once. Example usage: "I'm going to shop my story around."

slanting a story   Focusing on a certain aspect of an article based on the style of the magazine for which it is being written.

slush/slush pile   Unasked for manuscripts or queries sent to no particular editor.

spec/on spec   Writing an article with an assignment from an editor.

style   The rules of uniformity used by a magazine that concern punctuation, capitalization, word division, and spelling. The two major stylebooks are *AP* and *Chicago*. Also, a way of writing that conveys a certain idea to a reader.

T

tag line   Writer's byline appearing at the end of the story.

target audience   The audience which the magazine hopes to attract.

trade magazines   Publications used within certain industries and not found on the newsstands.

U

unsolicited manuscript   Article sent to an editor who did not ask for it.

W

Web site   A location on the Internet that provides information using text, pictures, audio, and video. Most major magazines are developing Web sites where the magazine's content can be accessed and updated.

well   Also feature well. The core of a magazine containing feature stories.

writer's guidelines   General information about a magazine for a prospective writer. Usually includes the type of stories most likely to get published, style of the magazine, circulation information, query letter addresses, and payment information.

Writer's Market   Reference book containing a comprehensive list of addresses, phone numbers, and contact names for freelance writers.

Index